LESBIAN AND GAY STUDIES AND THE TEACHING OF ENGLISH

Lesbian and Gay Studies and the Teaching of English

Positions, Pedagogies, and Cultural Politics

Edited by

WILLIAM J. SPURLIN
Cardiff University, Wales, United Kingdom

National Council of Teachers of English
1111 W. Kenyon Road, Urbana, Illinois 61801-1096

Staff Editor: Bonny Graham
Interior Design: Jenny Jensen Greenleaf
Cover Design: Evelyn C. Shapiro

NCTE Stock Number: 27940-3050

It is the policy of NCTE in its journals and other publications to provide a forum for the open discussion of ideas concerning the content and the teaching of English and the language arts. Publicity accorded to any particular point of view does not imply endorsement by the Executive Committee, the Board of Directors, or the membership at large, except in announcements of policy, where such endorsement is clearly specified.

Library of Congress Cataloging-in-Publication Data

Lesbian and gay studies and the teaching of English: positions, pedagogies, and cultural politics/edited by William J. Spurlin.
    p. cm.
    Includes bibliographical references and index.
    ISBN 0-8141-2794-0 (pbk.)
    1. English philology—Study and teaching. 2. English philology—Study and teaching—Political aspects. 3. Homosexuality and literature—Study and teaching. 4. Gays' writings—Study and teaching. 5. Homosexuality—Study and teaching. 6. Gay and lesbian studies. 7. Lesbians in literature. 8. Gay men in literature. I. Spurlin, William J., 1954–

PE66.L45 2000
420'.71—dc21

                                                  00-030567

For David,
again

CONTENTS

Contents

III **The Politics of Culture**

ACKNOWLEDGMENTS

I would like to express my deepest gratitude to those without whom the successful completion of this book would not have been possible. I am most grateful for the wonderful support of the National Council of Teachers of English for soliciting this project and for encouraging its completion. The contributors of this volume and I are most honored to be part of NCTE's *first* lesbian and gay studies book title. I would like to also express heartfelt thanks and appreciation to those members of the NCTE Executive Committee who have vigilantly supported and continue to espouse the greater visibility and awareness of lesbian and gay studies within the teaching of English across the levels of instruction. These individuals include NCTE Executive Director Faith Schullstrom; past, present, and future NCTE Presidents Carol Avery, Joan Naomi Steiner, Jerome C. Harste, Anne Ruggles Gere, and Leila Christenbury; and other members of the current Executive Committee, especially Nancy McCracken, Charleen Silva Delfino, Victor Villanueva, Jr., Kathy Egawa, and Dale Allender. I have been encouraged, both in my work in lesbian and gay studies and in putting together this collection, by the time spent with each of them in thoughtful conversation and in endless e-mail and written correspondence.

This book would not be possible without the creation of a new forum at NCTE, the Gay and Straight Educators Assembly (GSEA, formerly AGLAIA), for which I served as program chair from 1994 to 1999. Several of the essays that appear here began as papers presented at GSEA sessions at NCTE's Annual Convention and were subsequently revised for publication in this collection. I mention this because I did not want to lose the important connection to those early sessions at NCTE conventions that provided a space in which to seriously address and theorize same-sex desire, queer difference(s), the teaching of lesbian and gay authors, homophobic student writing, lesbian and gay narratives of the Holocaust, the psychic violences directed toward gender-atypical children, and other related queer issues and struggles in relation to the teaching of English, not only in the United States but in non-Euramerican locations, and not only in university class-rooms but in elementary language arts and secondary English classrooms as well. I would like to give special thanks to my wonderful colleagues in GSEA, including Roxanne Henkin, with whom I now co-chair the NCTE Advisory Committee on Les-bian, Gay, and Bisexual Issues, Debra Goodman, Mary Bixby, Rose Casement, Jim Sullivan, Marcy Rayher, and Hannah Fur-row. Early versions of the essays written by Marcia Blumberg, Claudia Mitchell, Karen Lee Osborne, Jim Reese, and Ann Smith were originally given as papers at GSEA sessions, and I am most grateful for their contributions in helping to open up lesbian and gay studies as a viable site of inquiry at NCTE.

Some of the essays collected here were not originally pub-lished for this volume; permission acknowledgments to reprint this material appear on the copyright page. The invaluable assis-tance and outstanding contribution of the NCTE editorial staff and those intimately connected to the reading of the manuscript and to book production warrant my personal thanks. They are an author's absolute dream! I am grateful to Michael Greer for soliciting this book on behalf of NCTE and for the lunches and dinners with which he bribed me at the 1996 and 1997 NCTE and MLA annual conventions! Equally important, I appreciate the help and dedication of NCTE Senior Editor Zarina Hock, especially when things got bumpy along the way. I am thankful to the Editorial Board for its insightful comments and to the pro-duction staff, especially Kurt Austin for his superb technical ex-pertise and Bonny Graham for her careful copyediting and proofing.

I would like to thank sincerely the authors collected herein for their fine contribution to this project and for their remark-able patience during the writing, editing, evaluation, and pro-duction processes. It is their contribution that has truly made editing this collection worthwhile. Lastly, I would like to thank my partner, David A. Smith, for his abundant love and support, which continue to remain a source of inspiration.

Permissions

Lee Lynch's "Cruising the Libraries" originally appeared in *Lesbian Texts and Contexts: Radical Revisions*, eds. Karla Jay and Joanne Glasgow (New York: New York University Press, 1990), pp. 39–48. Copyright © 1990 by Lee Lynch.

Lillian Faderman's "The Uses of History" was first published in a slightly different version as "History in the Making" in *The Advocate* on 28 May 1996: p. 80. Copyright © 1996 by Liberation Publications Incorporated. Reprinted with permission of *The Advocate*.

Debbie Epstein's "Reading Gender, Reading Sexualities: Children and the Negotiation of Meaning in 'Alternative' Texts" first appeared in a slightly different version as "Sex Play: Romantic Significations, Sexism and Silences in the Schoolyard" in *A Dangerous Knowing: Sexuality, Pedagogy and Popular Culture*, eds. Debbie Epstein and James T. Sears (London: Cassell, 1999), pp. 25–42. Copyright © 1999 by Debbie Epstein, James T. Sears, and the contributors. Essay reprinted by permission of Cassell, Wellington House, 125 Strand, London, England. The author is especially thankful to Cassell for giving permission to reprint this chapter so soon after its first publication.

Photograph in Chapter 12 by Brenda Prince/ Format Photographers.

Richard E. Miller's "Fault Lines in the Contact Zone: Assessing Homophobic Student Writing" originally appeared as "Fault Lines in the Contact Zone" in *College English* 56 (April 1994): 389–408. Copyright © 1994 by NCTE.

INTRODUCTION: QUEER STUDIES/ENGLISH STUDIES

WILLIAM J. SPURLIN

Cardiff University, Wales, United Kingdom

Imagine, if you will, a rather naive American teacher of Sixth Form English literature in Southeast Asia. Because his class in Singapore has just finished reading Shakespeare's *King Lear*, a "set" text on the syllabus that would appear on that year's Cambridge General Certificate of Education A-Level Examination, students are given a choice of essay topics on the play and asked to write on one of them. One student has written an essay on Cordelia, arguing against the more conventional interpretation (and the one already discussed at length in class) that she is the source of Lear's tragic downfall and subsequent regeneration. Influenced by her Singaporean Chinese background, the student reads irony and subtle deception on Cordelia's part early in the play; in response to her father's pleas that she speak of her love for him "more opulent than your sisters" (1.1.85), Cordelia replies:

> . . . I love your Majesty
> According to my bond; no more nor less. . . .
> You have begot me, bred me, lov'd me: I
> Return those duties back as are right fit,
> Obey you, love you, and most honour you. (1.1.91–92, 95–97)

According to this student, when Cordelia tells Lear she loves him "according to my bond," she is asserting that she loves him as her filial obligation dictates. And if she truly followed through on her filial duties, Cordelia, the student continues in her essay, should have told her father more or less what he wanted to hear, which, we realize later in the play, was her genuine love for him as opposed to the flattering accolades produced by her sisters. The student supports her position not only from the text but also from the context in which she has read and interpreted it; she argues that in Eastern cultures, a high value is placed on piety toward the parent, in contrast to the emphasis that Western culture places on the individual often at the expense of social and familial obligations. The young teacher is stunned by this student's essay, mostly because it is so eloquently argued and makes such perfect sense when Shakespeare is being read and studied in Singapore, something he had not even considered, and also because the stringent examination system in Singapore, and the kinds of teaching practices it imposes, generally do not encourage students to take that kind of risk. The teacher shares his student's response with a British colleague who seems quite knowledgeable about Shakespeare; yet when told of the student's argument, the colleague lets out an exasperated sigh and remarks that if one were to logically follow that ridiculous interpretation, "there wouldn't be much of a plot left, now would there?"

The next day the teacher asks the student if she would like to read her essay to the class; she agrees, and the teacher, still not knowing what to do with this interpretation and wondering if he, like Lear, is abdicating responsibility, asks the class to respond to the essay. At first, silence. . . . Some students shake their heads, others look puzzled, waiting for the teacher to respond. Gradually, a lively discussion follows in which others in the class begin to reread the play from an altogether different trajectory by imagining what might have happened if Cordelia had actually given her father the declaration of love he had hoped to hear. In class the following day, another student theorizes Cordelia as the *villain* of the play, while others argue for the more conventional interpretation of her pivotal role in Lear's renewal. Another student asks about the possibility of reading Cordelia as the tragic heroine of the play, arguing that she should have had the title role rather than Lear since she was stronger and more dignified than him and the other characters. The teacher, now visibly distraught, begins to worry that something vital is absent from his academic preparation. For the first time in three years of teaching English literature in Singapore, he wonders about his position as an American teaching *Lear* from a Western humanist perspective, and he begins to seriously doubt his own authority in the classroom. What, he ponders, if the student had written her interpretation of Cordelia in response to a question on the A-level examination? Would or could she pass the Shakespeare paper? This entire incident is something for which the teacher is not prepared, and when his contract in Singapore expires at the end of the academic year, he does not renew it; in fact, he is so troubled and confused that he flees Singapore and is not heard from again. . . .

————————

Well, . . . not quite! I merely fled to New York, to graduate school, where, from the mid- to late 1980s, I studied critical theory, which in turn generated more questions rather than giving me the simplistic, straightforward solutions I had hoped to find. In Singapore, while I was not yet familiar with the discourse of theory and the possibilities for critique it opens, and therefore was unable to deal with my sense of pedagogical (dis)location at the time, I did know that the classroom discussions I had with my Singaporean students on Shakespeare's text were the most *impassioned,* the most productive, indeed, the most genuine and engaging I had ever experienced. More important, this epistemological crisis was a turning point because it radically politicized my teaching; my student's (re)reading of *Lear* enabled me to interrogate more fully the relationship between the text and the cultural context in which it is read and interpreted, to examine the ways in which my own certitudes about how and what I teach could be rooted in the perpetuation of normative ideologies, and to see critical reading as a struggle to (re)write the text against, indeed transgress, the grain of dominant discourses, hegemonic images, and received knowledge.

Such contentious practices of reading and writing are central to investigations of cultural difference. As Paulo Freire reminds us, "A pedagogy will be that much more critical and radical the more investigative and less certain of 'certainties' it is. The more 'unquiet' a pedagogy, the more critical it will become. . . . This pedagogy is thus much more a pedagogy of *question* than a pedagogy of answer" (Freire and Macedo 54; emphasis added). But have the contemporary cultural debates helped to truly transform our classrooms, to unsettle our pedagogies? Rather than simply subordinating differences according to race, gender, and class (and sexuality when it is credibly addressed in the classroom) under normative teaching practices that still value the authority of text and teacher (thereby neutralizing any subversive modes of inquiry into language, literature, culture, and teaching itself), investigations of culture can become more critical if, following the implications of Freire, we do not see difference as a solution to a problem (e.g., adding a more diverse representation of writers to the literary canon) but as an ongoing site of inquiry. Susan Stewart speaks of multicultural pedagogy as the practice of an *interpretive* strategy that demands a radical *re*consideration and *re*thinking of our grounds of judgment and "an ethical imperative to examine the relation of forms of knowledge to the democratization of expression, articulation, and access" (13). This involves continual questioning, not the mere substitution of a new set of teaching practices as a simple solution. A question that should be raised again and again, in and out of the classroom, is whether the culture, as it exists at any particular moment, is legitimate in the eyes of *all* of its participants. Despite the transformative potential of this question, and despite innovative work in lesbian and gay studies and academic queer theory, much scholarship in English and language arts pedagogy organized around the rubric of cultural difference has woefully undertheorized same-sex desire as a viable position from which to speak, read, write, and locate oneself in the world. Likewise, it has failed to ask the ways in which heterosexism and homophobia also shape the world of hegemonic power and the extent to which other vectors of domination, as well as new possibilities for cultural production, are obscured in the absence of same-sex desire as a significant axis of pedagogical inquiry.

Indeed, our queer "tinkerings" with texts, similar to my colleague's response to my student's (re)reading of Shakespeare's text in Singapore, are thought to produce no plot at all, and any kind of queer inquiry in English studies and English language arts classrooms is often similarly dismissed as having little or no intellectual or pedagogical significance. We see this especially reflected in the current backlash against cultural diversity and difference in general, in the hostility particularly directed toward lesbians and gay men among political leaders, and in more or less conservative proposals for educational "reform." Looking back over the 1990s, a decade which also marked the centennial anniversary of the Oscar Wilde trials (and similarly fed off and (re)produced social phobias about homosexuality), we have witnessed the tirades of William J. Bennett, Dinesh D'Souza, Roger Kimball, Harold Bloom, and others who lament that intellectual and aesthetic standards are being abdicated in the humanities in the name of social justice and identity politics, a position which speaks in the name of depoliticizing humanities teaching. Yet, hypocritically, appeals to traditional "standards" and to more traditional English and language arts curricula operate as obvious political attempts to keep issues of race, gender, popular culture, and *especially* sexual identity safely out of the classroom. The backlash against the teaching of lesbian and gay studies in particular has been especially fierce in primary and secondary schooling, ranging from heterosexism—insofar as schools generally tend to acculturate students toward the heterosexual imperative, often through the enforcement of gender norms—to more blatant forms of homophobia. The enforcement of gender norms, however, is not as innocent as it seems; nor is it entirely separate from homophobia—Judith Butler has argued for maintaining a theoretical apparatus that accounts for how "sexuality is regulated through the *policing* and the *shaming* of gender" (238; emphasis added). Butler's point is particularly telling in the context of elementary and secondary schooling given the relentless pressures placed on gender-atypical children from teachers, peers, and their families to conform to prescribed gender expectations. We must be especially skeptical of the methods and justifications for ensuring gender conformity, including, as I have pointed out elsewhere, "counseling" and therapeutic intervention (especially for feminine boys), self-righteously performed in the name of the "best interest" of the gender-atypical child but specifically tied to adult anxieties about the possibility that a child may become gay or lesbian (Spurlin 83).

Of course, one cannot ignore the more obvious forms of homophobia in schools, where, Eve Sedgwick and others remind us, in addition to the psychic and physical assaults on gender-atypical children and young people who identify as lesbian or gay, teachers are subject to being harassed, censured, and possibly fired, not only for being visibly gay, but—*whatever their sexuality*—for providing any intimation that homosexual desires, identities, cultures, children, or adolescents have a right to expression or existence (Sedgwick, "Queer and Now" 2). Speaking more specifically on the institutionalization of homophobia and the socially sanctioned violence that often accompanies it, Sedgwick writes:

> [T]he scope of institutions whose programmatic undertaking is to prevent the development of gay people is unimaginably large. There is no major institutionalized discourse that offers a firm resistance to that undertaking: in the United States, at any rate, most sites of the state, the military, *education*, law, penal institutions, the church, medicine, and mass culture enforce it all but unquestioningly, and with little hesitation at even the recourse to invasive violence. ("How to Bring Your Kids Up Gay" 161; emphasis added)

At the college level, despite common yet highly questionable perceptions of a more liberal or progressive stance toward variant sexual identities, many English faculty, despite a wealth of new scholarship in queer studies, often downplay the homosexuality of canonical authors, remain unfamiliar with contemporary gay and lesbian authors, do not create adequate spaces in classroom discussion for lesbian or gay readings of texts to emerge, and do not adequately sustain classroom discussion on the politics of sexuality as it comes up in student writing. As long as heteronormative thinking insists that "humanity and heterosexuality are synonymous" (Warner xxiii), and as long as such thinking is carried over and left unexamined in the classroom, we fail to acknowledge the various forms of expression and lived experiences of lesbians, gay men, and other sexual minorities that name, and possibly transform, the world.

In an effort to question further pedagogical certitudes that foreclose other possibilities of inquiry and mask the ways in which teaching practices can serve the interests of dominant social groups, and in an effort to speak to many of the problematic assumptions of the current debates about culture, *Lesbian and Gay Studies and the Teaching of English: Positions, Pedagogies, and Cultural Politics* provides a critical forum within the profession of English teaching across the teaching levels in order to engage sexual difference as a site of pedagogical inquiry, while at the same time keeping in mind that merely including lesbian and gay teachers, students, texts, and subject positions in a theory of teaching that remains otherwise unaltered is highly problematic. Certainly our positions as lesbian, gay, or bisexual teachers, as well as the antihomophobic positions proactively taken by teachers who are transgender identified and/or sexually straight, affect the ways in which we read, write, and teach. But we must take care to resist grounding our pedagogies in a new set of certitudes. While the rupturing of my own pedagogical presumptions in Singapore helped to transform my teaching and served as a valuable reference point that enabled me to later (re)position myself in the classroom and in my academic work as queer, I do not wish the narrative of my Singapore experience to be read quite as seductively as I may have told it. Suspicious of Foucault's faith in epistemological "breaks," Diana Fuss makes the instructive point that we need to be skeptical of such so-called shifts if new orientations, new objectives, or new vocabularies simply serve to reassert what they had sought to supersede (7); and for that reason, it is important to keep in mind that the processes of *re*seeing, *re*thinking, and *re*considering our cultural and pedagogical assumptions need to be ongoing.

All of the essays in this volume theorize, to varying degrees, queer difference as a lens through which to read, interpret, and produce texts, or as a way of reading the classroom and indeed the world, but they also remind us that this in itself is not sufficient to move us toward a more critical pedagogy. Rather than perpetuating the simplistic logic in the cultural debates that usually encodes and articulates differences according to race, gender, social class, and sexuality as if they are in parallel relation to one another without accounting for the ways in which they socially intersect and converge, the essays in this book explore and express queerness in a variety of ways while resisting the urge to name queer identity, as Phillip Brian Harper puts it, "as a primary identificatory principle, uninflected by the pressures of other subjectivizing factors" (26). Likewise, as bell hooks reminds us that "patriarchal domination shares an ideological foundation with racism and other forms of group oppression [and] that there is no hope that it can be eradicated while these systems remain intact" (22), any interrogation of homophobia as an axis of domination implies further thinking about where various forms of power intersect in culture. Given the diverse positions from which the contributors of this volume speak, the essays collected address the ways in which sexual identity is always already mediated by race, gender, class, and geopolitical spatialization; elucidate how queer identity can take multiple, contingent, and fluid meanings in a variety of contexts; question the hetero/homo opposition that has historically structured discourses on sexuality; analyze how *interarticulations* of power, including gender oppression, racism, heterosexism, homophobia, and nationalism, impinge on classroom analyses of difference; and examine the broader implications of these and other issues for the teaching of English.

In addition to this philosophical orientation, these essays explore the teaching of lesbian and gay studies from a range of disciplinary perspectives within the field of English, including composition studies, literary studies, cultural studies, film, English education, children's and young adult literature, and language arts; the essays also make use of relevant interdisciplinary work in such areas as academic feminism, Latina studies, Native American studies, critical literacy, and postcolonial studies. This book is also unique in that it is not limited to university teaching but instead contains essays that specifically investigate the teaching of lesbian and gay studies in elementary language arts and secondary English classrooms, where, given the current backlash, the risks are sometimes especially fierce. Antigay rhetoric, as Simon Watney notes, has identified elementary and secondary schools as sites where the "threat" of homosexuality is most acute and where preemptive measures are most needed (393–94). Not concerned entirely with teaching levels, however, and not making any attempt to erase or elide specific differences between elementary, secondary, and university teaching, the collection explores important issues and questions that center on the teaching of lesbian and gay studies; these include, for example, theorizations of the pedagogical closet; the neglect of transgender studies in academic feminism, queer theory, and pedagogical practices; the ways in which reconstructions of the sexual discourses in the English Renaissance can open up a range of historical, theoretical, and political issues in the teaching of Shakespeare and other historical authors; and the cultural influences that make homophobic student writing possible. Other essays are ethnographic studies. One essay, for example, studies the ways in which children reconstruct differences along lines of gender and sexuality in the context of discussions of texts about families headed by same-sex partners, and how the culture of heteronormativity is imbricated with these discussions. Another essay studies a lesbian faculty member in an English department who resists the imperative to "come out" in the classroom because she sees "lesbian" not as a fixed position for the teacher to occupy in the classroom but as a relational process of shifting identifications. In addition to the diverse geographic locations from which the authors of this volume write, which include various parts of the United States, as well as Canada and Europe, and in an effort to address how lesbian and gay identities and cultural formations have taken shape and operate outside of the Euramerican axis, other essays ask how assumptions of homosexuality—seen as an "import" of empire or as a Western aberration in much of the postcolonial world—affect English teaching and curricula in India and in South Africa. The essays in the book, then, generally concern themselves with how lesbian, gay, and transgendered positions rupture heterosexist assumptions about pedagogy, disciplinary knowledge, and culture and thus transform the teaching of English.

———————

The book is divided into three major sections—positions, pedagogies, and cultural politics. Each section addresses, but is not limited to, theoretical perspectives, pedagogical strategies, and the various social, cultural, and political contexts that surround the teaching of lesbian and gay studies within the discipline of English. The essays in Part I, Positions, primarily though not exclusively address the specific, often multifaceted positions held by the authors and call attention to the complexity of theorizing a lesbian, gay, or transgendered position in the classroom, whether as teachers, students, researchers, academics, or creative writers. What is the place of lived experience and personal history in the lesbian and gay studies classroom, and in what ways might such experiences and histories unsettle (or perhaps reinvent) many of the fixities built into current teaching assumptions and practices? Some of the essays in this section appear to be theoretically complex, but finding a viable position from which to speak and be heard as queer in the classroom is also about *finding a language*. The section opens with a reprint of a moving memoir, "Cruising the Libraries," by Lee Lynch, who writes poignantly of her intense search while a young reader for images of herself reflected in literature, of the pleasure she first experienced in identifying with the character Frankie Addams in Carson McCuller's *The Member of the Wedding,* and of her later ability to read with a "variant eye" to discover lesbian difference in work by other authors "who hinted at lives behind the heterosexual stories they wrote." More than simply anecdotal, a criticism which often works to silence the lived experience of those marginalized as Other, Lynch's essay speaks forcefully to all English and language arts teachers about the viability of reading texts and the world with a variant eye and of the important pedagogical consequences of the texts we choose to teach and the perspectives we choose to highlight or ignore.

Edward J. Ingebretsen, in "When the Cave Is a Closet: Pedagogies of the (Re)Pressed," explores the confusions that arise when the teacher's private sexual identification or subjectivity becomes the public subject under scrutiny. In his reflections on a new course he designed at Georgetown University—Unspeakable Lives: Gay and Lesbian Narratives—that was part of relentless media attacks on the university's slightly revised English curriculum, Ingebretsen asks what happens when the teacher (the one who "knows") becomes aligned with the monstrous (whose "knowing" is unspeakable) which must be repudiated for the "common" good, especially if that teacher is, like himself, gay, Catholic, and a priest. Not only does this social trajectory operate for the queer teacher, who gives voice to the unspeakable and simultaneously evokes the spectacle of the monstrous, but Ingebretsen also describes how it similarly works for students, particularly for those identifying as sexually straight, who, when they take his class, can no longer comfortably think of themselves "outside the scrutinizing apparatus of the closet," since they too become the objects of the sexualized gaze. In refusing institutional and cultural pressures that urge the lesbian or gay teacher to "stay put" or remain under erasure, Ingebretsen reimagines Plato's allegory of the cave as similar to the closet and the classroom, where learning becomes an act of "negotiating the passage out of the specular." This does not imply a romanticized movement from ignorance to enlightenment, but one beyond the fixities of dominant teaching practices and the fixations reinforced by the closet.

Jay Kent Lorenz's essay "Blame It on the Weatherman" is a refreshingly honest recollection of his own queer adolescence, particularly how growing up queer sometimes puts us in a position to reproduce homophobia as a defense in order to prevent detection of our emerging sexual identity. Lorenz reflects on how the internalized homophobia he experienced earlier reappeared in a slightly different form in his initial anxiety about being "marked" as gay when first asked to teach the film component of the lesbian and gay studies course, Unspeakable Lives, taught by Edward Ingebretsen at Georgetown University, and the conflict he experienced in trying to maintain the authority to speak as a teacher without bracketing, or altogether denying, his queer identity. Like other essayists in this section, Lorenz critiques the historical discrediting of lived experience in academic contexts. As long as lived experience and personal history are not fetishized, he argues, they can become both viable political strategies and powerful pedagogical tools to resist the silencing, erasive gestures of heteroculture and its insistence that classroom analyses of (sexual) difference taint the "purity" of English studies and pedagogical praxis.

Susan Talburt, in "On Not Coming Out: or, Reimagining Limits," an ethnographic study of one lesbian faculty member's understanding and enactment of the constructs "lesbian" and "intellectual" in her academic practice, shows how the category "lesbian," when attached to "identity" or "community," can potentially operate as another fixity and therefore can be intellectually and pedagogically limiting. Challenging the idea of a "lesbian personal," the essay questions the recent wave of pedagogical "coming out" manifestos and reconstructs "lesbian" as a site of *shifting* identifications that enables both teacher and students to enact multiple positions in relation to the texts they study. This is not to say that the option is for the lesbian or gay teacher to simply remain closeted; rather, the essay examines contexts in which "it might be more efficacious to rethink the intentional mediation of subjects of study through 'personal positioning' as an inherently valid pedagogical strategy," and to see ambiguity and the refusal of fixity as the effect of multiple personal and pedagogical commitments.

Taking a different perspective on the place of lived experience and personal positioning in the classroom, Jody Norton describes the problematic historical shift in English studies from the critic's demeanor of detachment to the position of critic/theorist/teacher as emblematic of the social and discursive communities out of which and for whom he or she speaks. S/he begins with a critique of feminist theory as being ensconced in a binary paradigm of gender. In "(Trans)Gendering English Studies," Norton argues that the explanatory incapacity of the binary model of sex/gender difference obscures other differences and especially fails to account for the specificity of transgender. Picking up from queer theory, s/he argues that we need to read specifically for marginalized genderings; his/her readings of works by Truman Capote, Delton Welch, Richard McCann, and Minnie Bruce Pratt insightfully call attention to forms of subjectivity that wander habitually from the fixations and constraints of gender "normalcy." Theorizing his/her own position as a teacher who is transgender identified, Norton discusses how it contributes to the kinds of pedagogical interventions s/he practices in the classroom as one who is "never *in*, but *passing through*, genders, sexualities, discourses, economies, and institutions."

The essays in Part II, Pedagogies, address strategies for teaching lesbian and gay studies in English classrooms and review relevant texts and instructional materials. Yet this shift of focus is not intended to examine classroom practices at the expense of a theoretical or philosophical framework. This section begins with a short but pointed introductory chapter by Lillian Faderman titled "The Uses of History." More than a mere collection or transcription of objective data, Faderman reminds us, the rendering of history, including literary history, is a narrative usually proffered by socially dominant groups. Though historically the (homo)sexuality of certain canonical writers, such as Socrates and Shakespeare, was often deemed irrelevant to the serious work of literary analysis, Faderman argues that when English teachers openly address the lesbian desires of Emily Dickinson or Willa Cather, or straightforwardly acknowledge that writers such as Walt Whitman and James Baldwin loved and desired men, lesbian and gay youth are provided with a sense of a *usable past*.

Skeptical of the fixed narratives of history and ideology to which Faderman refers, Claudia Mitchell and Jim Reese, in focusing on elementary language arts and secondary English classrooms respectively, offer teaching strategies that resist heteronormative ways of reading texts and reading the world. In "'What's Out There?'," Mitchell lays out a pedagogical framework from which to examine lesbian and gay identity in fiction for children and young adults that contests received assumptions about family, gender, and sexuality. She critically reviews the kinds of books that are available, examines possible points of entry for discussing with young readers texts about same-sex desire, and challenges language arts teachers and teacher educators, as they think about using these texts in their classrooms, to consider their own sexuality as constructed and the ways in which they imaginatively construct the sexuality of others. In "Creating a Place for Lesbian and Gay Readings in Secondary English Classrooms," Reese, a high school English teacher at the International School of Brussels, offers a gay (re)reading and analysis of the 1992 Australian film *Strictly Ballroom* by Baz Luhrmann. Informed by theories of reader response and by feminist theories of reading, Reese questions dominant reading practices in secondary schools that tend to suppress same-sex desire as a vantage point from which to read. Following the lucid trajectory he traces through the film that opens it to a gay interpretation, Reese argues for the pedagogical and cultural importance of resistant reading in the teaching of literature in secondary schools.

Attacks on lesbian and gay studies as being frivolous and as unnecessarily politicizing the English curriculum become particularly pronounced when historical writers such as Shakespeare are associated with the "sordid obsessions" of homosexuals, such as transvestitism, anal eroticism, and sadomasochism. Responding to these attacks, Mario DiGangi, in "Shakespeare's Sexuality: Who Needs It?," examines the ways in which modern studies of Shakespeare have been (re)appropriated to serve the ideological agenda of locating Shakespeare's work within the normalizing matrix of marital heterosexuality. He argues that scholarship on the English Renaissance that reconstructs the sexual discourses particular to Shakespeare's era can serve as a useful paradigm for helping both secondary and college students think critically about historical and political constructions of the sexual and gender ideologies they have inherited, including the myth of universal heterosexuality. This myth is often left unexamined in the study of premodern literature, insofar as it is assumed that queer readings apply only to modern and contemporary works.

Tatiana de la tierra discusses the political and academic concerns of consciously trying to address lesbian and gay subject positions in the pedagogical discourses and approaches used to teach English composition. Acknowledging the influence of her own positions as Latina, American immigrant, bilingual/bicultural, and lesbian in her teaching, and unapologetically responding to reductive criticisms that any teaching of lesbian and gay studies is nothing more than indoctrinating students to a gay "agenda," de la tierra's essay "Coming Out and Creating Queer Awareness in the Classroom" outlines specific classroom approaches for integrating queer and other perspectives of difference into the teaching of composition in order to enable students to think more critically and to become better writers. Given the multiplicity of her positions in the classroom, de la tierra theorizes homophobia as distinct but not entirely separate from other vectors of domination while simultaneously questioning heterosexist representations of people of color. More than writing about her experience of coming out to her students, she exposes problematic appropriations of cultural difference that silence queer perspectives in the classroom, especially when it is assumed that students who come from specific cultural groups that historically have had taboos against homosexuality may be offended. While this is sometimes the case with the Mexican American student population she teaches, de la tierra asks the extent to which the writing classroom, as a discourse community, is obligated to challenge the rhetorical appeal to these taboos in student writing, and the extent to which the code of silence that often surrounds them further normalizes the articulation of homophobic ideas and the concomitant denigration of gays and lesbians in the public sphere of the classroom.

"'Swimming Upstream': Recovering the Lesbian in Native American Literature" offers an alternative to existing practices of teaching Native American literature, especially if teachers wish to resist sentimentalizing the all-too-familiar presentation of Native Americans as victims. Through a careful reading of the short story "Swimming Upstream" by Beth Brant, a Bay of Quinte Mohawk, Karen Lee Osborne explores how contemporary Native Americans face multiple questions of identity and oppression, particularly if she is Native American, lesbian, and a recovering alcoholic. Osborne's analysis of the story invites literature teachers to (re)read Native American authors by looking for "threads of resistance, subversion, and strength that are neither masculinized nor heterosexist," and to explore lesbian identity as a site densely occupied by multiple and intersecting subjectivities.

Of course, it is not possible to theorize lesbian and gay positions in the classroom or to discuss and analyze resistant pedagogical strategies as if these transcend, or remain disembodied from, social and political struggles. A central focus of the essays in Part III is on the cultural and social contexts that shape and affect the teaching of lesbian and gay studies in English classrooms both in the United States and abroad. These contexts include the effects of gender norms on young children, hate speech directed against gay men and lesbians, postapartheid politics in South Africa, nationalism, and the politics of AIDS, all of which affect English studies and language arts, and, as the authors of these essays argue, have broader theoretical and pedagogical implications. Drawing from her ethnographic research on a multiethnic primary school in London, Debbie Epstein documents how children imaginatively reconstruct differences along lines of gender and sexuality through their play and in classroom discussions. Analyzing children's responses to texts about lesbian families and to their teacher's coming out to the class, her essay pays particular attention to the ways in which their responses are embedded in, and in some cases constrained by, master narratives of compulsory heterosexuality, which, of course, cannot be dissociated from hegemonic notions of gender, which also find their way into the children's responses. But because she found that some of the children were able to resist heterosexualizing the lesbian characters in the texts they read and discussed, and that they were able to inhabit an alternative worldview in response to their teacher's attempts to shift master narratives of compulsory heterosexuality in his teaching, Epstein suggests that language arts teachers mediate discussions of texts about lesbians and gay men rather than rely on the texts themselves to reflect "positive" images of groups already socially coded homophobically.

In discussing a disturbing, homophobically written student essay, "Queers, Bums, and Magic," in a pre-college-level community college composition class, and responding to a subsequent Conference on College Composition and Communication (CCCC) paper titled "How Would You Grade a Gay-Bashing?" given by the instructor of that class, Richard E. Miller, in "Fault Lines in the Contact Zone: Assessing Homophobic Student Writing," disputes the efficacy of such common pedagogical moves as removing the writer from the classroom or overlooking the offensive aspects of the student paper in order to attend to its surface and structural features. Miller asserts the need for creating classrooms "in which part of the work involves articulating, investigating, and questioning the affiliated cultural forces that underwrite the ways of thinking that find expression in this student's essay." In other words, rather than merely silencing voices that seek to oppose the work of constructing knowledge in the classroom by reinstating asymmetrical relations of power (i.e., "there will be no homophobic writing in this classroom"), or simply giving free rein to a student's self-righteous indignation and allowing that to pass as a "political intervention," the focus of classroom inquiry needs to be shifted to the cultural forces that make the gay-bashing essay not only permissible but prevalent in a homophobic culture. In this sense, Miller argues, writing becomes a site of investigation for students to critically examine the cultural conflicts that serve to define and limit their lived experience.

Acknowledging some of the erasures historically built into the teaching of literature, Ann Smith, in "Queer Pedagogy and Social Change," writes about her conceptualization and implementation of the first course ever offered on lesbian literature in the Department of English at the University of the Witwatersrand, Johannesburg, in 1995. Her essay and the course she discusses are framed by her work as a committed lesbian activist in apartheid South Africa (which was also a misogynistic and homophobic regime in addition to the racial oppression it legitimated and brutally enforced) and in the current postapartheid era. Smith calls attention to the historical split between activism, still often viewed as the teacher's personal business *outside* of the classroom, and teaching. For Smith, as for many teachers of lesbian and gay studies, teaching *is* activism. Her essay speaks powerfully to American English teachers about the ways in which her approaches to literature are shaped by her political commitments as lesbian, as feminist, and as advocate for racial equality, and by the changing social and political context in South Africa's transition from apartheid to democracy.

Likewise, Ruth Vanita, formerly of Delhi University and now teaching in the United States, addresses issues peculiar to the teaching of lesbian and gay literature in India in her essay "The Straight Path to Postcolonial Salvation: Heterosexism and the Teaching of English in India Today." Even though English studies in the Indian academy has questioned the traditional canon of English authors and, largely through the influence of postcolonial inquiry, has embraced radical texts that focus on victimization and resistance, Vanita demonstrates how any homoerotically charged writing in literature in English that could provide gay and lesbian students with a sense of past is virtually absent because any foregrounding of homosexuality is still dismissed as not indicative of "Indian-ness" and is regarded as a Western perversion imported through the capitalist free market.

"Rememorating: Quilt Readings" by Marcia Blumberg, the final chapter in this collection, speaks evocatively of the ways in which the AIDS Memorial Quilt both employs and displaces conventional art forms and how the Quilt's postmodern performance of mourning is connected to the practice of critical pedagogy insofar as it "celebrates lives, creates healing narratives, challenges and refutes elitism, values creativity, raises awareness, and inspires action." Refusing the simplistic equation of AIDS with gay men, the Quilt's multiplicity of panels of men, women, and children emphasizes the nexus of gender, race, class, religion, sexual identity, and ethnicity. Blumberg's essay makes a convincing case for including this powerful text in our classrooms without sentimentalizing or patronizing those who suffer and have died from AIDS-related causes, since preoccupation with emotional responses and their cathartic effects can engender political passivity and impede active engagement in the social issues that reading the Quilt raises. Blumberg's analysis not only situates the Quilt as text but also points to how its component panels—and other texts produced by those who are positioned in the margins of hegemonic social formations—push the boundaries of standard notions of textuality and are inextricably linked to political spheres of life. The author pays particular attention to how studying the Quilt's interwoven and politicized signs functions metaphorically as a critical praxis of reading that *acts* on the world.

———

While taking the discipline of English studies as its central concern, *Lesbian and Gay Studies and the Teaching of English* extends work on the teaching of lesbian and gay studies beyond the confines of the academy, beyond the more traditional domains of literary and composition studies, and beyond the geographic boundaries of the United States without replacing any of these sites as they are expanded. At the same time, it is important not to conflate the institutional affiliations of particular authors with the pedagogical issues they raise. Although a small number of essays are directed predominately to university teachers and teaching, most of the writing collected here speaks to a wider audience. For instance, tatiana de la tierra's theorizations of the ways in which her Latina, lesbian, and activist positions in the classroom contribute to her approaches to the teaching of writing; Karen Lee Osborne's focus on the intersections of multiple sites of subjectivity in her teaching of Native American literature that allows lesbian readings to emerge without ignoring other differences; and Edward J. Ingebretsen's (re)reading of Plato's allegory of the cave in relation to the pedagogical closet have significance for primary and secondary English and language arts teachers as well as for those concerned with college or university teaching. Certainly the same can be said of Richard Miller's analysis of homophobic student writing, Mario DiGangi's critique of heterosexist appropriations of Shakespeare in the dominant body of Shakespeare criticism, and Marcia Blumberg's reading of the AIDS Memorial Quilt. Likewise, Debbie Epstein's study of children's readings of gender and sexuality, Claudia Mitchell's overview and analysis of texts for children and young adults that address lesbian and gay identity, Jim Reese's reflections on reading from gay perspectives in secondary schools, and Lee Lynch's search for images of her emerging lesbian identity as a young reader address educators in general as well as language arts or secondary English teachers in particular.

While this book challenges fixed assumptions about (sexual) identity, gender, language, literacy, culture, political advocacy, and coming out in relation to English teaching, it also exposes the instability of borders and questions totalizing structures that oppress and exclude. We must be attentive to the ways in which narrow reinventions of the dichotomies between university and pre-university teaching inform our work insofar as they limit the breadth and potential of lesbian and gay studies as a discipline and impose problematic boundaries, which can operate oppressively when they are permitted to define or delimit the professional and intellectual space one may occupy as a teacher. Scholars who work in academic queer theory and lesbian and gay studies need to widen the interrogatory lens through which they read and analyze sexual difference and queer pedagogy as those sites of inquiry shift considerably in the specific contexts of elementary and secondary classrooms. At the same time, elementary and secondary teachers of English and language arts need to be familiar with the range of radical (re)readings of gender, sexuality, culture, textuality, reading, and writing made possible by queer inquiry, which can better inform their pedagogical decisions and allow them to bring to the field of lesbian and gay studies the insistent pressures of their different questions, their different claims. The juxtaposition of queer studies and English studies has the potential to broaden both disciplines and, it is hoped, to produce new insights in each.

Works Cited

Bennett, William J. *The De-valuing of America: The Fight for Our Culture and Our Children.* New York: Summit, 1992.

Bloom, Harold. *The Western Canon: The Books and School of the Ages.* New York: Harcourt, 1994.

Butler, Judith. *Bodies That Matter: On the Discursive Limits of "Sex."* New York: Routledge, 1993.

D'Souza, Dinesh. *Illiberal Education: The Politics of Race and Sex on Campus.* New York: Vintage, 1992.

Freire, Paulo, and Donaldo Macedo. *Literacy: Reading the Word and the World.* South Hadley, MA: Bergin, 1987.

Fuss, Diana, ed. *Inside/Out: Lesbian Theories, Gay Theories.* New York: Routledge, 1991.

Harper, Phillip Brian. "Gay Male Identities, Personal Privacy, and Relations of Public Exchange: Notes on Directions for Queer Critique." *Social Text* 15.3–4 (1997): 5–29.

hooks, bell. *Talking Back: Thinking Feminist, Thinking Black.* Boston: South End, 1989.

Kimball, Roger. *Tenured Radicals: How Politics Has Corrupted Higher Education.* New York: Harper, 1990. Introduction by Kimball. Chicago: Elephant Paperbacks, 1998.

Sedgwick, Eve Kosofsky. "How to Bring Your Kids Up Gay: The War on Effeminate Boys." *Tendencies*. Eve Kosofsky Sedgwick. Durham: Duke UP, 1993. 154–64.

———. "Queer and Now." Sedgwick 1–20.

Shakespeare, William. *King Lear*. Ed. Kenneth Muir. 1972. Arden Shakespeare. London: Methuen, 1982.

Spurlin, William J. "Sissies and Sisters: Gender, Sexuality and the Possibilities of Coalition." *Coming Out of Feminism?* Ed. Mandy Merck, Naomi Segal, and Elizabeth Wright. Oxford: Blackwell, 1998. 74–101.

Stewart, Susan. "The State of Cultural Theory and the Future of Literary Form." *Profession 93*. New York: MLA, 1993. 12–15.

Warner, Michael, ed. *Fear of a Queer Planet: Queer Politics and Social Theory*. Minneapolis: U of Minnesota P, 1993.

Watney, Simon. "School's Out." Fuss 387–401.

I

POSITIONS

CHAPTER ONE

Cruising the Libraries

LEE LYNCH

L ittle Ms. Muffet? Phooey. Cinderella? You have to be kidding. *Maybe* Prince Charming, but he was pretty innocuous, as well as male. Certainly no one in Grimm and Andersen. As a matter of fact, all those nursery rhymes and fairy tales, where the women were stolen or disappeared in a puff of smoke, where animals were hurt and men were not just powerful but superhuman, frightened me.

Nancy Drew? Now, she had promise. Dr. Doolittle? Absolutely. Young dykes are often more comfortable with animals than with humans—except who could identify with a bumbling, middle-aged man? Wasn't there anyone in literature like little Lee? I felt a real affinity with the fairies of Ireland, but all the available stories had them stealing babies, like queers corrupting Anita Bryant's children. Besides, they'd been shrunk to less than life size and I felt diminutive enough, lost enough in the crowd of rapacious, roughnecking boys and primping girls who were my peers.

Where were the stories of tomboys? Of little kids growing up with same-sex or single parents? Why did Nancy Drew have to have a boyfriend? Why couldn't a writer portray puppy love between best girlfriends? Why wouldn't a librarian order such books? Wasn't there one picture book, when I was five, of a little girl fighting to the death the horror of being skirted-up for a first day at school—and winning? Did Jill never save Jack? Or Jane, Jill?

This essay is dedicated to my high school English teacher, Mr. James Fechheimer, Flushing High School, Flushing, New York, 1962–1963.

At about the age of thirteen I stumbled across Carson McCullers's *The Member of the Wedding*. I totally understood Frankie Addams. Her anguish at not belonging in the world was mine. Her aborted attempts to relate to the wedding couple, to the femmy little girlfriend, and to the sailor who picked her up were so like my own search. When I found *The Heart Is a Lonely Hunter*, Carson McCullers gifted me with hope. Wasn't Mick in this situation just like me?

> Are you just going to tramp around the room all day? It makes me sick to see you in those silly boys' clothes. Somebody ought to clamp down on you, Mick Kelly, and make you behave," Etta said.

> "Shut up," said Mick. "I wear shorts because I don't want to wear your old hand-me-downs. I don't want to look like either of you. And I won't. That's why I wear shorts. I'd rather be a boy any day." (35)

Still, Mick and all McCullers's characters seemed to live in a twisted place nearly as frightening as a fairy tale. In *The Member of the Wedding*, Frankie feared that her own difference would trap her in a world of "freaks" like the ones she'd seen at the circus.

Throughout childhood and adolescence, I searched and searched for images of myself in literature, on television, in movies. I identified not with Scarlett, but with Rhett. At fourteen I thought Thomas Wolfe's passion was my own; I began to pour my heart onto paper just like him. Jean-Paul Sartre described exactly my feelings of discomfort in the world; I despaired and grew cynical.

At fifteen I came out. I accepted my Rhettness, but no one else did. My feeling of exclusion only deepened. I grew more fairylike, lost in the dells of my ire-land.

I found Radclyffe Hall's *The Well of Loneliness*, Ann Bannon's books, Vin Packer and her other pseudonym, Ann Aldrich. At last, lesbians! I devoured the books, loved the characters, identified completely. This was a mistake. These books, while validating because they acknowledged the existence of lesbians by portraying us, destroyed any incipient pride I might have had in my true fairy self. Titles like *Queer Patterns*, *The Evil Friendship*, and *The Sex Between* were instant signals of gay books. The characters were more miserable than Sartre's, and despised as well.

Ann Aldrich's *Take a Lesbian to Lunch*, while not released until 1971, illustrates the tone of books I read in the early sixties, her heyday. (I suspect this was written then and only published when the women's movement began to take hold, as if it reflected that spirit!) Aldrich purports to interview a straight male "host" in a Mafia-run lesbian bar. He declaims:

> "The pretty ones who come in here—they're twisted somewhere in their heads. I'm better buddies with the butches. I know what they're about. No man would want them in the first place. As females they're mistakes, pukes. Half of them got faces like little midgets—I've observed that about them—something about their faces, baby faces—they didn't develop right. Something in their genes. . . . But the goodlooking ones who could pass for my wife or daughter . . . They become gay to spit in men's eyes." (95)

I had found models of lesbians in literature at last, but inside them lurked Frankie Addams without her innocence. Radclyffe Hall's Stephen Gordon asserts in *The Well of Loneliness* what we homosexuals "must realize more clearly than ever, that love is only permissible to those who are cut in every respect to life's pattern" (188). These lessons were hard, but I took them with pride, a sexual rebel.

So I joined the underground of my own supposedly tormented kind, rejecting the far from baby-faced butches and the occasional spitting-mad femme, even as I followed them around New York City and learned their ways. I fell in love with many young women, some of whom wanted to come out, some of whom I refused in order to spare them my fate. At the same time I exulted in my lot, celebrated it with the girls (and boys) who were either of it already or who proved more persistent than my scruples. I felt as torn as the lovers in Valerie Taylor's 1957 novel, *Whisper Their Love*.

"I don't care. I'd like to tell everybody."

"I care," Edith said sharply. "I like my job, apart from having to earn a living. You don't know how they crucify people like us, tear us limb from limb and laugh when we suffer. . . . Everybody hates us." (56)

Although I read every one of these mass-market paperbacks I could get my hands on, always hungry for my life in literature, I yearned for more substance. I started to search the libraries and used bookstores to discover more authors like McCullers, who hinted at lives behind the heterosexual stories they wrote. It is amazing how unerring a kid with a variant eye can be, like a musical child prodigy with a perfect ear. Katherine Hume wasn't uncloseted for years, nor were Edna St. Vincent Millay, Mary Renault, or Virginia Woolf, but they felt variant to me. I even checked Cecil Beaton's photographs out of the library, and stared at the work of Louise Nevelson at the Museum of Modern Art, fascinated by the variance I sensed in their images.

Sherwood Anderson became my new hero when I found his *Beyond Desire*. John O'Hara was obviously fascinated by lesbians in work like his novel *The Ewings*. I found poets, Charlotte Mew and H. D., for example, before the gay scholars had at them. I could have taught a course in gay lit. by the time I hit college.

For the next several years, even into the start of women's and gay liberation, I continued the activity I came to call "cruising the libraries." Identifying variant books was as subtle, frustrating, and exciting a process as spotting lesbians on the street. Success depended on a vigilant desperation. I *had* to find reflections of myself to be assured that I was a valuable human being and not alone in the world.

This slightly tinged lavender culture was all I had, this and, later, the liquid solace of the bars. From fifteen to twenty-five, when the revolution finally reached me personally, I was driven, searching for my nourishment like a starveling, grabbing at any crumb that looked, tasted, or smelled digestible. Often wrong, always hopeful, my gay antennae never rested. Most of the passages quoted here I have taken from a yellowing collection of index cards I began to gather at age fifteen. These are the words which taught me who and what I was, which frightened and comforted me, which gave me my own life's work.

It's hard to reconstruct that literary cruising process. My tools were few and crude. There was the obvious one: the card catalog, though it yielded little enough. I can remember poring through it at my local library in Queens, New York, fruitlessly searching for other books by Radclyffe Hall. I was shaken by the intellectual thrill of finding, at Manhattan's 42nd Street library, a cross-reference to Una Troubridge and a book called *The Life and Death of Radclyffe Hall.* Until then, I hadn't been certain that Hall was anything more than a straight writer who'd written a chance novel about lesbians, but Troubridge's book, its cover, and photographs were fairly convincing evidence—and I took this evidence, hoarding it like a lone jewel in an otherwise empty case. Not only had I found lesbian characters, but a definitely lesbian writer, as I wanted to be.

How, though, had I first located *The Well of Loneliness?* I recall that moment, too. These were, after all, not simply formative, but decisive episodes at the start of a career I would dedicate to lesbians and lesbian words. There were no bookstores in my city, but next to the Paramount Theater in Queens was a stationery store. I must have drifted out of a Doris Day feature and into the stationery store to browse through the books. I'd already discovered paperback racks in the corner drugstore. My brother had bought me my first adult book there: *The Hunchback of Notre Dame.* Now *there's* a story of an outcast, and a love that dared not speak its name. But on this newly discovered rack I found *The Well of Loneliness.* The title had a provocative ring to it. Hadn't I fallen into just such a well? I peered inside. Imagine the effect of this passage on a gay, sixteen-year-old, would-be writer:

> "You're neither unnatural, nor abominable, nor mad; you're as much a part of what people call nature as anyone else; only you're unexplained as yet—you've not got your niche in creation. But some day that will come, and meanwhile don't shrink from yourself, but just face yourself calmly and bravely. Have courage; do the best you can with your burden. For their sakes show the world that people like you and they can be quite as

selfless and kind as the rest of mankind. Let your life go to prove this—it would be a really great life-work, Stephen." (154)

These words, spoken by Puddle in the novel, still move and inspire me.

Other racks over the years would yield further rewards. I found Gore Vidal on a shelf in a little bookshop at Grand Central Station. On Main Street in Bridgeport, Connecticut, there was a newspaper store where regular vigilance turned up books I was petrified to take to the cashier. Their ludicrous and blatantly sensational cover copy were both my signals and my shame. Valerie Taylor's *The Girls in Three-B* and Randy Salem's *Man among Women:* these books I would savor alone, heart pounding from both lust and terror of discovery, poised to plunge the tainted tome into hiding.

From *Spring Fire* by Vin Packer: "her hands found Leda's body. Then for the first time she was the aggressor. The strength that was sleeping in her awakened. A powerful compulsion welled up inside Mitch as she felt the pliant curves of Leda's body. Then they lay together, breathless and filled with a new peace." (78). I recognized this compulsion that heterosexuals called passion; I knew the peace "normal" people called love.

Just as other gays dotted the street populations of my young world, turning it into an endless exciting cruising ground, so a few of these compatriots led me, by word of mouth, to more precious books. This is how I originally heard of Ann Aldrich and Vin Packer, whom I was to learn years later are one and the same. Ann Bannon's books were so well loved I never even read one until much later. Some treasures were so priceless no one would lend them.

The other gay kids acted as a grapevine. (The word *grapevine* itself would tip me off to Jess Stern's work of the same name, an exploitative exposé of lesbians.) We had an oral *Who's Who* which included not only peers, movie stars, and pop singers, but authors. How did the famous names—Somerset Maugham, for example, or Marianne Moore—filter down to the sticky tables of Pam Pam's, the baby gays' ice-cream parlor on Sixth Avenue? It could be a hint as small as one I recently ran across in a movie review about a male character who wore nail polish to work.

Immediately my feelers twitched and I was searching for more. A long, deeply ingrained habit—or has it become an instinct for survival?

Traditionally, Clue Number One would always be marital status. A wedding ring in our circle did not mean quite the same thing that it would to a young het stalking husbands. Single was suspect and sometimes proof. Of course, married people were not safe either. We knew all about marriages of convenience. Someone always knew someone who was married because of her parents. Cover photographs were scrutinized for short hair on women, a pinky ring, and the indefinable "look" we sought on everyone: that dyke or faggot stamp that is utterly indefinable. These tactics did not always work. Françoise Sagan finally disappointed me. She'd had the short hair, the right face, and it was so easy to assume that she'd changed the pronouns in her slightly decadent love stories.

Also indefinable was variant content. McCullers was obvious, with her tomboys and otherly characters. I sought writers like her in the style I would later learn was Southern Gothic. Though Flannery O'Connor and William Faulkner proved worthless for my cause, Truman Capote, with his sissified young men, was as obvious as McCullers. My first taste of Tennessee Williams was through the mysterious but undeniably homosexual Sebastian in *Suddenly Last Summer.*

What did I find in these and other books which made the *New York Times Book Review*? Everything from shadows of my life to reflections of my mind—seldom out front, mostly nuance, never certain, always terribly exciting. Why was this so important? Simply, I suspected that all of these authors might be queer like me. Yet they belonged, truly had a place in the world, were valued. Even the fact that those who were gay were closeted thrilled me because I was part of their secret society. Someday I, too, might be valued *even though I was gay.*

Still, the words I needed to see in print remained invisible. It was all guesswork on my part: a photograph of no-frills Willa Cather; the literary whisper of a close friendship between Virginia Woolf and Vita Sackville-West; the frank, unabashed eyes and crew cut of Gertrude Stein; certain themes like the idyllic childhood scenes of Louisa May Alcott and Mazo de la Roche.

The latter panned out much later, though I could not have named the attraction of the Jalna novels when I read them. I only remember being hooked, completely. Was Rennie really a woman in de la Roche's mind? Alcott, of course, married, but having recently visited her home, and stood in those tiny rooms where privacy was obviously unheard of, I can understand why she would not come out. Even the desk where she wrote was totally exposed.

And the words, the lovely discriminating words of the poets, non-gender specific like Emily Dickinson and Louise Bogan, or full of Christina Rossetti's fiery passion, or of imagery which suggested variance.

Other tip-offs, as unreliable as short hair, were androgynous names. This was my original route to Carson McCullers. It also led me to Djuna Barnes. Although her lesbians were remote to me—as disturbed as Randy Salem's and as distant in terms of class as Radclyffe Hall's—Barnes's writing was brilliant. If I couldn't imagine knowing her characters, or creating a world like hers when I became a writer, I could at least dream, in adolescence, of writing as poetically. Though Barnes was later to deny her lesbian sexuality, at least I had someone to idolize when it counted. I visited Patchin Place, where she lived, like a shrine.

> What is this love we have for the invert, boy or girl? It was they who were spoken of in every romance that we ever read. The girl lost, what is she but the prince found? The prince on the white horse that we have always been seeking. And the pretty lad who is a girl, what but the prince-princess in pointlace— neither one and half the other, the painting on the fan! . . . for in the girl it is the prince, and in the boy it is the girl that makes a prince a prince—and not a man. (Barnes, *Nightwood* 136–37)

Then, in a magazine shop in Greenwich Village, I found *The Ladder*. This small, rough periodical was not full of unhappy endings. I sensed that its very existence proclaimed a kind of healthy survival I hadn't imagined possible. There were stories and poems and articles, advertisements and letters and editorials, just like in a real magazine. To a sadsack little kid who'd been badly beaten by blows dealt her from the hands of literary gays and straights alike, blows of persuasion to hide and mourn her very being, *The Ladder* allowed entry into a legitimate universe.

I was too young. I've told this tale on myself many times, about my disappointment when, reading the subscription blank, it said I had to be twenty-one to subscribe. Not that I had any place where I could have received the priceless journals by mail. Not that I would have had the price of a subscription.

But I now knew *The Ladder* existed, a magazine for me when I grew up. Most important, I had something, as a young writer, to which I could aspire.

Oh, I'm not saying that as a teenager my whole goal in life was to write lesbian materials for lesbians and to be published in a lesbian periodical and to be part of a growing gay publishing empire. No, I wanted to be Wolfe still, and Kerouac and Dreiser. Little by little, though, I began to wonder what a lesbian Wolfe would sound like.

Much later Jane Rule's work came into my life. *The Desert of the Heart,* first published in 1964, put together good writing with healthy, respectable lesbians. Rule had the magical ability to treat her gay characters as if they could function normally in a world large enough to hold them. No longer did I just want to write for *The Ladder,* which I was, by then, doing. Now I wanted to write like Jane Rule. The only words I could put to this yearning were the ones I use still: I wanted to make gay people feel as good about themselves as Jane Rule made me feel: "Evelyn saw Ann. It had not been her intention at first. It had not been her intention ever. And it was not her intention now, but it was her desire to be here or anywhere with Ann, a desire which all her intentions denied" (Rule 221).

Now when I read from the vast selection of lesbian and gay literature, I am looking for that same uplifting experience. I don't want the tormented complaints of our past abuse, unless they're turned around into hope and acceptance. I don't want melodramatic stories of desolation. I want our protagonists and heroes to be rounded people living in the world. I want our literature to project our own newfound or newly acknowledged health and I don't care if it's in mysteries and romances, or heady intellectual novels and perfect short stories. I want us thriving through our words.

I do care who writes the words. Straight authors writing gay characters are likely to fall as flat as I now realize John O'Hara did when creating those stiff, sexless lesbians of his. I'm not that hungry anymore. Though straight writers are not the only ones who carry homophobia like an illness in the blood (especially if they want to make a buck), they have little motivation to practice safe writing: writing that's not dangerous to the gay psyche.

I want gay characters to be as honestly passionate as gay people are. To throb with love and greed and hunger and all the driving forces of life which make for a common humanity. Gay characters do not have to thrash around obsessed with sexuality, though as long as it's an issue in the world at large it will be part of our literary thrashings.

I don't believe in prettying up our world for readers. Like heterosexuals, some of us are sick, or mean, or criminal. I don't believe in pretending happy endings when they aren't appropriate. On the other hand, there's a whole world of people who think they have no stake in our future and who continue to perpetuate the negative stereotypes of gays that heterosexual fear has invented. Vin Packer's bar host Arty was ignorant; he need be no longer.

I have been through years of self-destructive behavior, therapy, and recovery. I've experienced the damage of all that negativity. I want to create an alternative literature; to embrace where we were, but to deliberately flood our culture with the positive images which will make a better future; to create real characters with all their foibles, but to let them loose into a universe which will support them.

Writing about Radclyffe Hall, Una Troubridge asserted: "She had long wanted to write a book on sexual inversion. . . . It was her absolute conviction that such a book could only be written by a sexual invert, who alone could be qualified by personal knowledge and experience to speak on behalf of a misjudged and misunderstood minority" (81–82).

There is no way Little Miss Muffet or Cinderella was gay, but Judy Grahn in *Another Mother Tongue* has traced a gay connection to the Fairy people. And I was fervently grateful when I stumbled across Hall who had achieved her aim and made possible every bit of lesbian literature which has followed.

Jane Rule's *Desert* wasn't there for me then, but it's pushed back even further the walls which squeezed us, sometimes to death. The young dyke writers growing up will be stronger for Hall and for Rule, and will create a literature ever freer of doom because of their foremothers. There is no way the constantly expanded freedoms of the press won't affect everyone who reads our work. Where it will evolve I can't imagine, as I once could not imagine our current culture. My interest is that no little Lee ever suffer alone again.

Works Cited

Aldrich, Ann. *Take a Lesbian to Lunch*. New York: Macfadden-Bartell, 1972.

Barnes, Djuna. *Nightwood*. 1937. New York: New Directions, 1961.

Grahn, Judy. *Another Mother Tongue: Gay Words, Gay Worlds*. Boston: Beacon, 1984.

Hall, Radclyffe. *The Well of Loneliness*. 1928. New York: Pocket, 1950.

McCullers, Carson. *The Heart Is a Lonely Hunter*. 1940. New York: Bantam, 1953.

———. *The Member of the Wedding*. Boston: Houghton, 1946.

Packer, Vin. *Spring Fire*. Greenwich: Fawcett, 1952.

Rule, Jane. *The Desert of the Heart*. Cleveland: World, 1964.

Salem, Randy. *Man among Women*. Boston: Beacon, 1960.

Taylor, Valerie. *The Girls in Three-B*. New York: Crest, 1959.

———. *Whisper Their Love*. New York: Crest, 1957.

Troubridge, Una. *The Life and Death of Radclyffe Hall*. London: Hammond, 1961.

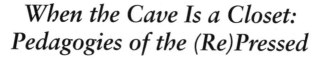

CHAPTER TWO

When the Cave Is a Closet: Pedagogies of the (Re)Pressed

EDWARD J. INGEBRETSEN, S.J.
Georgetown University

Fear, then, begins the story, and, with no apparent bridge across the abyss, the story for many of us ends abruptly there—at the hard place.

MARY ELLIOTT, "Coming Out"

"It's a strange image you're describing, and strange prisoners."

PLATO, *The Republic*

For a queer teacher to achieve a degree of safety in the classroom entails a complex choreography. He or she must negotiate multiple and generally disguised fault lines of power: civil, legal, popular, academic. When that queer teacher is Catholic, at a Catholic university, energies of the ecclesiastical kind figure in. When that queer Catholic is, in addition, a priest, a rhetoric of the monstrous is activated—a civic rubric of reprisal derived in large part from the cinema. This essay explores the confusions that arise—often with political forethought—when an instructor's private sexual identification or subjectivity becomes the subject under academic scrutiny. What happens when the teacher (the one who "knows," according to traditional pedagogical models) becomes aligned with the monstrous—a "knowing" that is, civically speaking, unspeakable? For the hapless lesbian or gay teacher, an unthinking use of Christian theology finds support from civic ideology, while media-organized fear politics noisily confirm both church and state: *monsters cannot be allowed to live.*

At the Front

Let me begin with some initial considerations about pedagogy as it is currently practiced. The classroom is the most public of the "private" sectors—the site most liable to "violent ideological contestation" (Watney 390). In it, the boundaries between the ostensibly private and the necessarily public stand revealed as a politically useful fantasy. Indeed, the public classroom is the place where the panopticon of social maintenance most exerts itself. Karen Harbeck writes, for instance, that "monitoring the activities of the teacher has been an affirmative community responsibility" (1). Public institutions at all levels face endless varieties of administrative interventions, usually routinized as calls for "departmental consistency" and "pedagogic evaluation." Like its public cousin in this respect, the Catholic classroom also supports a network of interlaced authoritative surveillances. Sometimes these privileged entries are gained in the name of social welfare, for reasons of health and civic safety, or for economic and public accountability. The Catholic classroom, however, presumes in addition a further, ecclesiastical intervention. The resulting tension between the secular and the religious has marked Catholic parochial education since its inception in the early nineteenth century. It continues to the present, as evidenced in Rome's most recent document on American Catholic universities, "Ex Corde Ecclesiae" (1990).

While ecclesiastical authority can sometimes be doctrinally specific, more often it works less directly, its force being felt as appeals for "moral tone," "orthodoxy," or "traditional values." Both secular and religious classrooms, then, are highly evaluative, intensely moralized sites. As a consequence, they are places of potential distress for many students as well as instructors. The latter, however, are under particular pressure. Whether the instructor is untenured and class evaluations are part of a tenuring process, or already tenured and in theory free of such interventions, these evaluative moments function as routine de facto policing.

It should be clear from the foregoing that no classroom is free of ideological pressure. When arranging a class or a curriculum around gender or sexuality, social investments in the facts and values of sexuality—both hotly contested—only compound the difficulties. Writes Mary Elliott, "Neutrality . . . is a universal cultural default setting which is almost always presumed to be heterosexual and white; it is not available to those who cannot 'pass' as either or both" (698). Under conditions that can sometimes be called academic vigilantism—whether encouraged by social policing, departmental micromanaging, or ecclesiastical zeal—pedagogy in a class featuring sex or gender issues is further problematized when the teacher is lesbian or gay, since those identities are still almost inevitably morally marked. In the first place, the self-identified lesbian or gay is *already* stigmatized as possibly diseased, potentially illegal, and certainly deviant. Ecclesiastical censure only increases the pressure, because from the Church's point of view—at least according to Catholics who do not bother to nuance church teachings on this issue—to be gay is to be *necessarily* sinful, as well. At best, the condition of homosexuality, however unwilled it might be, is thought to be a "near occasion" of sin, as the old moral manuals would term it. So whatever its private politics, being gay or lesbian in a public educational context is a social performance requiring skill and finesse to manage well. The athleticism, stamina, and sometimes sheer luck needed to negotiate these complexities can be formidable. Sometimes, in the process of negotiating them, education threatens to give way to a different set of explanatory terms entirely: specifically, confession, spectacle, and horror.

Lifting the Curtain, Opening the Closet

> [C]onfessions are the hottest of all stories. Ask any priest.
> MATTHEW RETTEMUND, *Boy Culture*

> What counts as experience is neither self-evident nor straightforward; it is always contested, and always therefore political.
> JOAN R. SCOTT, *"The Value of Experience"*

In the densely written social palimpsest of the classroom, the lesbian or gay teacher easily becomes entangled in a grammar of the pornographic. That is, the teacher performs a skin dance, a public baring of his or her emotional body that is generally not permitted under other conditions. The only problem, of course, is that the dance is forced. Indeed, framed as potentially scandalous, the public deviant presents a spectacle that is much in demand in eroticized popular culture. Like all prejudice, this focus on the instructor's presumed (anticipated?) sexual deviancy fetishizes the visible body in an accustomed cultural manner, framing it within a libidinal discourse of violation, contamination, and seduction. Theological discourse adds a fourth term—temptation. Setting up the queer instructor as a potential *political* spectacle, then, incites a civic panic that, no matter how it is framed (medically, morally, legally, or socially), activates a ritual of monster staking. In this civic rite of degradation, whose form is generally adapted from the cinema, the body politic defends moral or social boundaries by exposing and eliminating the monster that threatens the common weal.

In historical usage, the monster (from the Latin *monstrare,* meaning "to show," and *monere,* "to warn") was an individual whose private life became semiotically charged with public intent by virtue of his or her anomalous body. The "spectacle of the extraordinary body" (Thomson 1) was an interpretive event with consequences that crossed social and class boundaries and affected moral discourses as well as cultural practices. In contemporary usage, monstrosity still functions as it has for centuries, as an emotional shorthand term for civic reprisal. Nonetheless, the monster's time-honored role—lubricating social phobias of different kinds—barely disguises the commercial and erotic energies that fuel its politics. That is, erotic energy, unnamed as such, becomes the means by which public interest in the monster is aroused, since in current usage he or she is generally engaged in some sort of illicit intimacy. In turn, this libidinal energy converts easily enough into repudiation, not only of the monster but also of the monster's illicit activities. This then is the dilemma confronting gay or lesbian teachers long before they enter the classroom; they are coerced against their will into becoming agents of an eroticized show of sorts. As a consequence, focusing on the reported or potential erotic interest of the teacher, the tabloidal classroom takes its place as one of the means available in popular culture by which the erotic and the horrible elicit and secure social cohesion (see Crew and Norton; Abelove, Ohmann, and Potter).

To take a specific instance: I am a Catholic priest teaching in the English department at a Catholic university. Since 1995 I have taught a course examining the uses of social deviancy in American popular culture. English 118, Unspeakable Lives: Gay and Lesbian Narrative, focuses on a variety of self-identified lesbian and gay texts, as well as ideologically diverse commentary about them. The title of the course sets out the paradox under review; despite their highly visible position in United States public discourse, lesbians and gays are nonetheless disavowed in a variety of ways. How, then, can lives under social, medical, legal, and religious erasure prompt narrative of any kind, either public or private? How, that is, can a subject under erasure also be under scrutiny? What happens when discredited private experience becomes speakable only to the extent that it functions as a "deviancy," moralized for "the public good"? And, finally, if homosexuality *is* so unspeakable, why then in this culture is there so much spoken about it?

In English 118, education, censorious spectacle, and public morality entangle, and their various civic energies overlap. Nonetheless, the stated goal of the class is fairly conventional. It intends to untangle the spectacular from the educational and to reshape public thinking about the discourses of entertainment, education, and morality. The fact that the link between entertainment and deviancy is as commonplace as it is unspoken is one reason this course seeks to examine the linkage. Thus a course popularly perceived to be *about* social deviants actually poses more complicated questions about the reach and scope of deviancy as a social grammar—questioning in particular the pleasures clearly taken in the public display of "perversities." How, for example, is deviancy productive—of talk, of sales, of moral discourse itself? Ultimately this class examines the discursive practices in which lives of deviants are made to signify in purposely contradictory ways in order to produce a civic text often at odds with itself.

In its emphasis on language and text, English 118 is not all that different from more traditionally formulated courses in literature and linguistic studies. It differs from others, however, in that its scope is potentially wider—concerned as it is with the complications of *all* speech acts—as it assesses the grave consequences that follow from deflections and erasures in the discursive domain. To take a case in point: Freedom of speech is acclaimed everywhere. Congressional and presidential addresses extol it, while newspaper and tabloid alike hail it as the essential American freedom. Yet, to the contrary, in contemporary American society it is not *what* is said in public that is problematic—rather, it is what is not and what *will not* be said. That is the burden of this course's double-edged title. On the one hand, "unspeakable" refers to the social stigmas of taboo and horror attached to (and sustaining) the suspect lives and social narratives of homosexuals—which presumably the course organizes for dispassionate study. On the other hand, in very practical ways "unspeakable" is what students in the class find themselves becoming as they are forced to enact their own minigothic monster shows under the intense glare of publicity.

What do I mean by this? An initial insight into the social machinery of deviancy occurs when students find themselves becoming its scrutinized objects—their choice to take this class coming under evaluation by friends, acquaintances, even complete strangers. In particular, an unreflected taboo *about* the course leads to a pervasive inability to *speak* about it to peers, other professors, or parents. In the first place, in the erotic rhythms of pop culture, private lives become public by being sexualized. This publicity is one of the primary ways by which erotic interest is kept free-floating and culturally available for purchase, whether economically or semiotically. Partly because of this already intense pressure, going public with participation in a course like this seems tantamount to confession. How, students wonder, do they talk about the course to the prurient or merely curious of their friends without at the same time implicating themselves in the voyeuristic patterns the questions set up? The students become for a time the very lives on display; their "private experience" is evaluated publicly as "unspeakable" and triangulated as gossip in a direct but nonetheless ironic way, while the discourse of deviancy slips and slops around them. It soon becomes evident that being socially marked as gay depends less on biology than on social need. Anyone, that is, can assume the position of the socially abject—and at one time or another most of us have experienced the repudiatory uses of failed gender.

For a handful of students, the class's first lesson is having to acknowledge (and then manage) anxiety over how the course will be registered on their transcript. Should the terms "gay" or "lesbian" in the course title be listed? How, in other words, will their private learning be publicly signified? Will it be perceived as "orientation" (and scandalous) or as "learning" (and thus read as a sign of liberality and "tolerance")? These initial confusions are soon followed by others, and, when asked what they are studying, in a sort of cognitive overload students often take immediate and unreflected evasive action: "Oh, just some English course." This initial act of voluntary self-erasure may not trouble them at the time. By semester's end, however, even the most unreflecting student can recall this moment as a shame-drenched act of abjection publicly performed for others.

In retrospect, what stops students in their tracks is the speed by which, without ever thinking about it, even otherwise "straight" students silence themselves. In effect, such students become socially "queer," finding themselves engaged in the same stigma management common to their lesbian and gay friends— having to deal with knowledges, presumed yet not validated, and their consequences, real or imagined. As a result, they find themselves constructing their own defensive structures, from which vantage point they come to know an anxiety familiar to their closeted friends: Is the closet closeted enough? Are they "passing" and is their performance adequate enough? Here, as Sedgwick observes, the "precisely unnamed . . . delineation between 'the sexual' and 'the nonsexual'" creates "threshold effects" (45). This fosters the responsibility-less voyeurism that locates itself on students' bodies. Better than any theoretical lecture, this shifting threshold demonstrates the course's wider reach: all private lives have moments of forced public interpellation when, by the dictates of "politeness," of legal or religious constraints, or through other established mechanisms, private or personal experience is rendered unspeakable. Silence is a powerful, purposeful weapon.

"Nice" speech—the kind that receives social approbation—is, students learn, paradoxically a matter of not speaking at all. They also come to see how lesbian and gay persons, unlike other socially constrained populations, suffer this effect in particularly acute ways. In other words, *any* speech about the most common details of such stigmatized lives is, by definition, not "nice": "I don't care what they do, but why do they always have to flaunt it?" Rather than being a set of orders pragmatically governing military duplicity, "don't ask, don't tell" is a pervasive cultural phenomenon.

Another instance of the closet's compulsory, and perhaps compulsive, performance occurs when a student, enrolled in the class, mentions it to another—only, in response, to be asked not to describe the class, nor what texts will be read, but "Who *else* is in the class?" Suddenly the student—seemingly outside the scrutinizing apparatus of the closet and perhaps thinking *herself* looking in at others—finds instead that *she* is now the object of the sexualized gaze. Indeed, she now understands experientially that the closet's social usefulness is its punitive flexibility; it organizes the visual field of speculation in such a way that *no one*, not even she herself, is outside its potential frame. In this case, the student realizes that her inquiring friend thinks her to be *in* the closet, not just peering through the door at others. This is where the blackmail that burdens the daily lives of lesbians and gays works its effect. That is, the price exacted for being released from the suspicion of "being one" is informing on others. A certain kind of painful education happens here, of course, but one for which this student and others receive no academic credit. Yet by that same token, under this pressure the educative process again risks being hijacked by emotional terrorism of a fairly banal kind. What was once a class becomes an ongoing series of mini-outings staged as confessional moments in a model typically associated with TV entertainment.

The swirl of prohibitions and fascinations around the course, then, perhaps prompts its general narrative unspeakability. This contradiction alone increases the course's availability for fantasy, as evidenced in three different melodramas that play out around it, two of which will be discussed in each of the following sections. The first script I have already been discussing: the use of the spectatorial mechanics of the "closet." Powerful social emotions permeate any public contesting of "the homosexual question"—as courses like this one are rightly seen to do. The fear that a range of experiences socially constrained as taboo might actually be spoken accounts for the furious mobilization of public speech against it. An example of the virulence at work would be Mike Wallace's 1998 *20/20* television exposé on the academic study of sexuality and gender issues. Wallace's show explored the shift in the college curriculum from "traditional" topics to "pop" studies of deviancy, sex, and gender; he noted in particular, with alarm, the efflorescence of courses about homosexuality.

A slightly ajar closet door permits policing as well as display. Thus, from the outside, the closet serves the comfort and enjoyment of those watching for hints of movement around the closet door. The wandering eyes of those outside may cross the threshold unheeded, at their convenience and as the colonizing reaches of their fantasies demand. On the other hand, opening closet doors is thought to permit persons held captive to "come out." Yet just how liberating a movement is this? Such a passage is not unlike an antebellum American South rite, the degrading cakewalk, although its use is affectional rather than racial in this case—the voyeuristic scrutiny by others must be undergone by instructor as well as by any student who, as a consequence of enrolling in this course, finds himself or herself standing everywhere in the closet's glare. This of course is exactly why the passage out of the closet is never a cakewalk, in the now customary sense of the word. Instead, it is like negotiating the so-called demilitarized zone—one journeys across this heavily armored space at public risk, under the gossipy gaze of those whose "right" to look is never challenged.[1]

The intrusive, sexualizing gaze of those in the dominant position—authorities, other students, the curious or downright prurient—passes without comment. The extent of the social power wielded by those presumably not in sexually marked closets is evidenced in the fact that *their* prying gaze is never acknowledged as such, nor is it ever returned by those thus exhibited in positions of subordination. Cultural supremacy, then, is demonstrated by an ability to pass visually *into* the closet whenever desired, without occasioning remark. For this reason, being marked gay is often less a statement of biological necessity than a pragmatic social assessment. It is, after all, the privilege of the dominant, who do the looking, "to know" these things. In an ironic way, the closet can be viewed as an extension of the academy, since the evaluating gaze that organizes its use can be authorized, even justified, in the name of knowledge—a point I will consider in a moment.

Murray Kempton writes, "The closet happens to be the single human invention whose consequences have been universally benevolent" (qtd. in McCarthy 31–32). Of course. Like beauty, benevolence is in the eye of the one who controls the discourse. Further, in a commodity culture in which the traffic in erotizing bodies is as pornographic as in a gothic slasher film, the closet is especially benevolent when circulation of information about "the body"—someone else's in all cases—functions as "entertainment." The closet is designed in the first place to ensure a habit of passive watching that, like entertainment, guarantees the visual as a regulatory field. Either from within or outside the closet, the closet's social force depends upon the same specious, untheorized notion of visibility that cheers the occasional Ellen who is permitted to "come out" on TV, performing deviance for the titillating pleasures of the always phantasmatic "general public"—those whose common virtue lies in their untroubled straightness.

Teacher as Tour Guide

After being listed in the school's catalog for three years and regularly appearing in departmental announcements, English 118 achieved a semblance of conventionality. For many students, the course seemed similar to various programs abroad, a kind of academic tourism. Understood as a safely managed excursion to a world of exotica and prohibition, somewhat akin to the semester-at-sea program, students initially expected that course requirements would be light (How hard is *watching*, after all?!). For this reason, it was thought that the course would be "safe" for those nonexotic and nonprohibited (i.e., straight-identified) students who wished, in an old phrase, to take a walk "on the wild side." That is, an exposure that would ordinarily be taboo (hanging out with queers, reading "their" literature) was rendered permissible. Any potential threat or social stigma was sanitized by being encapsulated within the morally privileged discourse of "learning"—students would be "exposed" to experience that would confirm their benevolent tolerance in the first place.

For some students, however, less laudable reasons motivated their interest in the course; inquiries about it tacitly assumed that the course would facilitate the unveiling of hitherto hidden deviancies (not to mention the deviants themselves) that would be numbered and arranged, socially located, and made conveniently visible to the not always benign gaze of others. Initial comments suggested that many students (gay- as well as straight-identified) presumed that the course would function in precisely this fashion, supporting their own self-constructed, naive liberality. Viewed in this manner, however, the course could only be one more in a series of closets, socially arranged and approved. In addition, such views merely collude in a culturalwide liberalism in which altruism and abjection are reverse sides of the same mechanism of entrenched social power. Further, these expectations register the way homophobia plays from within and without, a position toxic to gay as well as straight. As time went on, students understood how such a taxonomizing project (and the leering fascination it evidences) targeted each of them in differing, though equally pernicious, ways. Gay students found themselves trotted out as spectacle and moral program, straight students found themselves dispensing a toxic compassion, and a third group, avoiding identity politics altogether, silently enacted the passive watching of spectator culture.

At any moment, as we have seen, the "subject" under study in this classroom could shift to a different subject or set of subjects entirely. Nor were students the only ones who faced potential entrapment in the series of scrutinies set up by dynamics within and outside the classroom. The second script prompted by this course, while making similar presumptions about student as well as teacher, focuses attention on the teacher. It dictates that I, at the front of the classroom as instructor, must therefore "be" one of the subjects I professed (or was assumed to profess) to place under scrutiny. This illogical conclusion depended in turn on a series of faulty premises, most particularly that I could only be interested in the topic because I *need* to be—being "one" myself. The speciousness and phobic circularity of this reasoning is stunning, especially when one considers the range of crossover teaching done by colleagues. For instance, I can easily name male instructors teaching in women's studies, or a woman colleague of color who teaches a course on Dead White Males. These and others routinely cross gender, racial, cultural, and temporal demarcations without suffering similar categorical collapse.

But in the case of the queer, or even slightly askew, classroom, logic evacuates. The conclusion that the teacher *must* be gay or lesbian is often arrived at with no necessary involvement on behalf of the instructor. One might say the conclusion precedes the actual course itself, and is warranted by, if not guaranteed by, the course's existence since, in popular reasoning, theoretical interest must devolve from prior experience. This is a dubious pedagogical principle, to be sure, but the swift movement to closure demonstrates the elegant simplicity and operational malice of stereotype. Prejudice, like all narrative, always gestures toward the formulaic and depends for its effects on the authority of the already known, or even the already speculated—or perhaps on the already unspoken presumptions and rumors that pass as "common knowledge."

It is still the case in many civic settings across the United States that a gay identity is tantamount to "criminality"—a sort of moral felony which automatically debars an individual from social and political, if not legal, due process. This is nowhere more obvious than in the classroom.[2] Indeed, the political wind shear buffeting courses such as these, I argue, is *intended* to circulate around the instructor, precisely to destabilize her or his authority as instructor.[3] It was hardly an accident, then, that media attention was focused on Unspeakable Lives during a contentious battle over English curricula at Georgetown. One can see the connections readily enough. In a period of intense political agitation concerning how and what the English department is teaching, as the most "visible" person in the classroom the instructor becomes perhaps its chief subject. The instructor's "confession"—simply being there—is read as deviancy of a speculative and customarily spectacular kind. Deviancy, of course, has its public uses as entertainment of sorts, as talk show, tabloid, and news broadcasts all demonstrate. The creation of public deviancy as moral exemplum is in fact the accustomed political work of scandal, by which stigmatized persons are used to establish boundaries considered "civil" and normal.

So there is some irony in noting that at this Catholic university a classroom podium becomes refitted as a confessional, although one quite unlike the anonymous and historically sealed confessional of Roman Catholic practice. Rather, this confessional is by definition public—its large bay windows intensifying the gaze of many upon an isolated individual in the manner of an auction block or police lineup. Configured in this manner under the pressure of intense media scrutiny, the classroom podium thus facilitates the twin social economies of commodity culture: that is, the body is sold as erotic commodity or policed as taboo—often both at once. Thus, to refer to my original point, whether framed as a moralized spectacle of the forbidden or as tabooed desire to be revealed, sexuality in the academy has consequences far in excess of the presumed subject. Pedagogy risks being hijacked by camp while the educative process succumbs to tabloid spectacle.

Although my identity as a priest is not directly related to my teaching duties, my presence as a priest in such a pedagogic hot zone activated another order of myth altogether. That is, while popularly speaking I "must" be gay in order to have the presumptive moral authority to teach this class, according to at least a grassroots Catholic sensibility I could not "be" gay in the sense the word is rhetorically leveraged. That is, I could not be "actively political"—a phrase with coded strictures that preclude experience of either a personal or public nature. Rather, I could only be homosexual—thereby accepting without demure a framing narrative of insufficiency that is as pervasive in church politics as it is in civil. In other words, homosexuals as such are accepted within the scheme of things to the extent that they are properly subordinate, accepting as their due the terms of a pathologizing discourse that indicates illegality, immorality, and failed gender. Unlike the self-identified gay man, the homosexual knows his place and so does not speak. The gay man or lesbian is one who speaks (and therefore "flaunts"). Rather than performing deviancy for the alternately altruistic and titillating needs of an undeviant majority, the self-identified gay or lesbian explicitly disrupts the formulaic narrative. How? Because their self-avowal does not depend on someone else's review or evaluation. They have no part in the social cakewalk of formulaic deviancy.

Yet to announce oneself as gay is already to be folded into Geraldo-like strip-search confessional politics, despite one's best intentions. As instructor in English 118, then, my very presence becomes confessional, viewed as scandalous by many Catholics. This is particularly the case in the present historical moment of the Catholic Church when, as Andrew Sullivan puts it, "uniquely among failings, homosexuality [is] so abominable it [can] not even be mentioned" (Sullivan 47). Catholics, however, do not have a corner on the market of prejudice, and in many churches (perhaps most) being gay-identified is tantamount to an act of social insolence and religious insubordination. Why? Because, finally, being gay means refusing the contradictory imperatives of silencing and provocative speaking that construe the homosexual as "the question" to be adjudicated.

The mechanics of scandal and spectacle upon which homosocial institutions depend manipulate socially tabooed speech for energy and political cohesion. Those who suffer these effects are the demonized persons or social misfits whose chief civic virtue is their political dispensability. Sometimes these persons are marked by race, other times by disease, often by an entangled code of criminality and failed gender. To some degree or other, however, the bodies of lesbian- or gay-identified teachers are marked by these stresses; speech is demanded of them in public, while their private subjectivities are denied in public. Enjoined to speak truth as a function of education, nonetheless they are constrained to lie. Thus any teacher thought to be gay (or even actually *being*—it doesn't matter which; state-of-the-art prejudice easily conflates the two) gets no respect but a lot of attention. Further, as educators, gay or lesbian persons must deal with the effects of a thoroughgoing gendering, since teaching is generally perceived to be a feminine occupation, or at least not economically "masculine" like business and the corporate world. Finally, the visibility of any lesbian or gay teacher can be punitively held against her or him by civic or ecclesiastical sanction as well as by social custom. Often this happens in ways that do not admit legal redress. In the final analysis, homosexual taint does not depend on proof. To the contrary, it depends on how inter-esting—how erotic, in a word—the suspicions of homosexuality are or can be made to be. The more outlandish the suspect, the better. Yet it is also true that however threatening any particular homosexual's presence might be, isolated instances of homosexual "visibility" can be rendered institutionally benign. For instance, my presence makes possible a means by which a farsighted eccle-siastical authority can demonstrate its earnest liberality: "Why, yes, we *are* very supportive of homosexuals. In fact we *have* one. Consider Father Ed, for example." Like any racial or gendered subaltern, the homosexual is burdened with shouldering an institution's duplicities, his or her body held as ransom against its lies.

Caves and Closets: An Allegory in Which the Monster Speaks

> A room for privacy or retirement; a private room; an inner chamber . . . *esp.* Such a room as the place of private devotion.
> "CLOSET," *Oxford English Dictionary*

Gothic tropes of the unspeakable and the monstrous might help us rethink the ethics of the silenced but speculative classroom of Unspeakable Lives. Indeed, the course title presumes and antici-pates them. I wish to conclude by examining the third phantas-matic script activated by English 118, in which pedagogy gives way to another discourse entirely, becoming entertainment, scan-dal, perhaps even horror show.

It is the function of scandal to ensure that deviancy, properly displayed, does important work. If readily visible as spectacle and moralized example, those who are marked as deviant or immoral authorize and confirm, by negation, a common civic life. Indeed, the watching of deviants is something of a national pastime, as indicated by tabloid (*National Enquirer* or *Time* magazine) or TV talk show. The myth of the "safe" or "benevo-lent" closet leaves unspoken its cachet as good theater: coming out, in such a context—or like being *in*, for that matter—is little more than performing deviancy for people whose straightness is not unquestioned. It is schooling them to the normative by means of a necessary scandal of the abnormal. Thus, to return to an earlier question, what happens when, in effect and purpose, education mimics the methods and cadences of entertainment?

What might not be immediately noticed is how similarly education and entertainment employ common methodologies—passivity and spectacle—while elaborating approved versions of social morality. For this reason, the "deviance-exposed-and-repudiated" format that underwrites the moral uplift of *Oprah* or other talk shows can easily find its way into the classroom. At the same time, it can also be found in an entirely different entertainment genre, the cine-porn narratives of gothic fright film. In these tales of the flesh ripped and torn, immorality is marked as monstrous and unspeakable although always on display in generous quantities. In either talk show or cinema, exposure leads to staking, since monsters of affection *or* action cannot be permitted to live.

The monster's privileged role is to be the unspeakable marker of social distress—the Hannibal Lecter or Jeffrey Dahmer who is exposed to titillating public scrutiny and then eliminated for the civic good. According to gothic convention, however, the monster rarely has a voice; often he cannot be spoken about directly, only gestured at, pointed to. There are reasons for this enforced silence: the monster's speechlessness cinematically aligns him or her with the "unhuman." A similar rhetoric and silencing effect often frame the gay or lesbian teacher as something of a monster. Such rhetoric of course serves a variety of civic purposes. In the first place, just as the monster permits the ritual drama of civic horror, the teacher, similarly portrayed as a moral or sexual monster, makes possible the specular theatrics of an entertainment-modeled pedagogy that already has its end in sight. Because finally, of course, the monster must die, and it can never be the fault of the viewer, who although complicit in and desirous of the death, walks away with unbloodied hands.

The first time I taught English 118, Miramax films had just released the film *Priest*. Early in the semester, a student approached me and said, with something of a smile, "Father, there is a film out about you." Now, there are at least three priests in the film—four, if one includes the bishop—and so, while the cinematic logic of the student's statement was unclear, her aggressively phobic point was not. The film, she intended to say, was about my homosexuality—the fact of which she was presuming in the first place, for reasons previously stated. The film, although ambiguously titled and not limited to *a* (or *the*) priest, was in her view about the homosexual. As presumptive heterosexuals, the remaining priests, including the bishop, exercise the privilege of the unmarked and so remain invisible to the gazing eye. Yet the point must be made that in the year 2000, *any* priest who could imagine himself in such a film would have to be homosexual and not gay—at least as I have defined the terms. Doubly bound by exterior ideological silencing as well as by internalized self-erasure, such a priest would probably never be found performing gay in so visible a site as the classroom. Why? Because giving homosexuals voice in a classroom is clearly more transgressive and socially destabilizing than having frantic, groping sex in a darkened automobile. Knowing the truth, to paraphrase Jesus, sets us free, and freedom is what systems of managerial spirituality (or education)—and those who are colonized by them—fear most.

Being an educator today is, like being queer, a public role suffused with deviancy. Almost by definition, the point of education is to teach transgression of—or at least a questioning of—traditions or habits or ways of thinking that have preceded us. But in addition, as noted earlier, the social role of teaching is complicated by its routine gendering. In an aggressively masculinist culture characterized by bottom lines and cash flows, I occupy a social position that is rhetorically privileged but economically and practically dismissed. It was from these twin social deviancies of being queer and effeminized as an instructor —not to mention being the presumptive subject of a film—that I recalled Plato's "Allegory of the Cave." It seems to me that Plato's *figura* offers a useful insight into the toxic closets of American popular education. It does so, I add, read "straight," without any Foucauldian or Sedgwickian gloss whatsoever. Consider the elements common to both cave and closet: the flickering fire that deceptively illuminates the cave's illusory relations; the bound spectators' mute immobility and the powerful ignorances thus normalized and secured, from inside the cave as well as from outside it; the fatuous, because speculative, swirl of what is known, or supposed as known; finally, the resistance provoked by those who, in a word, come out.

I came to self-possession as an educator long before achieving self-possession as a gay man. My understanding of Plato is, as a result, properly Platonic—that is, understood as a matter of retrospection. My education has been about revisiting and rethinking, revisioning—recovery in its original sense. And the places I most had to revisit were those small places in which, as a young boy, I took solace and comfort or in which I hid. For sometimes the hiding was the comfort—whether in confessionals in the church, closets at home, or those barricaded rooms in my heart. It comes as no surprise, then, that now I see education to be all *about* closets. Like the densely publicized "private space" of the closet, public educational structures (the "classroom") contrast the lure of secrets with the illusory nature of the visible. From the perspective of a student, education signifies the labor of coming out of illusion and speculation. As instructors, however, education is also concerned with managing the resistance that can quite directly get the teacher killed. As Plato remarks to Glaucon, "And, as for anyone who tried to free them and lead them upward, if they could somehow get their hands on him, wouldn't they kill him?" (189).

Let me not project all of this resistance elsewhere, however. Much of it is internal and self-generated by my need to dance for my masters. Thus, from either position—as student or teacher—education is an acknowledgment of the various pressures that urge us to stay put, to settle for the specular, for the speculative as well as the spectacular. To perform the cakewalk, in other words. Cast in contemporary terms, Plato's scene highlights the tension between the static furiousness of melodrama and the graceful mobilities of narrative. In other words, he contrasts a position of abjection in which the "caved"—in education, teacher as well as student—are chained side by side. No possibility exists for movement or change—in short, for narrative. This commonality of privileged ignorances, and the suppression of speech it dictates, sustains and enforces spectacle on the one hand and speculation and formula on the other. The drift between spectacle and speculation—scandal—is the dramatic scene played out in many classrooms, as well.

Because of the fixities built into the educational model, and because of the fixations enforced by the closet, the queer teacher is forever under erasure. His or her face must always be locked toward the light of the opening door—not to anticipate release but, sadly enough, to be alert to threat. After all, the monster must be silenced, lest fearsome spectacle be diluted by the compassion provoked by speech. (James Whale's *Frankenstein* [1931] eliminated the creature's speaking role for this very reason.) Yet the gay or lesbian teacher has another possibility; he or she can subvert spectacle altogether by thwarting prejudicial formulas that depend for their energy on cliché. Offered up as sacrifice in the rites of civic scrutiny, the monstrous gay or lesbian teacher can shatter the filmic illusion by having something to say, something to teach more substantive, perhaps, than what might be on the syllabus.

It is fear of this moment that drives the furious public energy circulating around a "known" homosexual who teaches, because, by virtue of his or her presence, myth collapses. By their silence, "unknown" homosexuals confirm the taboo on speech that cages them in silent accommodation, and so they can teach whomever and wherever they wish without reprisal. On the other hand, becoming "visible" engages the enchantments of specularity. Becoming vocal dis-spells the spell. The resulting collapse of structured, enforced silence reflects back to a society its immobilizing theatrics, the "don't ask, don't tell, just stare" rubrics of the Monstrous. With these politics and policies, society makes and sustains its monsters, flattening human narrative into formula, and reducing human complexity to public melodrama. These scenes of social crisis conjure up much speculation, but in the end nothing of substance changes.

Plato concludes that caves are never empty. The same can be said for closets. Plato underscores the fundamental pedagogic crisis faced by a technocratic commodity culture: wanting to leave the cave of ignorance "for the sake of enlightenment" must be thought to be the queerest idea of all. Nor should we romanticize the hard work of education, as the bleakness of Plato's allegory is often sentimentalized away. After all, the passage out of the cave is not a journey into knowledge but, paradoxically, a stepping forward into ignorance. In the Platonic figure, education results in freedom from specious and illusory knowledge; the enlightened are those who have been made aware only of their bondage and immobility. Recognition of entrapment—indeed, the resistance to being *untrapped*—is the enlightened's only point of privilege.

Plato's cave instructs us in the metaphors of ignorance, but like the closet, the cave can be reimagined within another discourse entirely—that of worship, in which submission also plays a role. What do I mean? I have been arguing that education should be about converting fixities to movements, melodramas to narrative. Additionally, it also can be about putting closets to new use—perhaps by expanding them into something resembling older ones. The closet once was more commodious than we now imagine it—more than a place of accidental storage in which to deposit and forget so much of life's baggage. Rather, closets were private places, places of self-possession. They were places of one's own, sites of prayer, meditation, devotion. Perhaps they again can be sites and occasions of interiority, in which, paradoxically, self-possession is part submission to the disciplines of letting go, going up, coming out. Plato's allegory can instruct the potentially queer student (lesbian and gay, perhaps, but surely *anyone* in a commodity culture who values learning over ignorance) in the hard human task of coming to terms with the demands made by an interior life. Perhaps this is what St. Paul meant when he encouraged the Romans, "Remember that with them that are bound you are bound" (Romans 15:3). The teacher appears when learning is to happen, and learning in the queer classroom is negotiating the passage out of the specular. It invites us out of the compellingly solitary gravity of ignorance that holds us bound, always solitary, in low dark places. Plato invites pedagogues, straight or gay, out of social melodramas in which nothing happens into narratives of grace by which we—and our students—become better persons than we ever could have imagined. Better, at least, than our culture permits us to be, bound and tied, prisoners of our own fear.

Notes

1. Richard Mohr in *Gay Ideas* argues that being "out" of the closet is a moral imperative since "living in the truth" (39) sets the standard for any normative morality.

2. See Rhoads for further discussion of this point.

3. Sears outlines some startling figures regarding the negativity with which teachers-in-training regard homosexuality: "Eight out of ten prospective teachers surveyed harbored negative feelings toward lesbians and gay men; fully one third of these persons, using the Index of Homophobia classification, are 'high grade homophobics'—nearly five times as many as classified by Hudson and Rickets (1980) in their study of college students a decade ago" (39–40).

Works Cited

Abelove, Henry, Richard Ohmann, and Claire B. Potter. "Introduction." *Radical Teacher* 45 (Winter 1994): 2–3.

Crew, Louie, and Rictor Norton. "The Homophobic Imagination: An Editorial." *College English* 36 (1974): 272–90.

Elliott, Mary. "Coming Out." *College English* 58 (1986): 693–708.

Harbeck, Karen. "Introduction." *Coming Out of the Classroom Closet: Gay and Lesbian Students, Teachers, and Curricula.* Ed. Karen Harbeck. New York: Harrington Park, 1992. 1–7.

McCarthy, Jeremiah. "The Closet and the Ethics of Outing." *Gay Ethics: Controversies in Outing, Civil Rights, and Sexual Science.* Ed. Timothy F. Murphy. New York: Haworth, 1994. 27–45.

Mohr, Richard D. *Gay Ideas: Outing and Other Controversies.* Boston: Beacon, 1992.

National Conference of Catholic Bishops. *Ex Corde Ecclesiae: The Application to the United States.* United States Catholic Conference. 1990. <http://www.nccbuscc.org/bishops/excorde.htm>.

Plato. *The Republic.* Trans. G. M. A. Grube. Indianapolis: Hackett, 1992.

Rettemund, Matthew. *Boy Culture.* New York: St. Martin's, 1997.

Rhoads, Robert A. *Coming Out in College: The Struggle for a Queer Identity.* Westport, CT: Bergin, 1994.

Scott, Joan R. "The Value of Experience." *The Lesbian and Gay Studies Reader.* Ed. Henry Abelove, Michele Aina Barale, and David M. Halperin. New York: Routledge, 1993. 397–415.

Sears, James. "Educators, Homosexuality, and Homosexual Students." *Coming Out of the Classroom Closet: Gay and Lesbian Students, Teachers, and Curricula.* Ed. Karen Harbeck. New York: Harrington Park, 1992. 29–79.

Sedgwick, Eve Kosofsky. *Tendencies.* Durham: Duke UP, 1993.

Sullivan, Andrew. "Alone Again, Naturally." *New Republic* 28 Nov. 1994: 47–55.

Thomson, Rosemarie Garland, ed. *Freakery: Cultural Spectacles of the Extraordinary Body.* New York: New York UP, 1996.

Watney, Simon. "School's Out." *Inside/Out: Lesbian Theories, Gay Theories.* Ed. Diana Fuss. New York: Routledge, 1991. 387–401.

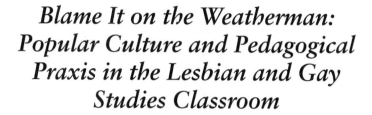

CHAPTER THREE

Blame It on the Weatherman: Popular Culture and Pedagogical Praxis in the Lesbian and Gay Studies Classroom

JAY KENT LORENZ
University of California, Irvine

All survivors, however they accommodate or fail to re-member it, bear the inexorable guilt of the survivor.
JAMES BALDWIN, *The Evidence of Things Not Seen*

I had stumbled across something which must be love but I had no language.
JEANETTE WINTERSON, *Art Objects: Essays on Ecstasy and Effrontery*

The term *experience,* in its most recent permutation, has be-come the whipping boy of postmodernity, a bad girl who tenaciously clings to her memories as if they alone contain the privileged signifier. Bearing that in mind, please permit me to share with you a remembrance of performance, love, and sur-vival. I do not claim to be the ultimate authority on the develop-ment of the queer adolescent; I merely wish to relate some of the motivation behind what I do.

In 1976, in my thirteenth year, the NBC television affiliate in Chicago hired a meteorologist whose tenure at the station would be remarkably short. Exhibiting a smart fashion sense and a flam-boyant delivery light years removed from his boxy and bland male colleagues, the weatherman became an object of derision in my working-class neighborhood. Those children skilled enough in employing the most outrageous embellishments when impersonating the weatherman were rewarded with requests to perform before the neighborhood adults. Hoping to be cacheted into the inner circle of grown-up galas, I fine-tuned a showstopper, laminated with genderfuck accoutrements courtesy of my mother's closet.

It was my father who cued me into the equation: gender performance = sexual orientation, a spurious relation but one that provided him with much mirth when I enacted the weatherman while simultaneously fulfilling the cultural imperative of exposing the homosexual. Performing the *swish* (my father's term) is compulsory in a culture that since the mid-nineteenth century, according to Eve Sedgwick, has been organized along a hetero/homo binary—the hetero, of course, occupying the privileged position—with other dualistic categories, most notably that of masculine/feminine, relying on the unbalanced oppositional divisions of sexuality to provide a prototype (111). As a child for whom the inside/outside overdeterminant of sexual orientation was not yet an issue, I came to comprehend that to be homosexual is to be incompatible with masculinity, a reductive, fatuous assumption but one made because I had aligned the gay male alongside the feminine, the devalued, the unloved. Love had become a conditional, and I believed that survival depended on the approval of the father. Passing was to be accomplished by excelling in athletics and through my flaming impersonation of the weatherman, a spectacle so amusing because the humor always lies in the *straight* male performing the homo; a gay male enacting hyperbolic homosexual stereotypes in 1976 would have been perceived as redundant. And so I existed, as I believe many adolescents did, as a queer Steppin Fetchit, trapped and speaking the language of the enemy in a twilight world somewhere between the homo and the hetero, uncomfortably complicit in my own oppression.

It is this memory that prodded me into a commitment, two years in succession, to teach the film component of a lesbian and gay studies course offered by the Department of English at Georgetown University during the spring 1995 and 1996 semesters. While I hesitated about attending graduate school and all the difficulties that would entail—beginning a master's program in English at age thirty-two, undergoing an abrupt shift from comfortable development director to full-time graduate student—the decision to enter Georgetown was relatively painless in comparison to tackling the lesbian and gay studies dilemma. I procrastinated for as long as possible before agreeing to teach the 1995 lesbian and gay studies class because I was reluctant to be marked as gay, which I believe, however erroneously, is the inevitable conclusion others draw when one assents to teach such a course. But the memory of the weatherman, among much more unsettling ghosts, provoked my guilt, and I agreed to design and teach Lesbian and Gay Representations in Film and Popular Culture, an optional section of Edward Ingebretsen's Unspeakable Lives: Gay and Lesbian Narratives course, during my second semester as a graduate student. Moreover, the classroom appeared to have changed since I was an undergraduate during the 1980s, with the instructor (under whom I had studied) now morphing into a performance artist whose job it has become, according to Peruvian novelist Harry Belevan, to entertain a new generation of "spectator-students" (16). My dormant thespian skills might be useful here; and I had certainly honed the fine art of performance during adolescence!

The incitement to perform straightness as a means of survival can prove irresistible to lesbian and gay youngsters. Yet while passing as straight may function as an avoidance of scorn and violence, the portrayal still leaves the performer deprived of a reasonable nurturing network and in a state of thwarted development. If much of secondary education is strictly acculturation to the heterosexual contract, just how relevant has this education been for lesbian and gay youths? Ideally, the university functions as a remedial dock for the queer young adult seeking autonomy, empowerment, language, voice. The lesbian and gay studies classroom assists the university with this crucial responsibility by inviting students to investigate heretofore unacknowledged areas of study—the polymorphous edge in Shakespearean sonnets, the queer cryptography sneaking into Hollywood film when the industry was subject to regulation by the Catholic Church, or the shifting definitions of *sodomy* under English common law—those areas erased by what Anthony D'Augelli terms the homophobic "'hidden curriculum' that devalues the existence and concerns of gay men and lesbians" (214).

I ignored the (willfully) hidden curriculum while trusting in the ability of the classroom to "rescue imaginative space from the onslaught of heterosexual society" (Shewey xiii). I enacted the role of "saboteur" and conceptualized a course that would ask questions about aspects of the relationship between lesbians and gay men and film/popular culture. These queries hold a particular relevance for a generation that has come of age in a time when the image acts as the privileged signifier, when representations in the visual economy hold pride of place over the written word. If literacy is a dialectic "between human beings and the world, on the one hand, and language and transformative agency, on the other" (7), as Giroux insists, then that world is rife with synthetic images which are readily absorbed and seldom unpacked. However dangerously my own teaching moves toward a romanticized notion of Friere's and Giroux's theories of critical pedagogy, I believe it is my job to empower students with the tools of resistant reading, that is, to help them achieve cultural literacy by recognizing, and perhaps sabotaging, the representational mirror of the surrounding heterosexual imperative.

Firmly believing in my mission, I whittled down the syllabus of my section of Unspeakable Lives to a concentration on the Hollywood film for the spring 1995 class. This initially seemed an astute strategy that would employ a more popular, accessible cinema as an aid in offsetting the often abstruse theoretical readings of the larger class. David Román elucidates the distrust often felt by undergraduates toward "high" theory:

> My students were suspicious of the sometimes "inaccessible" academic writing, questioning its utility outside the classroom. If it takes a PhD to read some of these critics, they wondered, what practical purpose do the texts serve for lesbian and gay people who are not academics? . . . In other words, the politics of theory seemed only to duplicate the hegemonic power structures that alienate the disenfranchised. (115)

I am forced to report that the "practical purpose" of queer theory was thrust in my face during the second week of class: Jason, struggling with Sedgwick's "Axiomatic," demanded to know why the essay had been written in such an oblique style: "Why does Sedgwick use words like *pellucid* instead of writing 'easy to understand'? Who will even attempt to read this outside the university? Maybe someone should buy her a copy of Strunk and White." Although I am weary of the hoary debates about academic jargon, the specialized lingo of much queer theory *does* promote dissension between two groups—queer academics and grassroots organizers—that share many political goals. Therefore I indulged the fantasy that engaging commercial cinematic texts alongside dense scholarly concepts—"popular/low culture" juxtaposed with "high theory," if you will—might somehow fuse the ivory tower and the workaday world.

So much energy was swirling around Unspeakable Lives during the first few weeks of the spring 1995 class that there was no time to revamp a syllabus which I now realized was one-dimensional, somewhat stale, uniform. As the projector flickered on the Hollywood flashback—Garbo in *Queen Christina,* Hitchcock's *Rope,* the histrionics of *Tea and Sympathy*—my concerns were with how to deflect personal accusations about my authority to teach such a course and how to create an atmosphere in which students were comfortable enough to attempt the personal voice in their writing. Perhaps the lesbian and gay studies classroom could be the university site in which we welcome a more personalized expression, in contrast to that often dry academic monotone, the monolithic impersonal writing style instilled when I was an undergraduate in the 1980s. As if a godsend, African American law professor Patricia J. Williams's essay "Crimes without Passion" fell into my hands and gave me impetus to gently push those students willing to experiment with voice:

> Q asks whether I am not afraid that my personal style is "too much" for an academic audience. . . . What is impersonal writing but denial of self? . . . empowerment without communion . . . lack of risk. . . . I think the personal has fallen into disrepute as sloppy because we have lost the courage and the vocabulary to describe it in the face of enormous social pressure to keep it to ourselves—but this is where our most idealistic and our deadliest politics are lodged, and revealed. (92–93)

In "keeping it to ourselves," scholarly writing has traditionally played a prominent role in silencing the Other insofar as the impersonal style of academic discourse relies on the elision of difference. My students willing to experiment might find empowerment in daring to articulate the personal voice, and I was experimenting alongside them, venturing to write a tricky essay (which you are now reading in substantially revised form) for a graduate course in composition studies while allowing—for the first time and after years of safe, glib film reviews—my own voice to creep in. Writing was thus functioning as a coming-out process for me and those students—of whatever persuasion—courageous enough to expose part of themselves.

How were the final results? I found that my initial attempt to create my own self-narrative-cum-academic essay suffered from evasiveness, a manifest reluctance at self-disclosure that impaired its effectiveness, and I intended to rewrite extensively over the summer. But several of the interesting topics that my ten students chose to write about—the love rescue of the lesbian vampire, the rationale behind the queer hagiography of Judy Garland and Greta Garbo, the sanitation of the AIDS pandemic in mainstream cinema—were cast into wonderful papers in which the "I" came into play. Perhaps having been inspired by gay film critic and historian Richard Dyer, a splendid scholar whose personal history is integral to his writing on cinema, students attempted to incorporate the self as a means of boosting their own authority as writers.

My self-congratulatory humor subsided quickly, however, when a faculty member, upon seeing my syllabus, remarked that the course was shockingly devoid of any representations that were not Anglo-Saxon. While I included lesbian images, those lesbian representations were as racially biased as the typical gay male depictions. Automatic admission based on group affiliation is seldom the policy for those gay men and lesbians not perceived as Anglo; instead, membership must be proven before they are allowed entrance. Audre Lorde speaks of the triple exclusion of lesbians of color: "We knew we were outside the pale."[1] Her words made me shamefully grateful that all of my students during the 1995 semester were white, as my trepidation about teaching the section led me to employ a Hollywood cinema that ignores multiple perspectives.

When it was syllabus preparation time for the next year's film component of Unspeakable Lives, I labored diligently over the 1996 section with the intent of creating a more expansive course; simultaneously, I attempted to avoid the trap of tokenism. Blessed with the extravagance of being able to participate in the larger class as teacher-cum-student and to utilize extensive film theory/queer theory in my section (because of a shift in the holistic design of Unspeakable Lives), I aimed for a syncretic film and reading selection. I interwove commercial U.S. films, independent releases, and foreign titles with pertinent essays to be read solely by the students in the film section, and always in consideration of the larger class readings. Hopefully, this strategy would encompass difference and challenge students. Some examples of pedagogical praxes planned in the second syllabus included screening Néstor Almendros and Orlando Jiménez-Leal's 1984 documentary *Mauvaise conduite (Improper Conduct)*, an indictment of Castro's reform policies aimed at the "nonexistent" Cuban homosexual, in conjunction with a discussion about the fall of communism in eastern Europe and the unsettling boom in gay pornographic video production aimed at a western market; reading Esther Newton's work on the "mythic mannish lesbian," illuminating why butch/femme role-playing was integral to the early lesbian community, before we viewed *Forbidden Love: The Unashamed Stories of Lesbian Lives,* Lynne Fernie and Aerlyn Weissman's Canadian documentary about women who chose to live openly as lesbians during the 1940s; and watching Black Brit Isaac Julien's fantasy about Harlem Renaissance poet Langston Hughes, *Looking for Langston,* in juxtaposition with Madonna's "Vogue," a music video shamelessly aping Julien's celluloid style and containing rap lyrics that sanctify white superstars of the past. The intricacy of the second syllabus had a salutary effect on me, and I was anxiously looking forward to teaching the spring 1996 class.

When the 1996 semester began, Professor Ingebretsen and I discovered that we had the most popular offering in the English department: we overenrolled the course at forty-five students and placed another forty on a waiting list. I spent the second large-class session projecting a compilation reel that had been created using film clips conducive to a subsequent discussion on the social construction of gender behavior and sexual orientation. I had painstakingly assembled footage—utilizing popular films from *Bringing Up Baby*, with Cary Grant and Katharine Hepburn, to *The Brady Bunch Movie*—to create a visual essay that contained its own, I hoped, amusing narrative. I reasoned that as I was essentially advertising myself to students who might desire to take the film section, this minimovie could sell the sizzle. I was rewarded with twenty students—refreshingly from across the multicultural spectrum, most of whom subsequently displayed an outward heterosexual identity—who signed up eagerly and barraged me with suggestions about possible screenings.

I was pleased with the lively results during the screening of my compilation reel—there would be no impassive spectator-students in this class—and requested, amidst some groans, that film section students begin a weekly journal in which they write about class screenings and readings or about outside media and print representations of gay and lesbian lives. While the groans initially appeared somewhat justified—Elizabeth bemoaned the requirement as she was already maintaining journals for three other classes—requiring students to record their thoughts in a less anxiety-ridden venue than a formal paper is a useful strategy for class involvement. In addition, journal writing functioned excellently as a seedbed for subsequent essay assignments.[2] But a predicament arose from my *reading* of student journals: I of course had no wish to apply letter grades to this assignment but, considering the subject matter of the class, considering that some students might be struggling with their own coming-out issues, should I merely check to ensure that journals were being maintained? Would a quick glance suffice? If I collected and read them, would students be more reserved in subject matter and less courageous in expository style? As I was only a second-year instructor, and because I did wish to be a good teacher, I elected to read the journals so that I could get a sense of what was working in the course and what was not, which would be especially helpful if I taught another course on lesbian and gay film representations in the future.

As I brainstormed and planned for the 1996 course, a second swell of legislation aimed at barring "the promotion of homosexuality" in public education—that is, any discussion of homosexuality that does not use words of condemnation—also politically threatened the open-forum policy of the private university.[3] Fueled by the media focus on both the presence of homosexual subject matter in the high school classroom *and* the neoconservative response to the ever-shifting intellectual climate of the university, right-wing gadflies were then castigating Georgetown in the conservative press because of changes in the English curriculum. "Promo homo" could be the rallying cry of the opportunistic politician or the overzealous columnist who was tipped off about this course.[4] But I attempted not to let paranoia rule my actions, even though it was doubtful that I could count on institutional support in light of Georgetown's own ignominious efforts to silence lesbian and gay students: in 1987, after prohibiting a lesbian and gay student association from meeting on campus, Georgetown changed its policy and granted the organization the privilege of institutional space but denied it university recognition or financial support. This "privilege" had been bestowed because disgruntled students had instigated a lawsuit against Georgetown, and the university feared losing in the D.C. court of appeals. In a contemptible fund-raising letter to alumni, Georgetown portrayed its actions in the language of self-sacrifice, patting itself on the back for avoiding a possible legal precedent that would lead to the "promotion of homosexuality" at other private universities.

"Promoting," or rather the academic inclusion of, a sincere inquiry into the representations of, the cultural artifacts created by, the legal concerns pertinent to, or the social existence lived by gay men and lesbians is but one of a number of potentially suspect scholarly pursuits. While the canon garrison maintains that there simply exists, indeed always has existed, an elite group of texts worthy of study, this seemingly benign posture betrays its pernicious intent through the enmity directed toward minority literatures and emerging fields of academic inquiry. Some evidence? Look no further than to what Mary Louise Pratt terms the "astoundingly racist remarks" of canon palace guard Saul Bellow: " . . . [W]hen the Zulus have a Tolstoy, we will read him" (15).

It was into the fury of the curriculum wars that I swam during the second spring of teaching, but I had had the advantage of acting out my insecurities during the previous year and was sufficiently equipped to handle a department under siege. Oh, but that first spring was excruciating: if I was struggling for authority when instructing First-Year Literature and Writing, imagine the pressures of designing my *own* section as a first-year graduate student for a course that some of the faculty deemed worthless, while simultaneously being forced into a coming-out posture that elicited a recoding of me from the department and student body. My initial mindset was an inescapable paranoia, a self-ingested terror that I lacked authority and would be discredited no matter what I did. David Halperin writes eloquently of "the problem of authorization" confronting the gay and lesbian academic:

> How can I acquire and maintain the authority to speak, to be heard, and to be taken seriously *without* denying or bracketing my gayness . . . [when] a claimed homosexual identity operates as an instant disqualification, exposes you to accusations of pathology and partisanship, and grants everyone else an absolute epistemological privilege over you. (8)

While Halperin's claim can be witnessed functioning outside academe with a more pronounced vengeance, "instant disqualification" exists at the university level in the "feminization" and dismissal of lesbian and gay studies programs and practitioners, often in the form of decreased funding. Yet paradoxically, a salutary space might be constructed under the lesbian and gay studies rubric where the authority of the instructor in *this* particular classroom receives a boost because of a professed queer identity. It was in this idealistic assertion that I took comfort when I realized how much energy I was expending distressing over my Q rating among students, daydreaming of an impressive popularity score as if that would somehow alchemize into respect. So I worried when, first semester, I turned around to discover a sea of angry faces fresh from Alfred Hitchcock's 1948 *Rope,* a film that even the late director dismissed with a wave of his hand as an unsuccessful exercise in style. But I responded to student bafflement as to what my motivation could have been for screening this film by first questioning their assumption that if the text to be investigated is a film, then said text *must* first function as entertainment. While *Rope* is not, I admitted to the class, a "good" film, it is worthy of consideration for several reasons: its *intentional* ability to sneak in a strong homosexual subtext under the restrictive Hays code; the disquieting, almost hysterical invective employed by the closeted homosexual character when denouncing the two homosexually active villains, a speech act which functions as a homophobic means of survival; and the overdetermined, self-conscious cinematic style that entangles and punishes "artistic" stereotypes in its intricate design. Students seemed impressed with my responses during our impromptu postscreening discussion, and while some of their respect appeared to emanate from their awareness of my tenure as a film critic, I believe that the majority stemmed from the authority I brought to the conversation as an out queer, my visibility increasing when I organized, among other campus involvements, a queer theory discussion group.

Along with that authority comes the risk that the instructor becomes the entitled signifier—something that, unfortunately, occurred during the 1995 class when students seemed reluctant to speak or to challenge me. But the students in the 1996 class managed to be open, outspoken, aggressive, fierce, never hesitant in stating opinions that might not be shared by me or universally admired. As an illustration, when reading Paul Monette's *Becoming a Man*, Sonia, perhaps the most conservative student in the section, articulated a concern about what was for her an unnerving, abnormal amount of attention paid by Monette to sexual matters during his preadolescence. She wondered if this appeared unusual to anyone else in the class. The responses were amazingly quick in forthcoming and constituted a pedagogical magic moment: recollections of playing doctor and fractured Freudian glimpses of parental nudity briefly gave the classroom a tinge of the confessional. Sonia discovered that she was a minority of one and attributed this to cultural differences, presumably her rigidly traditional Mexican upbringing. What functioned as the catalyst here? What made the 1996 classroom so frank and energetic in comparison with the previous year? Was it the group dynamic, my new self-assurance, or a combination of both?

I was not certain but suspected that an awareness of, and the focus on, difference—the unique perspective that each individual brings to a cultural artifact (something I stressed so firmly the second year)—contributed to our success. Culpable the first spring in abetting an "exclusionary" academic apparatus hazarding "the establishment of programs that might as well call themselves white lesbian and gay studies" (Yarbro-Bejarano 125), I forcefully emphasized in the 1996 class that any reading of the filmic cultural mirror is individually accomplished through the multifaceted lens of class, race, ethnicity, nationality, gender, personal history, *and* sexual orientation. Furthermore, screening such films as the Taiwanese *The Wedding Banquet,* with its conflicts between East and West, young and old, gay and straight, or the American independent *The Incredibly True Adventure of Two Girls in Love,* a lesbian bildungsroman entangled in the frictions of race and class, facilitated an appreciation of what Homi K. Bhabha terms "the vernacular cosmopolitan"—the mixture of identities confronting modern cultures (qtd. in Greenbaum). In our exceptionally multilayered classroom, it became strikingly evident that sexual orientation must be negotiated among other competing identities, a postmodern inevitability of the way we perceive.

Yet the postmodern take on personal history—that is, the bracketing, if not the outright discrediting, of lived experience—proved particularly troublesome in a class such as this. We flirted precariously with the possibility of establishing "truths," but I would not silence those students who chose to reveal memories, often painful, of those experiences that might possibly enhance our understanding of lesbian and gay issues. During the second year, there was Thomas, an older student, an African American veteran who spoke to us of the isolation he endured when stationed in Germany: the fear that the most subtle homosexual gesture would be decoded and result in a court martial. And Karen, an Anglo West Point transfer whose presence in our classroom appeared odd until she shared with us her memories of losing a father to AIDS three years previously, shortly after first being confronted with his homosexuality. Their recollections were palpable, unique, invaluable, providing firsthand accounts of current controversies—such as gays serving openly in the military or the horrors of the AIDS pandemic. I recollected the lesson of the weatherman and noted that if we unpacked the remembrances of Thomas, Karen, and others, if we unmoored the ideological underpinnings of these memories, then experience emerges from discreditation as a valuable analytical tool.

Inquiry into the relevance of lived experience, specifically as it assists in constructing the subject, became an unforeseen consequence of showing David Cronenberg's *They Came from Within*. Unplanned on my end, the disturbing 1975 horror film pressed the class into entering the social constructivism/biological determinism debate surrounding sexual identity. The rapacious sexual appetite exhibited by characters who have ingested a combination aphrodisiac/venereal disease prompted some students, a bit surprisingly, to view *They Came from Within* as the confirmation of desire as an innate urge. This viewpoint encouraged some genuine provocation among students surrounding the nurture vs. nature debate, an issue often contested in the workaday world but usually ignored by an academe that genuflects at the altar of Foucauldian-inspired constructivism. While I tend to embrace the constructivist side of the contention, I am nonetheless appalled at how the holy writ of nurture thoughtlessly annihilates the possibility of a biological component under the auspices of an antifoundationalism that disingenuously establishes a new foundation.

Our heated discussion about the constructivism vs. determinism dispute was representative of the pedagogical approach that promotes exposing students to ongoing struggles within (and, in this instance, also outside) academe. Perhaps one of the most engrossing ivory tower and workaday contestations confronted in this classroom concerns language, predominately the positive and negative energies generated by the term *queer*. Is the neologistic reinvention of *queer*, in which the word supposedly communicates positive connotations, working to promote "coalition between and among lesbians and gay men" or functioning as "an effacement of the subject position delineated by these two groups" (Haggerty and Zimmerman 4)? Furthermore, is *queer* a term so embedded in a history of hatred that its use conceivably alienates an older generation of gay men and lesbians? It is relevant to note that students in the spring 1995 course vehemently opposed the use of *queer* on historical grounds, but their response was apropos considering that *gay* and *lesbian* were hardly ever uttered during this semester, and discussions invariably worked backward toward gender performatives discussed during the first weeks of class. Students in the second offering of my section, however, became split between those anxious about yet another erasure of the lesbian or gay subject and those optimistic that employing *queer* in all situations would result in a contented pluralism.

When these conflicts began to find their way onto paper during the spring 1996 term, the gentle prodding on my part that was so much a part of the previous year was replaced by my asking students to concentrate on the passages that appeared most hazy, most hesitant, most promising. As I considered similarities between the processes of composition and coming out, processes that involve rewriting and restaging, I found it especially imperative to attack those drafts in which the student displayed the most trepidation and force the writer, in Nancy Sommers's words, "back into the chaos, back to the point where they are shaping and restructuring their meaning" (154). This entailed cajoling Russell into employing his own observations from time spent in London in his writing about homosexual representations in British films of the Thatcher era, even though Russell didn't "want to be pinned down." Or asking David to flesh out the link he discovered between communism and homosexuality during the McCarthy years, as it is quite relevant to his discussion of 1950s gender models. The overall quality of the final papers turned in at the end of the 1996 session was noticeably higher than those of the previous year. I was pleased.

Four years later, now struggling through a doctoral program in visual studies at the University of California, Irvine, I am more inquisitive than when I began teaching, struggling even more fiercely to gain a foothold, to grasp the intricacies of pedagogical praxis, and, with a tip of my hat toward the solipsistic, to understand why I do what I do. The "why" must partially lie in the satisfaction of encouraging inquiry into a field that I adore, learning from my students, and inhabiting the quixotic fantasy that I may actually make a small contribution to students' lives. So it is gratifying to recollect Russell making an unannounced visit to my office during the spring of 1996 to compliment me on the arbitration skills I had employed when ideological skirmishes erupted in our section. And equally reassuring in 2000 is the memory of the time when, while I was experiencing a low point during April 1995, Professor Ingebretsen informed me that I had been performing my teaching duties with felicity, and students had encouraged him to offer the film option the following year.

The latter incident could not have come at a more opportune time. I had just returned from signing my name to a contract to coach soccer at a middle school in Arlington, Virginia. I had broken the rules of my graduate fellowship because I had to do something in which I could be *certain* of my competence. Walking across the playing field toward my car, I acknowledged that the issue had never really been about the weatherman; the blame had been shifted onto him as part of a tangled scheme to evade the history of the self.

My parody of the weatherman was also an unconscious attempt to erase the memory of a little boy named Michael, a quiet, blindingly beautiful seventh grader taunted by peers and teachers for his aversion to athletics, his effeminacy, and his Asian American ethnicity. Beholding Michael in the doorway of a seventh-grade English class is the first time I experienced desire, and alongside that attraction existed the urge to annihilate, as if by destroying Michael I could permanently vanquish an unsanctioned urge. Always fearful of exposure and, of course, consulting no one—for what language would I use to tell?—I surmised that the survival of my secret depended on my participation in the verbal and physical abuse.

Matters reached critical mass during a rainy April day. Forced to stay indoors because of weather conditions, we organized an impromptu dodgeball game in the school gymnasium. Michael never once threw any of the red "safety" balls during the game, but remarkably he did manage to evade all the balls until he was one of only two boys remaining on the opposing team. Annoyed with Michael's refusal to fully participate, I picked up one of the smaller balls, lined him up in the position of fire, and threw that ball with the intent to maim. When the ball impacted—at the ideal moment it was surging with maximum velocity—it first broke Michael's nose. The force caused him to lose his balance and fall backward, his head the first body part to hit the concrete floor.

The relevance of lived experience? With me forever is a memory of myself committing violence against another young man who could not play dodgeball, who did not possess the ability to pass, but who was beautiful enough to unsettle me. I teach, therefore, as an act of atonement.

Notes

1. Lorde's quote is taken from the documentary *Before Stonewall*, dirs. Greta Schiller and Robert Rosenberg, 1985.

2. For a detailed discussion of journal writing, see Toby Fulwiler.

3. The first wave of legislation aggressively aimed at intimidating and silencing gay and lesbian students and teachers occurred in the late 1970s and was spearheaded by advertising pitchperson Anita Bryant and California state senator John Briggs. See Yarbeck. The second swell of antigay legislation occurring during the mid- to late 1990s uses a variant of Bryant's "Save Our Children" platform—children must be protected from the "allure" of homosexuality—as its blueprint.

4. The media brouhaha over the changes in requirements for English majors at Georgetown began when the *Washington Times* published several unflattering op-ed pieces in late 1995. See, for example, Clevenger. Subsequently, other local and national publications weighed in with their verdicts on the three new English tracks, of which only one made a course in Chaucer, Shakespeare, or Milton no longer mandatory. See Dowd; Pollit.

Works Cited

Belevan, Harry. "The American Professor: That's Entertainment!" *Washington Post Education Review* 6 Aug. 1995: 16.

Clevenger, Ty. "GU Pays Big Price for PC English." *Washington Times* 25 Feb. 1996: A1.

D'Augelli, Anthony. "Teaching Lesbian/Gay Development: From Oppression to Exceptionality." *Coming Out of the Classroom Closet: Gay and Lesbian Students, Teachers, and Curricula.* Ed. Karen Harbeck. New York: Haworth, 1992.

Dowd, Maureen. "A Winter's Tale." *New York Times* 28 Dec. 1995: A21.

Fulwiler, Toby. "The Personal Connection: Journal Writing Across the Curriculum." *Language Connections: Writing and Reading Across the Curriculum*. Ed. Toby Fulwiler and Art Young. Urbana, IL: NCTE, 1982. 15–32.

Giroux, Henry. Introduction. *Literacy: Reading the Word and the World*. Paulo Freire and Donaldo Macedo. South Hadley, MA: Bergin, 1987. 1–27.

Greenbaum, Steve. "A Cadre of New Scholars." *Chronicle of Higher Education* 22 Mar. 1996: A15.

Haggerty, George, and Bonnie Zimmerman. Introduction. *Professions of Desire: Lesbian and Gay Studies in Literature*. Ed. George Haggerty and Bonnie Zimmerman. New York: MLA, 1995. 1–7.

Halperin, David M. *Saint Foucault: Towards a Gay Hagiography*. New York: Oxford UP, 1995.

Pollit, Katha. "Sweet Swan of Avon!" *Nation* 4 Mar. 1996: 9.

Pratt, Mary Louise. "Humanities for the Future: Reflections on the Western Cultural Debate at Stanford." *The Politics of Liberal Education*. Ed. Darryl J. Gless and Barbara Herrnstein Smith. Durham: Duke UP, 1992. 13–31.

Román, David. "Teaching Differences: Theory and Practice in a Lesbian and Gay Studies Seminar." *Professions of Desire: Lesbian and Gay Studies in Literature*. Ed. George Haggerty and Bonnie Zimmerman. 113–23.

Sedgwick, Eve Kosofsky. *Epistemology of the Closet*. Berkeley: U of California P, 1990.

Shewey, Don. Introduction. *Out Front: Contemporary Gay and Lesbian Plays*. Ed. Don Shewey. New York: Grove, 1988. xi–xxii.

Sommers, Nancy. "Responding to Student Writing." *College Composition and Communication* 33 (1982): 148–56.

Williams, Patricia J. "Crimes without Passion." *The Alchemy of Race and Rights*. Ed. Patricia J. Williams. Cambridge: Harvard UP, 1991. 80–97.

Yarbeck, Karen Y. "Personal Freedoms/Public Constraints: An Analysis of the Controversy over the Employment of Homosexuals as School Teachers." Diss. Stanford U, 1987. Appendix C.

Yarbro-Bejarano, Yvonne. "Expanding the Categories of Race and Sexuality in Lesbian and Gay Studies." *Professions of Desire: Lesbian and Gay Studies in Literature*. Ed. George Haggerty and Bonnie Zimmerman. 124–35.

CHAPTER FOUR

On Not Coming Out:
or, Reimagining Limits

SUSAN TALBURT
Georgia State University

There is no innocent way to wear the category, no categorical innocence.

ROBYN WIEGMAN, "Introduction:
Mapping the Lesbian Postmodern"

In her recent book about gay men and lesbians in the academy, Toni McNaron describes the impact of her sexuality on her intellectual life, saying, "Lesbian is an intellectual lens through which I sift all the data that enter my consciousness daily" (110). Speaking of coming out and beginning to teach and conduct research in gay and lesbian studies after being closeted for years in the English department at the University of Minnesota, McNaron posits that the challenge for lesbians in the academy is "integrating our personal identities into our intellectual pursuits" (112). I suspect that even those who perceive themselves as not having the option of being "out" or working in gay and lesbian studies might agree with her. But while I do not wish to minimize the difficulties faced by those who would like but are unable to integrate their sexuality with their academic and pedagogical pursuits, it may be helpful to put a bit of pressure on an unquestioned

Portions of this essay were adapted for inclusion in my book *Subject to Identity: Knowledge, Sexuality, and Academic Practices in Higher Education*, Albany: SUNY Press, 2000.

desirability of such an integration. What if "lesbian" is not a lens? Or the most salient lens? What if "lesbian" is not a "personal" identity? What if a "lesbian" feels no need for such conscious integration?

McNaron's concerns follow several currents in antihomophobic and feminist thought. Gay and lesbian writing on pedagogy has been influenced by political incitements for instructors to come out in order to combat heterosexism and homophobia, to offer gay and lesbian students role models, and to counter institutionalized silencing of gays and lesbians. George Haggerty, for example, has argued that gay and lesbian faculty members have a "duty" to be open about their sexuality because they "offer one of the few contexts in which the thoughtless and demeaning label can be reinvested with personal and cultural meaning. But we must also teach our students to be gay and lesbian, to show them that it is possible to flourish as lesbians and gay men in a culture that does everything it can to silence and oppress us" (12). Along similar lines, Amy Blumenthal explains, "As an educator, I want to be a positive role model for all my students and a special support for lesbian and gay students. . . . I also believe that one of my professional obligations is to be a change agent, especially when that change leads to greater understanding" (Mittler and Blumenthal 4). Following calls for gay and lesbian voice and visibility, there is an imperative—indeed, an obligation—for teachers to figure themselves as classroom texts, to represent and embody a category of sexuality so that their very presence is pedagogical.

The logic of taking a gay or lesbian subject position is linked to oppositional pedagogies that would challenge ideologies of the instructor as universal bearer of truth, knowledge as disinterested, and pedagogy as properly detached from political concerns. A primary impetus behind such stances has been the feminist mantra "the personal is the political" as it has been translated into an emphasis on the personal in the classroom.[1] Broadly construed, these pedagogies argue that instructors should name their subject positions and personal stakes in the subject matter in order to demonstrate the situated relations of knowers and known: "By assuming a position in the classroom, on the contrary, the teacher makes it possible for the student to become aware of his [or her] position, of his [or her] own relations to power/knowledge formations" (Zavarzadeh and Morton 11). For the gay or lesbian academic, the personal becomes the sexual; sexual identity becomes the political. Presumably, a sort of osmotic modeling occurs: see my personal-sexual-political position and you will know your position.

Despite the dangers of a slippage between identity, positioning, and the personal, this "personalization" of pedagogy has not been without positive effects. It partakes of a moment of ferment in the academy characterized by efforts to democratize access to higher education and to challenge institutional norms brought about by civil rights and social movements since the 1960s. With political and demographic changes on campuses, programs in racial, ethnic, women's, and gay and lesbian studies have proliferated in order to accommodate the demands of newly vocal minority groups. The institutionalization of these identity-recognizing and identity-constituting programs has profoundly affected the content and methods of academic research and teaching and in many cases has enabled the work of minority and oppositional scholars. At the same time, however, the rhetoric of identity politics and universities' responses to it have had the social and academic effect of conflating identity with minority group affiliation. Social categories of identity have thus become structuring forces in higher education. In this context, feminist and other challenges to universality and objectivity, and the related trend of bringing the "margins" to the "center," have been constraining even as they have been enabling. For example, with pushes for the representation of "new voices" in the academy have come increasing pressure for scholars to account for what Roof and Wiegman describe as the "inescapable epistemic contingencies" (ix) in their scholarship and classrooms. As a result, demands on minoritized faculty have shifted so that a privileged few become representatives of a social position, contained in "a new, deafening 'authenticity,' one that disturbingly reduces the complexity of social subjectivity" (x). As David Palumbo-Liu points out, scholars who were once asked to universalize them-

selves—to ignore, for example, their gendered and racialized beings—are now being asked "not only to recognize the personal
as racial but to foreground it particularly in their scholarly duties" (1078).

With demands for (knowledge of) multicultural subjects, faculty hired on the basis of their identities or areas of "identity
scholarship" become objects of exchange on the academic market, filling niches that demonstrate institutional commitments to
diversity. The recognition of differences, however, is structured
by a dichotomy of dominant and subordinate that sets the terms
for the behaviors of minority faculty. Roof and Wiegman write:
"In return for being adopted as a token member and for gaining
entry into the privileges of the canon and/or scholarly authority,
the representative of the subordinate group complies with a variety of critical demands, including acting true to 'type'" (152).
But even with the salience of identity politics, ideologies of objectivity persist, creating a duality in which the erasure and the
highlighting of identity are simultaneous and contradictory ide-
als that structure academic and pedagogical authority.

In the face of these constraints, faculty have begun to question professorial identity politics in and out of the classroom.
Indira Karamcheti, for example, has written against "the
commodification of the multicultural body" (145). She argues:

> The demand on the minority teacher for the personal (a de-
> mand which often forms the grounds for pedagogical author-
> ity) appears in many places: in teaching strategy, in subject
> matter, certainly in the power dynamics and the erotics of the
> classroom. More important, it moves the marketplace into the
> classroom. The personal is something we narrativize and pro-
> duce as part of the package as well. The personal is part of our
> academic, economic product. (145)

What Karamcheti points to is a shift in which the "personal" is
becoming less a force in transforming academic norms and increasingly a function of the "institutional incitement to discourse" (Foucault, *History* 18) that completes the multicultural contract. What
happens, then, when a teacher rejects discourses of the personal?

An Ethnographic Reading That
Succumbs to the Intentional Fallacy

In this essay, I theorize the academic and social positioning of Olivia Moran, an associate professor of English at a prestigious public research institution.[2] Olivia is a white lesbian with a national reputation in lesbian theory, an area increasingly marketed in literary studies. She brings to her department a prolific publishing record and teaching abilities in Shakespeare, British and American twentieth-century literature, feminist critical theory, gay and lesbian studies, film studies, and cultural studies. In framing Olivia's pedagogical stances and actions, I begin with her relation to "lesbian," a category that, when attached to "identity" or "community," she finds limiting, static, and contradictory to her intellectual project of questioning to create new forms of thought. This relation is enacted most clearly in her departmental "anti-identity" performances against assumptions attached to "lesbian/lesbian theorist." At the same time, her experience of being a lesbian and her academic goals inform her pedagogy, but instead of constituting herself as a legible classroom text by naming her sexuality, Olivia creates situations in which she and her students must enact positions in relation to the texts under study. The juxtaposition of her words to my observations of her class suggest that at stake in her teaching is the constitution of a community based in relations to ideas rather than identities. What I offer, then, are my readings of both Olivia's actions and her readings of her actions.

By reading Olivia's departmental and pedagogical actions in relation to her articulated stances, I in a sense read against her words, for Olivia does not locate her work in relation to "self" or personal history. In fact, she is a vocal critic of authorial intentionality in biographical literary criticism, concerned that readers not think there is a "real" against which they can read an author's work. Olivia does not often offer a "real," describing her intellectual pursuits much as she describes identity: multiple, shifting, and relational. Experiences and intentions are not personal, but expressions of culture. I thus understand her actions as responses to what she perceives to be social and institutional exigencies. My reading is informed by Foucault's understanding of human practices as the creative use of existing systems. He describes "practices of the self," or "the way in which the subject constitutes himself [or herself] in an active fashion" ("Ethic" 11) as inventions that are suggested or imposed by social and cultural discourses. At times my analysis merges with Olivia's and at times it departs from it, for I read both with and against her understandings and actions.

Being a Cranky Lesbian Critic

For Olivia, "lesbian" is not a category to represent, voice, or make visible, but a relational process of shifting identifications. Her approach to what a lesbian is or is not—a verb rather than a noun, identifications rather than an identity, a source of limitation rather than liberation—is constitutive of much of her academic work and serves as a backdrop to understanding her performance against location and a lesbian "personal." In describing "identity," Olivia drew on the psychoanalytic notion of an ego fiction, "the thing that deludes you into believing there's something whole that you're speaking from," something that can speak but that is usually spoken: "This is identification, it's a process, it's not a static thing, it's not a category, it's not a thing. I prefer that as a way of understanding this because it allows flux, it allows the tensions, dynamics, and shifts, whereas "identity" seems to provide the fiction that there is this thing, this stable thing that's sort of unchanging through time." Not fully constituted, "identities" are situationally evoked:

> We have a legion of things that are providing identities; they're not that full, they're like attachments in some way. . . . They're always there, but they recede and they're more prominent at times and they recede at times. They're like a whole wardrobe, and sometimes, they're there, they're in the closet, you take them off and put them on, but it's more involuntary than that, I think. They come. They're called up by certain stimuli; it may be contextual, it may be environmental.

Her unsettling and evocative mixture of theatrical and closet metaphors suggests not a unified subject but a contextual self that is constituted transactionally.

For Olivia, understanding identity as a substance is implicated in the construction of "counterpoint identities," in which the meanings of inferior terms in hierarchized oppositions (such as man/woman, white/black, straight/gay) become overdetermined in their specificity vis-à-vis unmarked universals. Counterpoint identities such as "lesbian" conflate difference and identity, and elide their constitution within the recognitions of others. She thus understands the use of positionality ("As a white male heterosexual, I . . .") as a rhetorical strategy in which "identities are nouns rather than verbs, and that somehow is seen as a legitimate rhetorical move that authorizes even as it excuses." Rhetorical strategies are dependent on context, which defines "what a relevant identity category is there." Olivia seeks to sidestep the contextual relevance of "lesbian" by not naming a "personal." As Khayatt observes, "for a statement on the order of 'I am a lesbian' to have any coherence, there has to be an understanding of the term 'identity' as stable and unchanging or a recognition that the statement is momentary or necessary in a particular context" (132). If "lesbian" is a shifting process, if neither sexual categories nor our relations to them are static, what are the benefits of positioning oneself categorically? To reverse the question, what might be the benefits of questioning the category in practice? Olivia's response is to enact a performance that has as its point of departure location within the category but that, as David Román describes, "due to its *discontinuity*, offers neither a fixed subject position nor an essential representation of the 'real'" ("Performing" 212).

She takes on this performance in the context of her scholarly visibility as lesbian in a department she understands as attaching certain roles to her status of "lesbian/lesbian theorist." Olivia described colleagues' treatment of her and Karen, a colleague who also works in lesbian studies: "We will be our countercultural figures, we will be relied upon to do certain kinds of things and we speak for all gay people, and all that kind of stereotypical association kind of crap that you get." Such expectations play

themselves out across the university as Olivia is granted authority to speak for gay and lesbian persons and issues. After being
asked to take a lesbian candidate for a faculty position in another department to dinner and to be interviewed for an article
on gay and lesbian rights for a university publication, Olivia spoke
of her use of her token position:

> I use the opportunity to debunk the notion of the category. . . .
> I don't know to what extent the privilege I have is because of
> [the category] and because I produce a helluva lot—I can't fig-
> ure that, I don't know which it is. But that work has to be
> done. And the work means providing an interesting discussion
> about what these issues and categories are, in the place of an
> assumption about the category.

Her wariness of "lesbian" echoes Michel Foucault's claim
that "[v]isibility is a trap" (*Discipline* 200) that disciplines the
subject and inherently perpetuates itself:

> If you say that any identity category is limiting, then why isn't
> being lesbian limiting? . . . I really have a problem with the
> whole idea of role models and all of that stuff, particularly
> with sexuality, because it involves a reification of stereotypes
> and the entrapment of people in a particular place. So what I
> see as the virtue of debunking the sexual category is that it
> allows—not flexibility—but it allows you to move beyond that
> category which is a self-delimiting category. It's not an acci-
> dent that you get "I am what I am" in the middle of *La Cage
> aux Folles*. That's the tautological "What is a gay person like?
> They're gay." Over and over again. . . . It's a version of narcis-
> sism, but it's also a self-limiting narrative of self-discovery that
> keeps circling on itself, and if people treat you like that's the
> only salient fact about you, it actually is playing on the ho-
> mophobia that you would like to get rid of. In other words,
> there's a way in which coming out and reifying that category is
> exactly the opposite of what one would want to happen.

Inverting the efficacy of identity politics, Olivia suggests that to
claim the category is to become complicit with the structure of
the closet and to confirm the construction of sexuality as an identity. To model a role presumes an ideal that can be taught and
copied, that is transparent, self-identical, and unchanging.

Olivia's rejection of centering sexuality as a locus of identity is linked to her disconnection from lesbian communities. In one of our interviews, after she mentioned an uncharacteristically personal paragraph in one of her books, I asked, "Are you implicated in what you study?"

> I don't know. I have an odd position in relation to it, partly because I've never been able to be part of a lesbian community in my life. I mean, any time I was around them I was always put off by it in some way, like I don't really fit here. Nor was I actually ever allowed to fit, and it's not like a vendetta or anything, but it's more like "what the hell's going on here," what are the assumptions of these communities? What is the self-portrait being drawn of lesbians? I mean, lesbian literature is a pretty dismal self-portrait. . . . They [lesbian communities] tend to be, well now, but then they were focused around celebrating women and then walked around sort of screwing each other over, and they were terribly anti-intellectual, and most of them never did a goddamn thing, and they'd sit around—this was during the bar years mostly—they'd sit around and drink in bars and they would never do anything. . . . I have made a choice that academe is the most political place that you can be.

In separating herself from bar-dyke and lesbian feminist communities, Olivia overgeneralizes negative elements of "lesbian community" and ignores individual and collective changes they have enabled; however, her critique enacts her rejection of assumptions that identity is coextensive with sexuality and her disdain for the solipsistic tendencies of identity politics.[3] Across the multiple domains of Olivia's scholarship, there has been a persistent thread in lesbian studies that takes up these concerns, a fact that leads me to read her work to some extent autobiographically. Part of what leads me to do so is based in a connection she drew in one interview:

> Well, talk about bogus, if you want activism to have credibility, and then you end up with Rita Mae Brown, who has none, but a lot among people who are not academics. God, her novels get worse and worse. *Rubyfruit Jungle*, I don't know why, I think that started my career as the cranky lesbian critic, actually. . . . I don't celebrate. What is this trash I'm forced to read?

> Yuck, gag writing. This does not . . . very little of it is actually
> intellectually exciting, very little of it is titillating.

An interpretive leap I pursue is that lived experience and academic structures intersect to construct Olivia's performance
against "lesbian" as the personal. It may be that Olivia is, as
McNaron says, integrating her personal experience of "lesbian"
with her intellectual work. To consider that she is doing so leads
to a rethinking of what that integration can look like, what forms
it can take, and what effects it can have. In Olivia's case, that
integration entails an intellectual interrogation of meanings attached to the category and an academic enactment of anti-essentialism. As a result, she works in something of a performative
contradiction: known for her work in "the commodity category"
of lesbian theory, she uses the premises on which she is called to
speak to challenge—even decommodify—the very category that
has enabled her academic success.

Undisciplining Subjects

> I find my commodity category deeply annoying.
> OLIVIA

As a symptom of the assumptions surrounding "lesbian/lesbian
theorist" in her department, Olivia explained, "Karen and I are
often confused; like how the hell could they do that? It's not
based on physics or appearance or anything like that, it's based
on that identity business. 'They're both lesbians, ergo they're both
the same.'" An anecdote suggests how "lesbian" can narrow the
ways in which she and Karen are understood:

> There is a course that is required of all incoming students in
> the department, . . . which is deeply, deeply badly conceived. It
> has always been team taught. The teams have always, for rea-
> sons that are historical in the department, tended to represent
> the modern and historical areas, but they've also reflected other
> kinds of difference; usually it has been male/female, often the
> male has been senior, the female has been junior—it's not been
> a terribly good thing. Occasionally they will have white male,

black female or senior woman and middle man, but it's always been this hetero configuration. They have trouble finding people to teach this course. . . . So Karen and I decided we'd like to teach this course, and we volunteered to teach it. The graduate director went to the former director of graduate studies and said, "Olivia and Karen put in for this course, should I let them teach it?" He said basically, "Why the hell not?" "Well, because they're the same, they do the same thing." Well, Karen and I don't do the same thing; we're both twentieth century, we don't do the same thing. Well, the graduate director e-mailed Karen and said, "Well, you and Olivia are too much the same, but would you be willing to teach this with Bob?" this white guy that does twentieth-century American literature, which is what she does. And Karen said, "No, I'm not going to do this with anybody besides Olivia, and what's the difference between Bob and me?" Karen went on and said she [the graduate director] was being homophobic. So the graduate director goes and gets two other groups of people to do it. Her real coup was having a white male who does nineteenth-century British [literature] teach it with another white male who does nineteenth-century British.

In order to combat their conflation and open up "lesbian" for their colleagues, Olivia explained that in departmental contexts she and Karen "come from different angles, on purpose, to keep enacting the fact that we are not the same." Olivia reiterated a Foucauldian concern with disciplining persons as subjects—as well as with disciplining disciplines—as she performs against the predictable role of lesbian theorist who implements predictable gay and lesbian studies courses:

Why is it that sexuality is given the prominence it is in this culture, which is a fairly modern invention, and it's politically efficacious to do that, but hell, that's a control, that's a discipline here. In what way do we delimit people by naming it—and it's just the delimitation that one wants to fight against. In other words, if you're a lesbian and you don't act like one, you're supposed to, but you don't, but you still are, do you screw up the disciplinary function? I don't know. It's an interesting question, I'm playing it out to see what happens. I have the perfect setup for it [with Karen]. . . . We are not going to act according to type. We are not going to do the things you think we are supposed to do. We would never give a course on

> gay and lesbian studies, we would give a course called Studies in Sexuality. . . . That's what the discipline has to do and it can only do it by seeping into things other than its discipline, which is what Karen and I do, seep into other things than THAT THING, that isn't really a discipline but people keep trying to call one. We're going for versatility here. . . . What we need to do . . . is to not reify the categories that they want to reify via us, but rather to explode that by being anything or everything in addition to and but that. We need to show how it is always an element of interrogation, not ignore it nor overly include it, but do it in intelligent relation to other things.

Not wanting to participate in a discipline that turns in on itself as categories of identity turn in on themselves, Olivia seeks multiple locations. Rather than accept a place as lesbian subject or create a place for a discipline of gay and lesbian studies, Olivia in a sense performs the slogan "we are everywhere." "Everywhere" is undisciplined, unpredictable, and unlocatable. The fact that her work is not confined to feminist and lesbian studies enables her project of seeping into canonical period- and genre-based courses. If the vitality of feminist theory can be attributed to its integral role in textual and cultural inquiry across a number of topics, a goal for lesbian studies may be parallel: "It's just that my idea is that it needs to be like feminist theory, integrated into questions about other material, which is one of the reasons I don't like identity politics very much."

Olivia's self-conscious performances may be understood as a "doing" that disclaims "being" in a static social and academic location. To speak of performance to describe her work is not to suggest that she enacts a role (see Sayre); rather, her performances seek to transform roles and constitute new relations. They are productive precisely because they engage norms that already exist and are continually being reconstructed. In other words, the meanings of her iterations depend on context for their legitimation, as what is normative is articulated with what is not. Thus at times her performances are performative, in that they iterate yet refigure extant norms in practice.[4] It is this play with expectations that characterizes Olivia's use of the assumptions by which she and her work would be constructed and located to deconstruct and dis-locate her subject and disciplinary positions:

If you're a commodified category, it gives you an entrée, it's up to you to change it. You know, maybe this is idealistic, but okay, they hired me because they want someone in feminist theory that does gay and lesbian studies. But they don't really want anybody to do gay and lesbian studies, so you don't really do gay and lesbian studies in a way that anyone can understand as gay and lesbian studies. So instead you do something else that's even worse than gay and lesbian studies, which they think is more benign because it looks more traditional. Sexuality or American literature that's chock-full—you saw what we did in my performativity class.

Even as Olivia's performances of dis-location challenge the wisdom that transparent voice and visibility as lesbian are necessary to transform areas of study, Olivia is bound to the recognition of others in order to effect change. Her project of "being anything or everything in addition to and but that" depends precisely on a "that" not to be. By playing deliberately against expectations, Olivia depends on visibility as "lesbian" and on others' social knowledge of "lesbian" in order to achieve a debunking. While her performances may not be those of an essential self or an essential field, they rely on essential knowledges for their effects. Olivia claims, "I don't walk around thinking of myself as a lesbian. I walk around thinking of myself as me, and I relate to people the way I relate to people and I don't even think about that." But her disavowal of the relevance of "lesbian" in her interactions is belied by the ways the recognitions of others define her articulated tactics for unraveling assumptions attached to "lesbian/lesbian theorist." The fact that Olivia sees the goal of "breaking down the tokenism" as successful at "times when your agenda is not assumed to be gay studies" suggests that her rejection of thinking of herself as lesbian creates the paradoxical situation of thinking of herself as lesbian.[5]

What happens in a classroom in which the instructor seeks to avoid the entrapment of the location of gay and lesbian subjects? What can "lesbian" mean in a pedagogy that claims an anti-essential subject? Again, performance comes into play. Teaching as performance may be understood as an instantiation of self in interaction with others, what Gallop refers to as im-person-ation, or "*appearing as a person*" (9). Appearing as a person is not a presentation of self in relation to students and subject matter but a representation, for an appearance is mediated transactionally within a context, particularly as it is constituted by the (mis)recognitions of others. To turn to Olivia's classroom is not only to ask how her personal experiences and theoretical understandings of "lesbian" are enacted pedagogically but also to inquire into how her antidisciplinarity informs her pedagogy. Her responses to expectations of "lesbian/lesbian theorist" are most evident in her department; even though she did not problematize these same expectations from students, she performed her desires to "un-fix" subjects in her classroom.

Although I have not dwelled on Olivia's academic work beyond her goals of challenging the cultural construction of "lesbian," I should note that in defining her intellectual life as directed toward change, she places her political efficacy in the classroom. While she situates academics who question the category "lesbian" as speaking primarily to each other, she explains, "The answer is not that the books are going to effect cultural change. They're not. The process of thinking through the work that you do gets translated into the classroom, and it's via the classroom that very small changes are made." Because these changes are unpredictable and impossible to control, however, pedagogy cannot assume its effects beforehand. Olivia thus emphasizes processes of questioning and eschews the notion that students can take a "product" from her classes.

Is There a Text in This Class?

> About the change, the effect in the classroom, it wouldn't be around any specific theme of particular thought about something, but about ways of thinking about, instilling, or suggesting—I can't instill much—but suggesting that those questions are (a) worth asking, and (b) worth answering. I'm not sure they [students] know they can ask those questions themselves, and I think teaching is teaching them to ask those questions, because I'm not sure they do, or if they do, they're not posing them. So the change comes in simply asking questions.
>
> OLIVIA

I think she perceives students' function as taking material that's almost a non sequitur and to constantly question it.
FRANK, *a student in Olivia's American Fiction course*

To speak of Olivia's pedagogy is to speak of method and goals together, of a process that seeks to engender new habits of questioning through classroom experiences. In her earlier comment about doing something that is "even worse than gay and lesbian studies," Olivia referred to her graduate class titled American Fiction, which she had dubbed "Performativity Paranoia." She spoke of this class as "an exploration rather than something that's an accomplished fact," in which she sought for students to "perform a model of inquiry, a particular kind of questioning that I want them to be able to do in their own fashion." Her antidisciplinarity was enacted in a course that looked benign because it sounded "traditional," but that subverted the traditional through its analysis and choice of texts. For example, the structure of the class was designed to question academic practices that define boundaries of knowledge, such as area definitions (including Duras and Brossard in a class on American fiction) or generic divisions (in at least one class, the "literary" text showed itself to be theoretical and the "theoretical" text literary). And the class was indeed "chock-full" of gender and sexuality, even as these issues were not consistently at the center of analysis.[6]

In order to achieve a questioning that unsettles expectations, Olivia strives for authentic inquiry that is improvisational. Although she structured the class and positioned herself as asker of questions, students were to participate in shaping the inquiry that emerged:

> There are moments . . . of actual excitement, and that comes when there is actually a question, and they know when I really don't know the answer to a question, and I'm looking for an answer. And you can't fake that; maybe you can fake an orgasm, but you can't fake that. So if you go in there and try to play that, it really is improv in the sense that it happens at the moment and it's not preplanned. I think what happens with me is that there is very much a plan, but I don't know it, I will not tell myself what the plan is, so I maintain this disavowal stance.

Integral to the creation of spontaneity is Olivia's position of not "being the text," for the text is the process of inquiry. She thus performs herself as tabula rasa in order to perform the absence of professorial intentions: "They know when you have certain things in mind, and it limits what they're going to do. It also limits what you do, so you can't be active in relation to what they're saying, and let it push you, then nothing you say is going to push them." She explains,

> [Graduate students'] whole project is figuring out what the teacher's agenda is. It's a game. They'll figure out the teacher's agenda and then play along, and if you flip it on them and make the agenda based on their questions, it shifts the balance, it shifts the activity/passivity scale in the class. I wouldn't say it empowers them, because I don't think they are empowered in that way, but it enables them to be part of a community that's working together in relation to certain texts, where there are not preconceived ideas about how these texts work, and where everyone in the class should come out having learned something, including me.

This detextualization not only shifts responsibility to students but also allows for her seeming neutrality, so that students do not have preconceived notions about how Olivia works as text: "You can never actually aim at a political agenda because students pick that up and dismiss it. They read it as political and they dismiss it. It has to be a by-product, you have to actually teach so that it's a by-product." In order to avoid closing down inquiry by locating herself, Olivia shares few aspects of herself with students, although she is aware that graduate students draw conclusions about her sexuality based on her work in lesbian studies:

> I make no secret. I make no point. My sexual preferences are not a text in any class I teach, just as I am not a text in any class I teach, except for what I have to say that is relevant to that course. . . . I don't find it necessary whatsoever to announce it, just like I don't find it necessary to announce my religious upbringing, my tastes in pasta, or my political leanings. I think they all might be deeply evident, but I'm not going to announce them.

A "personal" is not only irrelevant but would also undermine her pedagogical efficacy by mediating the subject matter and closing down possibilities for new forms of thought:

> Being the text means that people are studying you instead of— they study whatever the subject matter is through you. Their total lens is, it's more like, what does she want here? To a certain extent, it's unavoidable given the pedagogical circumstances, but you really have to work against that because to some extent, yeah, that's exactly what they're getting, is my version of this, and if you say that, it tends to sort of debunk it. But what you want them to do is to begin to think independently, and as long as they're reading *you* as the text, they won't do that.

Unwilling to accept teaching as mimetic, Olivia does not position herself or her stances as a model; rather, she posits the proliferation of questioning and the disruption of assumptions as a model of sorts. Thus the "personal" as text represents closure that enables students to read and conform to a professor's preexisting intentions, whereas processes of inquiry as text represent openness that enables the appropriation of questioning for new uses and purposes.

Olivia's pedagogy—encouraging students to create questions whose effects cannot be known in advance—resonates with Foucault's description of the work of the specific intellectual as "not to shape others' political will; it is, through the analyses that he carries out in his own field, to question over and over again what is postulated as self-evident, to disturb people's mental habits, the way they do and think things, to dissipate what is familiar and accepted" (qtd. in Kritzman 265). Because intellectuals are not outside social and institutional discourses, they play a part in "forming" will through questioning the discourses in which they are implicated. In Foucault's formulation, as in Olivia's pedagogy, discursive formations rather than identity per se are constitutive of intellectual work. In fact, it could be argued that Olivia's nonpersonal questioning cites a norm of objectivity in order to engage students with the subject matter rather than with herself as a subject who matters. Her pedagogical anti-essentialism may function as a strategy of legitimation in which knowledge is detached from person as social knower.

Rather than suggest an assimilationist strategy, I think it more important to highlight the fact that Olivia's intellectual, academic, social, and political commitments are not based in articulating or representing "lesbian identity" as such but in positing alternative forms of thought and practice. Her choice not to teach "as lesbian"—her refusal to occupy a category she understands as constraining—constitutes a performative response to pedagogical coming-out manifestos that urge instructors to come out in classrooms in order to represent homosexuality and to have a place from which to speak. She thus offers a nuanced counterbalance to what are often decontextualized imperatives for professorial identity politics. "Coming out" in classrooms is not a simple either/or dichotomy but a highly idiosyncratic act made in the context of social and academic knowledges; intellectual, political, and personal commitments; and pedagogical goals and relations. Although intuitively appealing in their basis in "personal authenticity," calls for teachers to name their sexuality ignore the contextualized circumstances under which it might be more efficacious to rethink the intentional mediation of subjects of study through "personal positioning" as an inherently valid pedagogical strategy. While Adams and Emery argue, "You say it so that you can say something else. You say it because doing so allows you to say so many other things" (30–31), they fail to ask what other things one may not be able to say, how what one says is received and transformed, and how one's speech affects what others may say. Litvak has rather simplistically asserted that "the closeted gay or lesbian teacher's compulsory ambiguity seems, like all compulsions, forced on him or her" (25). His defeatist tone ignores the way that ambiguity, or, better said, refusal of fixity, is less forced than it is the effect of multiple personal and pedagogical commitments, albeit constructed within given discourses. Khayatt has remarked: "To come out is not simply to inform others of one's sexuality; it is a process whereby the speaker reiterates a certain relation, and perhaps a commitment to an identity, even if momentarily, and always in context" (140). Is a refusal to commit to lesbian identity tantamount to capitulating to compulsory ambiguity? Or could it be thought of as a performance of anti-essentialism—itself a commitment?

Pressures to "take a position" by embracing the "personal"

break down, as sexuality may not necessarily be a "personal" to reveal. To be placed as lesbian is to be put into place. To enact relations to ideas rather than invoking identities is to dwell in spaces that may be endlessly expanded and changed. Putting ideas into play rather than representing, embodying, or fixing them challenges the sexuality-identity nexus. To reject the "duties" of the lesbian instructor is akin to Agamben's understanding of ethics as born of unpredictability, of irreducible singularity. He argues that "there is no essence, no historical or spiritual vocation, no biological destiny that humans must enact or realize. This is the only reason why something like an ethics can exist, because it is clear that if humans were or had to be this or that substance, this or that destiny, no ethical experience would be possible— there would only be tasks to be done" (43). Rather than the closure of a "lesbian personal," a multiplicity of positions and actions may be made possible by a "lesbian impersonal."

Shifting Institutional Limits with/out Identities

Although the rise of gay and lesbian studies offers significant new sites from which to work, fetishizing the visibility of gay and lesbian studies, identities, and bodies as signs of progress in the academy endangers sustained critical analysis of the social and economic relations that make their circulation possible and that may limit their transformative potential. The segmentation of gay and lesbian studies into what Judith Roof calls a "consumer discipline" directly affects scholars' work: "The link between identity, epistemology, and discipline appears to open the academy, while in practice it restricts thought, limits and consolidates authority under the guise of distributing it, and sequesters individuals within manageable consumer groups with discrete market interests" (182). In a consumer culture that constructs freedom as individual choice, differences become self-fashioned consumer lifestyles that, as Clark argues, are depoliticized as the marketplace appropriates subcultural practices of resistance under the guise of tolerance. With the commodification of multiculturalism, critical identity becomes overdetermined as academics are contained in what Karamcheti describes as a "proper and personal field" (141) that would reduce them to roles of representing, embodying, and speaking as or about their reified categories—offering consumers informational commodities. If, as Lauren Berlant has ventured, the public sphere is "a marketplace where people participate through consumption" (175), gay and lesbian faculty may be entering the academic public sphere as ostensible subjects in order to become consumable objects of knowledge. Thus, despite the potential uses to which a new location could be put, liberal pluralist inclusion may operate to contain differences. Such is the skepticism Olivia enacts in relation to the liberatory nature of her social and disciplinary positions. Given present social discourses, to accept a "lesbian personal" would be to represent an identity to which she is not committed and to limit herself as metonym for a field of study. Although there are contradictions in her project—she embodies "lesbian" even as she disavows its relevance—the contradictions themselves may perform a questioning of how personal the lesbian position is. They may also perform the impossibility of the containment of faculty or subject matter in a field of study.

Despite the haltingly persistent advances of gay and lesbian studies and scholars, it is premature to describe either as institutionalized in the academy. David Román has argued that to do so "imagines commodity fetishism and the rhetoric of tolerance as viable sites for gay and lesbian agency. The task at hand is to critically locate sites of agency in order to challenge the commodification and depoliticization of lesbian and gay studies within institutional movements based on tolerance and market trends" ("Speaking" 171). Román would suggest a liminality for the field of gay and lesbian studies, so that it is perpetually in process, never fully legitimated, acculturated, or defined. The liminal is a temporal space that "enacts the move toward canonicity: it produces the illusion of assimilation while still holding license to remain temporarily outside of disciplinary control, even as it presupposes a narrative that will conclude in the initiation of customary norms" (173). Parallel to Román's antidisciplinary stance, Elizabeth Grosz's caution against overtheorizing, naming, and codifying lesbian pleasure serves as a warning against regarding gay and lesbian studies as a project of representation. Resistance to transparency allows limits and boundaries to remain open. The unknowable, that which cannot be contained ontologically or epistemologically through disciplinary representation or canonization, must be allowed free play: "To submit one's pleasures and desires to enumeration and definitive articulation is to submit processes and becomings to entities, locations, and boundaries, to become welded to an organizing nucleus of fantasy whose goal is not simply pleasure and expansion but control, the production of endless repetition, endless variations of the same" (Grosz 226).

I am inclined to argue that Grosz's and Román's proposals against codification and for perpetual liminality may be overly optimistic views of the ways in which lesbian and gay scholars can combat forces that simultaneously contain and tolerate, particularly in light of both oppositional and mainstream pressures for legitimation, inclusion, and location. Even as fields and scholars begin to embody that which cannot be fixed or personalized, however, they may do so in ways that preclude the closure that naming brings through performances and interactions that rearrange the meanings of those names—performances that, in short, surprise. Although not without contradictions, projects such as Olivia's suggest that even with the limitations of incipient canonization and disciplining, the theoretical insights of gay and lesbian studies may seep into other areas, and the disciplined subjects who work under its aegis may confuse the terms by which they would be located. Commodification allows for Olivia's presence; the challenge is to appropriate the terms of disciplined presences in order to perform alternatives to fixed categories. This appropriation may occur by moving in and out of disciplinary norms, both in departmental interactions and in a pedagogy of questioning in which expectations are never fulfilled but always rearranged. Although codification, representation, and market trends may contain thought and action, they may also offer resources with which to maneuver, allowing academics to rewrite the terms of their location by being there, nowhere, and everywhere, in and out of proper places. In this way, there may be a continual shifting of limits.

Notes

1. For an early text, see Culley and Portuges; on classroom positionality, see Maher and Tetreault; for a history of feminist pedagogy, see Weiler; on the personal as "mantra," see Gallop.

2. This essay constitutes a reflection drawn from an ethnographic inquiry into three lesbian faculty members' enactments of the constructs *lesbian, intellectual,* and *academic* in their research, teaching, and collegial relations (see Talburt). All names given here are pseudonyms.

3. On identity politics' implication in bar-dyke and lesbian feminist practices and divides between "academic" and "activist" lesbians, see Faderman; Krieger; and Phelan.

4. Derrida argued that the "success" of performatives does not lie in the originality of a statement but in the citation of an "iterable model" (326). Butler locates agency in citationality, arguing that performativity is "a reiteration of a norm or set of norms" (12). A performative *"accumulates the force of authority through the repetition or citation of a prior, authoritative set of practices"* (227). The citation of a norm enables its appropriation for new uses in new contexts.

5. Olivia would rewrite interactions that the knowledge of others would define: "You have to interact with a person enough to get that out of the way; [for] the more homophobic people, it'll be a lot longer. . . . If you make a big deal out of it, they'll make a big deal out of it. People have a way of picking up from you what they're supposed to do." Although she understands performance as beyond an actor's control, creating a Barthesian "writerly text" in which the reader is "no longer a consumer but a producer of the text" (4), she claims an ability to set the stage for others' readings. This contradiction reveals both the ways the recognitions of others construct her actions and her hope that a lesbian "impersonal" may discourage fixed readings.

6. The texts for the class included Barnes, *Nightwood*; Acker, *Portrait of an Eye*; Pynchon, *Crying of Lot 49*; DeLillo, *White Noise*; Nabokov, *Lolita*; Dürrenmatt, *The Assignment*; Harris, *Lover*; Brossard, *Picture Theory*; Duras, *The Malady of Death*; and Baudrillard, *Cool Memories*.

Works Cited

Adams, Kate, and Kim Emery. "Classroom Coming Out Stories: Practical Strategies for Productive Self-Disclosure." Garber 25–34.

Agamben, Giorgio. *The Coming Community.* Trans. Michael Hardt. Minneapolis: U of Minnesota P, 1993.

Barthes, Roland. *S/Z.* Trans. Richard Miller. New York: Hill, 1974.

Berlant, Lauren. "National Brands/National Body: *Imitation of Life.*" *The Phantom Public Sphere.* Ed. Bruce Robbins. Minneapolis: U of Minnesota P, 1993.

Butler, Judith. *Bodies That Matter: On the Discursive Limits of "Sex."* New York: Routledge, 1993.

Clark, Danae. "Commodity Lesbianism." *The Lesbian and Gay Studies Reader.* Ed. Henry Abelove, Michèle A. Barale, and David M. Halperin. New York: Routledge, 1993. 186–201.

Culley, Margo, and Catherine Portuges, eds. *Gendered Subjects: The Dynamics of Feminist Teaching.* Boston: Routledge, 1985.

Derrida, Jacques. *Margins of Philosophy.* Chicago: U of Chicago P, 1982.

Faderman, Lillian. *Odd Girls and Twilight Lovers: A History of Lesbian Life in Twentieth-Century America.* New York: Columbia UP, 1991.

Foucault, Michel. *Discipline and Punish: The Birth of the Prison.* Trans. Alan Sheridan. New York: Pantheon, 1977.

———. "The Ethic of Care for the Self as a Practice of Freedom: An Interview with Michel Foucault on January 20, 1984." Conducted by Raúl Fornet-Betancourt, Helmut Becker, and Alfredo Gomez-Müller. Trans. J.D. Gauthier. *The Final Foucault.* Ed. James Bernauer and David Rasmussen. Cambridge: MIT P, 1988. 1–20.

———. *The History of Sexuality: An Introduction.* Trans. Robert Hurley. New York: Vintage, 1978.

Gallop, Jane. "Im-personation: A Reading in the Guise of an Introduction." Gallop, *Pedagogy* 1–18.

———, ed. *Pedagogy: The Question of Impersonation.* Bloomington: Indiana UP, 1995.

Garber, Linda, ed. *Tilting the Tower: Lesbians Teaching Queer Subjects*. New York: Routledge, 1994.

Grosz, Elizabeth. "Bodies and Pleasures in Queer Theory." Roof and Wiegman 221–30.

Haggerty, George E. "'Promoting Homosexuality' in the Classroom." Haggerty and Zimmerman 1–18.

Haggerty, George E., and Bonnie Zimmerman, eds. *Professions of Desire: Lesbian and Gay Studies in Literature*. New York: MLA, 1995.

Karamcheti, Indira. "Caliban in the Classroom." Gallop, *Pedagogy* 138–46.

Khayatt, Madiha Didi. "Sex and the Teacher: Should We Come Out in Class?" *Harvard Educational Review* 67.1 (1997): 126–43.

Krieger, Susan. *The Mirror Dance: Identity in a Women's Community*. Philadelphia: Temple UP, 1983.

Kritzman, Lawrence D., ed. *Michel Foucault: Politics, Philosophy, Culture: Interviews and Other Writings 1977–1984*. Trans. Alan Sheridan et al. New York: Routledge, 1988.

Litvak, Joseph. "Pedagogy and Sexuality." Haggerty and Zimmerman 19–30.

Maher, Frances A., and Mary Kay Thompson Tetreault. *The Feminist Classroom*. New York: Basic, 1994.

Mittler, Mary L., and Amy Blumenthal. "On Being a Change Agent: Teacher as Text, Homophobia as Context." Garber 3–10.

McNaron, Toni A. H. *Poisoned Ivy: Lesbian and Gay Academics Confronting Homophobia*. Philadelphia: Temple UP, 1997.

Palumbo-Liu, David. "Historical Permutations of the Place of Race." *PMLA* 111.5 (1996): 1075–78.

Phelan, Shane. *Identity Politics: Lesbian-Feminism and the Limits of Community*. Philadelphia: Temple UP, 1989.

Román, David. "Performing All Our Lives: AIDS, Performance, Community." *Critical Theory and Performance*. Ed. Janelle G. Reinelt and Joseph R. Roach. Ann Arbor: U of Michigan P, 1992. 208–21.

——. "Speaking with the Dead." Roof and Wiegman 165–79.

Roof, Judith. "Buckling Down or Knuckling Under: Discipline or Punish in Gay and Lesbian Studies." Roof and Wiegman 180–92.

Roof, Judith, and Robyn Wiegman, eds. *Who Can Speak? Authority and Critical Identity*. Urbana: U of Illinois P, 1995.

Sayre, Henry. "Performance." *Critical Terms for Literary Study*. Ed. Frank Lentricchia and Thomas McLaughlin. Chicago: U of Chicago P, 1990. 91–104.

Talburt, Susan. *Troubling Lesbian Identities: Intellectual Voice and Visibility in Academia*. Albany: SUNY P, 2000.

Weiler, Kathleen. "Freire and a Feminist Pedagogy of Difference." *Harvard Educational Review* 61.4 (1991): 449–74.

Wiegman, Robyn. (1994). "Introduction: Mapping the Lesbian Postmodern." *The Lesbian Postmodern*. Ed. Laura Doan. New York: Columbia UP. 1–20.

Zavarzadeh, Mas'ud, and Donald Morton. "Theory Pedagogy Politics: The Crisis of 'the Subject' in the Humanities." *Theory/Pedagogy/Politics: Texts for Change*. Ed. Donald Morton and Mas'ud Zavarzadeh. Urbana: U of Illinois P, 1991. 1–32.

CHAPTER FIVE

(Trans)Gendering English Studies

JODY NORTON
Eastern Michigan University

*[T]he English language is rigid, and the thought patterns
that form it are rigid, so that gender also becomes rigid.*
LESLIE FEINBERG, *Transgender Warriors:
Making History from Joan of Arc to RuPaul*

One way of viewing the history of English studies from the
1960s to the present, and in particular the history of literary criticism, is to conceive it as having defined itself through a
series of gendered denials: the systematic, if not always explicit,
denial by men of the existence, importance, or interest of women—
especially as writers, critics, and scholars—and of those who are
neither women nor men; and the subsequent collusional denial
by many women, caught up in the struggle for equality and identity, of the existence, importance, and interest of transgenders
and intersexed persons.[1] In the 1970s, *gender* came to connote
the particularities of women in culture, in opposition to the ob-
tuse universalism of the term *man*; but the essentialist sex/gender
binary *male/female* remained largely uninterrogated until the
1990s, and continues its de facto dominance over our pedagogies,
curricula, and critical writing to this day.

In this essay, I want to open up the question of the representation, misrepresentation, and lack of representation of women,
within the context of the developmental history of English studies, to the more complex historical-theoretical question of gender. Specifically, I want to ask about the nature of the shifts in the
last thirty years in what we thought we knew about gender, point

to certain superficialities in what we take to be our more sophis-ticated contemporary awareness of gender, and suggest that as practitioners of English and cultural studies, we should avoid the classic predeconstructive error of declaring one truth while en-acting another. In effect, I will argue that this means we need to work out our collective spiritual, intellectual, and political re-covery from the paralyzing (and largely unconscious) commit-ment to the heteronormative fiction that two (and only two) sexes ground the cultural expression of two (and only two) genders.

In the 1960s, literature was not just taken to be about male power and ability but about the relative importance and interest of some forms of experience (war, politics, courtship, and similar forms of adventurous competition) as opposed to others (peace, community, intimacy, the everyday, the domestic). This disposi-tion toward the masculine was supported by masculine critical and pedagogical paradigms and methods. Standards of literary aesthetics valorized a dense textual allusiveness, intricate formal patterning, and intellectual complexity. Kinds of writing and other modes of cultural representation that did not seem to accord them-selves to the values of academic formalism were trivialized or dismissed (including popular culture *tout cours*).

The mutually enabling relations among male domination, masculinist sociopolitical ideologies, and monologic language is nowhere more clearly legible than in literary textbooks from this period. The third edition of Cleanth Brooks and Robert Penn Warren's classic *Understanding Poetry*, published in 1960, ap-propriates Coleridgean poetics to assert the organic character of the poem and the relation of reciprocal metaphoricity between the poem and the reader, each of which is whole—that is, com-plete in itself (a point on which Western men have expended a great deal of ink and nervous energy).[2] At the same time, how-ever (and quite un-Romantically), poetry is not crucially a mat-ter of the capacity to attune one's imagination to the harmonies of nature. *It is a matter of establishing control over the chaos of the meaningless*—which, of course, theorists from Aristotle to Lacan have given the name of woman.

For Aristotle, the female is fundamentally without formal capacity. The male principle is "the efficient cause of generation" (1112), and in general, "the female always provides the material, the male that which fashions it" (1146). For Lacan, in Jacqueline Rose's words, "woman . . . is *not*, because she is defined purely against the man" (49). That is, "woman is constituted as 'not all,' in so far as the phallic function rests on an exception (the 'not') which is assigned to her" (Rose 49). It is ironic, as Rose points out, that "[a]s negative to the man, woman becomes a total object of fantasy (or an object of total fantasy), elevated into the place of the Other and made to stand for its truth. Since the place of the Other is also the place of God, this is the ultimate form of mystification" (50). Symbolic control over woman is thus at the same time (the fantasy of) symbolic control over God. According to Brooks and Warren, finally, "The sense of order and control in the vital act . . . is what in a successful poem confirms us in the faith that experience itself may be made meaningful" (343). We can appreciate the poem, they explain, "for the sense of the conquest over disorder and meaninglessness which it gives us" (343).

In the fourth edition of *The Norton Introduction to Poetry,* J. Paul Hunter, writing about interpretation, echoes Brooks and Warren's concern with unity ("a literary text is unified" [501]) and wholeness ("the overall effect and meaning of the work of poetry" [501]; "*the* theme or whole" [501]). But in Hunter's mind, poetic meaning is also characterized by a certain privilege and pride of place. We are told that "[i]n most instances" a poem can be made to reveal a "central theme" (501–2). There are thus conflicting imperatives for both poem and interpretation, on the one hand, to display total self-containment and homogeneity (unity, wholeness, creation of an "overall effect") and, on the other, to reveal themselves as collectivities of multiple meanings among which one reigns as chief (the imperial model). The suspicion that the meaning of a poetic text is never absolutely autonomous is registered in the slippage from "*the* theme or whole" to "central theme" and "central statement" (502), which suggests both that the poem must include marginal or peripheral themes or ideas that are not fully encompassed by "*the* theme," and that it cannot be fully unified.

The hesitancy over whether theme is the only, or the most important, meaning of the literary text mirrors a similar controversy described by Thomas Laqueur in *Making Sex: Body and*

Gender from the Greeks to Freud, and extending from Aristotle to the present, over whether man is the only sex or simply the most important. The issues are related in that each reflects masculine anxiety over how to understand and institute rhetorically the dynamics of domination. The act of writing is paradigmatically an act of mastery—one that establishes a necessary, triumphal relation between meaning and order. The language of Brooks and Warren and of Hunter in effect constitutes poetic value as the formalization of the social supremacy of masculinity. It is a hypostatization, not of literature or textuality, but of the masculine ego, metaphorized as text.

> Literature is not the business of a woman's life, and it cannot be.
>
> ROBERT SOUTHEY, *letter to Charlotte Brontë*

Sandra Gilbert and Susan Gubar begin their classic work of feminist criticism *The Madwoman in the Attic* by quoting Gerard Manley Hopkins on the gendered character of literary creativity. In a letter to R. W. Dixon in 1886, Hopkins writes that the "most essential quality" of the literary artist is "masterly execution, which is a kind of male gift, and especially marks off men from women, the begetting of one's thought on paper, in verse, or whatever the matter is" (Abbott 133). Upon further thought, Hopkins decides that, in fact, "The male quality is the creative gift" (Abbott 133)—that is, it is not that masterly execution (a male capacity) marks men's writing as superior to women's, nor even that men's creative abilities are, in toto, superior to women's; it is that maleness itself *is* creativity.

Concomitant with this identification of maleness with creativity, as Gilbert and Gubar and many other feminist critics from Virginia Woolf to Carolyn Heilbrun have shown, is the conviction of the inappropriateness of writing women and writing by women.[3] The initial tasks carried out by feminist critics in the early 1970s were to break the male monopoly of literature, criticism, and pedagogy, and to promote the recognition of women as equally legitimate subjects of letters.[4] Almost simultaneous with the critique of masculine hegemony in/over literature, and the discovery, creation, and critical validation of writing by women, feminist thinkers began to explore conceptual foundations for the specific political, social, spiritual, and aesthetic importance of women's writing as opposed to writing in general. In effect, this amounted to asking what gender, or sex/gender, is, and why it is significant. Marianne Hirsch writes that "seventies feminism . . . was very set on theorizing difference—in the sense of attempting to define the specificity of women. From the mid to the end of the seventies, difference, in this sense, was the operative term" (Gallop, Hirsch, and Miller 351).

But "difference," of course, turned out to be a much more treacherous intellectual and political concept than a naive liberationist of the early 1970s might have assumed. Most important, there is rarely any indication in feminist writing of the 1970s and 1980s that gender is not simply the name for the social formation of a female or a male, conceived as a kind of regimentation of the body of each—or, at best, as a psychic economy already named male or female by virtue of the anatomy of the individual it inhabits.[5] The idea that a female might become, or live as, a man (or vice versa)—that is, that one's gender destiny might not be fundamentally determined by one's body—is largely unimagined, ignored, or denied, even as biological essentialism is heatedly rejected. Nor is it generally acknowledged that the structure of sex "itself" is not simply dimorphic but indefinitely variable.[6]

Even after Sedgwick, Butler, and the various queer theory projects of the 1990s, the problem of difference continues to vex feminist theory. In her essay "The Doxa of Difference," Rita Felski argues that the second-wave effort to ground women's liberation in "the affirmation of their irreducible difference" (1) has led to a privileging of difference over identity that is obsessive and theoretically unfortunate, in that it tends to create a purely oppositional terrain within and outside feminist thought.[7] Felski reads Rosi Braidotti, Drucilla Cornell, and Ien Ang, all leading sexual difference theorists, as in effect re-essentializing women at a higher power of abstraction, at the cost of their putative commitment to an antifoundationalist theoretics.

I would suggest that Braidotti, Cornell, and Ang are in fact reliving the classic problem of poststructuralist feminism: how to think "woman" as both a material and a constructed category. For example, Ang asserts that "[t]he subjective knowledge of what it means to be a woman . . . is ultimately inaccessible to men" (60). But in order for there to be "subjective knowledge," or any other kind of knowledge, of "what it means to be a woman," "woman" must have a specificity of meaning. At the same time, if what constitutes being a woman cannot be defined in any explicit (and hence limiting) way, except by recourse to infinite regression (a woman is a woman is a woman), being a woman might mean anything—including being a man. Hence there could be no grounds for Ang's claim, since men, or some men at least, might be women.

Braidotti and Cornell each, at some point, takes the category "woman" to be patently meaningful—and indeed transparently referential. Braidotti, elucidating Irigaray, distinguishes between "[w]oman as institution and representation" and "real-life women" (36). What or who, we might ask, are these "women"? And if the usage is merely rhetorical, why specify "real-life"?

Cornell presses for the right of abortion at any point until "the cutting of the umbilical cord" (43) as a corollary of the right of all sexuate beings to bodily integrity. Yet the example of abortion indicates that women do indeed constitute a cognizable material class of persons with specific particularities. And the unqualifiedly indicative form of Cornell's statement that "women must have the right to abortion" (43) carries an almost performative force: "women" *become* women insofar as they are persons for whom "abortion" can have an immediate meaning— that is, persons for whom the choice/act of abortion is a logical and material possibility.

Can an intersexed person have "subjective knowledge" of "what it means to be a woman"? What about a male-to-female transsexual? What about a woman with a beard and/or constructed penis? What about a woman who has survived cancer but has had her uterus, or ovaries, or breasts removed? If the answers are no, no, yes, and yes, it looks a lot as though biology were indeed destiny in contemporary feminist philosophy, and that insofar as sexual identity is concerned, the fancy talk over the years about the social construction of gender has amounted to little more than a (philosophically, if not politically) trivial discussion of sex roles of people with XX chromosomes. In reliving the problem of the woman who is/is not "real," Ang and others relive as well the condition of denial that *constitutes* the problem: the incapacity to let go their resistance to the idea that women *do not* exist categorically (any more than do men). Women's experience, and consequent fear, of the historical consequences of a naturalization either of their existence or of their nonexistence has tended to block feminist thinkers from making what is arguably a necessary strategic separation between the category "woman" and the historical/material individuality of each female person (reading "female" under erasure). The problematic of transgender opens itself at the point of recognition of the explanatory incapacity of the binary model of sex/gender difference and of the fruitlessness of further attempts to conceptualize actual human beings on the basis of a radical constructionist model that understands personhood as the largely determinate, passive product of social discourse.

Jessica Benjamin argues that "even though the original feminist emphasis on the singular sexual opposition man-woman may have obscured many other differences, it opened up a necessary intellectual space . . . in which the real social and psychological effects of that opposition on our world could be observed" (11). I believe it is crucial not to forget this practical reason for maintaining a historical and political awareness of the hegemonic force of the binary model of sex difference in Western societies. It is also crucial to remember that the sociocultural and economic consequences of the reification of sexual difference have not only been real, but are ongoing. Having said this, I want to press the claim that we need considerably more complex and sophisticated theories of sex/gender than are explicitly or implicitly available in most of the existing work on gender, whether in the humanities or the social or biological sciences.

At the level of popular discourse, gender no longer constrains itself to the measure of our conventional assumptions. Talk shows, documentaries, TV specials, news articles, and mainstream and independent films are only a few of the media genres that have facilitated the Foucauldian proliferation of categories and meanings the signifier *gender* mobilizes. Gender is now a name, not for the culturally constructed "woman" or "man," but for the affinities, desires, and modes of self-presentation that mark the aesthetic/erotic/social character of the individual subject.

At the same time, while gender is never reducible to sex and/ or the body, it is rooted in the materiality of genetic, hormonal, and anatomical developmental processes. *Environment and experience shape only what is there to shape.* The social construction of gender, properly understood, is the process of the phenomenological morphing of the "is-ness" of the individual. This continually transformative structuring takes place through a complex psychophysical and sociocultural interactivity, in which mind/body and self/other relations are fluid, mutually sensitive, and co-responsive. In human being there is never an *it*—an idea of the self or an a priori template of the individual—since genes are themselves developmental hypertexts: historical narratives with multiple new narrative potentials. But there is always an *is*—a contingently individual being perpetually combining and recombining matter, energy, symbols, signs, and experience into a historical becoming. The topographies of conscious memory, of the unconscious, of genes (phyletic memory), and of the body as biograph (the myriad textualities of growth, psychosomatic transformation, disease, trauma, scarification, medical/technological intervention, ritual practices [circumcision, tattoos], and aging) all testify to the conditional reality—the perdurability— of the person as an identifiable entity.

In my own theoretical reflections on gender, I use the work of Jessica Benjamin and D. W. Winnicott to provide clinical support for the argument that gender takes on specificity as a form of creative play.[8] I use the term *play* not in the abstract, Butlerian sense, but in the more literal Winnicottian sense of imaginative, psychophysical acting/narrating into which other subjects are tentatively and experimentally invited. The playing of gender involves a certain freedom to be—polymorphously, fantastically—and to actualize, provisionally, possibilities of identification and relation, partially sexed, partially sexual, partially affectional, and partially stylistic—and always mediated by culture and context. My concern here, however, is not with the theorization of gender per se, but rather with a point that the foregoing reflection on the complexities of difference should by now have made obvious: we (male, female, and other-identified teachers of English) are not reading and teaching literature with the knowledge of gender we already possess, and we ought to be.

I have suggested that much of even the most sophisticated sexual difference theory remains trapped in binary paradigms of gender. Curricula always lag behind theoretical developments, and teaching anthologies, especially textbooks, follow at a still greater distance, striving, often vainly, to acquire the semiotics, if not the substance, of intellectual contemporaneity. Yet what English teacher who has studied literature and gender at the graduate level in the last ten years has not at least heard of Judith Butler? And if we have so much as cast a glance at *Gender Trouble* (and even if that glance has caused our brows to draw together in a frown of irritation), can we justify any longer an approach to the teaching of literature that, when all is said and done, adheres doggedly to the principle that sex is the only true "mark of gender" (Wittig 76)?

Three imperatives to teachers of English follow from the recognition that current approaches to questions of gender in both teaching and critical/cultural interpretation largely remain stuck within an absurdly reductive either/or:

1. We need to teach the transreading of texts that raise or represent, either covertly or explicitly, variations from the standard gender dichotomy of male/female. That is, after the manner of queer readings of canonical texts from the Renaissance to the modernists, we need to read specifically for "deviant," anomalous, fluid, creative, or marginalized genderings, either as characteristic of certain people in specific cultural/historical locations, or as moments, phases, hybridities, and countermemories within individual lives.

2. We need to teach more literature that foregrounds specifically transgender subjects or subjectivities for whom gender identity is a struggle not just to accommodate individual human complexity to cultural constraints (as it is for everyone), but for whom the specificity of their way(s) of being gendered, and the degree of intensity of feeling around the question of gender, is such that they cannot or will not readily assimilate themselves to prevailing gender norms.

3. We need to teach more writing by transgenders, or by people for whom the preceding description of gender-as-struggle holds true.

Truman Capote's *Other Voices, Other Rooms* is a kind of southern gothic bildungsroman. Capote's overt protagonist, thirteen-year-old Joel Harrison Knox, is both the masculine ego-ideal of the author ("a fine boy" [5] and *all* boy) and an airbrushed romanticization of the feminine gay boy Capote actually was. The first, Tom Sawyerish Joel is somewhat flattened by his creator's affective disengagement from him: he fights, belongs to a detective club, and flirts with and fantasizes about girls—in short, is conventionally boyish. The femme Joel is more visible, both aesthetically and dramatically. Joel is described as "too pretty, too delicate and fair-skinned; each of his features was shaped with a sensitive accuracy, and a girlish tenderness softened his eyes, which were brown and very large" (4). At one point, Zoo, the maid, compares him to Alicaster (alabaster?) Jones, "a Paradise Chapel boy what used to sing in the choir. Looks like a white angel, so pretty he got the preacher and all kinda mens and ladies lovin him up" (160). When Joel kisses Idabel, his "tomboy"/transboy friend, he winds up pinned to the ground, naked, his bottom penetrated painfully by shards of Idabel's dark glasses that have broken under him. And when the two are confronted by a water moccasin, it is Idabel who takes Jesus Fever's sword from the paralyzed Joel and successfully wields its phallic power.

However, the transphobic, homophobic conventions of the world in which Capote writes ultimately win out, narratively. Joel recognizes his own gender deviance and propensity for sexual "perversion" in the debauched, world-weary Cousin Randolph, the "queer lady" (67) who reminds Joel of his distorted mirror image.[9] But at the novel's end, Joel's femininity is split off definitively and wholly absorbed by Randolph. Joel sees Randolph's utter helplessness and futility, "the zero of his nothingness" (227), which, the novel suggests, is ineluctably implicit in his being "neither man nor woman" (211). Joel, on the other hand, becomes certain that he "knew who he was, he knew that he was strong" (228). Even though we leave Joel going to "be with" Cousin Randolph (for the time being), he goes as a young man, now sure of his masculinity (whether gay or nongay), not as a younger version of the gender-abject Randolph.[10] Capote thus allows the culturally constructed ego-ideal to triumph over the real of gendered desire. He concludes by resolutely closing the door on his hero's subtextual transgender potential, allowing young-man Joel to look "back" at the feminine "boy he had left behind" (231).

The novel's most consequential flaw, however, is its failure to legitimate formally its true protagonist: Idabel, the young transboy Joel's age who is marginalized in his family and his community—and even in his somewhat tense friendship with Joel—because of his nontraditional gender.[11] Idabel does everything "boylike" (129). He moves "as jerky and quick as a boy" (31), hooks his thumbs in his belt loops, talks tough, and beats up his bratty high-femme sister when he can catch her. He claims he never thinks "like I'm a girl" (132)—his Uncle August "says I'm not a girl" (130)—and adjures Joel, when he makes the mistake of obliquely suggesting marriage, to "behave like we're brothers, or don't you behave at all" (174).

Against the heteronormative tendency to read Idabel as simply a tomboy who will "naturally" feminize/hetero-eroticize himself over time are the coherence and consistency of his masculine identification, and the fact that his first crush is not on Joel but on Miss Wisteria, a tiny circus performer cast as the intergenerational femme to Idabel's butch. That Idabel is not just butch but trans is registered in a variety of ways, most dramatically by his identification with an escaped convict for whom the people of Noon City once scoured the countryside: "I kept thinking I was him and he was me and it was both of us they were out to catch" (177). This fantasy of Idabel's is of himself as gender outlaw: I am the criminal, the one who ought to be/will be hounded and pursued, as guilty of gender nonconformity.[12] It is significant that the convict is never caught, though "[s]ome folks hold that he's still about . . . hiding in the Cloud Hotel, maybe, or living at the Landing" (177)—where cross-dressing Cousin Randolph, that other gender outlaw, resides. Idabel too remains uncaught, however constrained his circumstances socially, economically, and ideologically may be and remain. For he escapes Joel, his family, Noon City, and the discipline of heterosexual femininity.

In "What Is an Author?" Foucault suggests that the initiation of a discursive practice—let us insert "transreading" here—must involve a return to a textuality, the reception of which has been constructed as misprision (borrowing Harold Bloom's term) through the ambivalently intentional failure of its author to limit its potential meaning. The selectivity of both writer and reader involves omission—omission which serves crucially to structure the text-as-it-is-received. Foucault writes:

> [T]he barrier and the means for its removal, this omission . . . can only be resolved by a return. In addition, it is always a return to a text in itself, specifically, to a primary and unadorned text with particular attention to those things registered in the interstices of the text, its gaps and absences. We return to those empty spaces that have been masked by omission or concealed in a false and misleading plenitude. (135)

In Foucauldian terms, *Other Voices, Other Rooms* constructs its own reception as misprision by creating a fictional world which, for all its bizarrerie, assumes the normativity of heterosexuality and dimorphic gender. Capote centers his project formally on a (putatively) conventional male protagonist and thus forces the misreading of a text in which the true hero—the true adventurer, wanderer, breaker of rules, and so on—is the unconventionally embodied male Idabel. Capote mistakenly takes the genuine affective register of his work to be the frisson of the gothic—everything that strikes Joel as weird, out of which he eventually matures.

But his book is really trying to get at what it feels like to be Other in specifically transgendered ways, within a rigidly dichotomized social space. The discursive field on which Idabel could be understood as the protagonist (and fully written into the role)—an operant conception of gender that exceeds (and supercedes) dimorphism—remains submerged and unrealized in *Other Voices*, and it is such a field that transreading, and the transgender theory that precedes and supports it, can extract and actualize.

———————

Denton Welch's *In Youth Is Pleasure* often does not initially register with students as involving either gay sexuality or gender nonconformity, in part because Orvil, the fifteen-year-old protagonist, does not recognize these categories within the field of hir own experience. That, in turn, is one of the aspects of Welch's novel that makes it particularly useful to teach. On the one hand, Orvil mirrors the typical naiveté of student readers on the subjects of gender and sexuality. At the same time, however, the narrative viewpoint enables these same readers, once pointed toward revelatory passages, to perceive that Orvil, though s/he remains unable to articulate to hirself the meaning of hir own desire, is plainly strongly magnetized by certain images and fantasies of men (as objects) and women (as identificatory subjects) that place hir at a rather distant remove from hir thoroughly masculine brothers.[13]

In one striking scene in *In Youth Is Pleasure*, after wishing s/he were a girl at a dance in the hotel ballroom (so that some young man might ask hir to dance), Orvil goes upstairs to hir room, takes out a stolen lipstick, and colors hir lips very sexily. But s/he doesn't stop there. S/he goes on to make hirself a clown, with red cheeks and nose, ultimately marking hir entire body with "gashes and spots"—miming, serially, hir cross-gender identification, hir sense of hir impossible absurdity as a woman (not, of course, that s/he is right about this), and hir symbolic self-mutilative punishment. At the end of the novel, s/he tells the Lawrencian schoolteacher with whom s/he has a passionate, violent, erotic (albeit nonsexual) romance, about the death of hir mother and hir own dilemma as a transgirl: "I don't understand how to live, what to do" (135). The man's simultaneously commonsensical and opaque response is, "you can't stop still at your mother's death" (137).

These and other narratives of the pain, guilt, and frustration of transgendered youths—from Henry James's Morgan Moreen, to Radclyffe Hall's Stephen Gordon, to Jean Genet's Louis Culafroy—serve, if the characters are read specifically as transgendered, as vehicles for the coming to voice of nontraditionally gendered individuals as a *kind* of human being.[14] Transreading such narratives can enable students to understand the transgender journey—whether toward a more, or less, stable identity—as more complex and processual than the singular, public-dramatic, readily assimilable event of coming out that (mis)informs so many popular conceptualizations of gay sexual awakening. Rather, "transitioning," as it is known in the gender community, can be comprehended as the primarily private coming to consciousness, often despite intense negative social pressure, of forms of being and relating to others that "deviate"—that wander habitually—from the fixities and constraints of gender normalcy. These narratives function to a certain extent as metaphors for the journey any human being must travel in order to establish a reasonably comfortable sense of self. The stories thus work both to particularize transgenders (while deconstructing normative ideologies of gender) and to link them to those whose experience of gender more nearly reflects cultural norms.

Richard McCann's brilliant short story "My Mother's Clothes: The School of Beauty and Shame" is not about abstract conceptualizations of gender, despite the acuity of its narrator's analyses. Indeed, the story suggests that gender "itself"—and this is a point that is almost universally missed in poststructural theoretical discussions—is not about abstractions and categories. Most consequentially, it is about the *affect* that drives, shapes, and conditions our engendering. Gender, effectively, is what we *feel* it to be in our individual lives, not what we *think* it is.

"My Mother's Clothes" centers on a boy and his difficult identificatory relation to the mother he adores. Reflecting on the affective meaning of gender to himself as a boy, the narrator describes his sense of himself cross-dressed as follows:

> no matter how elaborate my costume, I made no effort to camouflage my crew cut or my male body. How did I perceive myself in my mother's triple-mirrored vanity, its endless repetitions? I saw myself as doubled—both an image and he who studied it. I saw myself as beautiful, and guilty: the lipstick made my mouth seem the ripest rose, or a wound; the small rose on the black slip opened like my mother's heart disclosed, or like the Sacred Heart of Mary, aflame and pierced by arrows; the mantilla transformed me into a Mexican penitent or a Latin movie star, like Dolores Del Rio. The mirror was a silvery stream: on the far side, in a clearing, stood the woman who was icily immune from the boy's terror and contempt; on the close side, in the bedroom, stood the boy who feared and yet longed after her inviolability. (551)

Two issues come up in this passage, and in the story as a whole, that, if they are brought out in class, can transform the reading experience from one in which students readily distance themselves from a "weird" kid to one in which they must perforce examine their own gender anxieties. First of all, if the boy desires to be/have femininity, beauty, his mother, he also fears and scorns the feminine; and in his fear and his contempt, he—proto-trans kid that he is—mirrors the general position of men in Western societies. He worries about being feminine the way most boys worry about being masculine; and these seemingly polar foci amount, in "My Mother's Clothes" and in the cultural context of its production, fundamentally to the same thing. Anxiety about masculinity *is* anxiety about femininity. As a boy, what one is taught is to be *not* like a girl.[15]

The second issue that surfaces here, and that applies to all the female characters in the story, is the way in which material women are subsumed under the abstract positionality of the feminine. It is no accident that an article of clothing, worn in masquerade, transforms the narrator not into a woman in his fantasy, but into an allegory, and then into another instantiation of masquerade: Dolores Del Rio, the Hollywood movie star. McCann never addresses this phenomenon in his text, but a bit of metatextual reflection can uncover the omission as part of the legible political and ethical history of gender in the United States: *The root cause of the oppression of women, as a class, is the effacement of the actuality and significance of each woman as a historical individual.*

I would argue that social, ethical, and political acceptance of transgenders necessitates the prior acknowledgment and valuation of individual women. And I would argue further that a morally viable place of being for the male-to-female transperson that is not merely a series of hideouts from women and myths of feminine mystery and power—a place that is not, in other words, a series of misogynistic little boys' clubs in disguise—necessitates a similar commitment to the historical specificity and individual realness of women before any politically legitimate transitioning is possible. Unless we deal with our own issues as transpeople, we will continue to play them out on the backs of others, and we will appropriate oppressive forms of femininity while, to our shame, reenacting the most virulent masculinist forms and practices of disempowerment and depersonalization of women.

In addition to teaching literature that represents dilemmas of gender and complications of the impoverished male/female model (Capote; Welch), or that foregrounds more overtly transgender concerns (McCann), we need to recognize that transgenders are not purely mythical beasts or monstrous anomalies. This is best done by teaching and taking seriously—and teaching is itself, of course, a way of taking seriously—works by transfriendly or transgendered authors.[16]

In "Stripped," Minnie Bruce Pratt writes of her outrage at the treatment of Brandon Teena, the preoperative female-to-male transsexual stripped, raped, and eventually murdered by transphobic thugs in a small town in Nebraska (recently the subject of the documentary *The Brandon Teena Story* and the Hollywood film *Boys Don't Cry*). But Pratt's most bitter anger is reserved for the lesbian author of a *Village Voice* article on the case who strips Brandon once again, metaphorically, by treating him as "a confused lesbian" who couldn't get "her" sex straight. "The writer," Pratt points out, "never mentions he died when he insisted he would choose his own pronoun" (174). The Teena case itself makes real the danger of living transgendered, and implicitly underscores the need for gender not to be reduced to the drag farce or the freak show and thereby dismissed as a non-issue for "real" human beings, trans or nontrans. Pratt's contribution is to show us how our discursive reception of the events of a life like Teena's often repeats the physical violence the subject has already suffered, and in doing so legitimates that violence as a proving of the truth.

For student readers, such a text demonstrates the rhetorical power of language to construct misguided "understandings" of transpeople, and the violence inherent in the use of hegemonic constructions to manipulate people into being what one wants them to be. Pratt's writing also demonstrates the possibility of critique and reconstruction: we can point out in language the misappropriations of power that others attempt, and thereby subvert the false hierarchies of value they seek to establish.

———————

As a male-to-female transgender—one who identifies more closely with "women" than with "men," but who *is* neither—I take some care lest I overwhelm, or frighten, or antagonize my students. Each course I teach is about them much more than it is about me in relation to particular kinds of intellectual content and experience. Yet because my composition courses are always focused on critical thinking, dialoguing, and writing about significant sociocultural and political issues, most of which involve gender as one level of inquiry (though they may foreground race, sexuality, nationality, ethnicity, economic status, and so on); because I teach literature on the theory that literary experience necessarily involves readerly identification with character, rememoration by readers of their psychostructural history, and consequent transformation; and because, finally, I understand self-exploration as in some sense the end of reading and the beginning of responsibility, I must, if I wish to be consistent with my own pedagogical values, model the practice of introspection and the imperative to self-disclosure.

I was told by a colleague that on the first day of class this semester, one of my students didn't know whether I was a woman or a man. Before our formal work together had even begun, then, the problem of gender—which on one level is the problem of why "the problem of gender" *is* a problem—had been raised for her. Without the willingness to *be*, honestly, and to search actively for the sources of what is meaningful to me in the social worlds I inhabit, I can neither own nor offer my subjectivity. The students who share a learning community with me, like my friends in transgender communities, lesbian communities, gay communities, and recovery communities, need me, as I need them, to model the struggle to become intensely present in my own life, while striving to respond with equal passion to the calls of others to shared speech and feeling. To fail in my responsibility to make the effort toward openness and integrity that will facilitate the growth of communication, affection, and trust is for me to become spiritual—and pedagogical—deadwood. Exchanging knowledge about who we are helps build bridges over initially intimidating differences between s/he's and she's, between "make believe" and "real," between human being and human being.

At the same time, my relationship to my students is a mentoring one, and therefore one in which I must take the initiative to hear and respond both to the needs of the group as a whole and to those of particular individuals. I must balance the need for sharing sameness with the need for attention to, and validation of, particularities and differences; the need to speak with the need to listen; the need for security with the need for risk; the need to cover certain disciplinary ground with the need to wander out into the world outside the classroom; the need to nurture and support students in their efforts to make meaning out of experience with the need to challenge and, occasionally, to confront. Sensitivity to the feelings and needs of others is always central to good teaching. But those others need to be brought to develop their own sensitivities as well, and sometimes transitional discomfort is a necessary part of transformational growth, as it is of healing. It cannot always be the woman, or the teacher, who gives, and the man or student who receives.

In one form or another, the reception theory of Hans Robert Jauss and Wolfgang Iser, and the discourse theory of Bakhtin, insist on the centrality in literature of the Other as well as the self, and of the reader as well as the text. The "given human being" (Bakhtin, *Art* 230) is conceived as constitutive of the aesthetic value of the text, the task of which is to give form to the individual in her world. A character's existence as ethical subject becomes comprehensible to the reader through the establishment of an empathic moral/interpretive relation grounded in "one's own questions" (Bakhtin, *Speech* 7). If we find the theory of Iser, Jauss, and Bakhtin useful in even this most general and partial summarization, we can extrapolate from their work the thesis that interpretation involves a complex triangular negotiation between reader, text, and culture, the specific dynamics of which will vary, as will the meanings experienced in the reading process.[17]

Interpretation and critical thinking both become fuller and richer when the feelings and questions of others become, by sharing and dialogue, part of one's own matrix of feelings and questions. As a teacher of literature and composition, I can facilitate the passage back and forth of "others'" questions among students in whose consciousnesses they might otherwise never have surfaced. In English composition, we might ask, for example, whether it is necessary or right to alter the genitals of boys (in the United States), of girls (in many developing countries), or of intersexed children worldwide (including the United States); or, perhaps more tellingly, we might ask why partial or total ablation of female genitals is acceptable in some cultures in which ablation of male genitals would be reacted to with horror. We might ask whether it is anybody's business if a "boy" wears a dress or a "girl" wears a man's suit. Finally, we might ask whether it is surprising that some little boys with access to automatic weapons shoot other children and grownups, of whom a disproportionate number are female, for "no reason."

My ability to pose or facilitate these and myriad other gendered questions of value, identity, morality, history, culture, and politics, in literature and in the range of contemporary visual and linguistic discourses, is determined in part by my institutional position. Currently, I teach *through* a department of English language and literature and a women's studies program, but because I am not a tenured or tenure-track employee, I necessarily teach on the border between the inside and the outside of my university's institutional structure. It is likely that I will remain in this borderland for the rest of my academic career. If there is a certain loneliness and severity to this position, it also makes possible a critical distance on the sociality of the university that can provide a productive perspective for critique, both of the micropolitics of the "coordinator class" to which we teachers and scholars belong, and of the relentless desire of the administration to create an ideological justification for its (transparently gendered) investment in power, prestige, and capital (all of which depend on the principle of subordination).[18] Living on the margins of privilege, I am by no means necessarily purer than those at the center, but I am less invested.

Perhaps more important, by being "out there" in various political, economic, and social senses—never *in*, but *passing through*, genders, sexualities, discourses, economies, and institutions—I show my students that it is possible to do. One can survive with considerable freedom, frequent satisfaction, and occasional serenity. I can model that possibility for others far more marginalized and disempowered than myself. It is a point of faith for me that in doing so, I can help some students find the forms of consciousness, contentment, political awareness, and productivity that are most appropriate, on their terms, to their own subjectivities.

In this essay, I have discussed what I see as the need to expand drastically our conceptualizations and understandings of the problematics of gender as we encounter them in theory, in literature, in our sociopolitical worlds, and in our individual lives. Gender is not the only identificatory rack upon which the young are stretched. But gender, considered as more than a myth of sexual difference, is, I have argued, an inadequately represented problematic in the discourse of English studies; and it is one that leads potentially to vast interpretive, affective, spiritual, and theoretical riches for student and teacher, connecting as it does with virtually every other human concern. As English teachers, we must confront, and work through, our collective denial of the fact that gender can be neither uncontroversially linked to sex nor facilely accounted for as the product of discourse.

From one perspective, all males, at least, are transpeople, since not only does each male combine genetic inheritances from a mother and a father, as do we all, but he spends his first months literally as a woman—that is, as part of his mother's body, her blood his blood—before emerging as a "boy." But a boy is not simply the penis and testicles that may initially garner him that label from the obstetrician, or even the chromosomes, hormonal particularities, anatomy, physiology, and so forth that, in multiple ways, typically distinguish him from the "other" sex. The psyche has its own reality. And to complicate things still further, psychic reality often literally changes the materiality of the body— and vice versa. In short, as the French film *Ma Vie en Rose* so touchingly illustrates, all "boys" are not boys. And as the life of Brandon Teena demonstrates, not all "girls" are girls. Why do we refuse these truths? Why do we efface the gendered reality of others—and of ourselves? Why do so many of us never really teach *gender*, let alone transgender? If the answer is fear, we have some self-reflection to do. And if the indicative response is, "I never really thought about it," the imperative rejoinder is, "Start thinking."

Notes

1. I recognize that gender, as an analytic category, can be disengaged from the array of issues with which it is intertwined—sexuality, race, ethnicity, nationality, class—only strategically, for the purpose of making an argument about its particular significance in a local context (in this case, the history of the study of literature in English).

2. Brooks and Warren contend that "[t]he human being is a unity" (341). Similarly, "a poem, in so far as it is a good poem, is an organic unity in which all the elements are vitally interfused" (34).

3. On the history of gender bias in literary criticism and critical theory, see Abel; Heilbrun; Millett; Showalter; and Woolf for important and representative critiques.

4. Elaine Showalter writes:

> In its earliest years, feminist criticism concentrated on expos-
> ing the misogyny of literary practice: the stereotyped images of
> women in literature as angels or monsters, the literary abuse or
> textual harassment of women in classic and popular male lit-
> erature, and the exclusion of women from literary history. . . .
>   The second phase of feminist criticism was the discovery
> that women writers had a literature of their own, whose his-
> torical and thematic coherence, as well as artistic importance,
> had been obscured by the patriarchal values that dominate our
> culture. (5–6)

5. Even in feminist psychoanalytic theory of this era, the concept of the feminine often slips back into the female—unsurprisingly, since Freud's work, antedating the theoretical distinction between sex and gender, characteristically assumes the conjunction of bodily and psychic sex except in children and pathological adults.

6. See Epstein; Fausto-Sterling; and Kessler. When a freer relation be-tween sex and gender *is* recognized, as it is in the writing of Janice Raymond and a handful of followers, it is condemned (in the case of male-to-female transsexuals) as a masculine (medical/transsexual) plot to infiltrate the ranks of real women, and to reassert patriarchy from within. The notion of multiple sexes and genders became fully think-able in feminism only around 1990, with the publication of works such as Diana Fuss's *Essentially Speaking: Feminism, Nature and Difference*; Eve Kosofsky Sedgwick's *Epistemology of the Closet*; and especially Judith Butler's *Gender Trouble: Feminism and the Subversion of Iden-tity*.

7. Felski suggests Robert Young's concept of hybridity as a useful way to keep difference and sameness simultaneously in mind:

> Metaphors of hybridity and the like not only recognize differ-
> ences within the subject, fracturing and complicating holistic
> notions of identity, but also address connections between sub-

jects by recognizing affiliations, cross-pollinations, echoes, and repetitions, thereby unseating difference from a position of absolute privilege. (Felski 12)

8. See Benjamin; and Winnicott, especially Chapter 3, "Playing: A Theoretical Statement."

9. The whole novel plays off Hans Christian Andersen's fairy tale "The Snow Queen," most particularly the image of Old Nick's looking glass and the propensity of its broken slivers to penetrate the eyes and heart, thereby destroying the human capacity for love, compassion, and the perception of beauty. Cf. Idabel's "dark" glasses, above.

10. Marvin E. Mengeling suggests that Joel assumes "the position of husband . . . in relation to Randolph" (104).

11. I use masculine pronouns for Idabel and later, neologistic transpronouns for Orvil Pym, protagonist of Denton Welch's novel *In Youth Is Pleasure*. At this historical moment, in what is still a male-dominant world culture, it seems important to legitimate (female-to-male) transmen without qualification, lest people born "female" once again be denied the right of self-determination. It seems comparably important to avoid born-"male" appropriation/exploitation of females, and of the meaning of female bodies, by indicating an awareness of, and respect for, differences in the life experiences and present social potentials of born females and born males—differences that unequal amounts of social power have historically conditioned. Hence the male-to-female signifiers *hir* and *s/he*.

12. Staring down at Idabel from the ferris wheel, Miss Wisteria laments, "Poor child, is it that she believes she is a freak, too?" (195).

13. See note 11 on my use of *hir* and *s/he*.

14. See James; Hall; and Genet.

15. See Badinter for a theorization of masculinity as the Other of the feminine.

16. Jay Prosser's *Second Skins: The Body Narratives of Transsexuality* provides an excellent analysis of transsexual narratives. Prosser's book includes a chapter on Radclyffe Hall's *The Well of Loneliness*, which could be described as female-to-male fiction. Male-to-female fiction includes such works as Jean Genet's *Our Lady of the Flowers* and Hubert Selby Jr.'s "The Queen Is Dead" (a section of *Last Exit to Brooklyn*). Leslie Feinberg's *Stone Butch Blues* is the best fictional representation

so far of a transgender community in the late-twentieth-century, Western, medico-technological world. Herculine Barbin's autobiography (with a foreword by Foucault) is an important intersexual document. Recent biographies include Kate Summerscale's *The Queen of Whale Cay: The Eccentric Story of "Joe" Carstairs, Fastest Woman on Water* and Diane Wood Middlebrook's *Suits Me: The Double Life of Billy Tipton*. Significant photographic works include Nan Goldin's *The Other Side* and Loren Cameron's *Body Alchemy: Transsexual Portraits*. For a review of theory and historical scholarship on transgender, see Norton, "Transsexualism/Transgenderism: History and Politics," and Norton, "Transsexualism/Transgenderism: Psychological Accounts," in the *Reader's Guide to Lesbian and Gay Studies*.

17. See Bakhtin, *Art and Answerability* and *Speech Genres and Other Late Essays*; Iser, *The Act of Reading* and *The Implied Reader*; and Jauss, *Aesthetic Experience and Literary Hermeneutics* and *Toward an Aesthetic of Reception*.

18. See Readings, *The University in Ruins*, for a brilliantly provocative reflection on the intellectual future of the postnational university.

Works Cited

Abel, Elizabeth, ed. *Writing and Sexual Difference*. Chicago: U of Chicago P, 1982.

Abbott, C. C., ed. *The Correspondence of Gerard Manley Hopkins and Richard Watson Dixon*. London: Oxford UP, 1935.

Andersen, Hans Christian. "The Snow Queen." *Fairy Tales*. Trans. R. P. Keigwin. Ed. Svend Larsen. Vol. 1. Odense, Den.: Flensted, 1953. 296–366.

Ang, Ien. "Comment on Felski's 'The Doxa of Difference': The Uses of Incommensurability." *Signs: Journal of Women in Culture and Society* 23.1 (1997): 57–64.

Aristotle. *The Complete Works of Aristotle*. Ed. Jonathan Barnes. 2 vols. Princeton: Princeton UP, 1984.

Badinter, Elisabeth. *XY: On Masculine Identity*. Trans. Lydia Davis. New York: Columbia UP, 1995.

Bakhtin, Mikhail M. *Art and Answerability: Early Philosophical Essays*. Trans. Vadim Liapunov. Ed. Michael Holquist and Vadim Liapunov. Austin: U of Texas P, 1990.

———. *Speech Genres and Other Late Essays.* Trans. Vern W. McGee. Ed. Caryl Emerson and Michael Holquist. Austin: U of Texas P, 1986.

Barbin, Herculine. *Herculine Barbin: Being the Recently Discovered Memoirs of a Nineteenth-Century French Hermaphrodite.* Trans. Richard McDougall. New York: Pantheon, 1980.

Benjamin, Jessica. *Like Subjects, Love Objects: Essays on Recognition and Sexual Difference.* New Haven: Yale UP, 1995.

Boys Don't Cry. Dir. Kimberly Peirce. Twentieth-Century Fox/Searchlight, 1999.

Braidotti, Rosi. "Comment on Felski's 'The Doxa of Difference': Working through Sexual Difference." *Signs: Journal of Women in Culture and Society* 23.1 (1997): 23–40.

The Brandon Teena Story. Dir. Susan Muska and Greta Olafsdottir. Zeitgeist/New Video, 1999.

Brooks, Cleanth, and Robert Penn Warren. *Understanding Poetry.* 3rd ed. New York: Holt, 1960.

Butler, Judith P. *Gender Trouble: Feminism and the Subversion of Identity.* New York: Routledge, 1990.

Cameron, Loren. *Body Alchemy: Transsexual Portraits.* Pittsburgh: Cleis, 1996.

Capote, Truman. *Other Voices, Other Rooms.* 1948. New York: Vintage-Random, 1994.

Cornell, Drucilla. "Comment on Felski's 'The Doxa of Difference': Diverging Differences." *Signs: Journal of Women in Culture and Society* 23.1 (1997): 41–56.

Epstein, Julia. *Altered Conditions: Disease, Medicine, and Storytelling.* New York: Routledge, 1995.

Fausto-Sterling, Anne. "The Five Sexes: Why Male and Female Are Not Enough." *The Sciences* 33.2 (1993): 20–25.

Feinberg, Leslie. *Stone Butch Blues.* Ithaca: Firebrand, 1993.

———. *Transgender Warriors: Making History from Joan of Arc to RuPaul.* Boston: Beacon, 1996.

Felski, Rita. "The Doxa of Difference." *Signs: Journal of Women in Culture and Society* 23.1 (1997): 1–21.

Foucault, Michel. "What Is an Author?" *Language, Counter-Memory, Practice: Selected Essays and Interviews*. Trans. Donald F. Bouchard and Sherry Simon. Ed. Donald F. Bouchard. Ithaca: Cornell UP, 1977. 113–38.

Fuss, Diana. *Essentially Speaking: Feminism, Nature & Difference*. New York: Routledge, 1989.

Gallop, Jane, Marianne Hirsch, and Nancy K. Miller. "Criticizing Feminist Criticism." *Conflicts in Feminism*. Ed. Marianne Hirsch and Evelyn Fox Keller. New York: Routledge, 1990. 349–69.

Genet, Jean. *Our Lady of the Flowers*. Trans. Bernard Frechtman. 1963. New York: Grove, 1987.

Gerin, Winifred. *Charlotte Brontë: The Evolution of Genius*. Oxford: Oxford UP, 1967.

Gilbert, Sandra M., and Susan Gubar. *The Madwoman in the Attic: The Woman Writer and the Nineteenth-Century Literary Imagination*. New Haven: Yale UP, 1979.

Goldin, Nan. *The Other Side*. Ed. Nan Goldin, David Armstrong, and Walter Keller. Zurich: Alltag/Parkett, 1992.

Hall, Radclyffe. *The Well of Loneliness*. 1928. New York: Anchor-Doubleday, 1990.

Heilbrun, Carolyn G. *Writing a Woman's Life*. New York: Ballantine, 1988.

Hunter, J. Paul. *The Norton Introduction to Poetry*. 4th ed. New York: Norton, 1991.

Iser, Wolfgang. *The Act of Reading: A Theory of Aesthetic Response*. Baltimore: Johns Hopkins UP, 1978.

———. *The Implied Reader: Patterns of Communication in Prose Fiction from Bunyan to Beckett*. Baltimore: Johns Hopkins UP, 1974.

James, Henry. "The Pupil." *The Great Short Novels of Henry James*. Ed. Philip Rahv. 2nd ed. New York: Carroll, 1996. 565–619.

Jauss, Hans Robert. *Aesthetic Experience and Literary Hermeneutics*. Trans. Michael Shaw. Minneapolis: U of Minnesota P, 1982.

———. *Toward an Aesthetic of Reception*. Trans. Timothy Bahti. Minneapolis: U of Minnesota P, 1982.

Kessler, Suzanne J. "The Medical Construction of Gender: Case Management of Intersexed Infants." *Signs: Journal of Women in Culture and Society* 16 (1990): 3–26.

Laqueur, Thomas. *Making Sex: Body and Gender from the Greeks to Freud.* Cambridge: Harvard UP, 1990.

Ma Vie en Rose. Dir. Alain Berliner. Perf. Georges Du Fresne, Michele Laroque, Jean-Philippe Ecoffey, and Hélène Vincent. Sony Pictures Classics, 1997.

McCann, Richard. "My Mother's Clothes: The School of Beauty and Shame." *The Penguin Book of Gay Short Stories.* Ed. David Leavitt and Mark Mitchell. New York: Viking, 1994. 540–56.

Mengeling, Marvin E. "*Other Voices, Other Rooms*: Oedipus between the Covers." *The Critical Response to Truman Capote.* Ed. Joseph J. Waldmeir and John C. Waldmeir. Westport, CT: Greenwood, 1999. 99–108.

Middlebrook, Diane Wood. *Suits Me: The Double Life of Billy Tipton.* New York: Houghton, 1998.

Millett, Kate. *Sexual Politics.* Garden City: Doubleday, 1970.

Norton, Jody. "Transsexualism/Transgenderism: History and Politics." *Reader's Guide to Lesbian and Gay Studies.* Chicago: Fitzroy Dearborn, 2000. 586–89.

———. "Transsexualism/Transgenderism: Psychological Accounts." *Reader's Guide to Lesbian and Gay Studies.* Chicago: Fitzroy Dearborn, 2000. 589–92.

Pratt, Minnie Bruce. "Stripped." *S/HE.* Ithaca: Firebrand, 1995. 173–74.

Prosser, Jay. *Second Skins: The Body Narratives of Transsexuality.* New York: Columbia UP, 1998.

Raymond, Janice. *The Transsexual Empire: The Making of the She-Male.* 1979. New York: Teachers College P, 1994.

Readings, Bill. *The University in Ruins.* Cambridge: Harvard UP, 1996.

Rose, Jacqueline. "Introduction-II." *Feminine Sexuality: Jacques Lacan and the école freudienne.* Ed. Juliet Mitchell and Jacqueline Rose. New York: Norton, 1982. 27–57.

Sedgwick, Eve Kosofsky. *Epistemology of the Closet.* Berkeley: U of California P, 1990.

Selby, Hubert Jr. "The Queen Is Dead." Pt. II of *Last Exit to Brooklyn.* 1964. New York: Grove, 1988. 21–79.

Showalter, Elaine, ed. *The New Feminist Criticism: Essays on Women, Literature, and Theory.* New York: Pantheon, 1985.

Southey, Robert. Letter to Charlotte Brontë, Mar. 1837. Gerin 110.

Summerscale, Kate. *The Queen of Whale Cay: The Eccentric Story of "Joe" Carstairs, Fastest Woman on Water.* New York: Viking-Penguin, 1997.

Welch, Denton. *In Youth Is Pleasure.* 1945. Cambridge: Exact Change, 1994.

Winnicott, D. W. *Playing and Reality.* 1971. New York: Routledge, 1991.

Wittig, Monique. "The Mark of Gender." *The Straight Mind and Other Essays.* Boston: Beacon, 1992.

Woolf, Virginia. *A Room of One's Own.* 1928. New York: Harcourt, 1981.

Young, Robert. *Colonial Desire: Hybridity in Theory, Culture, and Race.* New York: Routledge, 1995.

II

PEDAGOGIES

CHAPTER SIX

The Uses of History

LILLIAN FADERMAN
California State University, Fresno

I n her book *Epistemology of the Closet,* Eve Sedgwick disarm-
ingly queries, "Has there ever been a gay Socrates? Has there
ever been a gay Shakespeare? Has there ever been a gay Proust?"
And she saucily responds, "Yes," and "their names are Socrates,
Shakespeare, and Proust" (52). But why should it matter whether
we can claim these icons of Western culture as our own? Why
should we go even so far as to commit the sin of ahistoricity
(imagine "gay" culture in sixth-century B.C.E. Greece or sixteenth-
century C.E. England!) for the sake of finding connections between those icons and us? Why do we need to know that there
were great men and women in the past who shared our traits or
our desires? What justification is there for outing people who are
now dead?

As lesbians and gays, it is in our interest to know the lesbian
or gay facts in the lives of the great and to acquaint others with
those facts. That certain historical figures had something in common with contemporary homosexuals would be of little importance in a world where gay was considered as good as straight,
where homosexuals had never been put in jails or insane asylums
or fired from their jobs or disowned by their families merely because they were lesbian or gay. We would not especially need to
lay claim to great figures of the past if our homosexuality were
never a factor by which we've been meanly judged.

What are the uses of history? The various furors over the last
years regarding changes in the guidelines for teaching history in
the public schools should serve as evidence that "history" is never
simply a collocation of objective facts. The public school battle
was about crucial conflicts such as whether American history

should be related by stories that emphasize an Anglo heritage or stories that emphasize slave rebellions and immigrant experiences. Both sides in the battle realized what is at stake in the relating of history: among the uses of history are its possibilities for providing role models to the young, for giving people reasons for pride in who they are, for teaching lessons about the past that we can incorporate in the present and use to plan the future. The recording and relating of history is always a matter of angle of vision and is seldom without some degree of chauvinism. History can provide something vital to any people who bond in a meaningful group; it can provide what Van Wyck Brooks has called in a different context *a usable past*.

Lesbian and gay history has been nonexistent until quite recently. Heterosexuals certainly had no reason to record lesbian and gay history for us, and it was virtually impossible for us to record it ourselves since an admission of interest in homosexuality (apart from its legal or medical connections) was tantamount to the perilous admission of being homosexual. Thus we had few heroes, we had no lessons of the past, we had little wisdom that was handed down to us by our "elders." Generations of lesbians and gays were never dignified with a history. The belief that nobody in history has lived or felt as they have—nobody sane or socially viable, at any rate—must surely have encouraged in more than a few homosexuals the self-hating conviction that nobody sane or decent *should* want to live or feel that way. Perhaps it's no wonder that the suicide rate among lesbian and gay teens, who generally have not learned our history, has been astronomically high relative to the general population of teens.

Will knowing that Shakespeare or Sappho was homosexual—or having access to books such as the Chelsea House series, Lives of Notable Gay Men and Lesbians—lower the suicide rate for homosexual teens? In fact, it might. Surely in a homophobic society that has had little good to say about us, it would help our young people to know (and have it known by others) that Jane Addams could not have done her great social work for the underprivileged and neglected of society were it not for the love of her life, wealthy and generous Mary Rozet Smith; that Walt Whitman wrote some of his best poems to his "manly comrades" whom he loved no differently from the ways that contemporary gay men love other men; that many of Emily Dickinson's most passionate love poems were written not to the elusive "Master" but to Sue Gilbert—the woman who later became her sister-in-law; that Willa Cather had a forty-year domestic partnership with Edith Lewis; that Virginia Woolf and Katherine Mansfield were bisexual; that Auden and Housman and Spender were gay; that though she was closeted, African American playwright Lorraine Hansberry identified as a lesbian; that we figure very heavily indeed among those who have created the very best that has been thought and said—and done—in the world.

It is absolutely vital for young gays and lesbians to know that individuals who have been respected and valued even in a homophobic society have shared with them that very trait that the rest of the world has claimed to despise. And surely those dead greats would not have begrudged being used for such necessary solace and aid.

Work Cited

Sedgwick, Eve Kosofsky. *Epistemology of the Closet*. Berkeley: U of California P, 1990.

CHAPTER SEVEN

"What's Out There?" Gay and Lesbian Literature for Children and Young Adults

CLAUDIA MITCHELL
McGill University

Educators would significantly benefit from acquainting themselves with the fields of gay and lesbian studies, not because it would access some distant other, but more immediately, reading gay and lesbian scholarship, representations, and expressions might compel a second look at one's own constructed sexuality and a different look at what it is that structures how the sexuality of another is imagined.

DEBORAH BRITZMAN, "What Is This Thing Called Love?"

In making this statement, teacher educator and activist Deborah Britzman is drawing our attention to the fact that the field of gay and lesbian studies is not simply for gays and lesbians, and not just for the purpose of having "them" understand "us" better. Rather, through contact with representations of gay identity, all educators can have what she terms a "second look" at themselves and their own constructed sexuality. Her point is an important one in that, amongst other possibilities, it supports the notion that as teachers and teacher educators we need to be engaged in studying ourselves as part of our efforts to transform our own teaching. As I have noted elsewhere, it benefits all teachers that a discourse community has recently emerged that closely examines (homo)sexuality in the context of teaching (Mitchell and Weber). This community, which includes such authors/works as Kissen's *The Last Closet: The Real Lives of Lesbian and Gay Teachers*; Jennings's *One Teacher in Ten*; Tobin's *Making a Place for Pleasure in Early Childhood Education*; and Khayatt's *Lesbian Teachers: An Invisible Presence,* has in a sense placed sexuality on the agenda within the professional literature on teacher education.

I highlight the significance of teachers and teaching here because Britzman's point also serves as a personal reminder of the number of times I am asked by either the beginning teachers in my classes in a Faculty of Education or by experienced teachers who come to workshops on literature for children and adolescents: "Can you suggest some books on gay and lesbian themes," "What's out there?," and "What teaches well?" Anxious to accommodate their requests, thereby ensuring that at least some of these books get into circulation, I usually leap at the chance to pass out annotated bibliographies, without necessarily stopping to ask such questions as "Good for what or whom?" Or "Teach *what* well?" The question "Does it teach well?" is one that can be highly problematic both for what it implies about literature and reading practices and for what it says about teaching itself. At the same time, the question, because of its frequency in one formulation or another, suggests the need for strategies for examining the kinds of books that are available for young people on gay and lesbian issues. The purpose of this essay is not to provide some grand scheme of categorization of books, but rather to offer those who work with young readers some strategies for questioning the very question "What teaches well?" and what that might mean both in our classrooms and for taking a second look at ourselves. The question then is really one of how gay and lesbian literature for young people can become a meaningful site for learning and teaching in our own classrooms.

Gay and Lesbian Literature for Young Children

One of the most frequently banned children's books in Canada is *Asha's Mums* (by Rosamund Elwin and Michele Paulse), a picture book which challenges both the heteronormative practices of schools, insofar as they assume that everyone's family (regardless of whether it is "intact," headed by a single parent, blended, or newly constituted) is heterosexual, and the impact of heteronormativity on students and teachers. In the story, Asha's teacher asks the class to bring back signed consent forms so that the class can visit the Science Centre. When Asha brings back her form with two signatures, the teacher insists on knowing which of the names belongs to the mum:

> I said, "Both."
> "It can't be both. You can't have two mums," she said briskly.
> "But I do! My brother and I have two mums," I protested. (np)

The problem (as the teacher sees it) is settled during a meeting with the two mothers; it becomes clear that for the school both mothers can be "Mummy Number One." The story is an important one historically because it is one of the first to challenge overtly the ways that schools regulate what counts as "family," who can be a mother, and so on. Since schools can either reproduce or challenge dominant discourses, the issue is significant. Peer groups—particularly those in school—often reinforce for children what is socially acceptable. Potentially, schools can offer a mediating space for questions such as, "Am I the only one? What is wrong with my family?" *Asha's Mums*, far from offering "lesbianism in your face," as several school boards have charged, foregrounds the issue of divergent family structures by unapologetically making the lesbian relationship of the mothers central to the text.

In relation to teaching, the book reveals a number of layers. Interestingly, or ironically, it is frequently put on a suggested reading list for lesbian parents (perhaps as a warning of what they may be up against with the school system). While it is important for gay and lesbian couples and their children to know that there are books "out there" about us, there is probably nothing in the book that any gay or lesbian couple with children has not already thought about, anticipated, or even experienced. As Erika Courvoisier observes in her case study of one lesbian family that is preparing for the entry of their three-year-old son into the school system:

> As Nicholas is still only three years old, there have been no school-related experiences for the family to engage in as an openly lesbian family. Nicholas has not attended daycare, but is currently registered for pre-kindergarten. . . . A significant portion of the interview was spent discussing the upcoming problems facing Nicholas as the son of openly lesbian parents. The first long, uncomfortable pause in the interview occurred when discussing their fears for Nicholas. As single adults or partners their strategies for reducing the effects of homophobia on self-esteem are practiced. For their son, they know that "there's going to be a lot of pain for that little kid." (32)

Perhaps the greatest teaching potential of the book is for straight teachers who might themselves become conscious of heteronormative teaching practices (such as insisting that students bring a note from home with signatures that designate "mother" or "father," or organizing activities such as making Mother's Day or Father's Day cards). Thus the point is not that a minority group—what Hardiman and Jackson call the "target group"—needs to read stories about its own members, but that members of the "agent group" (in this case the heterosexual community) need to become more aware of their own teaching practices. Additionally, *Asha's Mums* offers teachers all the "entry points" they could ever need for extending and enriching the notion of family, a theme that characterizes almost every language arts curriculum in North American primary education. In short, yes, the book "teaches well," but it also makes the point that schools are too often outdated, excluding, and in need of change.

Whereas the lesbian mothers and the heteronormative practices of schools are foregrounded in *Asha's Mums*, another picture book, *Saturday Is Pattyday* by Leslea Newman, focuses on what happens to the child when the lesbian couple breaks up. In this story, Frankie is upset because his two mums have split up and he worries about whether he will still be able to see Patty, who no longer lives with him. Like other stories which represent families in which the parents are no longer together, *Saturday Is Pattyday* is about children in the position of living with one parent and spending "custody time" with the other. Although this subject has received widespread treatment in children's books —

in those for very young children, such as *Mom and Dad Don't Live Together Any More* (by Kathy Stinson), and in the range of books for preteens and young adolescents—*Saturday Is Pattyday* might be regarded as groundbreaking in that it is one of the first books to describe honestly separation in nonheterosexual families. The focus is on Frankie's sense of loss and fear of separation, not on the fact that his mothers are lesbian. While the book is important for any young reader who might be experiencing a sense of loss, it also challenges adult mediators to confront their own sense of "what is a family." For adults who are themselves gay or lesbian, the book offers an interesting take on what is possible for family life. For example, while the myth of the happy heterosexual two-parent family has been challenged as the model of family life—so much so that the heterosexual parents in children's books are often separated or divorced—in the few books for children in a gay or lesbian family, there has generally been no room for anything but representations of the family as happy and cohesive. The point of these books is becoming a family, or being part of a nonheterosexual family, as in *Asha's Mums*. Aside from the fact that books about lesbian and gay families have the potential for so many other story lines, this formulation of "the *new* happy family" could become a type of colonization whereby gay and lesbian couples must stay together, if not for the sake of the children, then for the sake of the community. *Saturday Is Pattyday* subverts this master narrative.

Leslea Newman's *Gloria Goes to Gay Pride* explicitly explores a sense of community. We see a gay pride march through the eyes of Gloria, a little girl who attends the march with her lesbian mothers. The book offers an acknowledgment of what a number of authors might describe as biculturalism as a feature of gay culture. In using the term *biculturalism,* Allen and Demo and Lukes and Land refer to the possibility that many gay and lesbian families have strong support through the gay community and outside of the more mainstream networks. This support, though, may be *in addition to* some of the regular support systems to which these families already have access. While this may not be quite the same as the biculturalism of, say, a Greek Canadian family, which might have access to the Greek community (customs, rituals, friends) as well as access to the mainstream culture, a "first start" is to recognize that there are identifiable, visible cultural components such as Gay Pride Day that should be celebrated (as opposed to being dismissed or pathologized). As Courvoisier notes, "While gays and lesbians have grown up in and have largely embraced the dominant heterosexual culture, they also have a rich alternative culture, complete with language, symbols, organizations and icons" (14). A recognition of this community by schools is important both for an understanding of cultural diversity generally and as a way to help de-pathologize the family life of gays and lesbians, where the "Other" can often be taken to mean "less." Books such as *Gloria Goes to Gay Pride* challenge that idea by highlighting the gay and lesbian community as it features in Gloria's life.

The three books just discussed do not fall into an imaginative fictional mode. Rather, they are in keeping with a genre of literature for young children that employs a narrative style—sometimes in the third person but most often in the first person—that operates under the rubric of "This is my life." The books are meant to inform. In none of these books is there anything explicitly sexual, although the idea of two mums (or two dads) is read by some censors as blatantly sexual for what it implies about the relationships between adults of the same sex, and for the questions it might provoke in children: "How could you have two mummies?," "Who sleeps where?," "How do they have babies?" Beyond what such works might convey about gay and lesbian families or a sense of community, the books can also contribute to Britzman's idea of a second look for educators, both in relation to our own constructed sexuality and the ways in which we imaginatively construct the sexuality of others, including that of children. For example, at present we know of no books for young children that address the idea of childhood sexuality (outside of those of the "know your body" genre). Indeed, even some of those that deal with the body in a very straightforward way, such as Kathy Stinson's *The Bare Naked Book,* have sometimes been censored in school settings. Where sexuality does appear in literature for young children, it is more likely to involve social pathology or disease—either in the form of warnings against child molestation (for example, *Tom Doesn't Visit Us Anymore* by Maryleah Otto) or in relation to HIV and AIDS (for example, *Come Sit by Me* by Margaret Merrifield).

However important these works are for the issues of sexuality they address, they do not address any notions of sexuality which are not framed within adult sexuality. Valerie Walkerdine, in her work on the eroticizing spaces of some popular culture texts in relation to young girls, questions the silence that surrounds this space, noting that "even though most parents will be used to little girls dressing up, gyrating to their favorite pop music and fantasizing a starring role, nobody appears to have put this together with all the educational, moral and sexual concerns about young girls today" (3). Using the idea of "the presence of absence," we might begin to question what kinds of stories are *not* available—perhaps not even imaginable—and to consider the apparent discomfort many teachers feel with the relationship between childhood and sexuality. While these three books on lesbian and gay issues represent landmarks in children's publishing, they also need to be read as much for what they have not said—yet. Here we might think of Elizabeth Bishop's poem "In the Waiting Room," which is based on her memory of being seven years old and looking at images of African women in a *National Geographic* in the dentist's office. In her autobiographical writing, Bishop interprets the memory as "the dawning of lesbian consciousness," something that Corinne Blackmer explores in her analysis of what she describes as "lesbian childhood" (17).

Gay and Lesbian Themes as Social Change in Young Adult Literature

Some picture books clearly directed at young children might also be appropriate for older readers, providing "teachable moments" by serving as springboards to discussion. Beyond those books already mentioned, consider the description offered by a junior high teacher of his use of Michael Willhoite's *Uncle What-Is-It Is Coming to Visit*. As Les Parsons writes:

> With colorful, lively drawings and a straightforward, wry and

fast-moving text, this picture book is ideal for any level when questions need to be answered and stereotypes need to be dispelled. "The teachable moment" for my Grade 8 students came up in a spontaneous discussion of Gay Pride Day. The book was a great hit as a read aloud and was passed around the classroom for days afterwards. My partner used the picture book to similar effect with a Grade 3 class when the "Ooooh, that's gay!" syndrome popped up." (11)

Clearly, teachers who have a knowledge of the range of books being published on gay and lesbian themes can be poised to act.

At the same time, there is a wide range of adolescent novels dealing with gay and lesbian identity, some of them dating back to at least the mid-1970s. Marion Dane Bauer gives a sense of the diversity of issues that can be explored when she describes how she put together her anthology, *Am I Blue? Coming Out from the Silence:*

> [W]hat about the joys of falling in love? What about all the minute complexities involved in finding a relationship at all? Or the grief of losing someone? Or the deep relief when someone who might have been lost comes home? What about stories which involve people who happen to be homosexual simply living out their lives? That was my dream when I first conceived of the idea for a collection of original young adult short stories on gay and lesbian themes. (Walker and Bauer 28)

Her distinctions are important and should serve as a reminder that there is no unitary experience of gayness—nor are the readers themselves coming to or looking for the experience of reading in any homogeneous way. Indeed, to add to the distinctions Bauer makes, one might also consider the differences between coming-out stories, stories in which the protagonist is gay, stories in which the protagonist is questioning his or her sexuality, stories in which the protagonist is working on behalf of a family member or close friend who is gay, and so on. While the differences should of course be obvious to anyone who reads and works with young people, the issue of diverse experience can sometimes get lost amidst the idea of "here's a book on *that* theme."

Given the range of books on gay and lesbian identity available for adolescent readers, however, the questions "Does it teach well?," "Teach what well?," "Good for whom?" are no less frequently asked and no less relevant. In this section, I give consideration to the ways in which some of the books and short stories can be regarded as strategic entry points for embarking on a study of literary-social relations with twelve- to fifteen-year-old students. How, for example, might representations of otherness be explored? Where does the idea of voice figure into explorations of the Other? What do certain conflicts in these texts, such as the tensions between progressive and more conservative ways of thinking, contribute to an understanding of the Other?

Consider, for example, an examination of these conflicts through other axes of oppression found in a number of gay and lesbian texts. One such text is M. E. Kerr's short story "We Might as Well All Be Strangers," included in *Am I Blue?*. The protagonist, Alison, wants to tell her Jewish grandmother that she is a lesbian. Her mother, however, disagrees:

> "Alison, this coming out thing isn't working. You came out to me, all right, I'm your mother and maybe you had to come out to me. But where your grandmother's concerned: Keep quiet."
>
> "You think she'd want that?"
>
> "I think she doesn't even dream such a thing could come up! She's had enough *tsuris* in life. Back in the old country there were relatives lost in the Holocaust! Isn't that enough for one woman to suffer in a lifetime?"
>
> "Maybe that would make her more sympathetic."
>
> "Don't compare gays with Jews—there's no comparison."
>
> "I'm both. That's prejudice against both. And I didn't choose to be either."
>
> "If you want to kill an old woman before her time, tell her."
>
> "I think you have Grandmother all wrong."
>
> "If I have Grandmother all wrong," said my mother, "then I don't know her and you don't me and we might as well all be strangers." (26)

In explaining how and why she came to write this story, M. E. Kerr notes that the story was inspired by a friend of hers who came out to her Jewish grandmother in spite of her mother's warnings that "the old lady couldn't take it." As she observes,

"To my friend's amazement, her grandmother was the only sympathetic member of the family. She told her grandchild that she had seen more than enough of prejudice in her life-time and asked to meet 'your girlfriend'" (27).

In the same volume, Lois Lowry's story "Holding" tells of the hidden history of Willie, whose father's lover, Chris, has just died. Willie, we discover, has been misleading his friend Jon into thinking that his father's lover was a woman simply because of the lover's ambiguously gendered name, Chris.

> "Jesus. Your dad's wife died. Bummer."
> "They weren't married," I reminded Jon, continuing the lie I'd been living so long that it came easily. "They only lived together." (179)

When Willie returns from the funeral, he decides he can no longer tolerate perpetuating the "lie" and tells Jon that Chris was not a wife or a female "significant other":

> I ended the lie, then, and gave a tiny sliver of life back to Chris and to my father and to myself. "Chris was a guy. . . . My father's *significant other,* as you would put it, was a guy," I said clearly, looking at him.
> "All these years? What's it been, like eight or nine years? Since we were little kids? It's always been a guy? But you said—"
> I gave him what I thought was a disdainful, condescending look. I did my John Gielgud accent. "I said nothing, my good man. You made certain assumptions. I allowed you to do so. It suited my purposes." (185; emphasis added)

In this passage, there is a heightened sense of who can become "othered." Not only does it include Chris—referred to as the "significant other"—and Willie's father, whose relationship has been kept secret, but it also includes Willie's friend Jon. In lying about his father's relationship with Chris, Willie categorizes it as the unmentionable. Deceived all those years by Willie into thinking that the relationship between Chris and Willie's father was a heterosexual one, Jon is in the position at the end of the story of discovering that he too has been part of a lie, and he begins to question his own heteronormative assumptions.

We also see this kind of questioning of the Other in *Skindeep*, a novel by the South African novelist Toeckey Jones. First published in 1985 during the height of oppression in the apartheid era, the novel contains some of the first gay references in adolescent fiction in South Africa. Eighteen-year-old Rhonda, who is "putting in time" at a shorthand and typing school until the university term begins, meets and becomes romantically interested in Dave. Dave is mysterious from the very beginning. His head is completely shaven, for no apparent political or other reason, and his family connections remain ambiguous. At one point, he says that his brother and two sisters are dead. Rhonda senses there is more to know about Dave than what she has been told. She decides that Dave must be gay when she sees him at a party being attentive to a young man known to be gay. For Rhonda this is an end-of-the-world experience, and she becomes despondent at what she perceives as his deception. But her suspicions that Dave might be gay are dispelled and replaced by an equally "unthinkable" revelation—Dave is actually colored and has kept his head shaven so that he can pass as white. ("Colored" was the term used in South Africa during apartheid to refer to people of racially mixed heritage.) Rhonda learns that Dave was adopted by a white family in Johannesburg, but in actual fact his mother and siblings are alive in Cape Town. Eventually Dave "comes out" as colored and goes back to live with his family in Cape Town. Rhonda, who throughout most of the book has wanted to get out of South Africa, decides to stay and fight against the oppression that has made it necessary for Dave and others to live secret lives. The book is an important one for what it says about the kind of suspicion that Rhonda has of Dave; the status of the Other to which Dave is relegated by Rhonda is no small point. Indeed, in setting the story during some of the most oppressive years of the apartheid era, when being colored carried with it significant social stigma, Jones is drawing our attention to the seriousness of the stigma of being suspected of being gay.

Related to the status of the Other is the issue of voice and narrative authority: who can speak? Kirk Fuoss notes that one of the characteristics of many of the young adult novels dealing with male homosexuality is that the characters "are more often than not presented as characters in someone else's story [rather] than

[as] narrators of their own life stories" (163). On the one hand, this can provide a type of "speaking on behalf of" activism, as we see in M. E. Kerr's *Deliver Us from Evie*, where Parr, who is straight, is fighting against the injustices done to his lesbian sister, or in Bette Greene's *The Drowning of Stephan Jones*, where Carla must acknowledge, regardless to the consequences of their relationship, that her boyfriend is directly responsible for the harassment and ultimately the death of Stephan Jones. These books pick up on Anne Bishop's idea of "becoming an ally" in working toward breaking the cycle of oppression. Bishop is referring to the ways in which those who have been identified as or associated with being agents of oppression might learn to work alongside those who have been its targets. At the same time, as Fuoss points out, this "speaking on behalf of" can also be read as a "sustained resistance to the articulation, by a gay narrator, of his [or her] own story. The implication seems to be that while it's one thing to permit talk about homosexuality, it is quite another matter to permit a homosexual to talk" (165). In a sense, then, there is often a censoring of the gay voice to speak on its own behalf. While it is clearly "safer" to have someone speak on behalf of gay voices, this is not without political implications, something teachers may be able to take up with students who themselves may often be subjected to kinds of voicelessness in their own lives.

Teachers might also consider the ways in which this literature can be read as impelling social change, something that is central to much of the literature of social realism written for young people generally (Mitchell and Smith, "More Than Just a Love Story" and "Nervous Conditions and the Smell of Apples"). How do particular works or their reading provide a map for social change by offering what might be regarded as strategies for grappling with change? For example, when Rhonda in *Skindeep* realizes that she must stay in South Africa to fight against apartheid, she asks her best friend to get her some political books from her boyfriend who is politically active. She realizes that if she is going to stay and fight, she needs to know more. Likewise, students might be guided to look at the radical/conservative binary that impels action in many of these works as itself a type of mapping for social change. M. E. Kerr's *Deliver Us from Evie* provides a good example of this. What is particularly important about this book is that it takes oppression out of a purely personal mode and places it in a social framework. Parr, for example, cannot bear to see what is happening to his sister but he also comes to see how the issue is not just an individual one. When the family is ostracized by the bank, the church, and the community in general, he comes to understand some of the ways in which institutions exert power and control over social norms.

In *Deliver Us from Evie,* as well as in a number of other works, the radical/conservative tension is often encountered more directly. Bette Greene's novel *The Drowning of Stephan Jones* and Diane Wieler's *Bad Boy* each interrogates the kind of value system in which intolerance of gays and lesbians is quite open, largely a result of "small town-ness," the force of fundamentalist religions, and the conservatism of a family values ethos, especially in rural areas. While these may seem like rather blatant stereotypes of rural life and the way it often perpetuates homophobia, it is perhaps the contained world of rural life as presented in these novels that highlights the contrasts between the radical-thinking protagonists and those who hold more conservative views. At the same time, the representation of rural conservatism and more progressive thinking can raise questions for students to consider about the ways in which political systems of thought construct sexuality.

We also see this kind of tension interrogated by South African writer Barrie Hough in his novel *Vlerkdans,* first published in Afrikaans and prescribed as a "set work" in many Afrikaans-medium high schools in South Africa. Now translated into English as *In Full Flight,* the book describes the relationship between a young artist, Hannes, and his model, Anton, a dancer. While there is no explicit acknowledgment of a sexual relationship between Hannes and Anton (in fact, Hannes tells his father they only peed together at a urinal), through its focus on the intensity of the relationship, the novel provides an opening for the question of whether they *could* be gay. Like many books for young adults, *In Full Flight* uses generational conflict as a way to confront radical and more conservative modes of thought. Hough uses the surface feature of an earring as a way into this investigation. Thus the novel opens with the following passage:

> It's because of Anton that I started wearing the earring. I had it
> put in after I started sketching him. I'll never forget that first
> afternoon, a few weeks before the earring. It was the first time
> I felt like a real artist. With my own model. (1)

When Anton becomes ill with AIDS, Hannes in despair telephones
his father, a medical doctor who no longer lives with Hannes's
mother and who is living in Cape Town. On the way to the air-
port, Hannes's mother asks in her "please-do-it" voice, "'Won't
you please take off the earring? Until he's gone back to Cape Town?'
I keep quiet, don't look at her" (61). The earring, as the mother
predicts, is a source of conflict when Hannes's father arrives:

> I don't know when exactly he notices the earring. When he's in
> front of me, he puts the case down again and hugs me. "Hullo
> Hannes." He steps back, looks at me fixedly straight in the
> eye. It feels like time stands still. Pa is the first to look away.
> (62)

As the visit continues, Hannes's father finally gets around to acknowledging the source of his son's grief and asks him about
Anton. Their conversation, a stilted one made up of a series of short
questions and answers, reveals the conflict between father and son:

> "Do you know how he got AIDS?"
> "He used drugs for some time a few years ago . . . spiked."
> "Don't they realize what they are doing?"
> Pa stares in front of him. He frowns. His eyes are almost
> slits. "This . . . Anton . . . I didn't realize you'd met him at the
> Gym. I got the impression he was one of your classmates. Was
> he still at school when he got sick?"
> "He was doing matric at a college somewhere here in town
> . . . ."
> "And you're good friends?"
> "Yes."
> "Just good friends?"
> I clench my fist and take a deep breath. "Why don't you
> ask me outright? If he's gay? And me?" (65)

Hannes and his father part on a note of reconciliation, although
the earring continues to be a source of conflict. Just before the
father returns to Cape Town, he asks Hannes:

"The earring. Does it mean anything?"
"It makes me feel . . . different, Pa. . . ." (67)

The earring serves as a site of contestation between the conservative father and the more radical Hannes. For adolescent readers, these straightforward points make such books work in ways that are both personal and literary. As Hough points out in an interview I conducted with him in South Africa in 1995, the novel encourages the idea of raising consciousness about gay identity. In commenting on his visits to some Afrikaans secondary classrooms, he notes that one of the most frequent questions that students ask him about this book relates to whether Anton and Hannes sleep together. Hough says he puts the question back to the students: "What do you think?" He acknowledges that it is the "open-ended" nature of the text as well as his presence in the classroom as an openly gay man that makes room for discussion.

Hough's comments are important for what they tell us about the significance of going beyond the primary text. In participating in school visits, for example, Hough is adding a layer of textuality to the reading, an act in keeping with what John Fiske would describe as a cultural reading. Fiske talks about the significance of the overlapping yet separate nature of (a) the primary text, (b) the text of the reader (the reader's response), (c) the behind-the-scenes text of why writers write and why publishers publish, and (d) the texts of critical reception, or what adult critics might say about the work. Lesbian and gay works lend themselves to a multitextual reading for a variety of reasons, not the least of which is their consideration of issues of censorship; authors, critics, politicians, parents, school administrators, and teachers all have a great deal to say about these texts, in terms of either why they should be written or why they should not be read in schools. Built into some works such as Marion Bauer's *Am I Blue?* is the idea of the behind-the-scenes voice of the author and references to critical reception and censorship. For example, Bauer observes in the introduction (directed toward young readers) that she did not approach as potential contributors writers who were *necessarily* gay. Part of her motive in compiling the collection was to ensure that the participation of well-known popular writers, regardless of their sexual identity, would make it difficult for librarians to refuse to stock the book. She also addresses the issue of "who can write gay" and the significance of "the informed imagination." Thus the text *Am I Blue?*, as young readers encounter it, includes both short stories and short autobiographical accounts of the writers. In some cases, the writer is openly gay. For example, the editor herself, who is also author of one of the stories, "Dancing Backwards," acknowledges in her autobiographical narrative that she married right after high school and that it took her thirty years to realize what "direction I had been facing all along" (273). Nancy Garden, well known for her lesbian "coming-out" novel for adolescent readers *Annie on My Mind,* addresses the significance of political movements, dedicating her story "Parent's Night" "to the schools that have gay-straight-bisexual support groups, in hopes that all schools will soon have them" (128). What is interesting about Bauer's text is its invitation to young people to do more than just speculate about the question "Is he or is she (gay)?" It has an honesty to it, and at the same time offers an affirmation of the significance of readings which are informed by the primary text, by one's own response to the text, by the author's actual or imagined reasons for writing the text, and by the text's political context. *Am I Blue?* is exceptional in its inclusion of the behind-the-scenes accounts for the students to read. Too often only the teacher has background information on the author or the controversy surrounding the text, so there is always an added layer of mediation between the reader and the text. In making the behind-the-scenes accounts accessible to adolescent readers, books like Bauer's treat the readers as knowers.

The works for adolescent readers referred to in this essay represent only a small number of those available. While novels dealing with gay and lesbian identity are by no means the only ones suited to the kinds of interrogation I have been discussing, they are particularly suited to adolescent readers and their interest in their own sexuality. But I return to Britzman's notion of educators taking a second look at ourselves and our own constructed sexuality. As Nancy Boutlier writes in her essay on lesbian literature in the secondary classroom:

I have found that the process of bringing lesbian and gay literature into the classroom, like coming out, leaves no room for turning back. The experience has reaffirmed my personal commitment to challenging myself to face the worst of my fears. Because my school had a strong commitment to multicultural education, I was able to use the description of the course I taught to introduce students to gay and lesbian literature. I do not assume that all teachers are in such a happy circumstance, but everywhere there is *some boundary that needs exploring, some limit that needs to be pushed.* (141; emphasis added)

In drawing our attention to the idea of "some boundary that needs exploring" and "some limit that needs to be pushed," Boutlier reminds us of the significance of works on lesbian and gay identity written for young people as potential sites for teaching and for learning. While the phrase "what's out there" in the title of this essay might be read as a reference to literature which is "out," we might also take it as a complement to Boutlier's notion of boundaries and limits. Here I have focused on some of the ways in which these works and their various readings can operate as "points of entry" for teachers and students to work together to engage in exploring boundaries and pushing limits. In focusing in particular on the notion of otherness as a construct in social-literary criticism, as well as a construct for interrogating lived experience, we see possible ways in which these works operate as meaningful pedagogical sites.

Works Cited

Allen, Katherine R., and David H. Demo. "The Families of Lesbians and Gay Men: A New Frontier in Family Research." *Journal of Marriage and The Family* 57 (1995): 111–27.

Bauer, Marion Dane, ed. *Am I Blue? Coming Out from the Silence.* New York: HarperCollins, 1994.

Bishop, Anne. *Becoming an Ally: Breaking the Cycle of Oppression.* Halifax, Can.: Fernwood, 1994.

Blackmer, Corinne E. "Ethnoporn, Lesbian Childhood, and Native Maternal Culture: Reading National Geographic with Elizabeth Bishop." *GLQ: A Journal of Lesbian and Gay Studies* 4.1 (1998): 17–58.

Boutlier, Nancy. "Reading, Writing and Rita Mae Brown: Lesbian Literature in High School." *Tilting the Tower*. Ed. Linda Garber. New York: Routledge, 1994.

Britzman, Deborah. "What Is This Thing Called Love?" *Taboo: The Journal of Culture and Education* 1 (1995): 65–93.

Courvoisier, Erika. *Lesbian Families: An Emerging Phenomenon*. Unpublished ms. Dept. of Educational and Counselling Psychology, McGill U, 1998.

Elwin, Rosamund, and Michele Paulse. *Asha's Mums*. Toronto: Women's, 1990.

Fiske, John. "British Cultural Studies and Television." *Channels of Discourse, Reassembled: Television and Contemporary Criticism*. Ed. Robert Allen. London: Methuen, 1987. 254–89.

Fuoss, Kirk. "A Portrait of the Adolescent as a Young Gay: The Politics of Male Homosexuality in Young Adult Fiction." *Queer Words, Queer Images: Communication and the Construction of Homosexuality*. Ed. R. Jeffrey Ringer. New York: New York UP, 1994. 159–74.

Garden, Nancy. *Annie on My Mind*. New York: Farrar, 1982.

Greene, Bette. *The Drowning of Stephan Jones*. New York: Bantam, 1991.

Hardiman, Rita, and Bailey W. Jackson. "Conceptual Foundation for Social Justice Courses." *Teaching for Diversity and Social Justice: A Sourcebook*. Ed. Marianne Adams, Lee Anne Bell, and Pat Griffin. New York: Routledge, 1997. 16–29.

Hough, Barrie. *Vlerkdans*. Johannesburg: Tafelberg, 1992. *In Full Flight*. Trans. Wierenga Jelleke. Johannesburg: Heinemann, 1996.

Jennings, Kevin. *One Teacher in 10: Gay and Lesbian Educators Tell Their Stories*. Boston: Alyson, 1994.

Jones, Toeckey. *Skindeep*. London: Bodley Head, 1985.

Kerr, M. E. *Deliver Us From Evie*. New York: HarperTrophy, 1995.

Khayatt, Madiha Didi. *Lesbian Teachers: An Invisible Presence*. Albany: SUNY P, 1992.

Kissen, Rita. *The Last Closet: The Real Lives of Lesbian and Gay Teachers*. Portsmouth, NH: Heinemann, 1996.

Lowry, Lois. "Holding." Bauer 175–87.

Lukes, C.A., and H. Land. "Biculturality and Homosexuality." *Social Work* 35 (1990): 155–61.

Merrifield, Margaret. *Come Sit by Me*. Toronto: Women's, 1990.

Mitchell, Claudia, and Ann Smith. "More Than Just a Love Story: Investigating the Literary and Social Significance of the Young Adult Novel in South Africa." *Alternation* 3.2 (1996): 173–83.

———. "*Nervous Conditions* and *The Smell of Apples*: Investigations of Innocence and Trauma through Adolescence as a Literary Space in Some South African Contemporary Literature." Association for Bibliotherapy Conference. Ottawa, Ontario. 28–29 May 1998.

Mitchell, Claudia, and Sandra Weber. *Reinventing Ourselves as Teachers: Beyond Nostalgia*. London: Falmer, 1999.

Newman, Leslea. *Gloria Goes to Gay Pride*. Boston: Alyson Wonderland, 1991.

———. *Saturday Is Pattyday*. Toronto: Women's, 1993.

Otto, Maryleah. *Tom Doesn't Visit Us Anymore*. Toronto: Women's, 1987.

Parsons, Les. "Completing the Puzzle: Gay-Positive Literature in the Classroom." *The Rainbow Classroom* 3.1 (1998): 11.

Stinson, Kathy. *The Bare Naked Book*. Toronto: Annick, 1986.

———. *Mom and Dad Don't Live Together Any More*. Toronto: Annick, 1984.

Tobin, Joseph Jay, ed. *Making a Place for Pleasure in Early Childhood Education*. New Haven: Yale UP, 1997.

Walker, Kate, and Marion Dane Bauer. "The Gay/Lesbian Connection: Two Authors Talk about Their Books." *Bookbird* 32.2 (1999): 25–30.

Walkerdine, Valerie. *Daddy's Girl: Young Girls and Popular Culture*. Cambridge: Harvard UP, 1997.

Wieler, Diana. *Bad Boy*. Toronto: Douglas, 1989.

Willhoite, Michael. *Uncle What-Is-It is Coming to Visit!* Boston: Alyson, 1993.

CHAPTER EIGHT

Creating a Place for Lesbian and Gay Readings in Secondary English Classrooms

JIM REESE

The International School of Brussels, Belgium

> *A life lived in fear is a life half-lived.*
> *Strictly Ballroom*

As a cautionary note to readers, let me begin by stating my preferred title for this piece: "How Watching a Silly Film Initiated the Process of Rethinking My Own Approach to Reader-Response Theories." What that title lacks in pithiness it makes up for in accuracy. For in this essay, I will return to 1993 when I first saw the Australian comedy *Strictly Ballroom*, which evoked in me a powerful response. In considering that response, I, as a novice teacher and a gay man, began to think about the implications of the pattern of responses I have as a reader of film and literature. Why would this film strike a chord with me? Was I merely projecting my own desires as a gay reader onto the film? Or was I constructing meaning in a personal way, one that was perhaps similar to that of other gay spectators? In trying to answer these questions, I began to examine the place of lesbian and gay readers and readings in secondary English classrooms.

We Are Everywhere?

Since the Stonewall riots of 1969 and the advent of the gay rights movement, lesbian and gay visibility has increased dramatically in the culture at large. In the academic realm, we have seen the formation of a new discipline—lesbian and gay studies—and in many quarters we can honestly say that there is a better understanding of sexual difference. Secondary schools, however, for the most part seem to have resisted such change; while there are isolated instances of progress—gay-straight alliances, same-sex couples attending school dances—lesbians and gay males are still by and large an invisible minority in middle and senior high schools.

In facing the everyday reality that most lesbian and gay students would not dare to reveal their sexual identity to their peers or teachers, we have to push ourselves to understand why this is so. Describing the difficult psychosocial adjustments these students face, Harbeck and Uribe write:

> For [lesbian and gay adolescents, secondary] school is often a time of isolation, humiliation, and pain. Those who openly admit their sexual orientation or who depart from traditional sex-role stereotypes . . . are verbally harassed and physically abused. Those who conceal their homosexual feelings experience loneliness and alienation, a splitting of their gay, lesbian, or bisexual identity from the rest of their personality. . . . By developing elaborate concealment strategies these young people are often able to "pass as straight," but at some significant, unmeasurable cost to their developmental process, self-esteem, and sense of connection. . . . The traditional support structures that serve all other children do not serve gay, lesbian, and bisexual youth. (11–12)

My own experience with U.S. public schools and international schools abroad leads me to conclude that many teachers and administrators often turn a blind eye to blatant examples of homophobia such as name-calling or bullying of those thought to be lesbian or gay. In other words, institutionalized homophobia usually goes unchallenged. At the international school where I currently teach, when discussing with colleagues the general need to foster greater tolerance and understanding, I am impressed by the high level of awareness shown for various minority groups within the school, as well as a certain willingness to appreciate individual differences among students. The faculty seem genuinely eager to promote openness and curiosity, to have students look beyond themselves in order to consider the world at large, and to help them find a place for themselves in a rapidly changing society. Yet when I attempt to discuss the need for increased awareness of issues facing lesbian and gay people and the importance of confronting homophobia within the school community, I often encounter what at first seems to be ignorance. Many well-meaning colleagues say they would be more inclusive if only they had more knowledge; some say they would rather not talk about homosexuality at all because the issue makes them uncomfortable; still others cannot understand why such discussions are relevant in the classroom setting; and I even have heard a few say that so long as they have no students who identify as lesbian or gay, there is no need to raise the topic. There are times, of course, when I wonder if this ignorance is not in fact veiled hostility.

Have we not reached the point in the year 2000 where we can agree that lesbian and gay people do exist in significant numbers and in all walks of life? Why, then, do these arguments against their inclusion persist? Would social studies teachers be serving their students well by ignoring feminism in a unit on social movements of the past fifty years because they just did not know enough to include such information? Would science teachers be nurturing a healthy approach to scientific investigation if, during work on genetics, they bypassed topical discussions on research into genetic predisposition for, say, eye and hair color, because such discussions brought discomfort? Would we consider it acceptable for literature teachers to refuse to assign works by African American authors on the grounds that there were no African American students in their classrooms? So many of us fool ourselves into thinking that we have no lesbian or gay students or that discussions about homosexuality are irrelevant for our students who identify as straight. By making such decisions, teachers deny students the opportunity to develop understanding and open-mindedness toward other ways of being in the world.

If we consider the attempts made in the past few decades to end racism and sexism in schools, we certainly have not expected children from groups which have been excluded or marginalized to challenge the system on their own. Rather, we have counted on adults in schools to ensure the safety of all children and to help them develop to their fullest potential in academic and social realms.

Implications for the English Teacher

These questions about inclusion have evolved over the years as I have explored more deeply my role as a secondary English teacher in encouraging personal response to the literature my students and I read and discuss. Having been trained in reader-response theory, I have noted the "opening" many theorists provide for various types of discourse, from the subjective approach articulated by Bleich, for example, who asserts that "all people, young and old, think about themselves most of the time and think about the world in terms of themselves. . . . [U]nderstanding and reconceptualizing a work of literature can be best understood as expressions of the personalities of the reader. The role of personality in response is the most fundamental fact of criticism" (4); to Rosenblatt's theory that meaning emerges from "the reader's contribution in the two-way, 'transactional' relationship with the text" (*The Reader* ix). While I want to imagine the inclusion of lesbian and gay readers in these theories, never in the canon of reader-response texts have I found reference to the role sexual identity plays in the reader's efforts to read and understand literature.

Gradually a new set of questions emerged for me to ponder, such as: Don't lesbian and gay readers locate themselves in a text just as other groups of readers do? Moving beyond mere response and realizing that most works taught in the secondary English classroom ignore or pejoratively depict homosexuality, I asked myself: When confronted with heterosexist or homophobic bias in the text and subsequently in class discussions, do lesbian and gay adolescents, in order to protect themselves, efface their own identity for the sake of fitting in with "accepted" or "traditional" interpretations which validate those biases?

While at the university level such questioning has been elaborated under the auspices of queer theory, I have seen little interrogation of this issue at the secondary level. Yet let us look at the way Rosenblatt envisioned the ideal English classroom setting in her seminal text *Literature as Exploration*:

> The youth needs to be given the opportunity and the courage
> to approach literature personally, to let it mean something to

[him or her] directly. The classroom situation and the relationship with the teacher should create a feeling of security. [She or he] should be made to feel that [her or his] own response to books, even though it may not resemble the standard critical comments, is worth expressing. Such a liberating atmosphere will make it possible . . . to have an unself-conscious, spontaneous, and honest reaction. (66–67)

While Rosenblatt may not specifically have had lesbian and gay students in mind, her words should resonate with English teachers who, sensitive to the needs of all students, aim to foster "a liberating atmosphere" and "unself-conscious, spontaneous, and honest reaction[s]" in literature discussions. The contrary would be classrooms which inhibit or, worse, prohibit students (in the context of this argument, read lesbian and gay students) from participating fully and honestly in the study of literature.

In widening the reader-response approach, therefore, we can consider the work of a number of feminist critics who have argued for a new type of reading. Patrocinio Schweickart, in critiquing the androcentric bias in canonical literature, urges resistance in the act of reading:

Taking control of the reading experience means reading the text as it was *not* meant to be read, in fact, reading it against itself. Specifically, one must identify the nature of the choices proffered by the text and, equally important, what the text precludes—namely, the possibility of reading as a woman *without* putting one's self in the position of the other, of reading so as to affirm womanhood as another, equally valid, paradigm of human existence. (81–82)

This idea of the "resisting" reader is precisely what I have in mind when discussing lesbian and gay readers and readings. Yet it would be naive to assume that adolescents, especially those who identify as lesbian or gay, would come forward to challenge heterosexist readings of texts, especially in a school environment in which being identified as homosexual could lead to physical and/or psychological abuse. For that reason, we as teachers must not only encourage but also be willing to lead the broadening of dialogue in the classroom so that it is inclusive of *every* student, which in reality is just one step in the process of transforming an intolerant school environment into one which genuinely accommodates lesbian and gay people.

An English classroom which embraces lesbian and gay readers and readings would serve all students—those who are lesbian and gay themselves, those who have other differences which go unrecognized, and those who lack sensitivity to difference. Ultimately in this essay I would like to introduce such a scenario, but before we enter the classroom I want to go back to 1993 when I first saw the film *Strictly Ballroom,* the starting point of my own understanding of myself as a gay reader.

The Text: *Strictly Ballroom*

Strictly Ballroom focuses on the world of competitive ballroom dancing in Australia. By the time it was released in the United States, the film had already received much favorable attention in Australia and parts of Europe. Director Baz Luhrmann conceived the story, originally performed as a play, as an allegory of the suppression of artistic expression behind the Iron Curtain during the cold war (Brunette 26). The principal characters are Scott (Paul Mercurio), a rebellious young competitive dancer who bucks the system in the name of artistic freedom; Fran (Tara Morice), a shy young student in a ballroom dance school who aspires to be Scott's dancing partner; and Scott's father, Doug Hastings (Barry Otto), a rather detached and seemingly broken man who quietly encourages the pairing of Scott and Fran.

The film begins with on-screen red velvet stage curtains opening to reveal sparkly titles, perhaps serving as an enticement to enter another world. Such an opening—the film ends with the curtains closing—asks the audience to suspend its disbelief, thus allowing the director to introduce implausible plot shifts and fantasy sequences.

In the ensuing ninety minutes, Luhrmann concocts a fairly simple and somewhat silly story. Fortunately, he decorates it with wonderfully eccentric characters and intentionally exaggerated melodrama. Strauss's "Blue Danube Waltz" provides a backdrop for the opening scene, as we glimpse, behind half-opened double doors, silhouettes of dancers in slow motion warming up just before starting a competition. As the music ushers in twirling couples in slow motion, the lights come up and the camera zooms in on their garish costumes and highly stylized moves.

Luhrmann grabs our attention as we wonder at this artificial world. We laugh at the spectacle, yet we remain curious about who these people are. Suddenly, documentary-style, the camera jump-cuts to a living room where Scott's inconsolable mother, Shirley Hastings (Pat Thomson), disconsolately describes her agony over her son's audacity in trying new "crowd-pleasing" steps in a regional ballroom dance competition. "That's the tragedy—my son was a champion!" she laments.

Next, we flash back to the scene Shirley has just described. On the dance floor, Scott and his partner Liz (Gia Carides), moving to a samba beat, become boxed in by another couple, forcing Scott in an act of desperation to break out of his traditional steps. From this point on, he seems unable to control himself. We hear from Scott's coach, Les Kendall (Peter Whitford), who derides Scott's behavior; we recoil as dance federation head Barry Fife (Bill Hunter) moralistically admonishes those who would dare to try new steps; and then Scott's mother comes back on screen, this time even more upset, wailing, "I keep asking myself, Why? Did I do something wrong? Did I fail him as a mother?"

Less than ten minutes into the film, we are fully immersed in the lives of characters who take themselves so seriously; to add to their zaniness, Luhrmann often films them in extreme close-up. We quickly understand, though, who is being shaped as the hero: The camera loves Scott's handsome, angular face and his lithe body, which moves so elegantly; furthermore, his rebellious streak, brazen self-confidence, and youthful nature all stand in stark contrast to the oppressive stances taken by the older generation. Obviously he does not heed the federation's rules as the others do, as evidenced by his risking a chance at winning.

Once the dust has settled, Scott seems as shell-shocked as everyone else, although his confusion more likely stems from the overreaction of others to his behavior. The omnipotent and sleazy Barry Fife sums up the general reaction to Scott when he says, directly to the camera, "Well, of course you can dance any steps you like. That doesn't mean you'll win." We realize that Scott has effectively ruled out any future he might have had as a competitive dancer by challenging the authority of the dance federation.

The rest of the film charts Les and Shirley's frantic attempts to find Scott a suitable partner, Fran's newfound boldness in asking Scott to give her a chance as his partner, and Doug's vicarious thrill at seeing his son rebel against a system which years before had crushed him in a similar manner due to the machinations of Shirley, Les, and Barry. Although most of the film comes off as parody, Luhrmann never lets it get out of hand. The audience grows giddy with the bizarre goings-on, only to be reminded every so often that something important is at stake here; namely, artistic freedom.

If the film had been played straight—that is, without the winking of the camera's eye—*Strictly Ballroom* would have been no better than the standard Hollywood comedy. By using heavy doses of humor and irony, however, the director weaves a significant message and provides visual and textual clues which invite the viewer into an act of complicity in the interpretive process. We cannot help but cheer for Scott and Fran, and yet we revel in the depiction of the cartoonish characters who stand in their way, simply because they are larger than life.

Crafting a Gay Reading of the Film

As far back as I can remember, I have been most attracted to films and literary texts that reject the rules, that show me the world from an unusual perspective. My passion for a particular work stems from my attachment to characters with the ability to overcome obstacles, which often take the form of societal oppression. The three characters at the center of *Strictly Ballroom* all have some trait that sets them apart from and makes them the object of derision by the rest of the crowd; however, they retain dreams that translate into fierce optimism. If they were to accept the reality as laid down by the majority, they would never succeed.

As I became engrossed in the film, certain lines of dialogue took me beyond the surface story, allowing me to read the film in a deeply personal way. For example, Shirley Hastings's dismay over her son's refusal to conform ("Did I fail him as a mother?"), along with her disparaging comments about her ineffectual husband, strangely echo the misogynistic and homophobic cultural myths in our society, perpetuated through now-outdated medical and psychiatric discourses which have insisted that homosexuality in males is "caused" by a domineering mother and a weak father. Les Kendall, who appears to be a gay character, is called a "faggot" by Barry Fife when it is discovered that he has assisted Scott and Fran. In general, the lines spoken by the film's authority figures about preserving sacred traditions, conforming for the sake of upholding the status quo, and fighting the corrosive influence of nonconformist behavior mirrored the kinds of utterances I was reading daily in the conservative media in response to lesbian and gay visibility. As Barry prepares to wage war against Scott, he imperiously declares, "It's about time that lad learned some home truths about where this kind of thing can lead."

On another level, I was drawn into the film by Scott's physical appeal and his independent spirit, which pushes him to go against the grain. He rejects the regulation dance steps not just because they are not right for him but also because there is injustice in the dance federation's tyranny. He follows his instincts, and in doing so he disrupts the world around him. When he cannot understand why such fierce opposition is directed toward him for doing what he feels is natural, he cries out, "What's wrong with me? What is so wrong with the way I dance?" Reading the film as a gay man, it did not take long for me to develop an affinity with Scott.

Interestingly, Scott, who exudes sexuality on the dance floor yet appears to have no interest in anyone except himself and his dancing, falls for Fran by the end of the movie; it is not clear how serious their relationship will be, as Scott himself admits that it is the passion of the dance that has made him romantic. While one might assume that this blossoming romance defines Scott as heterosexual, I found Scott's hedging on his feelings an even more appealing aspect of his character. It gave me, the viewer, a further opening through which to project my own same-sex desire, knowing as I do how impossible it is to fix boundaries to desire. The moment when Scott shares a kiss with Fran comes across as the least authentic scene in the film and led me to read their romance as inconsequential.

Certainly *Strictly Ballroom* is not a gay film per se. Rather, I would argue that my reading of the film relies on my sensibility as a gay man. Charting this difficult terrain in his afterword to *The Celluloid Closet: Homosexuality in Movies,* Vito Russo cautions against defining a gay sensibility while acknowledging that it does exist:

> Gay sensibility is not something we have or share or use. It isn't even something that only gay people express. It's a blindness to sexual divisions, an inability to perceive that people are different simply because of sexuality, a natural conviction that difference exists but doesn't matter; that there's no such thing as normal even when a majority of people think so. (326)

In the past two decades, studies of the reception of film by gay viewers have placed the viewer/reader in focus alongside the "text" and "author," mirroring in many respects reader-response theories in literature. In a chapter on gay readings of film in *Interpreting Films: Studies in the Historical Reception of American Cinema,* Janet Staiger studies various gay male responses in the 1950s to film star Judy Garland, contending:

> One of the procedures gay men seem to have used is to find homologous image structures between themselves and others— of the same or different gender and sexual orientation—and to apply those individuals' experiences to their own circumstances. Without images of their own, this seems . . . a reading strategy much like that of any repressed group's struggle over the meaning of a sign. (176)

Staiger carefully stresses that she is not lumping together all gay males as a monolith but instead is analyzing a phenomenon which existed within a certain faction of the gay male population over forty years ago. For when we attempt to understand responses to texts, we look for patterns.

Beyond the aforementioned elements of my own construct of *Strictly Ballroom,* I also saw a camp quality to the film. As Susan

Sontag defines it, camp "is the farthest extension, in sensibility, of the metaphor of life as theater" (281). Director Luhrmann has put such effort into every detail of the film's look and sound that he sacrifices character development; dance and music do most of the storytelling for us. From the outlandish costumes to the outrageous personalities portrayed on screen, the entire film seemed to be true to Sontag's definition in that we can see a "proper mixture of the exaggerated, the fantastic, the passionate, and the naive" (285). While *Strictly Ballroom* might not appeal to all lesbian, gay, and knowing straight viewers, it would most likely resonate with many of them for these reasons.

Lesbian and Gay Readers and Readings in the Classroom

Imagine lesbian and gay students in an English classroom who might "read" a text similarly to the way I have read *Strictly Ballroom*. If not openly gay at school, they would face a dilemma over responding honestly to the text. Knowing that their teacher asks students to share responses, they most likely would be tempted to choose a response other than the one they instinctively feel, for obvious reasons reluctant to expose themselves as gay.

Imagine too that the only romantic relationships depicted in literary texts are heterosexual and that no reference whatsoever is made to the possibility of divergence from this "norm." In class discussions, lesbian and gay students would listen as classmates—most of whom probably self-identify as heterosexual—express strong reactions to and personal connections with the text at hand. They would sit by feeling marginalized, unable to speak their minds. The essay or presentation which could have emerged from an honest response might not have been brilliant, but it would have been heartfelt; most students are energized and motivated by the thought of sharing their original ideas. In suppressing their responses, however, lesbian and gay students learn a sad lesson about their sexual identity: neither the teacher nor their classmates will acknowledge it. They themselves fear asserting it in public, and even though they might share certain values with their peers, they are effectively silenced because of who they are. Fear prevents recognition, and with the absence of lesbian and gay voices, we easily develop and perpetuate stereotypes and prejudices.

I am not asserting that every lesbian and gay student reads the way I have done, or that such readings exclude or take precedence over other types of reading; rather, I am putting forward the idea that if we do not give students the opportunity to be truly genuine in their responses, no matter where they locate themselves in the text, we have fared poorly as teachers. We must try to imagine the world through their eyes by opening ourselves to the various possibilities of reading the texts we teach. We also surely must strive, as Rosenblatt urges, "to help the student arrive at a more balanced and lucid sense of the work [which] involves the parallel effort to help [the student] understand and evaluate [his or her] personal emphases" (*Literature* 96). Moreover, we must understand that "the nature of the student's rudimentary response is, perforce, part of our teaching materials" (51).

How does an English teacher create a place for lesbian and gay readers and readings in the secondary classroom? An important step would be to acknowledge publicly that there are lesbian and gay readings of texts and to find a way to express them in the classroom. This task is not necessarily easy to undertake, for again, reader-response theorists do not usually locate lesbian and gay readings in their theories although they do provide spaces for them. If we were to take, say, Richard Beach's approach to various perspectives of reader-response theories, which he labels textual, experiential, psychological, social, and cultural (8–9), we could locate lesbian and gay readings in most, if not all, of these categories. Opening ourselves as teachers to these possibilities would enable such readings to emerge and develop.

Furthermore, as texts concerning lesbian and gay studies are published in greater numbers each year, teachers can find valuable resources in bookstores and libraries and on the Internet. Several critical series which deal primarily with texts used in secondary schools are beginning to address issues of sexual identity. In teaching *The Catcher in the Rye*, for example, I have found Twayne's Masterwork Studies edition of this 1950s novel to be helpful in challenging overt homophobia in the text. Sanford Pinsker, in a chapter titled "And Holden Caulfield Had a Great Fall," discusses the protagonist's derogatory references toward homosexuality throughout the novel and his efforts to confront his feelings for his favorite English teacher, whom he suspects is "a flit." Presenting Pinsker's analysis as a basis for class discussion, I urge students to address Holden's homophobia in the course of seeing patterns in his behavior; not surprisingly, they can draw from their own experiences of hearing antigay comments from their peers. Students readily see that Holden often uses homophobic language when he grows defensive or confused on sexual matters, but as he matures he shows a willingness to reevaluate his attitude when faced with the possibility that a man he idolizes is gay.

I remember the profound effect *The Catcher in the Rye* had on me as a young reader. Holden's rebelliousness and his search for goodness in the world made him a hero in my eyes. At the same time I was admitting to myself my own desire for the same sex, sadly, homophobic comments made by peers, silence on the part of adults, and daily validation of heterosexism and even homophobia in school became powerful warnings to me against public disclosure of my own sexual identity. I accepted Holden's homophobia because I had no means with which to challenge it. Now, as a teacher of young people, I know that being complicitous through silence when encountering such antigay sentiment only reinforces oppressive social relations.

"A life lived in fear . . ."

Teachers must open up their own imaginations before they can expect their students to do the same. Rosenblatt, again writing in general terms but making a point which has a special meaning for gay people, defines the role a literature teacher must play in encouraging personal response:

> We must indeed forgo the wish for a single "correct" or absolute meaning for each text. *If we agree on criteria for validity of interpretation,* however, we can decide on the most defen-

sible interpretation or interpretations. Of course, there remains the possibility of equally valid alternative interpretations as well as for alternative criteria for validity of interpretation. Such an approach enables us to present a sophisticated understanding of the openness and the constraints of language to our students without abnegating the possibility of responsible reading of texts. (*The Reader* 183)

To take this a step further, we must see lesbian and gay readings as valid, but we also must question criteria for validity of interpretation when they are heterosexist, just as feminist critics have challenged sexist and masculinist criteria.

Creating space for lesbian and gay readings initiates a dialogue which in practice most secondary classrooms lack. This dialogue can lead to wholesale transformation of attitudes, for in reading and discussing texts we must remember that "the point is not merely to interpret literature in various ways; the point is to *change the world*. We cannot afford to ignore the activity of reading, for it is here that literature is realized as *praxis*. Literature acts on the world by acting on its readers" (Schweickart 70).

I would not want to conclude this essay without a return to *Strictly Ballroom,* to which I am indebted for my own initiation into appreciating lesbian and gay readings of texts. In an interesting turn, it is not until late in the film that Doug Hastings, the protagonist's father, is developed as a heroic character. His role in the film becomes transformed when he comes out of his shell and from behind his annoying home-video camera, and implores his son to follow his heart. Doug's redemption is the most satisfying and emotional moment of the film.

To me, Doug easily represents a past generation stymied by social pressures and an oppressive culture. Through the present generation—epitomized in brash and confident Scott but perhaps more subtly brought across through shy but strong-willed Fran, Doug's real soulmate—Doug is able to recapture the moment of glory stolen from him years earlier. While others might not read exactly the same meaning into Doug's role in the film, for me he exemplifies the film's motto, which Scott learns from Fran: "A life lived in fear is a life half-lived."

In the classroom, we should be able to understand that our lesbian and gay students who suppress their true responses out of fear resort to half responses to texts. In the same way, students who identify as straight lose the opportunity to understand and appreciate multiple readings if lesbian and gay readings are not given full expression. After all, an important aspect of our work as English teachers is to foster honest and genuine dialogue in our classrooms so that literature can help us and our students imagine worlds beyond the ones we normally inhabit. In doing so, we can take the lead in making schools better places for everyone.

Works Cited

Beach, Richard. *A Teacher's Introduction to Reader-Response Theories*. Urbana, IL: NCTE, 1993.

Bleich, David. *Readings and Feelings: An Introduction to Subjective Criticism*. Urbana, IL: NCTE, 1975.

Brunette, Peter. "More Than Romance Colors *Strictly Ballroom*." *New York Times* 7 Feb. 1993: 26.

Harbeck, Karen, and Virginia Uribe. "Addressing the Needs of Lesbian, Gay, and Bisexual Youth: The Origins of PROJECT 10 and School-Based Intervention." *Coming Out of the Classroom Closet: Gay and Lesbian Students, Teachers, and Curricula*. Ed. Karen Harbeck. New York: Harrington Park, 1992. 9–28.

Pinsker, Sanford. *The Catcher in the Rye: Innocence under Pressure*. New York: Twayne, 1993. 72–88.

Rosenblatt, Louise. *Literature as Exploration*. 1938. London: Heinemann, 1970.

———. *The Reader, the Text, the Poem: The Transactional Theory of the Literary Work*. Carbondale: Southern Illinois UP, 1994.

Russo, Vito. Afterword. *The Celluloid Closet: Homosexuality in the Movies*. New York: Harper, 1987. 325–26.

Schweickart, Patrocinio P. "Reading Ourselves: Toward a Feminist Theory of Reading." *Readers and Reading*. Ed. Andrew Bennett. London: Longman, 1995. 66–93.

Sontag, Susan. "Notes on 'Camp.'" *Against Interpretation, and Other Essays*. New York: Dell, 1966. 277–93.

Staiger, Janet. "The Logic of Alternative Readings: *A Star Is Born*." *Interpreting Films: Studies in the Historical Reception of American Cinema*. Princeton: Princeton UP, 1992. 154–77.

Strictly Ballroom. Dir. Baz Luhrmann. Buena Vista Pictures Distribution, 1992.

CHAPTER NINE

Shakespeare's Sexuality: Who Needs It?

MARIO DiGANGI

Lehman College, City University of New York

Acccoording to a familiar and enduring myth, the works of Shakespeare express universal truths of human nature and therefore transcend the limitations of historical contingency and political ideology. Tellingly, the proponents of this myth do not consider the virtue or naturalness of same-sex love to be among those "universal truths" they find in Shakespeare. To the contrary, they often regard any analysis of same-sex desire in Shakespeare's works as irrelevant at best and sordidly proselytizing at worst, especially in educational settings, where the "proper" transmission of high culture to the next generation is at stake. Why should students be asked to think about pederasty in *As You Like It*, lesbian desire in *Twelfth Night,* or anal eroticism in *Romeo and Juliet*? What would justify the discussion of AIDS, homophobia, or queer theory in a course devoted to Elizabethan drama? And how could a consideration of these issues possibly enhance appreciation for Shakespeare's genius, which is the goal, after all, of serious teaching?

Questions like these have become the familiar refrain of reactionary cultural critics, who frequently exploit the ostensible discrepancy between a revered body of work and a new critical approach. Because lesbian and gay studies has emerged as a distinct academic discipline only during the last decade, it is particularly vulnerable to dismissal as merely the latest fashion sported by the so-called intellectual left. Lesbian and gay studies has certainly displayed the characteristically rapid growth of a hot new trend.[1] Even a selective account of recent developments in publishing will reveal the degree to which queer inquiry has grown, both inside and outside academia, in forums old and new. Educational journals as different as *College English* and *Radical Teacher* have featured articles or issues on lesbian and gay pedagogy (Phillips); in 1995 the MLA published *Professions of Desire*, "the first collection of essays to address issues concerning lesbian and gay studies in the undergraduate classroom" (Haggerty and Zimmerman, back cover); new journals such as *The Journal of the History of Sexuality* (1990), *GLQ: A Journal of Gay, Lesbian, and Queer Studies* (1993), and *Sexualities* (1998) are featuring interdisciplinary approaches to the study of sexuality; and competition for the lesbian and gay studies book market continues to thrive among university and commercial publishers alike. From an unsympathetic perspective, however, this palpable excitement about lesbian and gay studies might be cited as evidence of its mere faddish appeal.

The increasing visibility of lesbian and gay scholarship has certainly been regarded in some quarters as undeniable proof of the decline of "legitimate" literary studies. Lesbian and gay inquiry has recently been scapegoated along these lines in the contentious "Forum" section of *PMLA*, widely regarded as the premier academic journal in the field of language and literature. For instance, in 1996 *PMLA* published a letter by one Thomas C. Greene, who accuses the journal's editors of rejecting essays that are "original," "apolitical," and "stubbornly not hip" in favor of essays that showcase "vogue names" and "vogue words" (473–74). When he offers a representative list of "vogue words," Greene draws widely from multiculturalist and poststructuralist jargon; however, many of the offending terms inhabit the particular domain of lesbian and gay studies: *Eros, feminine, gender, masculine, queer, sex,* and any word beginning with *homo-*. Greene uses "homo-" studies as a synecdoche for the absurdity of all "theoretical" approaches, much as a tabloid journalist might use a particular sex scandal to epitomize the decadence of celebrities in general.

Insinuating that lesbian and gay scholars exploit and unfairly profit from current academic fashion reproduces the techniques of homophobic silencing that prohibited queer modes of analysis in the past. Given the pervasive homophobia of the cold war era, it is not surprising that previous generations of U.S. scholars did not speak appreciatively, if at all, about homosexuality in history or literature. Nor is it surprising that the sudden explosion of openly lesbian and gay scholarship into this void should send powerful shock waves through conservative quarters. While they sometimes mask as sagacious and timely critiques of the postmodern academy, tirades against the visibility of lesbian and gay studies play a familiar homophobic card: reducing a meaningful lesbian and gay presence to a superficial "lifestyle" or a temporary "phase." Such complaints thus seem to be motivated by nostalgia for the values and etiquette of a more repressive era, when traditional works were interpreted through traditional methods—the study of genre, textual form, and historical background—and when queers remained silent and abject.

Appeals to tradition are nonetheless powerful, especially when the difference between an established tradition and an encroaching "trend" is represented as self-evident and absolute. Queer theory is indicted on just these grounds in another letter from the same volume of *PMLA* cited previously. Referring to the sessions at annual MLA conventions, Larry Isitt asks:

> Of the some twelve hundred panels of the last two years, how many deal with the canonical and not the trendy? How many place radical political agendas above simple literary analysis? How many panels, for example, have been given on William Faulkner at the last two conventions and how many on queer theory? (475)

Isitt offers the cataloging and counting of session titles as an objective scientific procedure that exposes the palpable bias of the MLA leadership. Yet the logic of the procedure requires queer theory to function as a transparent sign of all the radical political "agendas" and impenetrable poststructuralist methods that have corrupted a once respectable profession. An ideological agenda evidently motivates the primary distinction between "tradition" and "trend," as well as the narrative of queer decadence that distinction produces. Furthermore, the coherence of Isitt's attack requires that he remain blind to the manifold differences within the field of queer theory, and also between queer theory and other "radical" methodologies. Ignoring these significant internal differences bolsters the fantasy of a united radical front, the threatening advance of which justifies retaliation by equal force.

Attacks on lesbian and gay studies as the latest outgrowth of academic theory (poststructuralism) or identity politics (cultural studies, multiculturalism) falsely exaggerate its novelty. Lesbian and gay scholarship did not spontaneously issue from the minds of contemporary academics who have built high-profile careers on the merits of their brilliant work. Along with other critical discourses based on the differentials of gender, race, and class, queer cultural analysis emerged in the United States from the political and intellectual upheavals of the 1960s, and it flourished in the aftermath of the legendary Stonewall riots of 1969. According to sociologist Jeffrey Escoffier, post-Stonewall lesbian and gay intellectuals attempted to authenticate their newly affirmed sexual identities by promoting an awareness of homosexual history and culture (11). Groundbreaking works of this stamp include Karla Jay and Allen Young's anthology *Out of the Closets: Voices of Gay Liberation* (1972); a special volume of *College English*—*The Homosexual Imagination* (1974)—comprised of essays on literature, criticism, and pedagogy (Crew and Norton); and Jonathan Ned Katz's *Gay American History* (1976). Louie Crew, the co-editor of *The Homosexual Imagination* and editor of *The Gay Academic* (1978), recently reflected on his involvement in the lesbian and gay studies explosion of the early 1970s. It is no wonder, he observed, that lesbian, gay, and bisexual scholars during this period "poured forth such an abundance of manuscripts: in addition to sleuthing and reclaiming our past, we were writing ourselves into community" (52). Many scholars of this generation regarded their intellectual endeavors as a vital contribution to the struggle for homosexual emancipation.

Neither faddish nor frivolous, lesbian and gay cultural analysis has demonstrably contributed not only to the development of lesbian and gay communities since Stonewall, but also to the ongoing institutional changes in academia that are the legacy of 1960s radicalism. According to Gerald Graff, the political revolts of the 1960s finally made it clear "that there was no more consensus on the disciplinary foundations of English than there was about the social function of education in general" (18). Lesbian and gay scholarship helped to shatter this consensus, and it continues to expand the boundaries of English studies today. For instance, recent efforts to "queer the Renaissance" have furthered the methodological innovations that feminist and materialist critics brought to the study of English Renaissance literature in the early 1980s (Goldberg, *Queering*; Ferguson, Quilligan, and Vickers). Moreover, lesbian and gay scholarship on the Renaissance has provided significant insight into our own culture by revealing the historical foundations of modern constructions of sexuality, and by showing how these ideological constructions continue to shape our interpretation of premodern literary texts. The study of sexuality, then, is hardly the exclusive domain of a self-interested minority of contemporary lesbian and gay scholars. At its best, it has served as a model of cultural analysis, synthesizing history, theory, and politics.

In the analysis that follows, sexuality is revealed to be a highly charged site of past and present conflict over the meaning of, and uses for, "Shakespeare." Since the late eighteenth century, the significance of same-sex desire in Shakespeare's life and works has been a topic of debate in the arena not only of literary criticism but also of ethics, law, sexology, politics, religion, and psychology (Fisher; Porter; Radel; Shepherd; Stallybrass). After sketching the history of this debate, I will examine its present manifestation in academic scholarship and popular culture, with the aim of showing that lesbian and gay studies can be political as well as intellectually rigorous, theoretical as well as socially engaged. The thorny political and theoretical issues surrounding the introduction of queer material into the English literature classroom will be the focus of a concluding discussion on pedagogy and queer Shakespeare studies.

Queer Genealogies: Two Hundred Years of Shakespeare's Sexuality

English departments need Shakespeare. This, at least, is a governing assumption of contemporary Anglo-American culture. If that statement sounds more like an axiom than an assumption, however, it only proves the success of an ideological campaign launched over a century ago within a particular institutional configuration that has long since vanished. As Thomas Dabbs explains, "[m]ass Shakespearean education did not come to fruition until the second half of the nineteenth century, when the playwright, then one of the most popular cultural figures in England, was placed at the core of the new English literature curriculum" (89). Teaching Shakespeare's plays made university education more accessible to working middle-class students, who did not have the time to study the Latin and Greek texts that formed the basis of the traditional curriculum. To elevate Shakespeare into a legitimate academic subject, however, Victorian educators presented his plays as repositories of philosophical and philological knowledge, thereby draining them of the sexual energies that contributed to their enduring popularity in the theater (Dabbs 90).

Whereas Shakespeare's place in the English curriculum now seems unshakable, the place of sexuality in the English curriculum remains a topic of fierce contestation. In vehement polemics against "political correctness," conservative individuals and organizations such as the National Alumni Forum typically represent lesbian and gay course offerings as the symptom of a degenerate English department. In 1996, for instance, critics roundly attacked the English department at Georgetown University for not requiring majors to take courses in Chaucer, Shakespeare, and Milton (see Strauss). Writing in the *New York Times,* Maureen Dowd ridiculed the faculty for "dissing" these "timeless" classics and replacing them with the dogmatic, jargon-filled offerings of the "race and gender brigade." It is no accident that two of the three courses so mocked—History and Theories of Sexuality, Women, Revolution, and the Media, and Unspeakable Lives: Gay and Lesbian Narratives[2]—explicitly focus on lesbian and gay subjects. Presumably, the media outcry against the "political" and "theoretical" corruption of the English department was intended to intimidate minority faculty members at this Catholic institution and to delegitimize their concerns in the eyes of the university, the academic community, and the general public. Unspeakable lives indeed.

Even critics with more benign, less overtly political motives may feel that English professors do students a disservice by applying contemporary theories of sexuality to literary works of timeless genius. In the wake of the Georgetown controversy, an established Shakespearean actor expressed to me the conviction that only when discussing modern gay-themed plays such as *Marvin's Room* or *Bent* was a teacher justified in raising the issue of homosexuality. Teachers of Shakespeare, he insisted, are obliged to convey the brilliance of his achievements in dramatic art: rich language, engaging plots, and psychologically credible characters.

Yet it is misleading to imply that the study of sexuality and theatrical craft are fundamentally incompatible. As numerous studies have demonstrated, sexuality infuses the very texture of Shakespeare's plays: erotic meaning does not exist independently of its expression through language, plot, and character (Bredbeck; DiGangi; Goldberg, *Queering* and *Sodometries*; Orgel, *Impersonations*; Smith; Traub, "(In)significance" and *Desire*). The question, therefore, is not whether Shakespeare's plays portray homoerotic relations, but the kind of recognition we are willing to afford those portrayals. Unfortunately, too many scholars have chosen to ignore homoeroticism altogether. Stephen Orgel observes that as of 1995, not one edition of *As You Like It* had mentioned the unmistakable homoerotic allusion in Rosalind's choice of the name "Ganymede" for her male alias ("Teaching" 64). This is no innocent oversight. When Rosalind declares her intention to disguise herself as a boy and take the name of "Jove's own page" (1.3.120), she evokes the most famous narrative of homoerotic desire in classical mythology. Rosalind's homoerotic role-playing, moreover, is integral to the development of the comic plot: as "Ganymede," she initiates a romantic courtship with Orlando, the man she will marry at the end of the play (DiGangi 275–78).

Although contemporary lesbian and gay scholarship has certainly made it more difficult simply to ignore or dismiss the homoerotic aspects of plays such as *As You Like It,* Shakespeare's sexuality has in fact been a topic of scholarly interest for the past two hundred years. Attending to Shakespeare's sexuality, for all its postmodern currency, thus turns out to be a very traditional pursuit. In the eighteenth century, editor George Steevens was the first to argue that the *Sonnets* provided a record of Shakespeare's objectionable sexual morality. Beginning with

Edmond Malone in 1780, subsequent editors and critics anxiously strove to construct "a normative character and sexuality" for Shakespeare (Stallybrass 96). While modern interpretations of the *Sonnets* do not as regularly conflate the narrator of the poems with the biographical author, they take up the legacy of these defenses when they attempt to justify the speaker's desire for the young man he addresses in terms of platonic friendship or literary patronage. More than a local skirmish within literary criticism, the nineteenth-century discourse about the *Sonnets* played an important role in constructing the modern discourse of sexuality (Stallybrass 102). Conversely, Victorian historiographers and sexologists used contemporary notions of sexuality to construct "the Renaissance" as a historical period and to demonstrate Shakespeare's artistic superiority over playwrights such as Marlowe (Fisher; Radel).

First in "The Portrait of Mr. W. H." and then through his highly publicized trials, Oscar Wilde played a remarkable role in developing the late nineteenth-century narrative about Shakespeare's sexuality (Stallybrass 102–3). Accused by the Marquis of Queensbury of "posing as a sodomite," Wilde sued him for libel; consequently, Wilde was required to prove that Queensbury's charge was neither true nor conducive to the "public benefit" (Cohen 126–27). Having failed to prove his case against Queensbury, Wilde was himself tried for committing "acts of gross indecency." During the first trial, Wilde had justified an erotically suggestive letter he wrote to Lord Alfred Douglas as a "prose sonnet," a poetically phrased expression of one artist's regard for another (Cohen 150). In the second trial, he defended the letter again, this time as an expression of the "deep spiritual affection" between an older and a younger man found throughout history, as instanced in the biblical story of David and Jonathan, the philosophy of Plato, and the sonnets of Michaelangelo and Shakespeare (Cohen 200). Instead of serving to legitimate his associations with younger men, however, Wilde's "aesthetic" imitation of Shakespeare was regarded as further evidence of his morally suspicious "extraordinary character" (Cohen 159). For the media and the jury, Wilde's homoerotic writings and appropriations of Shakespeare established not his place within a genealogy of spiritual male love, but rather his embodiment of the popular stereotype of the male homosexual: an effeminate, leisured aesthete.

The notoriety of the Wilde trials thus served to crystallize the male homosexual as a "paradigmatic sexual figure," a deviant who was recognizably distinct from his "'normal' twin, 'the heterosexual'" (Cohen 102, 211). During the early decades of the twentieth century, emergent sexological discourses continued to establish heterosexuality as "the ruling sexual orthodoxy"; by 1930 this normative understanding of heterosexuality had entered into widespread popular usage (Katz, *Invention* 82, 92–94). As a result of these developments, the claims and counterclaims made on behalf of Shakespeare's sexuality began to be articulated in the terms of sexual object-choice. Early twentieth-century scholars attempted to stabilize Shakespeare's sexuality once and for all by fixing his identity as homosexual or heterosexual. Heterosexuals and homosexuals alike could then claim Shakespeare as "one of us." Whereas the appropriation of Shakespeare has remained a familiar strategy of gay pride rhetoric up to this day (Shepherd 97), the significance of heterosexual appropriations of Shakespeare during the earlier twentieth century should not be overlooked. To conclude this historical survey, then, I want to consider two striking instances of the heterosexist appropriation of Shakespeare's sexuality from this era: a Shakespeare lecture delivered in 1920 by noted Renaissance scholar C. H. Herford, and the introduction to *Shakespeare's Bawdy* (1947), Eric Partridge's influential glossary of Elizabethan sexual terminology.

In "The Normality of Shakespeare Illustrated in His Treatment of Love and Marriage," Herford surveys Shakespeare's development as a dramatist of love and marriage. While conceding that "Shakespeare's persons and plots are in a sense foreign to us," Herford affirms that "when compared with those of almost any of his contemporaries, [they] avoid eccentric, pathological, or fantastic types, and in this conform, as Marlowe or Webster, or even Jonson do not, to the broad highway of experience" (4). More is at stake here than Shakespeare's superiority to his contemporaries, for Herford aims to prove that Shakespeare's "mature" plays and *Sonnets* advance a supreme ideal of "normal" love. Although Herford does not employ the terminology of sexual identity, he unambiguously defines as "normal" the "joyous" and "healthy" love "between men and women" (4). A 1928 sex education pamphlet cited by Katz similarly describes conjugal love in terms of physical and emotional health, as "an unsurpassed joy, something which rightly belongs to every normal human being" (*Invention* 93). Herford thus appropriates the unique cultural status of Shakespeare for a particularly modern ideological agenda: the celebration of the "lofty Normality" of marital heterosexuality (15).

Although the distinction between normality and abnormality also informs *Shakespeare's Bawdy,* its use of prevalent discourses on sexual identity permits an even more thorough normalization of Shakespeare. Explaining his motives for compiling a glossary of sexual terms from Shakespeare's works, Partridge approvingly cites the homophobic quip of a contemporary scholar: "Pederasts and pedants have been the curse of Shakespearean biography and criticism." As "neither pederast nor pedant" (xi), Partridge believes that his normal heterosexual identity provides an objective position from which the oft-repeated "charge" of homosexuality brought against Shakespeare can finally be refuted. According to Partridge, it was "a homosexual"—Oscar Wilde—who first charged Shakespeare not merely with *sodomy* but with homosexual *identity* (12). There is a chilling irony in representing Wilde as the source of Shakespeare's criminal homosexual identity, a libel from which the maligned poet must be exonerated. Says Partridge, "Like most other heterosexual persons, I believe the charge against Shakespeare[—]that he was a homosexual[—]to be, in the legal sense, 'trivial': at worst, 'the case is not proven'; at best—and in strict accordance with the so-called evidence, as I see it—it is ludicrous" (11–12). Such positivism leads Partridge to the equally ludicrous conclusion that, had Shakespeare indeed been a homosexual, "he would have subtly yet irrefutably conveyed the fact" (16). Remarkably, however, Partridge also conveys the contradictory idea that rather than historical or textual evidence from the sixteenth century, the sexual identity of the modern critic will ultimately decide "the fact" of Shakespeare's sexuality. For despite the intention to adjudicate the matter scientifically, Partridge reveals his actual bias with the solipsistic assertion that he, like "most heterosexual persons," believes that Shakespeare was also heterosexual.

Queer Renaissance: Shakespeare's Sexuality in the 1990s

Partridge's blatant heterosexist partisanship refutes the myth that the proponents of "trendy" lesbian and gay studies are responsible for politicizing Shakespeare's sexuality. As this brief historical account shows, lesbian and gay critics have in fact entered into a perennial debate over the meaning of and uses for Shakespeare's sexuality (Shepherd 98–101). Undeniably, these critics have significantly altered the political terrain of the debate by openly addressing contemporary sexual issues. Nonetheless, the most compelling lesbian and gay accounts of the Renaissance have avoided projecting modern notions of sexual identity back onto Shakespeare and hence anachronistically claiming him as "a homosexual." Instead, they recognize the historical alterity of Shakespeare's texts even as they use their interpretations of these texts to intervene into present political concerns.

An excellent illustration of this critical strategy appears in Bruce Smith's influential study, *Homosexual Desire in Shakespeare's England* (1991). While producing a historicist account of Renaissance sexuality, Smith nevertheless links the present to the past by arguing that a modern male homosexual subjectivity first emerged in Marlowe's *Edward II* and Shakespeare's *Sonnets*. He explains that his "political purpose" in making such an argument was to show gay men that they "have not only a present community but a past history" (27). Smith's desire to use the past "to consolidate gay identity in the last decade of the twentieth century" (27) doubtless took impetus from his particular historical circumstances as a gay man writing in the late 1980s. Bolstering a sense of gay history, identity, and community would have been especially crucial during this period, when doubts had peaked about the ability of gay men to survive, individually and collectively, the ravages of AIDS.

Deriving a genealogy of male homosexual subjectivity from male-oriented Renaissance texts, Smith primarily appeals to the communal identifications of gay men. Other critics have opened up avenues of identification and affirmation for lesbian readers. In a historical analysis of female homoeroticism, Valerie Traub points to the analogous tendency in Renaissance and modern cultures to differentiate female lovers by gender and erotic role as "feminine" or "masculine" women ("(In)significance" 78–79). Even more suggestively, in her book *Desire and Anxiety* Traub concludes a theoretical excursus on "gender" and "sexuality" with a personal fantasy about Shakespeare's Olivia, the countess who falls in love with the cross-dressed Viola in *Twelfth Night*. Envisioning Olivia "sitting at her computer, wearing high heels," Traub intimates the complex personal and political investments a lesbian reader might bring to Shakespeare's plays (*Desire* 116). This modernized Olivia might represent a feminist academic, perhaps a version of Traub herself, writing to produce social change. But what kind of gender or erotic roles do Olivia's high heels signify? Is she legible as a feminine lesbian? Do the high heels suggest a parody of femininity or rather a concession to a professional role? Traub's fantasy does not make any truth claims about the sexuality of Shakespeare or his characters; rather, it acknowledges that interpretation is a dynamic process involving acts of identification, desire, and resistance.

Whereas Smith and Traub foreground positive models of reader identification with Shakespeare's poetic persona and dramatic characters, other approaches emphasize the repression of same-sex practices from the Renaissance to the present day. For instance, Jonathan Goldberg examines the legacy of the sixteenth-century juridical discourse of sodomy in the 1986 *Bowers v. Hardwick* ruling, in which the Supreme Court upheld the constitutionality of sodomy laws (*Sodometries* 6–18). For Goldberg, however, the presence of sodomitical discourses and acts in the Renaissance does not imply the existence of homosexual identities or individuals. His poststructuralist approach to Renaissance sexuality thus sharply contrasts with the essentialism of Joseph Cady, who posits the existence in Shakespeare's England of an oppressed minority of homosexuals. Nevertheless, Cady likewise applies his knowledge of Renaissance sexuality to contemporary political struggles. He argues that campaigns for lesbian and gay civil rights will gain credibility if scholars can prove that throughout Western history homosexuals have not only existed but have also suffered from the intolerance and animosity of the dominant culture.

As I hope to have shown, the overt politicizing of Shakespeare during the 1990s represents an important development in the queering of academic scholarship. Of course, the specialized readership and restricted circulation of academic criticism necessarily limits its political impact. Fortunately, lesbian and gay filmmakers and writers have brought queer appropriations of canonical Renaissance texts to a larger audience. For instance, by rewriting the history plays of Shakespeare and Marlowe, respectively, the films of Gus Van Sant (*My Own Private Idaho*) and Derek Jarman (*Edward II*) powerfully critique the repressive heterosexual institutions of family and state (see Jarman; Goldberg, "Hal's Desire"). Furthermore, these innovative and provocative films have generated significant debate about lesbian and gay politics, postmodern representational strategies, and the translation of high culture texts into more popular media.

In *Paris Is Burning* (1991), Jennie Livingston's enormously successful documentary about Harlem drag balls, a single allusion to Shakespeare delivers a powerful emotional and political charge. At one point in the film, a drag queen seemingly echoes Shylock, the usurer from *The Merchant of Venice,* when defending herself before a disapproving crowd. Just as Shylock insists that Jews share a common humanity with the Christian majority that persecutes them—"if you prick us do we not bleed?" (3.1.58)—so the queen affirms, "I am a person just like you: you cut me, I bleed the same red you do." She refuses, however, Shylock's role as abject and vengeful Other; instead, she makes her antagonists erupt into raucous laughter by identifying them as members of her community: "See, see, there goes my sister right there . . . she's a bulldagger; that's my husband back there; and that's my girlfriend." Transforming her vulnerable situation into a hilariously campy performance, the queen exemplifies the creative survival strategies for which Livingston's subjects are so memorable.

A similarly witty, if more deliberate, appropriation of Shylock appears in David Feinberg's novel *Spontaneous Combustion*

(1991). Gay, Jewish, and HIV-positive, the novel's protagonist, B. J. Rosenthal, wryly jokes, "If you prick us, we may bleed, but we try to clot as rapidly as possible" (193). More than a joke, Feinberg's alteration of Shylock's famous words parodies what Marjorie Garber calls the "penchant for quoting Shakespeare out of context, as a testimony simultaneously to the quoter's own erudition and the truth of the sentiment being uttered" (25). Garber points to the Senate hearings on Clarence Thomas's nomination to the Supreme Court, a forum in which Thomas's supporters used Shakespeare to elevate their own moral and political convictions to the status of unassailable truths about greed, envy, and the nature of women. Rejecting such tendentious and recuperative appropriations of Shakespeare's wisdom—or any conventional wisdom—Feinberg does not even mention Shakespeare as the source of B. J.'s quip. Instead, he tests lofty Shakespearean sentiment against hard reality, reminding us that, for the HIV-positive, "bleeding" has material as well as metaphorical consequences.

Queer Pedagogy: Shakespeare's Sexuality and Cultural Change

Having explored some paradigmatic appropriations of Shakespeare's sexuality in scholarship and popular culture, I want to end by considering the place of lesbian and gay studies in the Shakespeare classroom. Anachronism need not be a concern here, for whereas *homosexuality* properly speaking is a modern phenomenon, any literary analysis can include consideration of same-sex desires and homosocial relations. The survey of medieval and Renaissance literature I regularly teach, and which is a staple of many college English department curricula, offers the opportunity to discuss same-sex desire in the works of Chaucer, Marlowe, Shakespeare, and others. I would argue that a student has a greater chance of comprehending and appreciating these difficult works when challenged to think critically about the ways in which they may articulate the gender and sexual ideologies of their eras. Moreover, an understanding of premodern discourses of same-sex desire facilitates the understanding that "heterosexuality" and

"homosexuality" are modern inventions, not universal categories of experience. The historical distinctness of Shakespeare's
sexuality thus provides a valuable perspective on the erotic taxonomies we have inherited.

Of course, some students might not welcome this perspective, especially in a course on early English literature, in which
the issue of same-sex desire might not be expected to arise. As
one student remarked in an end-of-semester evaluation, "The
professor uses [the course] to support his own views on
homosexuality in both his interpretation of the texts and his choice
of texts." Even though I would question the reactionary thinking
behind this student's comment, I would not deny the basic truth
it expresses. My selection and interpretation of texts does indeed
reveal (hence "support") my "own views" on homosexuality. My
"own views" are not merely my own, however, for they are shared
by other scholars and historians, nor are they limited to
homosexuality, for I also express my views about gender roles,
social conflict, religious doctrine, courtly politics, literary influence, poetic form, and many other topics pertinent to the study
of early English literature. It makes little sense to argue that the
course is "about" medieval and Renaissance literature, not
homosexuality, for depictions and even occlusions of same-sex
desire contribute to what and how these texts might mean. My
reasons for teaching about same-sex desire are personal, political, and scholarly all at once, precisely because these realms cannot be completely separated. By the same token, the student
previously cited uses the course evaluation not merely to analyze
my teaching but also "to support" his own views on homosexuality.

Teaching openly about same-sex desire may strike students
as flagrantly political not only because homosexuality is a controversial subject but also because teaching controversial subjects powerfully debunks the myth of pedagogical objectivity. It
seems perfectly natural when English teachers discuss relationships between men and women, because heterosexuality is generally understood to be a "natural" condition, not an ideological
construct. Creating the illusion of the natural, which in this case
serves to render heterosexuality cognitively un(re)markable, is of
course a primary operation of ideology. It may take less natural-

ized topics such as homosexuality to alert students to the production of knowledge as inevitably an ideological and intellectual endeavor. A student who recognizes the motive behind one
teacher's discussion of homosexuality might then recognize the
motive behind another teacher's refusal to talk about
homosexuality. Especially when employed in a traditional (hence
presumptively heterosexual) space such as the Shakespeare classroom, queer approaches can have the salutary effect of challenging the myth of universal heterosexuality.

Rather than deny the ideological dimensions of my pedagogy, then, I would argue that teaching about homoerotic desire
in Shakespeare's texts constitutes a minor intervention in an educational system already dominated by heterosexist agendas and
assumptions. As I have suggested, the presumption of heterosexuality often makes these agendas invisible. To take a concrete
example, it may seem perfectly reasonable and unobjectionable
that *Romeo and Juliet* is one of the most commonly taught
Shakespeare plays at the high school level. Yet as queer critiques
of this play's symbolic cultural importance have shown, *Romeo
and Juliet* is regularly used, quite ahistorically and tendentiously,
to promote a transhistorical myth of heterosexual romance. The
ideological ends which the play can be made to serve become
especially apparent when teenage high school students are presumed (or encouraged) to identify with Shakespeare's sympathetic
young couple (see Goldberg, "Romeo"; Porter).

While the kind of heterosexism instanced above may seem
commonplace and relatively innocuous—images of the heterosexual couple, after all, dominate our media—homophobia is
being practiced more flagrantly in the educational system, perhaps most damagingly at the secondary level. Across the nation,
parents, school board members, and right-wing Christians have
been demonizing lesbians and gay men in an attempt to remove
all mention of homosexuality from the curriculum in the public
schools. In such a climate, insensitivity to the needs of lesbian
and gay students can produce devastating consequences. This
became painfully clear in a recent lawsuit involving a young gay
man who sued his former high school administration for failing
to protect him from the relentless verbal and physical abuse in-
flicted by his peers. Before finally dropping out of school, he had

attempted suicide several times (Chandler; "Agenda"). In the romantic fiction of *Romeo and Juliet,* suicide seals the tragic destiny of "star-crossed lovers"; in our own world, studies have shown that lesbian and gay teenagers are at least three times more likely to attempt suicide than their straight peers.

As an isolated practice, teaching about same-sex desire in Shakespeare's plays may not prevent suicides. Bringing lesbian and gay subjects into the classroom for serious analysis and discussion, however, can certainly help to change the generally homophobic climate that promotes suicidal self-hatred and despair in young people just coming to terms with their sexuality. As Lillian Faderman has argued,

> Surely in a homophobic society that has little good to say about us, it would help our young people to know (and to have it known by others) that Jane Addams and Lorraine Hansberry and Bayard Rustin and Willa Cather—individuals who have been respected and valued even in that homophobic society— have shared with us that very trait which the rest of the world has claimed to despise. (80)

Doubtless, many of us who teach courses in lesbian and gay studies hope to give queer students institutional and personal validation, as well as to provide all students with a rare opportunity to learn about lesbian and gay culture from an antihomophobic perspective. Since not all students will have the opportunity (or desire) to take a lesbian and gay studies course, however, it is imperative not to sequester queer analysis from the methods and spheres of inquiry that constitute English studies.

By stressing the value of bringing lesbian and gay subjects into the English classroom, I do not mean to imply that the more traditional goals of teaching reading, writing, and critical thinking are unimportant or merely secondary to more or less overt political struggles. To make such an argument would be to reestablish a version of the "tradition" versus "trend" dichotomy I have been challenging. Moreover, I would not want to dismiss out of hand Stanley Fish's argument that English teachers should embrace the importance of the pedagogical role they are generally expected to fulfill: "Someone, after all, should be taking care of verbs and adjectives. Someone should be codifying and refurbishing those verbal skills that on occasion move the world" (161). Despite the validity of this claim, however, members of minority communities might not see instruction in verbal skills as the most effective way to participate in immediate political struggles for social change. For me, and I suspect for others of my generation, the opportunity to teach and research lesbian and gay subjects within the discipline of English provided an important motivation for pursuing a career in academia instead of politics, law, journalism, social work, or AIDS services. The knowledge that students will not be responsibly exposed to lesbian and gay issues elsewhere raises the stakes of incorporating them into the classroom, a discursive arena where I influence the terms and direction of the discussion, if not its final outcome.

Treating homosexuality as a legitimate subject of classroom discussion does not mean preaching or propagandizing—methods best left to the homophobic right—but challenging students to confront, articulate, and question some of their most deeply held assumptions and beliefs. For some students, this process will feel unsettling, provocative, or even threatening. Already convinced that sexuality is an inherent, natural trait of persons, they might refuse to view it differently, as a messy tangle of historically variant significations. On the other hand, some students resent having to learn what they consider "useless" specialized information—such as the structure of a Shakespearean sonnet—relevant only to their grade in an English course.

Asking students to confront "controversial" social issues might produce resistance, but resistance can be a sign of growth. By participating in the ongoing discussion about the meaning of and uses for "Shakespeare's sexuality," students can learn just how much is at stake in the ways that questions of sexuality get framed, debated, and answered. If it can provide the opportunity for such an inquiry, Shakespeare's sexuality will have served a very real need.

Notes

1. Throughout this essay, I will use "lesbian and gay" and "queer" interchangeably when referring to modes of analysis and critique that

focus on same-sex relations. I will use "lesbian and gay," however, when I wish to stress the social and institutional formations that have arisen from a modern (post-Stonewall) political identification and movement (e.g., "lesbian and gay studies").

2. For further discussion on the Unspeakable Lives course at Georgetown, see essays by Edward Ingebretson and Jay Kent Lorenz in this volume. *Ed.*

Works Cited

"Agenda: Youth." *The Advocate* 24 Dec. 1996: 11–14.

Bredbeck, Gregory W. *Sodomy and Interpretation: Marlowe to Milton.* Ithaca: Cornell UP, 1991.

Cady, Joseph. "Renaissance Awareness and Language for Heterosexuality: 'Love' and 'Feminine Love.'" *Renaissance Discourses of Desire.* Ed. Claude J. Summers and Ted-Larry Pebworth. Columbia: U of Missouri P, 1993. 143–58.

Chandler, Kurt. "A Reluctant Hero." *The Advocate* 28 May 1996: 29–34.

Cohen, Ed. *Talk on the Wilde Side: Towards a Genealogy of a Discourse on Male Sexualities.* New York: Routledge, 1993.

Crew, Louie. "Back to the Future." Raymond 44–61.

Crew, Louie, and Rictor Norton, eds. *The Homosexual Imagination.* Spec. issue of *College English* 36 (1974): 271–401.

Dabbs, Thomas. "Shakespeare and the Department of English." Raymond 82–98.

DiGangi, Mario. "Queering the Shakespearean Family." *Shakespeare Quarterly* 47 (1996): 269–90.

Dowd, Maureen. "A Winter's Tale." *New York Times* 28 Dec. 1995: A21.

Escoffier, Jeffrey. "Generations and Paradigms: Mainstreams in Lesbian and Gay Studies." *Gay and Lesbian Studies.* Ed. Henry L. Minton. New York: Harrington Park, 1992. 7–26.

Faderman, Lillian. "History in the Making." *The Advocate* 28 May 1996: 80. Reprinted in revised form in this volume.

Feinberg, David B. *Spontaneous Combustion*. New York: Viking, 1991.

Ferguson, Margaret W., Maureen Quilligan, and Nancy Vickers, eds. *Rewriting the Renaissance: The Discourses of Sexual Difference in Early Modern Europe*. Chicago: U of Chicago P, 1986.

Fish, Stanley. "Them We Burn: Violence and Conviction in the English Department." Raymond 160–73.

Fisher, Will. "One Hundred Years of Queering the Renaissance." Historicizing Queerness Forum. MLA Convention. Washington, D.C. 29 Dec. 1996.

Garber, Marjorie. "Character Assassination: Shakespeare, Anita Hill, and JFK." *Media Spectacles*. Ed. Marjorie Garber, Jann Matlock, and Rebecca L. Walkowitz. New York: Routledge, 1993. 23–39.

Goldberg, Jonathan. "Hal's Desire, Shakespeare's Idaho." *Henry IV: Parts One and Two*. Ed. Nigel Wood. Theory in Practice Series. Buckingham, Eng.: Open UP, 1995. 35–64.

———, ed. *Queering the Renaissance*. Durham: Duke UP, 1994.

———. "*Romeo and Juliet*'s Open Rs." Goldberg, *Queering* 218–35.

———. *Sodometries: Renaissance Texts, Modern Sexualities*. Stanford: Stanford UP, 1992.

Graff, Gerald. "Is There a Conversation in This Curriculum? Or, Coherence without Disciplinarity." Raymond 11–28.

Greene, Thomas C. Letter. *PMLA* 111 (1996): 473–74.

Haggerty, George E., and Bonnie Zimmerman, eds. *Professions of Desire: Lesbian and Gay Studies in Literature*. New York: MLA, 1995.

Herford, C. H. "The Normality of Shakespeare Illustrated in His Treatment of Love and Marriage." Pamphlet 47. Oxford, Eng.: English Association, 1920.

Isitt, Larry R. Letter. *PMLA* 111 (1996): 474–75.

Jarman, Derek. *Queer Edward II*. London: BFI, 1991.

Jay, Karla, and Allen Young, eds. *Out of the Closets: Voices of Gay Liberation*. New York: Douglas Book Corp., 1972.

Katz, Jonathan Ned. *Gay American History: Lesbians and Gay Men in the U.S.A.* New York: Crowell, 1976.

———. *The Invention of Heterosexuality*. New York: Plume, 1996.

Orgel, Stephen. *Impersonations: The Performance of Gender in Shakespeare's England.* Cambridge: Cambridge UP, 1996.

———. "Teaching the Postmodern Renaissance." Haggerty and Zimmerman 60–71.

Paris Is Burning. Dir. Jennie Livingston. Prestige/Miramax, 1991.

Partridge, Eric. *Shakespeare's Bawdy.* 1947. 3rd ed. London: Routledge, 1968.

Phillips, Kathy J. "Billy Budd as Anti-Homophobic Text." *College English* 56 (1994): 896–910.

Porter, Joseph A. "Marlowe, Shakespeare, and the Canonization of Heterosexuality." *Displacing Homophobia: Gay Male Perspectives in Literature and Culture.* Ed. Ronald R. Butters, John Clum, and Michael Moon. Durham: Duke UP, 1989. 127–47.

Radel, Nicholas F. "Our Havelock Ellis: Queer Theory and the Uses of Shakespeare." The Uses of Shakespeare Seminar. Sixth World Shakespeare Congress. Los Angeles. 9 Apr. 1996.

Raymond, James C. *English as a Discipline; or, Is There a Plot in This Play?* Tuscaloosa: U of Alabama P, 1996.

Shakespeare, William. *As You Like It.* Ed. Agnes Latham. Arden Shakespeare. London: Routledge, 1989.

———. *The Merchant of Venice.* Ed. John Russell Brown. Arden Shakespeare. London: Routledge, 1988.

Shepherd, Simon. "Shakespeare's Private Drawer: Shakespeare and Homosexuality." *The Shakespeare Myth.* Ed. Graham Holderness. Manchester, Eng.: Manchester UP, 1988. 96–111.

Smith, Bruce R. *Homosexual Desire in Shakespeare's England: A Cultural Poetics.* Chicago: U of Chicago P, 1991.

Stallybrass, Peter. "Editing as Cultural Formation: The Sexing of Shakespeare's Sonnets." *MLQ* 54 (1993): 91–103.

Strauss, Valerie. "Relaxed Rules for English Majors Set Some at Georgetown University Muttering." *Washington Post* 12 Dec. 1995: E1+.

Traub, Valerie. *Desire and Anxiety: Circulations of Sexuality in Shakespearean Drama.* London: Routledge, 1992.

———. "The (In)Significance of 'Lesbian' Desire in Early Modern England." Goldberg, *Queering* 62–83.

CHAPTER TEN

Coming Out and Creating Queer Awareness in the Classroom: An Approach from the U.S.–Mexican Border

TATIANA DE LA TIERRA
University of Texas at El Paso

A fter being out for over fifteen years, not being out is not an option for me. When I began to teach English composition in 1996, I did not debate whether I would come out in the classroom. I did, however, consider the different ways it could be done, the timing and the theatrical aspects of it. I wondered and even worried about the response from my students and the administration. I considered my social responsibility to come out in an academic arena that was relatively foreign to me as a new graduate student in an M.F.A. creative writing program.

I did not consult with peers or conduct research on theory or pedagogy before coming out. I simply came up with ideas and organized them into a lesson plan. But before getting into that lesson plan and the strategies I subsequently developed, let me preface this essay with the identities that are at my core and drive most of my actions. I was born in Colombia and, at seven years of age, immigrated to Miami with my family in 1968. For all practical purposes, I am a product of the culture and educational system of the United States. But I am Colombian, fully bilingual and bicultural, as well as a lesbian.

What do my identities have to do with my approach to coming out in the classroom? Everything. When we walk into the classroom, we bring the entirety of ourselves with us. Beyond our political and religious inclinations and economic status are the particular ways in which we maneuver in society. In my case, I became a leftist when I came out as a lesbian in a heavily politicized antipatriarchal feminist environment. I am of working-class stock, a goddess worshiper, a lover of art, and a stickler for order.

I mention this because my background and personality have notable effects in the classroom. I am conscious of the amount of money students spend on materials for class. I ask them not to turn in assignments with unnecessary fancy plastic or cardboard covers. I design a syllabus not to be taken lightly; I expect students to come to class prepared, to turn in their assignments on time, and to participate. And finally, I strive to make the classroom fun. I am passionate about writing, and I know that many first-year students in English composition courses have negative attitudes as a result of being force-fed five-paragraph formulas and having their writings marked up in furious red ink by their previous teachers. I want students to walk out of my class refreshed by the power of the written word. I want them to appreciate the writing process, to be able to identify a good essay, to be inspired by a story or a poem, to realize that there are many approaches they can take to completing assignments, and to know that they are creative thinkers capable of producing good writing themselves.

Being out and making my political positions known as a composition teacher raises important pedagogical questions. Do I want my students to walk out of my classroom better informed about lesbian and gay issues? Do I want them to see gays and lesbians and all other sexual "outlaws" as human beings? Furthermore, do I expect students to be politically astute? Do I want them to realize that the nuclear dumping site proposed for Sierra Blanca, ninety miles from El Paso and twenty miles from the Mexican border, was the result of environmental racism and U.S. imperialism? Quite honestly, given my history and political convictions, I would love for my students to oppose anti-immigrant legislation and support gay rights. But do I expect my students to disregard the religious and cultural doctrines, bestowed on them by their parents and grandparents, that say homosexuality is a sin? Do I encourage them to eat less meat? Do I instruct them on how they too can be gay, if only they would allow themselves to experiment? Do I use the classroom as a political arena of my making, with conscious intent to change their convictions?

When I am teaching writing, whether it is English composition, research and critical thinking, or creative writing, my main priority is just that—to teach students to write. The way I do this, however, is influenced by my political ideology and personality, as well as by guidelines from the English department at my university. This combination of factors determines the materials and pedagogies that all instructors choose for a class, including syllabi, lesson plans, and class policies. It is not realistic or appropriate to use one's authority in the classroom to impose one's politics on students. Yet some may interpret my selection of materials or topics, or even the way I present myself, to have the same political overtones I claim to be avoiding. Regardless of intention or interpretation, the classroom works as a site of social transformation. On the cover of a membership brochure of the National Council of Teachers of English are words that confirm this idea: "Changing the Classroom. Changing the World."

Change occurs within a complex environment. Students and teachers both enter the classroom with preexisting ideologies that range from political convictions to expectations of the learning process. Inevitably, some of our differences will be revealed along the way, and these differences may affect the dynamics in the classroom. To further complicate things, even though most of us are in class by our choice, there is great resistance to being there. As a teacher, I have to lecture, lead discussions, and review my students' essays, regardless of my mood. I may be annoyed at the Bible-thumping student who sits in the front row and constantly makes comments that I find obnoxious, but still I have to teach. Meanwhile, my students may be overwhelmed with the workload, critical of my teaching methods, angry because it takes them half an hour to find a parking space, or frustrated with writing itself. Whatever the reasons, teachers sometimes resist teaching and students sometimes resist learning. And then there is the fact that the classroom is inherently politicized through the hierarchy between teacher and student, whereby students are disempowered by the very structure of the classroom. As Maxine Hairston writes in "Diversity, Ideology, and Teaching Writing," "The real truth about classrooms is that the teacher has all the power; she sets the agenda, she controls the discussion, and she gives the grades" (536). The change that occurs in the classroom, then, is the result of this complex mixture of elements.

Learning takes place when teachers acknowledge that ideological differences, resistance, and an unbalanced power structure are at work in the classroom. We need to recognize that education is ideological and that the classroom is a politicized space, instead of pretending that it is politically neutral ground. We need to engage our students' resistance, instead of trying to dismiss it. And we need to assure our students that even though teachers are in a position of power, we are there to facilitate their learning experiences. We need to be honest, to an extent, about who we are, and we also need to give students the opportunity to be honest about themselves. All of this allows the classroom to become an organic space in which ideas are debated, contested, redefined, and articulated in different ways. Acknowledging and working with factors already present in the classroom creates an opportunity for it to become a site of social transformation because students are then able to problematize their own positions.

The innate power of the classroom was a key concept in the work of Brazilian educator Paulo Freire. When Freire placed language within a political context and taught Brazilian students to read and write in their natural environment, he discovered just how empowering literacy skills were when the students were able to become political advocates for themselves. Scores of teachers were influenced by Freire's work and followed suit by deliberately using the classroom in ways that could greatly transform the lives of their students. While I do not advocate teaching with an "agenda," it is important to set up conditions that encourage students to think critically. I want students to open their minds to other perspectives, but I am not trying to force them to think the way I do.

So Much Social Responsibility, So Little Time

These are frightening times, however, and I am concerned, not only about queers who are not protected from bigotry, but also about immigrants under attack by the federal government and all people of color who are losing the battle against affirmative action. As Henry Giroux writes in "National Identity and the Politics of Multiculturalism," "Nationalism is currently being shaped to defend a beleaguered notion of national identity read as white, heterosexual, middle-class, and allegedly threatened by contamination from cultural, linguistic, racial and sexual differences" (48). Peter McLaren, in "Paulo Freire and the Academy: A Challenge from the U.S. Left," takes this concern into the classroom: "Teachers and students together face New Right constituencies of all types and stripes—in particular, fundamentalist Christians and political interest groups who are exercising an acrimonious appeal to a common culture monolithically unified by a desire for harmony in sameness" (152–53).

These mistaken ideas of a homogeneous society to which Giroux and McLaren refer can lead to the kind of bigotry at the root of two incidents that received national attention in 1998— the gay-bashing death of Matthew Shepard in Wyoming and the racially motivated murder of James Byrd Jr., an African American man who was dragged to death in Texas. While extreme examples, these events do represent the serious nature of hatred and fear of difference. And in my case, as someone whose legal identity in this country consisted of a green card that labeled me a "resident alien" for twenty-seven years, and as someone who is out as a lesbian, I am clearly "other." When I walk into the classroom, I am conscious of being a racialized, gendered body. The fact that I am a Latina lesbian affects me as a teacher, because in order to teach, at some level I have to break through my students' notions of the "mainstream." The classroom does not exist in isolation from the horrific deaths of Matthew Shepard and James Byrd Jr. As someone conscious of social inequities and as someone who is vulnerable to acts of hatred just because of who I am, I feel a measure of social responsibility.

What to do with this social responsibility? I have several strategies and coming out is one of them. I come out, not only as a courtesy to my gay students who deserve queer support, but also because coming out affirms a reality of the moment. Teachers today must acknowledge that there are gay students in the classroom and that we are in the midst of a queer revolution, one that spans the entire world. Every day I receive dozens of e-mails about queer conferences, demonstrations, and legislative challenges in places such as Madrid, São Paolo, Cologne, Buenos Aires, London, Mexico City, and so on. In September 1998, for instance, I received an e-mail from Infogay, an international listserv, with the subject heading "Latin American Briefs." The message informed me that Colombia's Constitutional Court ruled that schoolteachers cannot be fired for revealing they are gay. Beyond issues of gay rights, hate crimes, and social visibility, there is growing discourse on gender and sexuality as bisexuals, transvestites, and transsexuals contribute to public debate. "Father Knows Best" has been discarded by those of us who have come to realize that "family values" do not include our families or even us in our representations of ourselves. Regardless of where they stand in this discourse, or even if they have yet to consciously consider it, students form part of a society that is already actively working within queer solidarity or trying in various ways to eradicate it. Queer issues are relevant in English courses, just as are topics such as the death penalty, Ebonics, and English-only legislation. These are our contemporary issues, the ones that make headlines, that citizens cast their ballots on, and that students need to learn to consider in a critical manner in English composition classes. The arguments articulated in discussions and debates allow students to examine their positions.

Another strategy integral to my teaching methods is to include within the materials I select for my classes texts by and about people of color and queers. Each semester I compile a reader of essays and creative writing for my English composition courses with the purpose of using selected writings to show a variety of writing styles and techniques. I emphasize literature by people of color for several reasons. To begin with, perspectives of people of color are too often absent from English composition textbooks and from classrooms in general. The reality is that there is a significant and growing body of work by Latins, Caribbeans, Asians, African Americans, and Native Americans. If in the process of selecting material for my reader I choose to ignore this literature, then I am guilty of erasing important voices. One advantage to emphasizing writing by people of color is that, by interacting with the texts, students will see that no one model represents the experience of people of color. The literature offers the reader alternative worlds.

Another reason for using texts by people of color is that there is great power in representation, and our students of color deserve to have texts that reflect their lives. While white heterosexuals are presented with multitudes of images of themselves in the media, the classroom, and the political arena, gays and lesbians and people of color rarely see representations of ourselves, and when we do, they are usually negative ones. Throughout my education in this country, I seldom saw my Colombian or lesbian self reflected in any classroom. The challenge is for *all* educators to assume the responsibility of multicultural representation in the classroom.

Here at the University of Texas at El Paso, situated on the border between the United States and Juárez, Mexico, 74 percent of the undergraduate population is of Mexican descent. The dead-white-European-heterosexual-male canon, which has been sanctified and debated in literary circles for decades, is decidedly challenged in my classroom. What, then, are my students reading? Edwidge Danticat, Esmeralda Santiago, Nellie Campobello, Amy Tan, Amiri Baraka, Jamaica Kincaid, Cristina Garcia, Alice Walker, other writers of color, and even a few white males, such as Joe Brainard and Michael Cunningham, and white females, such as Susan Minot and Lucia Berlin. But because most of my students are Mexican American, I focus heavily on Chicano voices, such as Helena Maria Viramontes, Luis Valdez, Sandra Cisneros, Gloria Anzaldúa, and Rudolfo Anaya. I also include several pieces that touch upon gay experiences, such as fiction by Nice Rodriguez and John Rechy, as well as a contemporary gay-themed article from a magazine or newspaper.

Am I cramming ethnically and "politically correct" texts down my students' throats? Am I doing what I claim to be attempting not to do—politicizing the classroom? Am I guilty of using a model that, according to Hairston, "envisions required writing courses as vehicles for social reform rather than as student-centered workshops designed to build students' confidence and competence as writers" (530)? Well, yes and no. I am an out Latina lesbian who is using representation as a political tool, and I am using these texts to teach writing. Teaching composition goes beyond presenting formulas for cohesive essays—it involves teaching students to think critically and to develop skills in logic and argumentation. The materials I select prompt students to think, write, consider a variety of topics and perspectives, and teach them to write effective introductions. The reader I compile for my classes in many ways mirrors English composition textbooks; the main difference is the addition of creative writing and texts by queers and people of color.

I teach students to write essays through focusing on such contemporary methods as employing prewriting techniques and having a clear thesis statement, organizing information logically, and revising. In addition, I liberally use creative writing techniques, such as "showing" versus "telling," and ask students to attempt to emulate strategies used by published writers. Each selection in the reader has a corresponding writing assignment. At times the assignment is an open response, a page in length. Other times students are instructed to try out specific techniques or to comment on a specific aspect of the piece, such as the topic (i.e., love, grandparents, prostitution, language, movies, gays).

I also use creative texts to demonstrate important elements of composition and craft. For instance, we discuss thesis statements in class and then read Amy Tan's "Fish Cheeks" as an exercise to identify the thesis statement. To discuss distinctions between expressive, informative, and persuasive texts, I use Esmeralda Santiago's "How to Eat a Guava." For the persuasive essay, some texts focus on contemporary debates, such as smoking in public spaces, euthanasia, and English-only legislation. I use Gloria Anzaldúa's "How to Tame a Wild Tongue," Julia Alvarez's "Bilingual Sestina" and Luis Valdez's "Zoot Suit" as springboards to discussing the relationship between language and culture. Students turn in a creative writing journal three times in the semester and are graded for completing the assignments, not on the content. The grades are then combined at the end of the semester; they total a percentage of the final grade, usually between 10 and 20 percent. Students are never penalized for their response to my selections. The grades they receive on the final drafts of the four essays they write carry the greatest weight on their final grade.

If I were teaching in a predominantly white university, I would probably *still* use a large number of texts by writers of color and queers. My selection of material would depend on the course and the complexities of the geographical region and of the student population. I would use some texts that reflected the student body, though I would look for unique works that might be unfamiliar to them. Given the growing population of "minorities" and the rising visibility of gay issues in the mainstream, maintaining a multicultural and queer perspective in the classroom is essential regardless of the geographical location of the classroom.

"Speaking Secrets" from the "Hard Place"

I have been out in the classroom since I began teaching over two years ago, and I have employed a variety of strategies, from a full-blown presentation to simply allowing students to interact with the queer texts in the reader. Coming out is easy for me because the word *lesbian* is so integral to my identity. It is also comfortable for me to be out in an academic setting in El Paso, where I feel solidarity and even a sense of *familia*, Latin style, with the undergraduates. If I were somewhere else, maybe coming out would be a different issue for me. But here I am out in the community, I participate in local readings, date a butch in public, and dance in a gay bar. Most of my published writings reveal my lesbianism, one of my lesbian plays has been staged at this university, and students have prior knowledge of my sexuality (and word gets around)—so I can't keep a secret that clearly isn't one. And neither do I want to, for I chose many years ago to be vocal about being a lesbian.

It is too late for me to "hide" because I have already come to terms with my lesbianism. As Mariana Romo-Carmona writes in the introduction to *Compañeras: Latina Lesbians,* "When we weigh the benefits of being silent and saving the other people from the shock, or ourselves from the pain, we internalize the hatred against us. In essence, we begin to believe that our lives are less important, and we continue to hide a part of ourselves" (xxiii). There is little benefit to being silent in a course in which students are, in part, using writing to express their personal history and experience. By revealing my lesbianism, I am showing students there is no need to hide, that all of who we are is significant, and that silence is not required.

But my ease with coming out contrasts sharply with other teachers' experiences. As Mary Elliott writes in "Coming Out in the Classroom: A Return to the Hard Place": "Perhaps we feel that our political or personal development should have delivered us beyond 'the hard place'—the pounding hearts, shaking voices, sleepless nights, and hours of strategizing with friends" (694). Elliott cites deep fear as the cause of difficulties in coming out. She continues: "Fear, then, begins the story, and, with no apparent bridge across the abyss, the story for many of us ends abruptly there—at the hard place" (701). This "hard place" Elliott refers to is one with which I do not identify. It's not that I don't worry or consider the repercussions, but this visceral response, this intense fear embodied, is not my experience. Coming out does involve personal risk, though. It forces you to confront yourself, not only as a lavender-blooded queer with political overtones, but also as a human being willing to speak your truth.

If only I had done as my grandmother instructed me when I was a teenager: "Never reveal all that you are or all that you know." Putting yourself out there is dangerous. Some things are meant to be a secret. Deena J. González tackles secrets in her essay, "Speaking Secrets: Living Chicana Theory": "Speaking secrets is never easy. In many cultures, it is considered bad form because secrets stigmatize families and community, separate one from loved ones, and leave bad impressions" (46). What would my grandmother think of me now, I wonder? I never did come out to her, but then, she died before I had fully come out to myself. She was a keeper of secrets, and I doubt she would have approved. By coming out, and also by "speaking secrets" of other sorts, I hope to be part of the greater movement to which González alludes:

> To deal with these issues [woman-identification, lesbianism and misogyny] in an academic environment, and break the cycle of violence into which we have been socialized and accommodated, means that we must begin to name our fears, to ac-

knowledge that we cannot move forward alone, and that each step we take to tell secrets moves us one step closer toward what bell hooks and others term a liberatory, transformative life. (69)

Coming Out: A One-Dyke Version

Coming out, whether in El Paso or Manhattan, is a process that should be personalized by each instructor. There is no one way or "the" way to do it. How we choose to come out depends on us as individuals, on the setting of the classroom, and on the context of discussion in which it occurs. My Mexican American students are mostly Catholic and working class and tend to identify on the conservative side of the political spectrum. Many of them live with their parents, work, and are the first in their family to attend college. Most likely they grew up dancing to disco, listening to *rancheras*, and eating tortillas with one hand and French fries with the other. They have an image of the Virgen of Guadalupe in their homes. They rock with Maná and Shakira and croon with Juan Gabriel and Selena. They are well-dressed, well-mannered, and respectful. I, on the other hand, am a writer and a pagan. I am a melomaniac—a music lover—especially fond of salsa and *vallenato*. I drive too fast, live too hard, hibernate one day and travel the world the next. I love plastic flowers, loud colors, gaudy rings. These are simplistic generalizations, of course, of both my students and myself, but I include them here as a synopsis of the players involved in my act of coming out.

To reiterate a central point from my introduction, when we walk into the classroom, we bring the entirety of ourselves with us. Be yourself, and you will find a way to "be" queer. Come out because you want to, because it is a gift you can offer your students and your school or university, because you want to be socially responsible, because you want to check it out, because you can. Do not come out because of queer political pressure. Following, then, is a recounting of a coming-out lesson plan, along with other approaches I have used in coming out and creating queer awareness in the classroom. An analysis, as well as an overview of student responses from end-of-semester evaluation forms, follows this pedagogical section.

To begin with, coming out is a "process." You don't just yell "I am queer" into a bullhorn and leave it at that, because there is a reverberation, before-during-and-after effects. I am a "person" and a "lesbian" in the classroom. I am someone with particular characteristics that my students are able to identify as "me" in the form of my appearance, my personality, my response to them as people and as students. All of this makes me a "person" without emphasizing the fact that I am a woman who desires other women. This is not to say that I would lie or otherwise mislead if I were somehow put to the test before officially coming out. But if possible, I prefer to establish my personhood before being branded as the dyke that I am. As Elliott writes, "to announce my sexual orientation as I hand out the class syllabus unproductively fragments my identity and polarizes the students in relation to that fragmentary self-representation in a way that seems no less deceptive" (704). In her conclusion, she states: "Only if students can see the teacher as an individual rather than an 'agenda' is there hope of that teacher forging the kinds of new and productive ways of thinking, writing, and working with the students that most of the coming out testimonials describe" (706). I agree with this statement wholeheartedly; it is the gist of coming out. To give students the opportunity to see a lesbian as a person may sound simple, but considering that lesbians are commonly thought of as perverted, man-hating, and dangerous and indecent bulldaggers, the simplicity of being perceived as an individual is powerful.

The first time I came out in the classroom was the result of a lesson plan I had very carefully constructed. National Coming Out Day, celebrated on the 11th of October, was the magical date. It was also convenient that we were past the middle of the semester (so I was already a "person" in my students' eyes), and that we were about to commence working on the persuasive essay. By then my students and I had already established what I perceived to be a free-flowing relationship. Our collective purpose was to develop writing skills; this was accomplished in a friendly, familial environment. I had come to genuinely like and care for some of the students. What if my favorites turned out to be homophobic? Or if the laid-back atmosphere were to become charged with politics? Or if they walked out on me en masse, complained, rebelled, rejected me or my lesbianism? These were my concerns as The Day neared.

I began class by writing the words "gay" and "lesbian" on the board and instructed students to freewrite for five minutes on what these words meant to them. This process is one I had previously used in class with different topics, so this was familiar to them. They were free to turn their writing in with their journal, which was due at a later date, or to keep their initial opinions to themselves. As I noted later when I reviewed their journals, this generated a variety of (unedited) comments: "fags and homos should go back in the closet"; "If someone is a good person then his/her sexual preference has no ill effect on who they are"; "gays are people who don't like themselves"; "they bring diseases"; "it's unnatural"; "gays know how to dress"; "they make great room decorators"; "it's a disorder of the mind"; "people are usually born this way"; "glamorous world"; "freedom of choice"; "not accepted by God"; "doesn't bother me"; "power rangers"; "dirty jotos"; "lesbians are a turn-on"; and so on.

Then I asked students who had gay and lesbian people in their lives to raise their hands. About half of them did, which surprised me; I expected fewer. Later on I was to learn that my students had gay family and friends, and that several were themselves gay. I told those who had not raised their hand that from then on, they could say they knew a lesbian because, in fact, their teacher was one. I proceeded to give a brief overview of National Coming Out Day and to relate some of my personal history as a lesbian, such as how long I had been out and how my lesbian identity had evolved over the years. They responded with a rush of excitement, laughing at some of my anecdotes and shouting out questions.

Taking advantage of their enthusiasm about my personal revelations, I invited them to ask me lesbian-related questions. They asked: When did you first know that you were a lesbian? How did your mother react? Have you ever had a boyfriend? If lesbians like other women, then why do they dress as men? Have you ever wanted to marry another woman? Is it true that one woman acts like a man and the other one acts like a woman? How has society's rejection of lesbianism affected you? These are typical questions that most of them had never had an opportunity to ask a "live" lesbian. I answered their queries quickly and honestly. I related my lesbianism to current homophobic legislation that does not allow marriage or equal access to constitutional rights and employment benefits. I told them about the Colombian girlfriend I'd had whom I was not allowed to marry and bring into the United States. I also found out that a few students in each class already thought I was gay. I ended our question-and-answer session by getting on to the work as outlined in the syllabus.

The topic for the day was developing ideas and writing an effective introduction. I came prepared with lesbian-related examples for all of the techniques we were going to cover. I let the students know that if they listened closely they would learn to apply the techniques to their own essays. Following are several examples of the texts I wrote and used to demonstrate a variety of writing techniques.

Facts: Although statistics fluctuate, it is believed that about 10% of the general population is gay. Every large city has its share of gay bars, bookstores, groups, and events. There are also lesbian and gay publishing houses, electronic chat lines, and restaurants. There is even a gay credit card publicized by the lesbian tennis star, Martina Navaritalova.

Description: Imagine seven thousand women in the woods for a solid week. At night, beneath the starry skies, campfires burn throughout the land and women gather in circles, singing and talking. At one in the morning the amber flames are still flickering; by now the women are dancing and drumming. At some point, the women will crawl into their tents with each other beneath the twinkling stars. They are in nature and they are part of nature.

Classification: A separatist is a lesbian who attempts to eliminate male interference from her life. She does not want or need men for any reason, and she goes to great lengths to keep them out, even going as far as changing the spelling of certain words. A "woman" becomes "womon;" "women" becomes "womyn" or "wimmin;" "history" becomes "herstory," and so on. Thus, language is a key to asserting a separatist identity.

Examples: When she was eight years old, she was inseparable from her best friend, Lucia. Then it was Vicki, the girl with the golden hair, who held her in awe. When she was ten years old she became best friends with Amy and refused to do anything unless Amy was involved. By the time she was eleven she realized that these close friendships were more like the crushes that other girls her age had on boys. Although she hadn't realized it, she had had lesbian tendencies throughout her childhood.

If this had not been The Day, my students would have read about airplanes, Girl Scouts, softball teams, and musicians—the topics in the textbook at hand that semester, *Your Choice: A Basic Writing Guide with Readings* (see Mangelsdorf and Posey). Instead, they were presented with my lesbianized versions of texts that demonstrate strategies for developing ideas in an essay.

With a few minutes of class time remaining, I asked the students to freewrite once again on what "lesbian" and "gay" meant to them and to note if there were any changes. Then, to wrap up the coming-out class, I sang "Amazon ABC," a lesbian-pride song written and recorded by Alix Dobkin (510). The class ended with a healthy round of applause. My coming out was a theatrical event of sorts; I was on exhibit and my audience was scrutinizing me and the lesbianism I represented. My students were mostly respectful and naturally curious, even though there was some snickering during the question-and-answer segment. It wasn't until after the end of the semester, however, that I could really assess the impact my coming out had on my students.

The rest of that particular semester continued as planned in the syllabus. The only other significant in-class activity that focused on gay issues was an exercise several weeks later designed to show how to explore the pros and cons of an issue as preparation for the persuasive essay. I brought copies of "Gay Families Come Out," an article about gay adoption inside that week's *Newsweek,* which had a photograph of Melissa Etheridge and

Julie Cypher embracing on the cover. After reading the article aloud and leading a discussion on some of the points and anecdotes in the article, I instructed students to write "I do/do not support the adoption of children by gays." They were to freewrite on whichever statement reflected their opinion by listing ideas and information that supported their belief. Then, so that they could become adept at identifying the other side of the argument, I instructed them to support the opposing view. A few students resisted, claiming that their views were too strong. Did I overdo it? Am I guilty of manipulative teaching methods? Or did the students' homophobia get in the way of an exercise created to encourage them to think through both sides of an issue, regardless of the issue itself?

"Flesh and Blood" versus "Why Does Everything in this Class Have to Be Gay?"

Coming out that semester had an immediate effect in the classroom and affected my relationship with several students. For instance, one student complained, "Why does everything in this class have to be gay?" Another student, who was obviously angry about a D+ I had given him on his expressive essay, complained to the administration that I had been too personal and graphic in my coming-out presentation. In another case, a student addressed me in his journal: "But what I can't understand is why do gays want so much attention. I never saw any of my straight high school teachers read or talk so much about straight people like you do about gays. It seems you want to convert some of the students into what I call 'gayism.' p.s. nice try!" This was a student I liked and his hostility threw me. I responded, "No, I don't think it's even possible to 'convert' people into 'gayism' any more than you can convert others to 'heterosexualism.' What I do want to do is have it be an open issue that is okay to talk about in the classroom, and since there are so many different kinds of antigay legislative efforts in the works at this moment, it's also a timely issue."

On the other hand, there were some notable and surprising reactions from students. One, who had written "gross, sick fags" during the initial freewriting, approached me several days later seeking information for a pro–gay rights speech he had decided to write for his speech class. Nearly half of the students selected a gay-related issue for the persuasive essay. The essays included one that opposed gays in the military because they make heterosexuals uncomfortable; one that used the "all men are created equal" argument to support legislation that favors gay partnerships; and one that sanctioned homophobia as long as violence was not involved. Regardless of the positions students took, however, the most valuable result of my coming out was that they took the time to consider queer issues in a meaningful way. Most of them, for instance, opposed the adoption of children by gays, but their main reasoning was that it could be detrimental to the children because of the societal stigma against homosexuality. With the exception of some Christian fundamentalists, most of my students did not appear to be homophobic. They spoke freely to me about their gay relatives and friends, for instance. And the ones I had branded as "conservative" because of the topics of their previous essays, such as *quinceañeras* (a Latin version of a sweet sixteen cotillion, but done at fifteen years of age), church retreats, and traditional Mexican weddings, were surprisingly open-minded and sympathetic.

The most tremendous and positive result from having come out that semester, though, was that my gay students felt that they had someone on their side. One let me know through his journal that he was afraid the male students would interpret his friendliness as a come-on. Another student, who had written a personal essay about being gay, avoided coming to class on peer-review days, when students are required to comment on each other's essays. During the last week of the semester, this same student stood up in front of the entire class and read his coming-out essay, "Flesh and Blood," and received a respectful round of applause. (I have subsequently used his essay in my reader.) On the last day of class, I found out that I had at least two other gay students whom I hadn't known about. One wrote in his evaluation, "thanks for coming out. It made me feel better about myself as a gay." Another, my favorite student of all, trailed me to my office afterward for his true confessions. When he was fifteen, he had told his father that he was gay and was sent to a psychologist, who "cured" him. He lived with his parents, had a girlfriend, and pretended to be straight. A year after he spoke with me, he moved to California on his own. He wrote me a letter, saying, "Now all of my friends know I'm gay, so I am completely out!" Long after the semester was over, several of my gay students often visited me during office hours, seeking a gay connection. Clearly, the fact that I had come out had an impact on my gay students.

Overall, my assessment of having come out in the classroom that semester is, more than anything, a positive one. With the exceptions already noted, the majority of my students did not change how they related to me or how they approached their work. They continued to participate in class discussions, and as far as one could tell, English composition was just another one of their classes. Were they inhibited as a result of my having come out? Were they merely being polite and tolerant? And if this is the case, is this necessarily a bad thing? It is impossible for me to know what effect my lesbianism had on my students during or even after class. I do know there was healthy debate, pro and con, on all the issues discussed in class, including the gay ones.

I also know what they wrote in their class evaluations, and if this is a reliable measure, the results are decidedly favorable. During the last week of the semester, I pass out an evaluation form with specific questions. Students also fill out an official computerized evaluation that goes directly to the English department, the results of which I do not see until the following semester. I let students know that the evaluation I pass out is for my own information and that I am interested in their assessment of class because their viewpoints could affect how I plan future classes. I also ask them not to put their name on it (though some of them do) in the hope that they will be as honest as possible. One of the questions on the evaluation form that semester was, "How do you feel about the fact that your teacher came out as a lesbian?" The overwhelming responses were along the lines of "it's cool," "does not bother me," "it's her choice," and "it didn't change anything." Many wrote that they were initially shocked. A few commended me, with comments such as, "It took a lot of courage and I respect you for that." Only two students out of fifty wrote what I interpreted as negative comments. A few noted that I was, above all, a teacher. One wrote, "She is just as respected as all my other teachers." Finally, one of the student's responses hit home: "I thought you had confidence in us and shared what was a secret. By this the class became closer." That for me was at the heart of coming out. I was real, the students were open, and it was, above all, a revealing, human experience.

I have not come out again in quite the same way I did that first semester, mostly because I am curious to see how different approaches affect the classroom. Looking back, it was an in-your-face approach and it had correspondingly strong effects. Never since have I had nearly half the class select a gay-related topic for their persuasive essay. No other student has complained about me to the administration. I do not have gay students trailing me to the office, confiding in me. I do still come out, but I do it in the midst of a debate, in answer to a question, casually and unplanned. I do not make a big deal out of it. I don't even ask students the lesbian question on the evaluation forms at the end of the semester. Even though I eventually let my students know that I am a lesbian, I rely more and more on their responses to the queer texts in the reader, hoping that their minds are open to cultural and sexual diversity.

My subdued approach still garners hostile reactions from select students, evidenced through their responses to the writing assignments in the reader. In reaction to "The Land of the Free," an essay in favor of gay rights written by a previous student, one student wrote, "The constitution says all men are created equal therefore you must be a man not a homo sexual. the reason gays do not have the support of the government is because they chose to be gay. I did not choose to be a Mexican I was born one . . . gays are fighting for rights that are against the constitution and against the law of God." Another student, in response to a chapter from John Rechy's novel *City of Night*, wrote, "I have a solution to cure the worlds AIDS problem but when I called Hitler his secretary told me he was booked for life. Ha, ha, get it." I do not respond to these hostile and ignorant comments; there is no need to fuel hatred, and there is little hope that any reaction on my part will favorably influence this kind of homophobia.

Inclusion of texts by people of color in the reader and a focus on Chicano writings also drew notable criticism from a few students. The same student who made the Hitler reference wrote in his evaluation, in response to "What did you like least about this class?": "I felt I had to be Mexican to fit in. I felt I was discriminated against because I am a Christian." (Ironically, this same student's response to "What did you like most about this class?" was "The openness.") Another white student e-mailed me early one semester: "I suppose I could be considered as a bitter old white guy. . . . I get frustrated at all the material that seems to me to be either too TOUCHY/FEELY, or man-hating, or gay, or ethnic, or just plain boring for me. I have no prejudices, I am just not interested in this stuff." A week later, he wrote me again, saying, "I am starting to like 'ethnic-bicultural-gay-touchy/feely stuff' more by the minute. Seriously, I do like your class. I will try to keep my ignorance to myself, and get on with [the] lesson." These students are exceptions to mostly favorable responses to materials in the reader; I cite them to show the power of including certain texts.

My English composition classroom has my lesbian presence, queer and ethnic texts in the reader, creative writing assignments, strict class policies, a fun atmosphere, and an intense focus on writing. What has been, across the board, the main criticism students make of my class? Too much work. What are their "Additional comments, critiques, & praises" on the end-of-semester evaluations? Comments include: "It was the bomb." "I learned more about writing style in this class than any other English class." "I liked and appreciated the day you showed us yourself. Up until then I thought you were sort of slave driving." "You are an original teacher whose comments are helpful and direct." "The class went well because there wasn't much pressure on what topics to talk about, and everybody was pretty open minded." "This is the first English class that I have liked & actually learned something good in. I also liked the stories you picked for us to read." "I really liked the student-teacher interaction. I was really glad that you weren't no monotoned professor." "Everything here was off the wall and made me realize that there's always more than one way to get something done. . . .Thanks!"

Creating Queer Awareness for Queers and Allies

My approach to teaching, which emphasizes a personalized style in an environment with notable queer and multicultural presence, is one that can be used by any instructor. Creating queer awareness in English composition classes is quite simple when the instructor weaves gays and lesbians into the fabric of the course. A teacher need not be gay to do this, and in fact I strongly urge heterosexual allies to consciously make their classrooms queer-friendly.

There are many ways in which English composition teachers, gay or straight, can incorporate queer visibility into their teaching methods, and it can be done without deviating from the focus of the class. Coming out in a way that complements some aspect of the writing process, as I did with the lesbian-themed excerpts that exemplify writing techniques, is one way. If an instructor is not gay or does not want to come out, he or she can invite a local gay activist or artist to make a presentation to the class. This presentation can be used as a catalyst for in-class debates on gay issues, or the students can do an in-class writing that evaluates the presenter on his or her performance and on the content of the material presented. The presentation can simply be a creative reading that includes queer themes, something I have done in other English classes at the request of colleagues. Students can be assigned readings and responses aside from those in the textbooks, and gay authors or gay themes can be included in the options they have to select from. Multimedia presentations, including music, film, theatre, art, and photography, can be used to bring queers to life in a colorful and provocative way.

Queer topics can be presented or discussed when the teacher is introducing the range of topics appropriate for particular essays. A firsthand account of growing up gay and what it's like to have a gay relative, for instance, are good topics for expressive essays. An informative essay on cultural symbols can focus on gay symbols, such as the rainbow flag, the pink triangle, double-male and double-female signs, and the color lavender. Essays about cultural icons can include figures such as Audre Lorde, Frida Kahlo, Harvey Milk, Xena, Zorro, Sappho, Liberace, Wonder

Woman, and so on. Holidays can include Gay Pride Day, National Coming Out Day, and the anniversary of the Stonewall riots. Persuasive essays can tackle topics such as the expanding definition of "family," hate crime legislation, coming out on television, and queer texts in elementary school libraries. With a little knowledge and creativity, English composition teachers can easily support gays and lesbians within the classroom while teaching students to debate current issues and formulate ideas for their essays.

Each semester is a coming-out experiment for me. I am interested in gauging my students' reactions to homosexuality, in seeing how they respond to texts, how they respond to me as a teacher and as a human being. There is nothing scientific about my perception of their perception of me or of lesbianism. I read their gay-related commentaries (in their journals, essays, and creative writing responses) with great interest. Sometimes I respond to their comments, sometimes I don't. I have ended up, for now, taking a mellow, middle-of-the-road approach to coming out. I have a "que sera, sera" attitude. Coming out is my small contribution within a society that I hope will one day be just, inclusive, and progressive. I don't want to look back at my life years from now and wonder what would have happened if only I had come out, if only I had strived for racial equality, if only. . . . I have a clean conscience, and I have hope.

Works Cited

Dobkin, Alix. "Amazon ABC." *Lesbian Culture: An Anthology: The Lives, Work, Ideas, Art and Visions of Lesbians Past and Present.* Ed. Julia Penelope and Susan Wolfe. Freedom, CA: Crossing, 1993. 510.

Elliott, Mary. "Coming Out in the Classroom: A Return to the Hard Place." *College English* 58 (1996): 693–708.

Giroux, Henry A. "National Identity and the Politics of Multiculturalism." *College Literature* 22.2 (1995): 42–57.

González, Deena J. "Speaking Secrets: Living Chicana Theory." *Living Chicana Theory.* Ed. Carla Trujillo. Berkeley: Third, 1998. 46–77.

Hairston, Maxine. "Diversity, Ideology, and Teaching Writing." *Composition in Four Keys: Inquiring into the Field: Art, Nature, Science, Politics*. Ed. Mark Wiley, Barbara Gleason, and Louise Wetherbee Phelps. Mountain View, CA: Mayfield, 1996. 530–40.

Kantrowitz, Barbara. "Gay Families Come Out." *Newsweek* 4 Nov. 1996: 51–57.

"Latin American Briefs." Online posting. 13 Sept. 1998. Servicio de noticias para la comunidad lesbitgay. 13 Sept. 1998 <Infogay@ mx.gw.com>.

Mangelsdorf, Kate, and Evelyn Riggs Posey. "Writing an Effective Introduction." *Your Choice: A Basic Writing Guide with Readings*. New York: St. Martin's, 1997. 165–68.

McLaren, Peter. "Paulo Freire and the Academy: A Challenge from the U.S. Left." *Cultural Critique* 33 (1996): 151–84.

Romo-Carmona, Mariana. "Introduction." *Compañeras: Latina Lesbians: An Anthology*. Ed. Juanita Ramos. New York: Routledge, 1994. xx–xxix.

Scharrer, Gary. "Mexico Official: Dump Approval May Incite Protests." *El Paso Times* 8 Oct. 1998: 1B+.

CHAPTER ELEVEN

"Swimming Upstream": Recovering the Lesbian in Native American Literature

KAREN LEE OSBORNE
Columbia College of Chicago

T he landscape of American literature has dramatically changed during the past thirty-five years. Our curricula and syllabi have been transformed by postmodern literary theory and teachers and critics who have "recognized that underlying the questions of what is taught and to whom, what is anthologized, published, and written about, are ideas about what a culture values and why" (Lauter 148). African American, feminist, and lesbian/gay studies exposed the myth of a values-neutral profession of literature as early as the 1960s. Recent critical and pedagogical theory, by exploring not only the changing canon but also questions of authorship, social constructs, subject positions, and the relationship between the "literary" and the "political," has led teachers to question what we need to know in order to teach, and to consider more fully what our students bring with them into the classroom.

The growing attention by publishers, scholars, critics, theorists, and teachers to Native American literature has been a significant part of the changing canon. While commercial publishers have actively and successfully promoted the work of a few, a large group of less well-known Native American writers has also begun to receive attention. There was, of course, a body of literature by Native Americans long before this literature was formally studied. But it is not enough simply to enlarge the canon. Like feminist, lesbian/gay, and African American critics, scholars of Native American literature continue to bring our attention to texts that have been excluded from the dominant canon of literary study, but they also discuss culturally specific approaches to texts once they have been included. The question now is "*how* we teach what we teach and *why* we teach what we teach" (Abbott 1). Other critics have stressed the necessity for situating Native American texts within their tribal, cultural, mythological, religious, historical, and political contexts.[1] Additionally, Arnold Krupat has warned of the dangers of interpreting Native American literature from dominant Western perspectives.

> A multicultural commitment . . . does not particularly encourage one to urge additions to the curriculum or the canon in the name of . . . "diversity" or "tolerance" (important as these are), but, rather to urge the deconstruction of all dichotomized paradigms of the us/them, West/Rest type, and so to undo manichean allegories at every level (*Ethnocriticism* 237–38).

Even Native American postmodern theorists do not satisfy Krupat, who argues that postmodern approaches to Native American literature are still based on Western models and/or assumptions about vaguely understood, overgeneralized "Indian" modes. Krupat concludes that overgeneralization ignores intertribal diversity and is often useless if not dangerous. Well-meaning critics and readers have also developed a postcolonial revisionism that takes the form of "victimist history" depicting the same binary oppositions featuring "genocidal Euramericans" and "innocent and hapless Native Americans" (*Ethnocriticism* 20).

Ironically, the popular consumerist trend toward Native American culture tends to reinforce such binary oppositions. Non-Indian readers often take a proprietary stance toward Native American culture and romanticize Native Americans as all good, all natural, all spiritual. This can be as dangerous as racism. When reading texts by, say, African American authors, white readers do not frequently claim that they are really black, boast of their black spirituality, or suggest that their knowledge of matters African American qualifies them to write texts that can be classified as African American literature. Yet such appropriations of Native American identity by whites is common. Commentaries resisting this new form of cultural imperialism have been published by many Native American writers. Hilarious satires on Native American literature classrooms appear in Sherman Alexie's *Indian Killer* and in Dorris and Erdrich's *The Crown of Columbus*.[2]

Critics also tend to "dabble" in Native American literature. Although much progress has been made in transforming the canon since the publication of Krupat's *The Voice in the Margin* in 1989, it is still true that "too many Westerners have played carelessly in the realms of Otherness, taking what they wanted—a little of this, a little of that—and blithely moving on, 'savagizing' or 'orientalizing' the Other" (Krupat, *Ethnocriticism* 36). Although he has trouble with those who claim that Native American writers or contributors speak with one voice, and raises important questions about relying on essentialized categories of Native and non-Native, Krupat argues that "in the same way that one would not want to see the criticism of literature by women and African Americans largely in the hands of men or Euramericans, so too criticism of the literature of Native Americans should not be largely in the hands of non-Native people" (*Turn to the Native* 9).

I agree with Krupat. Non-native scholars should approach texts by Native American writers with some care. Yet in practice, the majority of teachers who teach Native American texts in the literature classroom are non-Native people. How can well-intentioned non-Native teachers include Native American texts in the curricula without perpetuating the kind of damage Alexie, Krupat, and others describe? By situating texts in their contexts, Native and non-Native scholars and teachers can do much to avoid the overgeneralizations just mentioned.

Simply put, teachers need to consider their own motives and those of their non-Indian students. Presumably, most teachers have abandoned the "banker" model of pedagogy long since and instead are making efforts to engage students as active learners and participants in a classroom community. Frantz Fanon, Paulo Freire, bell hooks, and others have shown that we need to consider what Henry Giroux has referred to as "the productive meanings that students, in all of their cultural and social differences, bring to classrooms as part of the production of knowledge" (Giroux 17). In teaching texts written by Native Americans about

Native Americans, the teacher must also consider how these texts and their audiences have reinforced or countered damaging stereotypes. It is not enough to teach the text as a great "literary" text or to teach it from a politically astute but oversimplified Indian–good, white–bad revisionist agenda. While Krupat believes that Native American critics should dominate the field of Native American literature, he also points out that this literature does not benefit from a reductively essentialist perspective, that one should "be wary of the tendency to essentialize difference" (*Ethnocriticism* 243). Ethnocriticism, Krupat says, "rejects all forms of manichean discourse whether of a traditional and neocolonial or of a revisionist, 'victimist' kind" (26). The challenge is to be "concerned with differences rather than oppositions" and to "replace *oppositional* with *dialogical* models" (26; emphasis added).

Such an approach, derived partially from the work of Mikhail Bakhtin, is valuable when examining gender and sexuality as axes of analysis in Native American texts. Many poststructuralist lesbian-feminist critics, such as Diana Fuss and Judith Butler, would probably reject, with Krupat, the tendency to reduce subjects to a singular position or to presume that all subjects who share a particular identity speak with a unitary voice. Our culture has difficulty with those who speak from multiple positions, and yet it is precisely when we move away from totalizing views of race, gender, and sexuality that explorations of *difference* become most illuminating. We must remember, however, that one can still honor a distinct axis of identity while speaking from multiple positions. Emma Pérez's advocacy of a "strategic essentialism" for Chicana lesbians has important implications for Native American lesbians as well. Although Pérez complains of the "invasionary politics" women of color in the academy face who are "essentialized from above" (110) when asked to speak as women of color, she affirms the need for lesbians of color to create their own "*sitios y lenguas,* spaces and languages, sites and discourses, apart from male-defined and/or Eurocentric arenas" (109). While potentially confining, these spaces and languages are necessary parts of "the process for finding and expressing one's multiple voices" (Pérez 109). Indeed, identities tend to be multiple and distinct, yet simultaneously fluid. As Biddy Martin has pointed out, lesbianism no longer constitutes "total political and self-identification, and yet it figures no less centrally. . . . It remains a position from which to speak, to organize, to act politically, but it ceases to be the exclusive and continuous ground of identity or politics" (289). Acknowledging the position of the lesbian as central but not exclusive in defining identity is helpful in examining texts about Native American lesbians. Otherwise, we impose and perpetuate the same limitations bell hooks writes of in *Teaching to Transgress* when she is expected to discuss feminism without honestly confronting the issues affecting black women, or when she is asked to discuss race while checking her feminism at the door.

The role of lesbian and gay characters and themes in Native American literature has not been fully explored. Many of our classrooms are silent about lesbians and gays both in general and within Native American literature in particular. Doubly marginalized, this sizable minority suffers from invisibility at best, and at worst from stereotypes and discrimination. Teachers of Native American literature have been inspired by Paula Gunn Allen's *The Sacred Hoop* to recognize how the male heroes of novels by Leslie Silko, N. Scott Momaday, and others achieve personal and communal healing through a feminine agency connected with the land. Yet most critics and teachers are less comfortable exploring lesbian and gay issues. Had, for example, Tayo, the male protagonist of Silko's *Ceremony,* been a woman, the response would have been far different, as it was originally to Paula Gunn Allen's own novel *The Woman Who Owned the Shadows.*

Annette Van Dyke, Vanessa Holford, and Tara Prince-Hughes have since recovered the lesbian in *The Woman Who Owned the Shadows.* "Critics and historians of American Indian women's literature and culture," writes Holford, "are often uneasy with the issue of homosexuality, some even going so far as to claim conspiracy amongst non-Indian gays and lesbians to appropriate Native American spiritual beliefs toward their own political ends" (108). But indeed the lesbianism is there, and throughout the novel those who hurt or thwart the heroine Ephanie's self-development and self-recovery also forbid or punish her lesbian tendencies. "Distrust of lesbianism is fear of women's renewed strength, self-value, and unity" (Holford 105). Because lesbians exist "outside of phallic patriarchy," they and their utterances are generally "incomprehensible to the male master discourse" (Luce Irigaray, qtd. in Moi 126). Ephanie and her childhood girlfriend were happy together until forced apart. They were linked to the creation story of Uretsete and Naotsete, double woman. "With each other they were each one doubled. They were thus complete" (Allen, *Woman* 22). Through her relationship with another woman later in the novel, Ephanie begins to recover her own history and her spirituality. Allen's novel, Van Dyke argues, "is an important offering to Native American lesbians" (351).

Native American writers such as Chrystos, Janice Gould, Vickie Sears, Anne Waters, and Beth Brant have also recovered the lesbian in their stories and poems. These texts cannot be treated as though they are exactly the same as all other Native American texts, nor can they be approached as if they are primarily or only lesbian texts. Whereas some critical work has challenged narrative conventions in texts that are nonetheless informed by heterosexist assumptions, these women writers further empower the voices of the oppressed by speaking in resistance to multiple oppressions, thus reinventing language in new ways. Beth Brant's story "Swimming Upstream" is worthy of close examination because it is a site where several subjectivities intersect. The story raises important questions and offers alternatives to existing practices of teaching Native American literature. It is helpful to teachers who wish to avoid sentimentalizing the presentation of Native Americans as victims and who wish instead to focus on threads of resistance, subversion, and strength that are neither masculinized nor heterosexist. The text affords an opportunity for engaged dialogues in which students can discuss and interrogate their own experiences of and assumptions about difference. Anna May, the protagonist, is an open lesbian who lives with another woman in a stable relationship. There is no ambiguity about this. She is treated unfairly by the white, patriarchal legal system, yet she is more than a victim, and the presentation of her character counteracts stereotypes about lesbians and about Native Americans.

One stereotype used to portray both lesbians and Native Americans is that of the alcoholic. Popular images of lesbians in general were until recently influenced by outdated definitions of pathology and perversion. For many years, the primary opportunities for women to meet other lesbians were in the bar culture. Lesbians also frequently faced poverty, discrimination, and harassment, all conditions often associated with alcoholism. Much of that has changed, though not completely and not everywhere. Lesbians in general now have higher visibility, greater acceptance, and more opportunities for building community apart from the bar culture. Lesbian characters in recent Native and non-Native texts are no longer as likely to be depicted as victims, with drunkenness or suicide their likely outcomes.

Unfortunately, the stereotype of the Native American alcoholic has continued to haunt literature, persisting since the nineteenth century, when the European American view of Native Americans as "savages" and the construction of "Indian nature" were used to justify expansion into Native territories. A significant part of this construction was the "drunken Indian." Many communities were "virtually destroyed" by alcohol. Nineteenth-century federal laws prohibiting the sale of alcohol to Native Americans were nearly impossible to enforce, and the belief that the liquor trade could not be stopped helped build support for the removal of Indians from their lands (Davis 216). The stereotype of the drunken Indian has continued to depersonalize and depoliticize the image of the Native American. If the Indian were not drunk, what then would he or she do? Even Native American authors seem to have had difficulty imagining this, although living examples of activists, artists, teachers, writers, and businessmen and businesswomen are all around them. Although many works by Native Americans have underscored the problem of alcoholism on the reservations, few have escaped the tendency to reinforce stereotypes. Novels by D'Arcy McNickle, James Welch, N. Scott Momaday, Leslie Silko, Louise Erdrich, and others show us the devastation wrought by alcoholism. Only rarely do we see recovery, and often it is only implicit at the end of long narratives about drinking.

Beth Brant, a Bay of Quinte Mohawk, is one of the few writers who has not only imagined the sociopolitical factors of Indian alcoholism, but also has focused on Indian political agency and what Indians do when they do *not* drink. She also creates lesbian characters situated as Natives within white culture and as outlaws within heterosexist patriarchy. In Brant's collection *Mohawk Trail*, "A Long Story" offers two, parallel plots. In an 1890s narrative thread based on historical fact, Native children are taken and put on trains to schools in other states, where they are assimilated. Their hair is cut and they are given new names. They are not allowed to retain their former language or their former identities. Brant links the parents' powerlessness to prevent the theft of their children to alcoholic despair. "I see this. My husband picks up the braids, wraps them in cloth; he takes the pieces of our son away. He walks outside, the eyes of the people on him. I see this. He will find a bottle and drink with the men. Some of the women will join him" ("A Long Story" 78). But one of the women "tried to board the train and search for my babies. The white men tell my husband to watch me. I am dangerous. I laugh and laugh. My husband is good only for tipping bottles and swallowing anger" (83). This woman is called crazy because she does not allow her children to be taken away without a fight. Rather than "swallowing anger," she expresses her outrage and is therefore considered both "crazy" and "dangerous." The character is dangerous because she resists the patriarchal control of the white government that has engineered the kidnapping of Native children. Throughout this and other pieces in *Mohawk Trail*, Brant explores the tensions between the master narrative of patriarchy and the feminine. By the "feminine" I refer to the determination to go beyond the norms of the legal system, defined in the patriarchal language of the oppressor, to create a new language, a subversive action necessary to healing and survival. The character's defiance and outrage are actually signs of finding her speaking voice, and through that, finding political agency, an alternative to alcoholic self-destruction in the face of oppression. Alcohol abuse is self-destructive, and like other self-destructive actions (such as violence against the self or against the fellow oppressed), prevents effective resistance.

The other plot of "A Long Story" takes place in the 1970s, when a father uses the patriarchal legal system to take a daughter from her mother and the mother's lesbian lover. This story also interrogates the dialectics of oppression and explores the development of voice and political agency as an alternative to self-destruction. This emphasis on voice against silence and rejection of the language and structure of patriarchy informs most of Brant's narratives. Marilyn Farwell has argued that "the lesbian body is the ultimate transgressor of narrative limits because even when absent it is the silent threat behind the excess attributed to the female body not under male control. . . . [T]he lesbian body terrifyingly ruptures the distinction on which male, heterosexual power depends" (Farwell 163). The legal system seeks to silence lesbians, to keep them out of the story. Alcoholism is another great silencer, creating passivity instead of active resistance.

In a story from the collection *Food and Spirits,* "Swimming Upstream," set along the shore of Lake Huron, Brant reconstructs both alcoholism and lesbianism while disrupting stereotypical expectations of narrative. This is a story about a lesbian recovering alcoholic in which the recovery, rather than the intoxication, is the central focus.

In "Swimming Upstream," Anna May's father was an alcoholic known as "Injun Charley" and "Good-time Charley." Her mother was a white orphan. She and her siblings were targets of ridicule as mixed bloods and the children of a "drunken Indian." Anna May felt abandoned by both her parents. She grew up angry with her father for "going away" into his intoxication and angry with her mother for never complaining. This frustration echoes that of the woman in "A Long Story" who in 1891 criticized her husband for drinking instead of trying, as she did, to keep the white people from taking her children.

Like her father, Anna May became an alcoholic herself, but she stopped drinking when she became pregnant with her son, Simon. By the time the action in the story begins, she has stayed sober for more than six years. Her sobriety does not stop the white judge from awarding custody to Simon's father. The judge, representative of white patriarchy, punishes her for her past history with alcohol and for her present lesbian relationship, a painfully ironic condemnation, because the Mohawk traditionally were a matriarchal and matrilineal tribe. The mother was the center of power; the lineage and identity of the mother often determined the child's future. The judge's actions in the story show how much the white legal system has infringed upon traditional tribal values. This forced removal of the child from the mother echoes "A Long Story," which juxtaposes the historical practice of kidnapping Native American children during the nine-teenth century with the action of a 1970s father who takes his daughter away from her lesbian mother. In "A Long Story," Brant suggests that those who use the power of the white legal system, then and now, to remove children from their mothers are blind to the destruction they cause.

In "Swimming Upstream," the same intractable blindness and heterosexism directly or indirectly causes harm to both mother and child. By the time the narrative begins, Anna May's self-esteem has already been damaged. She has felt the sting of racism for being an Indian and further disapprobation as a result of being a mixed breed, a recovering alcoholic, and a lesbian, not necessarily in that order. To be a mixed-blood lesbian recovering alcoholic is to be excluded from the dominant, privileged group and also to be perceived with some suspicion in the Native American community. (Interestingly enough, Beth Brant's Mohawk name, Degonwadonti, translates as "several against one.") In "Swimming Upstream," these contradictory subject positions create dual sites of narrative tension. It is a measure of Anna May's determination that she has managed to stay sober and to resist a victim identity. Yet the reader senses the fragility of her self-esteem and her sobriety.

Anna May associates her sobriety with her son, Simon. Even though she only sees him on weekends, she still believes that Simon's existence is what keeps her from drinking. "She had no need for alcohol. There was Simon" ("Swimming Upstream" 118). She lives for Simon more than for her lover Catherine, more than for herself. After Simon dies in a boating accident while out with his father, Anna May struggles against an overwhelming grief.

"Swimming Upstream" goes a bit further than "A Long Story" and much further than most lesbian fiction in portraying lesbians neither strictly as victims of an unjust legal system nor as romanticized saints. Anna May and Catherine are not perfect, and they are not—per the lesbian romance—"all" to each other either. Anna May does not live for Catherine, although theirs is a strong, loving relationship. Her lesbianism is part, but not all, of Anna May's identity; she is also the mother of a son. She has to experience her grief alone, and Catherine respects Anna May's need to go away. This respect for the partner's needs is evident in

"A Long Story" also, when Ellen offers to leave Mary "if it will make it better" (82). In "Swimming Upstream," Catherine makes no effort to stop Anna May from going away, even though she may have guessed (as the reader has) that Anna May is planning to drink.

Catherine has, however, suggested that Anna May needs to forgive Tony, her ex-husband. The reader senses that Anna May cannot forgive Tony for the accident because she has not forgiven herself. Anna May tells herself at one point that she "should have placated" Tony, that "she should have lived alone; she should have pretended to be straight; she should have never become an alcoholic; she should have never loved; she should have never been born" ("Swimming Upstream" 122). These are the messages she has received from the world, and in her grief they begin to insinuate themselves into her psyche. She cannot locate herself as a speaking subject. Like Ephanie in *The Woman Who Owned the Shadows,* she has forgotten her own strength and value.

These internalized messages amount to what Janice Gould calls the injunction against speaking the truth, the injunction against knowing oneself as a lesbian and as an American Indian. Disobedience for Gould means revealing the fact of one's lesbianism and establishing what it means to be Indian (41). In "A Long Story," Mary worries that her ex-husband will teach her daughter, Patricia, "to hate us" (79). Brant links the racism Native Americans face with the homophobia lesbians encounter, and like Gould, suggests that those oppressed by racism and homophobia must fight to preserve their identities. Just as the kidnapped children of 1890 assumed new identities and became strangers to their parents, so Mary nearly a century later fears that Patricia will forget her life with her mother. Mary finally recognizes, as did her ancestor, the "crazy woman" who fought unsuccessfully in 1890 to save her children, that "they want our power. They take our children to remove the inside of them. Our power. They steal our food, our sacred rattle, the stories, our names. What is left?" ("A Long Story" 84). At the end of the story, Mary is determined not to give in, despite the pressure to destroy herself: "The word *lesbian.* Lesbian. The word that makes them panic, makes them afraid, makes them destroy children. The word that dares them. Lesbian. *I am one.* Even for Patricia, even for her, *I will not cease to be!"* (85). By disobeying the dangerous injunction, Mary challenges the misconception that one can be a good mother only by sacrificing herself for her children. She continues the tradition of defiance she has inherited from her "crazy" ancestor and sounds a clarion call of sanity for all lesbian mothers. Her disobedience allows her to transform the external hatred into a stronger self-acceptance. Resisting silence and claiming her position as a speaking subject empowers her. As Giroux reminds us, "To be able to name one's experience is part of what is meant to 'read' the world and to begin to understand the political nature of the limits *and* possibilities that make up the larger society" (7). By repeating the word *lesbian* Mary is naming her experience and interrupting the narrative of the homophobic world that would prefer to write her out of existence.

Mary is not a recovering alcoholic, however, and her daughter, while absent, is still very much alive. In "Swimming Upstream," the injunction against lesbianism is further complicated by alcoholism and the death of the son. Anna May has suffered a far more profound loss in the death of her son. It is as though Brant raised the stakes in the more recent story. The reader wonders whether the injunction can be disobeyed in such a context, under such pressure. Anna May's name evokes the name of a historical person who questioned unjust authority and who is believed to have been murdered by white authority in the form of the FBI.[3] Through complicating the character's identity as not only Native American, not only mother, but also alcoholic, Brant explores lesbian identity as one of several intersecting subjectivities.

In "Swimming Upstream," Anna May drives north along the shore of Lake Huron with her bottle of wine, planning yet postponing her plan to destroy her sobriety. In this tension lies much of the story's power. She has viewed her son Simon as the counterweight to all the forces, including her father's genetic legacy, that threaten her own recovery. Now that Simon is gone, she feels there is nothing to stop her from fulfilling this doomed legacy. Although she pauses to attend an AA meeting, she does not speak up and say what's on her mind. For a moment, the narrative offers a slight tease of hope, when a woman comes up to Anna May and tells her she knows what she is planning. "Don't do it," the woman says, and offers to help (120). But Anna May refuses to let herself be helped. Thus the reader expects the character to drink, to act true to the stereotype. After all, who could possibly blame her, given the tragedy of losing a son? Brant critiques the stereotype of the tragic Indian both here and in her poem "Her Name Is Helen" in *Mohawk Trail*: "She's had lots of girlfriends./ White women who wanted to take care of her,/who liked Indians,/ who think she's a tragedy" (62). As Anna May nears the Bruce peninsula, she stops again at Sauble Falls. This is to be her last stop before going on to drink.

At Sauble Falls, Anna May sees a small crowd of people watching the salmon make their way to their spawning grounds. She notices one fish in particular and names him "Torn Fin" because of his wounds. This scarred salmon becomes the symbolic equivalent of her dead son, and his journey becomes her own symbolic journey of death and renewal. The title "Swimming Upstream" announces the symbolic connection of the journey of the salmon with that of the alcoholic, the lesbian, the Native American, and the mixed blood. To carry all of these labels is to be scarred many times by forces that impede a life's journey. It is not surprising that a character who is a lesbian, Native American recovering alcoholic would identify with such a struggle. To acknowledge only this aspect of the symbolism, however, is to miss perhaps the most important thread of the story, that of death and rebirth.

In several Native American tribal stories, salmon figure prominently, and in many stories it is also common for humans and animals to exchange shapes. Transformation is frequently key. In one story, a young man ponders the ancient mystery of the salmon. Why did the salmon return so joyously to the river when there was only death waiting? Surely they must know. By becoming a salmon and traveling with other fish, the young man learns about the gift that salmon make of themselves for the renewal of life (Harris 44). In another salmon story, Swimmer the Salmon says that he is "covered by scars." He is followed by nets, traps, and hooks "wherever I go as I look for my home" (Hausman). He is looking for home—that is, *looking for his own death*—knowing he will die as he spawns, but also knowing that he will give life and will live again in the salmon he spawns. The stories in Brant's collections *Mohawk Trail* and *Food and Spirits* reprise this theme of return, rebirth, coming home. In "This Place," a mother tells her gay son who has just called to tell her he has AIDS, "Come home to us" (49). Salmon are the perfect example of the instinctive drive to find home. Swimmer the Salmon doesn't think of stopping until he reaches the spawning grounds. "Now I am swimmer who dies, with the water reborn." He announces that he always returns (Bruchac).

Anna May's son has literally drowned in Lake Huron, dying in the water, as the salmon die. She sees the bleeding bodies of dead fish on the rock slabs, salmon that did not make it, even as the other fish keep leaping, battered by the rocks. She watches the fish she has named Torn Fin struggle as she calls out to him to go on, to fight, to survive. She waits for him to make it past the next barrier. This salmon is both a real fish and a spirit. "By the Indian view, everything that exists is spiritual. Every object—plants, rocks, water, air, the moon, animals, humans, the earth itself—has a spirit. The spirit of one thing (including a human) is not superior to the spirit of any other" (Williams 21). After the other people leave, Anna May stays to watch. Torn Fin, like Swimmer the Salmon, must always return to his home spawning waters, must always go to his own death, which is the place of his birth. Salmon die in the process of affirming life. This tremendous push for life, this sacrifice of the torn and bleeding body of the fish, cannot be interpreted as an excuse for complicity in her own death. The mystery of her son's death can never be explained, but as Anna May enters into the mystery of the salmon, the transformation of Torn Fin into her son becomes definite. She chants her son's name: "*Simon. Simon.* Anna May rocked and put her hands in the water, wanting to lift the fish over the dam and to life" ("Swimming Upstream" 124). She does not actually touch the fish, just as she cannot actually touch her dead son. But when "the fish turned a complete circle and made it over the dam" (124), she calls out her son's name again. Unable to locate herself as a speaking subject, she speaks somehow. Anna May watches as the fish "slapped his tail one last time and was gone, the dark body swimming home. She thought . . . she saw her son's face, his black hair streaming behind him, a look of joy transfixed on his little face before the image disappeared" (124–25). Parallel to the transformation Anna May imagines of the fish into her son is her own transformation, a transformation that involves a rene-gotiation of her own identity through shifting subject positions.

Anna May had believed that Simon was the only thing keep-ing her from drinking and that with his death her connection to him was gone. She failed to realize that her relationship with Simon continues even after his death and that Tony and she are connected through both the shared creation of life and their shared grief. In failing to forgive both Tony and herself, Anna May had failed to understand how inescapable these connections are. Ul-timately, "Swimming Upstream," like many other Native Ameri-can texts, is about healing. Through her epiphany, her connection with the salmon, Anna May realizes the full meaning of her other connections. She recognizes that she, like Torn Fin, is wounded in a way that makes direction and progress difficult. Torn Fin's successful motion demonstrates that the wound is part of the journey. In naming the fish, in saying her son's name, Anna May has begun to move, to take her place in language instead of obey-ing the injunction not to *be*. Instead of her earlier silence at the AA meeting, Anna May has decided, like Mary in "A Long Story," to reject silence, to refuse complicity in her own destruction.

When Anna May leaves her wine bottle untouched, the ste-reotype of the drunken Indian is shattered. We see that grief and homophobia do not necessarily construct a binaristic universe wherein the heroine must either triumph or fall. Rather, Brant's narrative suggests that the thread of transformation utilizing *both/ and* is a more effective structure. The recovering alcoholic is *both* an alcoholic *and* sober. Simon's struggle, his joyful life, and the joy he brought Anna May help to enact her own transformation from death to life. This does not mean that she will be free of her grief. Just as Torn Fin/Simon could not give up, so Anna May must struggle toward recovery, toward renewed life. Like the salmon she has just watched turn in a complete circle in order to push himself over the dam, she turns the car south, turns toward home. The salmon's mission, his gift to his community, was his death. Part of Anna May's mission, like that of her mother and her grandmother before her, is to fight for survival. Her commu-nity includes both her lover and her ex-husband. In constructing the story of Torn Fin for herself, she has begun to transform her

world. If "the spoken word flows from our reading of the world"
(Freire and Macedo 35), then Anna May has begun to read the
world differently, including the meaning of death. Like Mary's in
"A Long Story," Anna May's story is really the continuation of a
very old story, repeating itself over many generations. The stories never end, according to Native American beliefs, yet they
constantly undergo change. These women are part of a tradition
of women who fight oppression, who refuse to read or write
themselves out of the larger story. As N. Scott Momaday, Leslie
Silko, and Paula Gunn Allen have all shown in their novels, the
healing of the individual is always already inextricably connected
to the healing and survival of the community. These stories of
healing, of allowing readers "to participate in the curing ceremony" of the novels and stories themselves, can help to "re-
store balance to the community-at-large" (Van Dyke 351).

The ending gesture of "Swimming Upstream" involves the
speaking voice, this time a voice seeking dialogue. When Anna
May stops to make a phone call, the reader assumes she will call
Catherine, her lesbian lover. This call further signals her disobedience of the injunction not to *be*, a disobedience essential to
recovery. The final image of the story is that of the sober lesbian
who survives by claiming her voice, her identity, and her connection to others. She will complete the circle and return home. Now
she has her story and her place in the world, established through
her transgression of injunctions imposed by a world that has
sought to exclude her. But she will remain a mother who has lost
her only child. She will remain an alcoholic, although a recovering one. There is no absolute redemption from fallen to saved,
only a contingent recovery, constantly negotiated through the
shifting positions of the speaking subject. The world will remain
complicated for Anna May; heterosexism, racism, and stereotypes are not likely to disappear.

Because of the nature of the transformative process and the
theme of community so important in Native American literature,
I would argue that Anna May's ex-husband, Tony, is crucial in
the story. The process of reading the world with a lesbian/recov-
ering alcoholic/mother in it must involve her voice(s) as part of a
dialogue with voices such as his. Ultimately, if the limitations of
patriarchal language and the imposed silences on lesbians are to

be transgressed, the heterosexual male must become part of the collective transformation of the world. Catherine tells Anna May to forgive Tony because Catherine knows that the loss is their shared experience and not Anna May's alone. Tony's own experience of loss and grief may help lead him to critical consciousness and enable him to hear Anna May's voice as part of his community, his larger world. But the story refuses to lead us to this all by itself. Instead, it leaves us with the *possibility* of this connection. I would argue that this open-endedness enables readers themselves to address the question and empowers them to enter into the completion of that transformative process, both in the text and, ultimately, in the world.

Inviting students to rewrite the story from Tony's point of view, or to compose a letter from Tony to Anna May, can be a productive avenue for exploring the different worlds students themselves bring to the story. Students who are sexist or homophobic should not themselves feel silenced in the classroom. But their positions may be interrogated and thus may become part of the larger story of meaning the class constructs together.

> The classroom, with all its limitations, remains a location of possibility. In that field of possibility we have the opportunity to labor for freedom, to demand of ourselves and our comrades, an openness of mind and heart that allows us to face reality even as we collectively imagine ways to move beyond boundaries, to transgress. This is education as the practice of freedom (hooks 207).

If the purpose of multicultural pedagogy is not to reduce all differences toward some notion of universality or to show how other cultural productions are like those of the dominant culture, then it is important for readers to consider identities as fluid, as multivoiced, and as constituted by difference. We must also critically examine how these identities operate contextually within larger narrative frames and the larger world. Discussion of such complications by students and teachers who speak in different voices from a wide range of experiences and positions is one starting point. While many texts emphasize only one aspect of identity and remain crucial to our curriculum, texts such as "Swimming Upstream"—those that decenter subjectivity, challenge overdetermined stereotypes, and radically revise the narrative expectations of the reader—are also necessary to a truly multicultural education.

Notes

1. For a more thorough discussion, see Chris LaLonde's "New Stories and Broken Necks: Incorporating Native American Texts in the American Literature Survey." Much of Krupat's work also discusses this topic.

2. Julie La May Abner asks: "Is any document that an 'Indian' writes considered American Indian literature, or is a text that a 'non-Indian' writes using Indian themes and following certain accepted techniques . . . an Indian text?" (2). While many feminist theorists question categories such as "male" and "female" and insist that gender is constructed, not biological, many Native and non-Native theorists of American Indian literature and cultural studies insist that some degree of essentialism is necessary when studying Native American culture and literature (see Williams 272–73). I tend to agree. As recently as 1998, I heard a white colleague defend his choice to teach such books as *The Education of Little Tree* rather than texts written and respected by Native American writers and scholars.

3. The name "Anna May" could be a coincidence. Although Brant spells "May" with a "y" and not an "e," she dedicated a previous book, *A Gathering of Spirit,* to Anna Mae Aquash, a Micmac activist killed and mutilated in South Dakota in 1976. The story of Anna Mae Aquash is well known in Native American communities, where it is widely believed the FBI was responsible for her murder.

Works Cited

Abbott, Lawrence. "Introduction." *Studies in American Indian Literature (SAIL)* 3:2 (1991): 1–5.

Abner, Julie La May. "The Fusion of Identity, Literatures, and Pedagogy: Teaching American Indian Literatures." *Studies in American Indian Literature (SAIL)* 8:2 (1996): 1–6.

Alexie, Sherman. *Indian Killer.* New York: Atlantic Monthly, 1996.

Allen, Paula Gunn. *The Sacred Hoop: Recovering the Feminine in American Indian Traditions.* Boston: Beacon, 1992.

————. *The Woman Who Owned the Shadows*. San Francisco: Spinsters, 1983.

Brant, Beth. "Her Name Is Helen." *Mohawk Trail*. Ithaca: Firebrand, 1985: 61–65.

————. "A Long Story." *Mohawk Trail*. Ithaca: Firebrand, 1985: 77–85.

————. "Swimming Upstream." *Food and Spirits*. Ithaca: Firebrand, 1991: 117–25.

————. "This Place." *Food and Spirits*. Ithaca: Firebrand, 1991: 49–66.

Bruchac, Joseph. "Salmon Boy." *Keepers of the Animals: Native American Animal Stories*. Audiocassette. Golden, CO: Fulcrum, 1992.

Davis, Randall C. "Fire-Water in the Frontier Romance: James Fenimore Cooper and 'Indian Nature.'" *Studies in American Fiction* 22 (1994): 216–31.

Dorris, Michael, and Louise Erdrich. *The Crown of Columbus*. New York: HarperCollins, 1991.

Fanon, Frantz. *The Wretched of the Earth*. New York: Grove, 1963.

Farwell, Marilyn R. "The Lesbian Narrative: 'The Pursuit of the Inedible by the Unspeakable.'" *Professions of Desire: Lesbian and Gay Studies in Literature*. Ed. George E. Haggerty and Bonnie Zimmerman. New York: MLA, 1995: 156–68.

Freire, Paulo, and Donaldo Macedo. *Literacy: Reading the Word and the World*. Westport, CT: Bergin, 1987.

Giroux, Henry. "Introduction." Freire and Macedo 1–27.

Gould, Janice. "Disobedience (in Language) in Texts by Lesbian Native Americans." *Ariel: A Review of International English Literature* 25:1 (1994): 32–43.

Harris, Christie. *The Prince Who Was Taken Away by the Salmon*. New York: Atheneum, 1973.

Hausman, Gerald. *Swimmer the Salmon*. Audiocassette. Santa Fe: Sunset /Lotus, 1989.

Holford, Vanessa. "Re-Membering Ephanie: A Woman's Recreation of Self in Paula Gunn Allen's *The Woman Who Owned the Shadows*." *Studies in American Indian Literature (SAIL)* 6:1 (1994): 99–113.

hooks, bell. *Teaching to Transgress: Education as the Practice of Freedom.* New York: Routledge, 1994.

Krupat, Arnold. *Ethnocriticism: Ethnography, History, Literature.* Berkeley: U of California P, 1992.

———. *The Turn to the Native: Studies in Criticism and Culture.* Lincoln: U of Nebraska P, 1996.

———. *The Voice in the Margin: Native American Literature and the Canon.* Berkeley: U of California P, 1989.

LaLonde, Chris. "New Stories and Broken Necks: Incorporating Native American Texts in the American Literature Survey." *Studies in American Indian Literatures (SAIL)* 8:2 (1996): 7–20.

Lauter, Paul. *Canons and Contexts.* New York: Oxford UP, 1991.

Martin, Biddy. "Lesbian Identity/Autobiographical Difference[s]." *The Lesbian and Gay Studies Reader.* Ed. Henry Abelove, Michele Aina Barale, and David M. Halperin. New York: Routledge, 1993. 274–93.

Moi, Toril. *Sexual/Textual Politics: Feminist Literary Theory.* London: Routledge, 1985.

Pérez, Emma. "Irigaray's Female Symbolic in the Making of Chicana Lesbian *Sitios y Lenguas.*" *The Lesbian Postmodern.* Ed. Laura Doan. New York: Columbia UP, 1994.

Van Dyke, Annette. "The Journey Back to Female Roots: A Laguna Pueblo Model." *Lesbian Texts and Contexts: Radical Revisions.* Ed. Karla Jay and Joanne Glasgow. New York: New York UP, 1990. 339–54.

Williams, Walter L. *The Spirit and the Flesh: Sexual Diversity in American Indian Culture.* Boston: Beacon, 1986.

---III---

The Politics of Culture

Reading Gender, Reading Sexualities: Children and the Negotiation of Meaning in "Alternative" Texts

DEBBIE EPSTEIN

Institute of Education, University of London

During the 1995–96 school year, I carried out a small-scale research project in a primary school in north London, which I shall call Edendale School.[1] I spent most of my time with one Year 5 class (of nine- to ten-year-olds) in the classroom, in the playground, and at lunch. I was interested in how these children constituted themselves in relation to gender and sexuality both in class and through their play. I was already familiar with the school through the class teacher, Mr. Stuart,[2] and prior to the project we had discussed what we both hoped to gain from it.

My purposes were partly to begin the exploration of gender and sexuality at this age, an area which is both unresearched and controversial because of "common sense" (that is, what seem to be obvious and unquestionable) assumptions that young children neither know about nor are interested in sexuality. This so-called common sense runs alongside the notion that if children do know about or show any interest in sexuality, they are somehow tainted and perhaps even seductive—and that their very innocence is part of the seduction (see Kitzinger, "Defending Innocence" and "Who Are You Kidding?"). Indeed, the front page banner headline in the *Daily Mail* on March 6, 1996 reading "5-Year-Olds to Get Gay Lessons" (Halpin), which ran across three columns and occupied four and a half inches of prime space a third of the way down the page, was illustrative of this discourse of childhood innocence (for further discussion of this topic, see Epstein, "Too Small to Notice" and "Cultures of Schooling/Cultures of Sexuality"). For Mr. Stuart, an out and politically active gay teacher, the opportunity was to have a researcher in the classroom to help him understand and analyze how children in his class made sense of and understood issues of gender and sexuality, and how they *performed* gender (see Butler, *Gender Trouble* and *Bodies That Matter*). What, he wanted to know, did the texts he used in the classroom signify for the children with regard to the performance of gender?

Throughout the research, it was clear that, while these young children were not sexually active or aware in the ways that secondary school pupils often are, they nevertheless knew a great deal about (hetero)sexuality, which was part of the stuff of everyday life in their playground and classroom in a number ways:

- through imagined futures, particularly as heterosexual women in couples and families, which tend to dominate the fantasies of adulthood expressed by girls in their play and storytelling/writing

- through traditional games and rhymes, particularly those associated with skipping and newer games based particularly on popular television scenarios

- through versions of games involving running and catching, which become transmuted into arenas of sexualized chasing

- through the sexual/sexist harassment of girls by boys and sexually charged, frequently homophobic, insult exchange between children, often of the same sex

- through early assays into the world of "going out," "dating," "two-timing," and "dumping" of some of the children

- through the gossip networks of playground, staff room, and classroom

Here my focus will be on the children's cultures, including the formations and significance of their quasi-romantic relationships, on Mr. Stuart's use of particular "alternative" texts about family and how the children read them, and on significant silences in which the children actively engaged around Mr. Stuart's gayness. I argue that the children had complex and contradictory responses to Mr. Stuart's attempted normalization of homosexuality, sometimes rejecting and at others working with it, in ways which were strongly influenced by "master narratives" of compulsory heterosexuality as the inevitable and happy outcome of growing up.

Shereen Benjamin, writing about her work as a feminist teacher and researcher challenging hegemonic masculinities in her class, comments:

> Not surprisingly, one of my key challenges was in working with resistance. I found myself in a paradoxical situation. I was asking the boys to identify with me, an authority figure, probably perceived by them as middle-class, in resistance to a constellation of hegemonic and working-class masculinities that I had identified as oppressive. The boys could work out and choose from a variety of ways of working "with me" or "against me," but whichever way they decided to act they could not avoid being involved in resistance. (43)

Similarly, the pupils in Mr. Stuart's class were required either to resist his push toward a counterhegemonic discourse in which heterosexuality is not assumed and homosexuality is not condemned, or to resist dominant discourses presumptive of heterosexuality and dismissive of or hostile toward lesbian, gay, or bisexuality. This essay traces some of the strategies that the pupils and their teacher used in negotiating this particular discursive field. In so doing, I examine the ways in which an openly gay teacher like Mr. Stuart may both embody possibilities, especially for the boys in his class, of different ways of being a man (or performing masculinity) even before he makes any conscious intervention (see and cf. Redman and Mac an Ghaill) and, at the same time, be constrained by dominant discourses of compulsory and assumed heterosexuality, whose myths pervade the spaces of both classroom and playground.

A Teacher and His Class: A Thumbnail Sketch

Mr. Stuart was in his early thirties. Over six feet tall, he appeared at first sight to exemplify the male teacher who can exert power in class through his size and his voice. His body language and soft-spoken manner, however, gave this the lie. Rather than standing over the children, he tended to crouch, to get down to their level. His voice was seldom raised in class,[3] and he was more likely to display disappointment than anger in dealing with misbehavior or poor work. He was well organized and prepared in detail for each day's work, with immaculate record keeping, his pedagogic style mixing the formal and informal. For some lessons, he taught from the front of the classroom, with the children sitting quietly in neat rows in desks which had been assigned to them. At other times, they worked in small groups, chatting quietly as they did so. Barrie Thorne shows how:

> [i]n managing almost thirty lively children within relatively small spaces, Mrs. Smith, like other teachers and aides, drew on the general power of being an adult, as well as on the more institutionalized authority of her official position. She claimed the right to regulate the students' activities, movement, posture, talking, possessions, access to water, and time and manner of eating. (31)

Similarly, Mr. Stuart claimed the rights of the adult-as-teacher to control, regulate, and survey his class and the children's individual behaviors. Foucault's description of the panopticon as a prison, in which the prisoner can always be seen by the warder but cannot be sure when he [sic] is under observation and therefore modify his own behavior, could equally be a description of any classroom, and Mr. Stuart's was no exception. From his position at the desk or walking round the classroom, he could at a glance see any child, and there were certain children, typically boys rather than girls, who drew his attention (often through disruptive behavior) more frequently than others. He was profoundly aware of gender relations in his class and worked hard to encourage the girls to speak out, especially in "circle time" when every child had an opportunity to contribute to the discussion as a selected small object (often a shell) was passed from hand to hand. Mr. Stuart took his turn in the circle along with the children and, on the rare occasions when he interrupted (for example, to reprimand someone), he apologized to the class. Circle time was when class members could talk about a range of events and, in particular, when feelings could be expressed. Mr. Stuart modeled this by speaking about his own feelings whenever he felt it was appropriate. The children loved him and loved being in his class. When, in July 1997, he gave up teaching,[4] the parents in this working-class, ethnically mixed, inner-city school set about raising enough money to pay for him to work part-time at the school teaching music and working with children who have special educational needs. They raised over £300 within the first few days, and Mr. Stuart returned to teach one day a week at the school, a year after he had left.

Edendale School had a large ethnic minority pupil intake. The area it served had large, settled Cypriot populations, both Greek and Turkish, although many Greek Cypriots seemed to be moving further north into more suburban neighborhoods. More recently there had been an influx of Kurdish and Somali refugees. There were also children whose families originated in the Indian subcontinent, Africa, and the Caribbean, and children of Travellers. For the last dozen years at least, more people have emigrated from the UK than have come to live in the country from elsewhere. There is almost no primary immigration (that is, immigration by people who are the first members of their nuclear families to become residents in the country, as opposed to spouses and children joining those who had previously migrated and settled or had been born in the UK). This means that very few young children have migrated themselves, or have parents who have done so. Unusually, then, Edendale's roll included many children who were themselves fairly recent immigrants (refugees), often with horrendous experiences of persecution and war. There were over twenty different mother tongues spoken at the school and at least fourteen in Mr. Stuart's class. The largest single ethnic/language group was Turkish. Classes were kept quite small, usually between twenty and twenty-five pupils in each class, and many of the pupils were transient, spending a few weeks or months in the school before moving on to a more permanent setting, and their places taken by others. The London Borough, where the school was situated, was one of the poorer boroughs/Local Education Authorities in London and there was high unemployment within it. There was also a growing professional middle class and mainly white population buying up houses (which are significantly cheaper than in some other areas of London). Consequently, there were a few middle-class children in the school, but only one in Mr. Stuart's class when I was doing my research.

The class was roughly evenly divided between girls and boys, and I use the term "divided" advisedly. When left to their own devices, the boys and the girls hardly ever mixed in the classroom (even though there was some mixing in the playground, which I will discuss in more detail below). Mr. Stuart therefore made it a rule that, for circle time at least, boys must sit next to girls and vice versa. A small group of girls and boys seemed to be positioned by the other children (and to position themselves) as the class leaders. These children were not necessarily the most successful academically, though they were all fluent in English. It seemed that, for the most part, the "leading boys" were lively, noisy, and often quite troublesome, even rough, in their behavior. They were also the boys most likely to be at the center of the daily football games (U.S. soccer) during lunch recess and most likely to become involved in physical fights to prove their toughness. Indeed, it could be said that these boys occupied subject positions of hegemonic masculinity within a school context in which it was definitely not common (or even acceptable by the peer group) for boys to be seen to exert themselves over their schoolwork. They were much more likely to be working extremely hard at being boys, or performing "boyness."

In contrast, the girls in leadership positions in the class tended to be hard working and eschewed the kinds of horseplay the boys enjoyed. They were neither timid nor submissive, however, being strongly opinionated and ready to express themselves freely in front of the whole class. They were quite confident about schoolwork and, during play time, either chatted to each other in small groups or played in a mixed group with the boys in particular heterosexualized games, which I will discuss shortly. Indeed, one of the most striking aspects of the gendered dynamics of the class was that the children who seemed to be most attractive to the others and who, therefore, occupied the more dominant positions, were those who engaged in considerable talk about boyfriends/girlfriends, dating, dumping, "two-timing," and so on.

There are two particular children, one boy and one girl, who exemplify this group of leading children and were, indeed, at its center.

Elias was an outgoing boy of Greek Cypriot working-class origin. He had significant problems with his schoolwork, particularly reading, and Mr. Stuart paid him a great deal of attention. He was often charming but was also often in trouble for fighting or otherwise misbehaving. He was frequently the first to voice an opinion which seemed to be prejudiced (for example, "They're taking over London, the Turkish people are"), but was equally quick to withdraw such statements in favor of liberal sentiments (for example, "They're just people. Like Greeks, some people think that's not nice. Turkish, some people think that's not nice. We're all the same people."). He could be sensitive, even touchy, quick to take offense and quick to lash out when he did, but he was also eager to please and could be careful about other people's feelings.

Louise was the only child in the class whose background could be said to be middle class in terms of her parents' educational and professional qualifications. She was a tall girl of mixed Turkish/English origin and was easily the most articulate child in the class, able to present an opinion with great fluency, a confident reader, and generally academically able. She would frequently help other children with their work, particularly her girlfriends, but also Elias, with whom she had an ambivalent relationship. On the one hand, she found him irritating, particularly when he became involved in episodes of sexual harassment, invading the girls' changing-rooms during swimming sessions when Mr. Stuart was away from school on jury service and the class was being taught by a substitute teacher. On the other hand, she found him attractive, and the two of them declared themselves to be "boyfriend" and "girlfriend," although she had mixed feelings about this. She was an extremely perceptive child, both about other children and about the adult world.

Normalizing Heterosexuality: The Playground Context

Barrie Thorne uses the term "gender play" to describe the ways in which elementary school children in the United States insert themselves into gendered (and heterosexist) discourses. The playground was a major arena for this kind of play at Edendale. Girls particularly were often enthusiastic in performing gendered, heterosexual parts through skipping and other rhymes (for a collection of children's playground rhymes, see Opie and Opie). Whereas boys' playground games often involved running and ball games (usually football), the girls were much more frequently to be seen chatting or skipping to particular rhymes or playing clapping games which, more often than not, were about boyfriends, marriage, and children. Of course, girls can and do indulge in verses of this kind without thinking of their meaning, enjoying the rhythm and the skipping. Nevertheless, it is an activity through which heterosexuality is normalized/naturalized (even if not thought about reflectively). The fantasies developed through such rhymes, while not necessarily about sex as such, are certainly reproducing part of a culture of heterosexuality in which girls grow up to be women who marry men, go on a honeymoon, have babies, and otherwise perform their gendered, heterosexual feminine roles.

Other skipping and clapping rhymes performed by the girls gave particular pleasure to the players because they were sexually suggestive and somewhat risqué, and they were normally performed to gales of laughter. While skipping and clapping were almost exclusively girls' games, other games were played by both girls and boys. These were variants of chasing and catching games, in which gender was strongly marked and sexual connotations were introduced. One such game was based on the popular UK television show *Blind Date*. In this game, three girls stood behind a wall and numbered themselves from one to three. The boy then chose a number (the question-and-answer session of the original show having been dispensed with). The game finished with the chosen girl coming out from behind the wall, the boy running away, and all three girls chasing after him. When they caught him, as they invariably did, the "chosen" girl would kiss him on the cheek. This game, like "kiss, cuddle, torture," described and discussed below, could be seen as a reversal of the usual gendered power relations of the school playground. The fact that the boy was always younger and smaller placed him in a less powerful position than the girls he was playing with (and it is perhaps significant that no boy in their own year group would play this game with them). The chasing and catching of the boy by three girls provided the girls with an opportunity to display their own power, including the power to humiliate a boy. The fact that this took place literally on the margins of a playground dominated by bigger boys playing football is a paradox. So too is the fact that the power developed through playing this game could simultaneously be seen as helping to embed girls within the power relations of heterosexuality.

Blind Date as played here was a version of the ever popular "kiss-chase," usually seen in infant playgrounds (that is, amongst children aged four to seven). At Edendale School, the children had evolved another version of "kiss-chase" which they called "kiss, cuddle, torture." This was the subject not only of playground activity but also of much discussion in the classroom. When I interviewed the children, this was one of the key subjects of discussion. Samantha and Louise's account of the game was that the boys would nearly always choose "torture" rather than "kiss" or "cuddle" when the girls caught them. The girls, on the other hand, were most likely to choose "cuddle," since being kissed was embarrassing and being "tortured" unpleasant. As in *Blind Date,* gender difference was strongly marked, indeed exaggerated, as a binary and heterosexual opposition. Boys and girls, at least according to the girls, chose differently and, indeed, from my discussions with both boys and girls and from my playground observation, it seems that the girls literally never chose "torture," whereas the boys frequently did.

It is interesting to reflect on the signification of these gendered choices by the girls and boys involved in the game. The choice of "torture" by the boys seemed to signify that they were "real men" who could put up with being kicked (which, the girls explained, was what torture entailed) rather than being soft enough to be kissed by a girl. Connell suggests that masculinities are, at least in part, achieved through a circuit of production of cultural meaning related to bodily experiences. He argues that bodily experiences (in his particular example, of men enjoying sex with each other) are understood through the lens of what they signify in the culture, and then similar bodily experiences are entered into again with these culturally rich expectations (62). For both boys

and girls, "kiss, cuddle, torture" involved developing a repertoire of culturally interpreted bodily experiences. Rather than
just being painful (which it is), the experience of "torture" (being
kicked, as Elias explained to me, "in some place that's not nice")
is inscribed into the boys' "boyness." What is more, being tortured seemed to be more a marker of "proper" (i.e., macho) male
heterosexuality than being kissed. Indeed, kissing (of girls by
boys), because it was seen as feminized, also became an indication of being a sissy, which was immediately conflated with being gay (or, in the children's most common nomenclature, a
"poofter"). In fact, Elias appeared to be the only boy involved in
the game who could get away with choosing "kiss," possibly
because he was well established as a "real boy" and one who
was heterosexually attractive. Indeed, within classroom and playground gossip, his heterosexual attractiveness was legendary—
"everyone wants to go out with Elias," as one girl told me.

Girls too entered into a circuit of "bodily reflexive" experience. In the context of the game, they empowered themselves/
were empowered through their ability to "torture" and to choose
not to be "tortured." Of course, the terms of their power were
constrained by the more general relations of gendered power
within the school. As pointed out earlier, the playground, especially during lunchtime play, was completely dominated by boys
playing football, and this was frequently a subject of complaint
from the girls. Moreover, the choice of "cuddle" rather than "kiss"
was definitely related to the potential for a kiss given in the playground to be mythologized in classroom gossip, to the point that
it came to stand for excessive sexuality: the whore side of the
Madonna/whore binary. Engaging in the game but choosing
"cuddle" for the girls did establish their feminine/feminized heterosexual credentials, but without the danger of being identified
as, in some sense, "loose." Another constraint on the girls' ability to develop power in the gender dynamic of the playground
was that the hetero/sexist harassment[5] of girls by boys was a
constant presence, either in the girls' constantly retold narratives
of what it meant to be a girl or because it was actively taking
place.

Signifying Mothers/Signifying Heterosexuality

This was the context for the year-group topic adopted by Mr. Stuart and the other Year Five teacher, Ms. Allen (who, as it happened, was a lesbian), on "Me, My Family, and My History." This topic was intended to be an opportunity for antiracist, antisexist, and antiheterosexist work as the children explored different aspects of the topic, including their connections with other parts of the world, their own family histories and differing family formations, biology, and sex education. It was Mr. Stuart's intention that, should the opportunity arise within the topic, he would come out to his class (and, indeed, he hoped and intended that the topic would give rise to just such an opportunity). This was not a sudden decision; he had been out among the staff for a long time and had met with the school's governing body during the previous year and obtained their support for the idea that, should it be appropriate, he would come out to the children in the school. I discuss what happened when he did come out in the next section of the essay. In this section, I focus on the way children used and made sense of two particular texts introduced for their potential to show alternative family formations to the nuclear, heterosexual family, which, in popular culture if not in the children's lives, is usually represented as white and middle class. These texts were a Canadian children's picture book titled *Asha's Mums* (Elwin and Paulse) and a photopack titled *What Is a Family?* (Development Education Centre).

Bronwyn Davies shows how many children read feminist fairy tales in ways that recuperate the patriarchal gender order. The children's readings of *Asha's Mums* and of the photographs from *What Is a Family?* were somewhat more contingent on the particular context than those of Davies' subjects. *Asha's Mums* tells the story of a little girl who is required to get the permission of her parents to go on a class outing to the Science Museum. When she brings the permission note back to school signed by two women, the teacher says that no one can have two mothers and that permission must be given in a note signed by Asha's mother *and* father. The next day, both her mothers visit the teacher to explain their familial situation, and Asha is allowed to visit the Science Museum. Along the way, there is a discussion amongst the children in Asha's class about whether or not it is possible to have two mothers. The book is attractively illustrated and, though it is a little obvious in its righteous intentions, it did hold the children's interest.

Asha's Mums was one of several books available for small groups of children to do an activity in which they mapped the central characters' relationships to others in the story. Mr. Stuart had given each group a sheet of paper on which he had already drawn a set of concentric circles. The task was to read their chosen story together and to write the main character's name in the central circle and the names of the other characters elsewhere on the sheet within circles closer or nearer to the center, depending on the closeness of that character to the story's protagonist. Mr. Stuart suggested that they start by writing the characters' names on small pieces of paper, which they could move around on the larger sheet until the group agreed about the relative positioning of each, at which time they could transfer the names to the big sheet. Mr. Stuart moved around the classroom talking to the small groups as they worked. The group using *Asha's Mums* consisted of three girls (Christina, Aysegul, and Nadia). Much of their conversation about the book revolved around the question of how Asha came to have two mums, and the girls decided to place the names of both mums equally near to Asha. These names were followed by the names of Asha's baby brother and her best friend, then her teacher and the other children in the class. In this context, and in discussion with Mr. Stuart, they decided that Asha's two mums loved each other, and Nadia supplied the word *lesbian* when Mr. Stuart asked if they knew a word to describe women who loved other women. At the end of the session, however, when each group of children was asked to explain to the rest of the class what they had done, this explanation of Asha's parents vanished from use, and any number of other explanations, no matter how unlikely, was offered in preference:

MR. STUART: So why d'you think that Asha has two mums?

LEVI: [*to laughter*] They might have had, one of them might have had a sex change.

ELIAS: Might have a stepmum.

LOUISE: Maybe the kids are orphans and came to live with these two ladies.

CHRISTINA: I think they adopted the children.

[*General puzzlement in the class*]

MR. STUART: Do you think they might be two women who loved each other?

EDWARD: [*gasping, in a very shocked voice*] Lesbians!

LEVI: How d'you know which one's pregnant?

CHRISTINA: No. Maybe they're sisters.

(Conversation as noted in research diary, 29 September 1995)

It is worth noting that neither Nadia nor Aysegul contributed to the discussion despite the fact that Nadia had supplied the word *lesbian* when talking in the small group with Mr. Stuart. Moreover, Christina, who had been involved in the previous discussion, offered a new explanation of Asha's relationship with her two mums, which had been explicitly rejected by her small group earlier.

This raises two important questions. First, why were the girls either silent or unable to present the suggestion that Asha's mums might have been lesbian when they moved from their small group to the whole class situation? It seems that the presumption of heterosexuality within the class as a whole was overwhelming and that the explanation that there were lesbian mothers felt risky to the girls. Since the very term "mother" signifies heterosexuality in commonsense terms (Kaplan; VanEvery), the girls seemed to feel that using the term "lesbian mother" was in itself an admission of illegitimate knowledge. Effectively defying the normative definition of mothers as heterosexual by offering the explanation of lesbian motherhood identified the girls as themselves possible "lezzies," a term sometimes used within the playground as a form of abuse. Edward's shocked gasp of "Lesbians!" when Mr. Stuart suggested the possibility of two women loving each other was an indication of the reception the girls might have experienced if they had used the word themselves or implied its concept. As Sue Lees has shown in relation to older girls in secondary schools, the use of the epithet "lesbian" as a term of abuse is commonplace and applied to girls who do not conform to the status quo, socially or intellectually. Acceptance of lesbians (or lesbian mothers) as "normal" would, potentially, associate the girl using it with the (stigmatized) status of the lesbian.

Second, what was the difference for the girls between the small group and the whole class? I would suggest that for the three girls, all of them friends, working together in a small group constituted a kind of private space. In this context, transgression (or knowledge of transgression) of the myth that all mothers are inevitably heterosexual could be allowed without the danger of appearing to have been contaminated. But the whole class was a public space, no longer consisting of girls only or of chosen friends with whom one could risk, as Nadia did, using the word and concept *lesbian* in a noncondemnatory way. Edward, within the whole class context, knew the word but distanced himself from it by demonstrating his shock through the exaggerated expression in his voice.

When the children worked with the pictures in the *What Is a Family?* photopack, they also resisted reading a particular picture as depicting one of lesbian mothers.

The photograph shows two women, both smiling, one of them holding a baby on her lap as a cat climbs out of her hands, and the other sitting very close and stroking the cat. Both women are, to my (adult, lesbian) eye at least, coded as lesbian in their dress and self-presentation. Given the context of all these pictures being about "families," the preferred reading of the picture would seem to be that it is of a lesbian couple with their baby (and their cat). The children had been given several questions to address as they discussed their chosen photographs in pairs. One of these questions was, "How are the people in the picture connected to each other?" Elias and Brendan, who had chosen this photograph, were steadfast in refusing to admit the possibility of lesbian motherhood in their discussion of it, even when Mr. Stuart suggested this to them. They insisted instead that the picture showed two mums who were friends and one had come to visit the other, even though there was only one baby to be seen in the photograph. So, whereas the girls were prepared to entertain the possibility that Asha's mums might be lesbians while they were within the relative privacy and safety of their small group, the boys were not willing to do so even when working in a pair. This may be an illustration of boys' greater unwillingness to take risks, particularly the risk of appearing not to be "real boys," even (perhaps especially) with their closest friends and allies.

Given the children's abilities to read against the grain, which Bronwyn Davies discusses and I have traced in rather a different form here, it seems important that progressive teachers think about how they use "alternative" texts in the primary (and secondary) classroom. This is not to suggest that such texts are useless: after all, the girls did some important thinking in relation to *Asha's Mums*, and even the boys were asked to confront the possibility of a different way of being mothers, however resolutely they refused it. Nevertheless, language arts teachers in particular may wish to give some thought to the necessity of facilitating small-group work and classrooms in which they are able to talk with children in small groups about such texts. This is almost certainly more effective than relying on the texts themselves to do the work of providing "positive images" of groups of people normatively seen in negative ways or in stereotyped positions.

"Some Grown-Ups Aren't Very Grown Up": Coming Out in Class

In another activity for this project, Mr. Stuart asked the children to work in small groups to write down three "facts" about girls and three about boys. All the groups came to the conclusion fairly quickly that the only "facts" they could write down would be biological ones like "girls can have babies" and "girls have vaginas." When they came back to the whole class, Mr. Stuart went around the circle, asking each child to offer one "fact" their group had written down. After a few along the lines of "boys can stand up to go to the toilet" and "girls can have babies," Aysegul offered:

AYSEGUL:	[*very embarrassed, looking down at her feet and whispering*] Girls can marry, girls can't get married to girls.
MR STUART:	It's true that girls can't get married to girls because of the law, but girls can fall in love and live together.
EDWARD:	Maybe they're lesbians.
[*Lots of giggles*]	
LEVI:	I know a man, I think it's disgusting.
MR STUART:	Well, I'm gay and I'm not disgusting.
[*Lots of giggles*]	
MR STUART:	The person I happen to love is a man.
ELIAS:	A man is a man and a woman is a woman.
LOUISE:	Everyone says you're not gay and Ms. Allen is your girlfriend.
MR STUART:	Everyone is wrong. Ms. Allen is a very good friend, but I don't love her. . . .
SAMANTHA:	But we *saw* you and you were in the greengrocer's, laughing.

Clearly, the gossip networks had been active and the two teachers had been paired off in the children's minds. After all, shopping for fruit and vegetables is a domestic act, and laughing while doing so may well signify romantic, heterosexual involvement! What seemed to be operating here was the development of a narrative around these two popular teachers whereby linking them romantically worked as a potent enactment of the myth of "happy heterosexuality." The fact that the two teachers were evidently happy in each other's company (laughing while they shopped) was worked up into a kind of mythical, romantic, almost fairy story in which the two were destined to have the inevitable happy ending.

Much to my surprise (and indeed to Mr. Stuart's), his being gay did not spread around the school. Two weeks later, for example, a child in the other Year 5 class was in trouble for using homophobic insults and had no inkling that Mr. Stuart was gay. When I interviewed Samantha and Louise, I asked them about gossip and they told me that, although they did gossip about and at school, they did not gossip about Mr. Stuart because:

SAMANTHA: Yeah. Maybe, if he told us and then he might not want the whole school to know.

LOUISE: We wouldn't have done it.

Throughout this conversation (and the transcript of this section of it is several pages long), the girls refused to say that what they were not gossiping about was Mr. Stuart's coming out to them. Neither they nor I used the term "gay," and the girls were insistent that Mr. Stuart would not want "it" spread about:

SAMANTHA: Yeah, but, he doesn't want, really, everyone at the school to know.

LOUISE: Maybe he does but, I don't know, I wouldn't really spread it because . . .

SAMANTHA: 'Cos people go a bit funny in this school about . . .

LOUISE: Yeah and then they'd go, they'd jump around and tell . . .

SAMANTHA: Their mum and dad . . .

LOUISE: . . . and then they'd say "is it true?" or something. And maybe their mum and dad will think that he's a bad teacher and then they'll think that "oh no, my son is going to be, like, um, don't want my daughter, he's going to be like that, so I'm going to take

> my kid away from the school" and tell Mr. Snowden about him and he could be sacked.

DE: D'you think that would happen?

SAMANTHA: No.

LOUISE: No, not really, 'cos, most grown-ups are, um, grown-up about it but some aren't really. Some are.

We all knew what we were talking about. It was, in Eve Sedgwick's terms, the "open secret." Furthermore, the children were absolutely aware of homophobia as a feature of society that they had to negotiate. They knew that "most grown-ups are grown-up about it, but some aren't really" and seemed to have made a conscious (or semiconscious) decision to build a kind of closet around the classroom in order to protect their teacher, but maybe also to protect themselves from the contamination of having a gay teacher. If being gay seemed to them to be dangerous because of the reactions of adults, then maybe being taught by a gay man was dangerous because of the reactions both of adults, who might remove you from the class of a teacher you liked, and of other children, who might tease you and accuse you of being gay or lesbian yourself.

Conclusion

In the context of Mr. Stuart's teaching and, in particular, of his coming out to the class, opportunities were opened up for some radical shifts in the narratives by which these children had learned to understand gender and sexuality. But these possibilities were constrained in several ways. Talk about romance, dating, dumping, and going out, in which the most popular children were keenly involved, was an important aspect of the way the class as a whole made sense of heterosexual gender relations. The involvement of this particular popular group of children in games, in which both heterosexuality and gender were heavily marked, took place in ways that reinforced the hegemonic gender order: macho men and cuddly, caring women were enacted through the conduct of "kiss, cuddle, torture." The way that motherhood is made to signify heterosexuality was difficult to shift, especially in whole-class discussions of the "alternative" texts provided by Mr. Stuart, although the girls (unsurprisingly) showed more signs of shifting the narrative than the boys. Finally, the mythology of "happy heterosexuality" was perpetuated in the legend of Mr. Stuart's romance with Ms. Allen.

Nevertheless, the impact of Mr. Stuart's attempts to shift the master narrative and rewrite the myths of family and of happy heterosexuality should not be underestimated. Some of the girls in his class were able to articulate opinions about homophobia and heterosexism, even if they could not name them as such, and even for the boys he offered alternative ways of being masculine, thereby disrupting the heterosexual matrix which insists on fixed notions of gender. Coming out to the class, in a context in which the very term "family" was under consideration, constituted a radical challenge to these children, one which some of the boys initially responded to by making homophobic comments. Even Elias and Levi, however, were later (and, significantly, in private to me) moved to insist that they thought there was nothing wrong with being gay. In a way, it did not matter whether this was simply a version of trying to please the teacher, for as the boys took up an antihomophobic stance, they momentarily inhabited this alternative worldview and thus created, for themselves, the possibility of inhabiting it again in the future.

Notes

1. This project was a pilot for the Economic and Social Research Council–funded project (R000 23 7438) on "Children's 'Relationship Cultures' in Years 5 and 6," which began on 1 January 1998 and lasted for two years.

2. All names have been altered to retain anonymity for the school. Participants in the study were asked to choose their own pseudonyms. In some cases, children chose names that do not reflect their ethnicity.

3. This was characteristic of the school culture at Edendale. I had spent three full days in the school before I heard any adult (including lunch supervisors) raise their voice to a child. Those who are familiar with schools will recognize such an atmosphere as unusual.

4. The end of the 1996–97 school year saw an unparalleled level of resignations from school teaching in the United Kingdom. This appears to have been, in part, the culmination of years of what Jane Kenway, writing in an Australian context, labeled "discourses of derision" (see also Ball), combined with ever-increasing pseudo-accountability through paperwork and punitive inspection by the Office for Standards in Education (OFSTED). It was also due to alterations in superannuation rules introduced by the previous Conservative government, which made July 1997 the last opportunity for teachers to take early retirement with enhanced pensions. Edendale School was one among many that were hard hit by this: the head and four other teachers (including Mr. Stuart) left. For a small junior school (with two classes in each year group from Year three through Year six), this constituted almost half the staff.

5. See my essay "Keeping Them in Their Place" for a discussion of the reasons for moving from use of the term "sexual harassment" to using the term "hetero/sexist harassment," and see "Cultures of Schooling/ Cultures of Sexuality" for a discussion of harassment at Edendale School.

Works Cited

Ball, Stephen J. *Politics and Policy Making in Education: Explorations in Policy Sociology.* London: Routledge, 1990.

Benjamin, Shereen. "Fantasy Football League: Boys in a Special (SEN) School Constructing and Re-Constructing Masculinities." MA thesis. University of London Institute of Education, 1997.

Butler, Judith. *Bodies That Matter: On the Discursive Limits of "Sex."* New York: Routledge, 1993.

———. *Gender Trouble: Feminism and the Subversion of Identity.* New York: Routledge, 1990.

Connell, Robert W. *Masculinities.* Cambridge: Polity, 1995.

Davies, Bronwyn. *Frogs and Snails and Feminist Tales.* St. Leonards, NSW: Allen, 1989.

Development Education Centre. *What Is a Family? Photographs and Activities.* Birmingham, Eng.: Development Education Centre, 1990.

Elwin, Rosamund, and Michele Paulse. *Asha's Mums.* Illus. Dawn Lee. Toronto: Women's, 1990.

Epstein, Debbie. "Cultures of Schooling/Cultures of Sexuality." *International Journal of Inclusive Education* 1.1 (1997): 37–53.

————. "Keeping Them in Their Place: Hetero/Sexist Harassment, Gender and the Enforcement of Heterosexuality." *Sexualising the Social*. Ed. Lisa Adkins and Janet Holland. Basingstoke, Eng.: Macmillan, 1996.

————. "Too Small to Notice? Constructions of Childhood and Discourses of 'Race' in Predominantly White Contexts." *Curriculum Studies* 1 (1993): 317–34.

Foucault, Michel. *Discipline and Punish: The Birth of the Prison*. Trans. Alan Sheridan. Harmondsworth, Eng.: Penguin, 1977.

Halpin, Tony. "5-Year-Olds to Get Gay Lessons." *Daily Mail* 2 Mar. 1996: 1, 4.

Kaplan, E. Ann. *Motherhood and Representation : The Mother in Popular Culture and Melodrama*. London: Routledge, 1992.

Kenway, Jane. "Left Right Out: Australian Education and the Politics of Signification." *Journal of Education Policy* 2.3 (1987): 189–203.

Kitzinger, Jenny. "Defending Innocence: Ideologies of Childhood." *Family Secrets, Child Sexual Abuse*. Spec. issue of *Feminist Review* 28 (1988): 77–87.

————. "'Who Are You Kidding?' Children, Power and Sexual Assault." *Constructing and Reconstructing Childhood*. Ed. Alison James and Alan Prout. London: Falmer, 1990.

Lees, Sue. *Sugar and Spice: Sexuality and Adolescent Girls*. London: Penguin, 1993.

Opie, Iona, and Peter Opie. *Children's Games in Street and Playground: Chasing, Catching, Seeking, Hunting, Racing, Duelling, Exerting, Daring, Guessing, Acting, Pretending*. Oxford: Clarendon, 1969.

Redman, Peter, and Maírtín Mac an Ghaill. "Educating Peter: The Making of a History Man." *Border Patrols: Policing the Boundaries of Heterosexuality*. Ed. Deborah Lynn Steinberg, Debbie Epstein, and Richard Johnson. London: Cassell, 1997. 162–82.

Sedgwick, Eve Kosofsky. *Epistemology of the Closet*. Berkeley: U of California P, 1990.

Thorne, Barrie. *Gender Play: Boys and Girls in School*. Buckingham, Eng.: Open University P, 1993.

VanEvery, Jo. "Heterosexuality and Domestic Life." *Theorising Heterosexuality*. Ed. Diane Richardson. Buckingham, Eng.: Open University P, 1996.

CHAPTER THIRTEEN

Fault Lines in the Contact Zone: Assessing Homophobic Student Writing

RICHARD E. MILLER

Rutgers University

W hat is the place of unsolicited oppositional discourse, parody, resistance, critique in the imagined classroom community?" Mary Louise Pratt asks in "Arts of the Contact Zone" (39). In Pratt's essay, this question is occasioned by the fact that her son, Manuel, received "the usual star" from his teacher for writing a paragraph promoting a vaccine that would make school attendance unnecessary. Manuel's teacher, ignoring the critique of schooling leveled in the paragraph, registered only that the required work of responding to the assignment's questions about a helpful invention had been completed and, consequently, appended the silent, enigmatic star. For Pratt, the teacher's star labors to conceal a conflict in the classroom over what work is to be valued and why, presenting instead the image that everything is under control—students are writing and the teacher is evaluating. It is this other strategy for handling difficult material—namely, ignoring the content and focusing only on the outward forms of obedient behavior—that leads Pratt to wonder about the place

I want to thank Scott Lankford for making this student essay available for discussion, Jean Ferguson Carr for providing me with materials related to this panel, and Mariolina Salvatori for introducing me to the idea of the "position paper" that appears here, in modified form, in my discussion of my students' responses to Gloria Anzaldúa's essay. An earlier, unabridged version of "Fault Lines in the Contact Zone" appeared in *College English* 56 (1994): 389–408. See permissions page.

of unsolicited oppositional discourse in the classroom. With regard to Manuel's real classroom community, the answer to this question is clear: the place of unsolicited oppositional discourse is no place at all.

Given Pratt's promising suggestion that the classroom be reconceived as a "contact zone," which she defines as a social space "where cultures meet, clash, and grapple with each other, often in contexts of highly asymmetrical relations of power" (34), this example of the kind of writing produced in such a contact zone seems oddly benign. One might expect that the writing Pratt's students did in Stanford University's Culture, Ideas, Values course, which she goes on to discuss, would provide ample evidence of more highly charged conflicts involving "unsolicited oppositional discourse, parody, resistance, critique." Unfortunately, however, although Pratt avows that this course "put ideas and identities on the line" (39), she offers no example of how her students negotiated this struggle in their writing or of how their teachers participated in and responded to their struggles on and over "the line." Instead, Pratt leaves us with just two images of writers in the contact zone—her son, Manuel, and Guaman Poma, author of a largely unread sixteenth-century bilingual chronicle of Andean culture. Both, to be sure, are readily sympathetic figures, obviously deserving better readers and more thoughtful respondents, but what about those who parody or critique the notion that we ought to value individual and cultural differences? And what exactly are we to say or do when the kind of racist, sexist, and homophobic sentiments now signified by the term "hate speech" surface in our classrooms? What "Arts of the Contact Zone" are going to help us learn how to read and respond to voices such as these?

By attending to a student essay that is much less likely to arouse our sympathies than Manuel's inventive critique, my concern in what follows is to examine the heuristic value of the notion of the contact zone when applied not only to student writing, but also to our own academic discussions of that writing. The student essay I begin with was so offensive that when it was first mentioned at an MLA workshop on "Composition, Multiculturalism, and Political Correctness" in December 1991, provisions were quickly made to devote an entire panel to the essay at the Conference on College Composition and Communication (hereafter 4C's) in 1992, and this in turn led to a follow-up workshop on "The Politics of Response" at 4C's in 1993. Thus I would hazard to guess that this student essay, titled "Queers, Bums, and Magic," has seized the attention of more teachers, taken up more institutional time, and provoked more debate than any other single piece of unpublished undergraduate writing in recent memory. Before beginning my discussion of "Queers, Bums, and Magic," I should note, however, that in the ensuing discussion I have intentionally allowed the content of the student's essay and the wider sweep of its context to emerge in fragments, as they did in the contact zone of the national conferences, where competing modes of response served alternately to reveal and obscure both the text and information about its writer. This partial, hesitant, contradictory motion defines how business gets transacted in the contact zones of our classrooms and our conferences, where important questions often do not get heard, are ignored, or simply do not get posed in the heat of the moment, with the result that vital contextual information often is either never disclosed or comes to light very late in the discussion. I believe that following this motion provides a stark portrait of the ways in which dominant assumptions about students and student writing allow unsolicited oppositional discourse to pass through the classroom unread and unaffected.

The essay I will discuss, "Queers, Bums, and Magic," was written in a pre-college-level community college composition class taught by Scott Lankford at Foothill College in Los Altos Hills, California, in response to an assignment taken from *The Bedford Guide for College Writers* that asked students to write a report on group behavior. One of Lankford's students responded with an essay detailing a drunken trip he and some friends made to "San Fagcisco" to study "the lowest class . . . the queers and the bums." The essay recounts how the students stopped a man on Polk Street, informed him that they were doing a survey and needed to know if he was "a fag." From here, the narrative follows the students into a dark alleyway where they discover, as they relieve themselves drunkenly against the wall, that they have been urinating on a homeless person. In a frenzy, the students begin to kick the homeless person, stopping after "30 seconds of non-stop blows to the body," at which point the writer says he "thought the guy was dead." Terrified, the students make a run for their car and eventually escape the city.

It is a haunting piece, one that gave Lankford many sleepless nights and one that has traveled from conference to conference because it is so unsettling. When Lankford discussed it at 4C's in his paper titled "How Would You Grade a Gay-Bashing?" the engaged, provocative, and at times heated hour-long discussion that followed provided a forum for a range of competing commitments to, as Pratt might say, "meet, clash, and grapple" with one another. What was clear from this interchange was that part of what makes "Queers, Bums, and Magic" so powerful is that it disables the most familiar kinds of conference presentations and teacher responses. Here is writing that cannot easily be recuperated as somehow praiseworthy despite its numerous surface flaws, writing that instead offers direct access to a voice from the margins that seems to belong there. The reactions given to Lankford's request to know how those present "would have handled such a situation" (5) varied considerably, both in intensity and in detail, but most of them, I would say, fell into one of three categories: read the essay as factual and respond accordingly; read the essay as fictional and respond accordingly; momentarily suspend the question of the essay's factual or fictional status and respond accordingly.

In the first category, by far the most popular, I place all suggestions that the student be removed from the classroom and turned over either to a professional counselor or to the police. Such a response, audience members argued repeatedly, would be automatic if the student had described suicidal tendencies, involvement in a rape, or having been the victim of incest. To substantiate this point, one member of the audience spoke passionately about Marc LeClerc, saying that the Canadian gunman had revealed his hatred of women to many of his college professors prior to his murderous rampage. As compelling as such examples were at the time, it is important to realize that this line of argument assumes that the described events really occurred and, therefore, that the essay contains evidence either of a serious crime or of a vivid and potentially dangerous fantasy life. This assessment of the student essay is striking because the audience members had little to go on beyond the kind of brief outline that has been provided here. In other words, although no one in the audience had actually read the student essay, many felt quite confident recommending that, based on brief excerpts and a summary of the essay's content alone, the student ought to be turned over either to the legal or psychological authorities! These respondents, starting with the assumption of a stable and unified subjectivity for Lankford's student, went on to construct a student writer incapable of dissimulation. Within such a paradigm, the actual text the student produced was of secondary importance at best in relation to a hasty and, as we will see, partial summary of the student text's contents.

Lankford chose another route entirely, electing "to respond to the essay exactly as if it were a fictional short story" (4). What this meant in practice was that he restricted himself to commenting on the student's word choice, querying the student about his imagined audience, acknowledging the text's "reasonable detail," and "favorably comparing the essay to A Clockwork Orange in its straightforward depictions of nightmarish 'megaviolence' and surrealistic detail" (4). According to these criteria, Lankford determined the essay merited a low B. Although this strategy provoked the wrath of a large portion of the audience, Lankford argued that it was not without its virtues: by focusing only on the formal features of the essay and its surface errors, Lankford was able to successfully deflect the student writer's use of his writing to "bash" his professor, with the unexpected result that the student not only stayed in the course, but actually chose to study with Lankford again the next semester. Thus, despite Lankford's own assessment of his approach as "spineless," he was in a position to insist that it was nevertheless a "qualified success," since the student in question "learned to cope with an openly gay instructor with some measure of civility" (5).

Among those present who had access to the student's paper, there were those on the panel who agreed with Lankford's approach but disagreed with the grade assigned. These respondents spoke of the essay's faulty organization, the problems evident in its plot development, the number of mechanical errors. On these grounds alone, one panelist assured the audience, the paper ought to have received a failing mark. If the first category of response displays a curious willingness to dispense with the formality of reading the student's essay, Lankford's strategy asks teachers to look away from what the student's writing is attempting to do—at the havoc it is trying to wreak in the contact zone—and restrict their comments to the essay's surface features and formal qualities, affixing the "usual star" or black mark as the situation warrants. Such a strategy itself invites parody: would changing the word choice/spelling errors/verb agreement problems/organization/etc. really "improve" this student's essay? Would such changes help inch it toward being, say, an excellent gay-bashing essay, one worthy of an A?

I intend this question to verge on being offensive. The problem, however, is not that this approach is "spineless." To the contrary, in Lankford's hands this kind of response made it possible for both the teacher and the student to remain in the contact zone of his classroom, allowing them to negotiate the difficult business of working with and through important issues of cultural and sexual difference. By suggesting that his difficulty in responding to the student essay is a personal problem, that it revolves around a question of "spine," Lankford obscures the ways in which the difficulty that confronted him as he struggled to find a way to respond to "Queers, Bums, and Magic" is the trace of a broader institutional conflict over what it means for a teacher to work with student writing. Lankford and the others who spoke of responding to the essay as "a piece of fiction" did not suddenly invent this curiously decontextualized way of responding to writing that can imagine no other approach to discussing a piece of writing than to speak of how it is organized, the aptness of the writer's word choice, and the fit between the text and its audience. Such an approach to writing instruction has been proffered in the majority of grammars, rhetorics, and readers that have filled English classrooms since before the turn of the century: it has been around for so long that, despite the grand "turn to process" in writing instruction, it continues to suggest itself as the most "natural" or "reasonable" way to define the work of responding to student writing. All of which leaves us with this profoundly strange state of affairs in which a discipline explicitly devoted to studying and articulating the power of the written word gets thrown into crisis when a student produces a powerful piece of writing.

To sum up, then, these two lines of response to the student essay—the one recommending the removal of the offending writer from circulation, and the other overlooking the offensive aspects of the student text in order to attend to its surface and structural features—taken together dramatize how little professional training in English studies prepares teachers to read and respond to the kinds of parodic, critical, oppositional, dismissive, resistant, transgressive, and regressive writing that gets produced by students writing in the contact zone of the classroom. This absence of training, I would argue, actually comes into play every time a teacher sits down to comment on a student paper: it's just that the pedagogical shortcomings of restricting such commentary to the surface features and formal aspects of the writing are not as readily visible in a response to an essay on a summer vacation as they are in a response to an essay about beating up the homeless and bashing gays. Unfortunately, recent efforts to reimagine the work of responding to student writing provide little guidance for addressing this particular problem. Edward White's *Teaching and Assessing Writing,* for instance, argues for holistic scoring but offers no suggestions on how to go about holistically scoring essays that are racist, homophobic, misogynistic, and so forth. And, similarly, Anson's *Writing and Response: Theory, Practice, and Research,* which asserts that "real, substantive response is in one form or another fundamental to language development" (4), never gets around to the business of discussing how to produce a "real, substantive response" to the kind of unsolicited oppositional discourse discussed here. Since this is uncharted territory, it is not surprising that we often find ourselves at a loss, not knowing what to do, where to go, what to say.

And yet, granting this, one has to wonder why it is that, at a time when almost all of the current major theories on the rise celebrate partial readings, multiple subjectivities, marginalized positions, and subjugated knowledges, nearly all student essays remain essentially illegible, offered forth more often than not as the space in which error exercises its full reign, or, as here, the site where some untutored evil shows its face. There seems, in other words, to be little evidence of what one might call "poststructural" or "postcolonial" trickle down, little sign that the theoretical insights that carry so much weight in our journals actually make themselves known in the pedagogical practices deployed in classrooms across the country. There were, however, a few respondents to Lankford's presentation who saw a way to smuggle some of these insights into the classroom and thereby propose more fruitful responses than either expelling the student or ignoring the content of his essay. In proposing that "Queers, Bums, and Magic" be reproduced alongside legal definitions of hate speech for the entire class to read and discuss, one panelist found a way to pull the paper out of the private corridor running between the student writer and the teacher and move it into the public arena. This approach turns the essay into a "teachable object," enabling an investigation of the writing's performative aspect—how it does its work, what its imagined project might have been, and who or what might be the possible subjects of its critique. By situating the essay in relation to legal definitions of hate speech, this approach also puts the class in a position to consider both how words can work in the world and how and why that work has been regulated.

The prospect of having such a discussion would no doubt frighten some, since it would promise to be an explosive, tense, disturbing interchange. Some students would undoubtedly agree with the treatment meted out to the disenfranchised; others might speak of it as being funny; others might point to the references to "Elm Street," "nightmares," and "magic" in the essay to argue that it was a piece of fiction; and still others might be horrified by the essay and express their feelings to the class. Such a discussion would, in other words, place one squarely in the act of teaching in the contact zone where, as Pratt says, "No one [is] excluded, and no one [is] safe" (39). The point of having such discussions, however, is neither to establish a community where a simple pluralism rules and hate speech is just one of its many voices, nor is it to create an environment that is relentlessly threatening, where not feeling safe comes to mean the same thing as feeling terrified. Pratt, in fact, is careful to maintain the importance of establishing "safe houses" in the curriculum, courses in which a different kind of talk is supported and sustained. But for those courses that take as their subject how language works in the world, the central concern should be to provide students with moments taken from their own writing as well as from the writing collected in published texts where the written word is powerful. In such class-rooms, "teaching the conflicts" is not simply an empty slogan plastered over a practice that means "business as usual," but an actual set of practices whereby the conflicts that capture and con-struct both the students and their teachers become the proper subject of study for the course.

This third category of response argues for the necessity of seeing the way we structure our courses and the kinds of texts we read with our students as potential resources for commenting on the writing our students produce. Thinking along these lines, another member of the audience suggested responding to this essay with a revisionary assignment that required the student to rewrite the story from the perspective of either the gay man whom the students had harassed on Polk Street or the homeless person whom the students had beaten in the alleyway. This strategy of having the student do more writing about this event seems par-ticularly appropriate in a discipline that believes in the heuristic power of the composing process, and the further requirement to have the student shift perspective provides a meaningful avenue for re-seeing the described events. As useful as I believe it is to see the assignment of revision as a way of responding to student writing, though, I think the response called for in this instance is so obvious that it is most likely to solicit a seamless parody, one of those acts of hyperconformity regularly produced by those writing in the contact zone. In other words, while producing a writing situation in which the student is advised to mime the teacher's desired position would probably succeed in sweeping the most visible manifestations of the student's hateful thoughts and actions out of the classroom, it would not, I think, actually address the roots of that hatred. That hatred would simply curl up and go underground for the duration of the course.

At this point, it may seem that in assessing the range of reac-tions to "Queers, Bums, and Magic" I am holding out for some magical form of response that would not only make this student stop writing such things, but would actually put an end to his thinking them as well. My central concern, however, is not with this particular student essay or with what the student writer as an individual thinks, but with what this student essay and the professional activity that surrounds it can tell us about the cultural, political, and pedagogical complexities of composition instruction. With this distinction in mind, I would go so far as to argue that adopting any classroom strategy that isolates this essay and treats it as an anomaly misreads both the essay's cultural significance and its pedagogical possibilities. As the debate over military service's "don't ask, don't tell" policy made abundantly clear, Lankford's student has not expressed a unique and private hatred of gays, nor, to be sure, has he voiced a peculiar antipathy for the homeless. Rather, the homophobia this student articulates and the violence he describes as perpetrating against the disenfranchised are cultural commonplaces, drawn from the national symbolic imaginary. For these reasons, it seems much more important to me to produce a classroom in which part of the work involves articulating, investigating, and questioning the affiliated cultural forces that underwrite the ways of thinking that find expression in this student's essay—a classroom, in short, that studies the forces that make such thoughts not only permissible but prevalent.

From this perspective, one could say that the only truly surprising thing about "Queers, Bums, and Magic" is that it voices this particular set of cultural commonplaces in the classroom, since most students practiced in the conventions of reading teacher expectations know not to commit themselves to positions their teachers clearly oppose. In this regard, the following facts are not insignificant: the student writer grew up in Kuwait; English is his second language; he was writing during the onset of the Persian Gulf War. An outsider himself, Lankford's student almost certainly did not understand what was intended by the examples that accompanied the assignment in the *Bedford Guide* to: "Station yourself in a nearby place where you can mingle with a group of people gathered for some reason or occasion. Observe the group's behavior and in a short paper report on it. Then offer some insight" (Kennedy and Kennedy 41). Following these instructions, the student is informed that one writer "did an outstanding job of observing a group of people nervously awaiting a road test for their driver's licenses"; another observed a bar mitzvah; another an emergency room; and another a group of people looking at a luna moth on a telephone pole "including a man who viewed it with alarm, a wondering toddler, and an amateur entomologist" (42). Unschooled in the arts of reading the textbook, this student failed to pick up on the implicit directions: when you write this essay, report only on the behavior of a group that is of no particular interest or importance to you. Had the student been able to read the cues in the suggested examples, he might well have selected a less explosive topic and thereby kept his most familiar ways of knowing the world out of view.

If the assignment's examples direct students to topics guaranteed not to provoke offense, the assignment, by refraining from using any kind of critical terminology, encourages students not to wander beyond the business of reporting their immediate experiences. In lieu of inviting students to work with any of the central terms taken from anthropology, sociology, or cultural studies, say, the assignment merely informs the students that, after observing the behavior of their selected group, they are "to form some general impression of the group or come to some realization about it" (Kennedy and Kennedy 42). They can expect, the assignment concludes, that it will take at least two written pages "to cover" their subject. Grasping the import of these directives, Lankford's student did even more than was required, performing the kind of hyperconformity I suggested earlier characterizes one of the arts of the contact zone: he wrote, as required, for his "fellow students" (41); he handed in not two but four typed pages; and he made sure his essay concluded with "some realization." His final paragraph reads as follows:

> Although this night was supposed to be an observation on the people of the streets, it turned out that we were walking on "Elm Street," and it was a "nightmare." I will always remember one thing, next time I see bums and fags walking on the streets, I will never make fun of them or piss on them, or anything like that, because they did not want to be bums or fags. It was society that forced them out of their jobs and they could not beat the system. Now when I think about that bum we beat up I can't understand how he managed to follow us the whole time, after being kicked and being down for so long. I think it was one of two things; he is either psychic or it was just plain magic.

In miming the requisite better understanding that is supposed to come from studying groups, the student's essay concludes by disrupting all that has come before: did the beating actually take place or has the writer simply fabricated it, recasting the assignment within the readily available narrative frame of the film *Nightmare on Elm Street*? Is the student having one over on the system, manufacturing both the material for his response and his consequent realization, and thus, in one fell swoop, parodying, resisting, and critiquing the values that hold the classroom community together? Or—and this is obviously the more frightening possibility—is his conclusion some kind of penitential confession for events that really did happen?

These questions, slightly rephrased, are of central importance to any writing classroom: How does a writer establish authority? How does one distinguish between fact and fiction in a written document? What does it mean to read and to write dialogically? And yet it is important to realize that, had the assignment worked as it was supposed to, these questions would never have surfaced with the urgency they have here. That is, had Lankford's student been a better reader of classroom norms and textbook procedures, he might well have written about beekeepers or people at hair salons and left the surface calm of the educational community undisturbed. If we step back from "Queers, Bums, and Magic" for a moment and consider the fact that the mixture of anger, rage, ignorance, and confusion that produced this student essay are present in varying degrees on college and secondary school campuses across the country, what is truly significant about this event is not that it occurred, but that it occurs so rarely. This, surely, is a testament to the immense pressures exerted by the classroom environment, the presentation of the assigned readings, the directions included in the writing assignments, and the range of teaching practices which work together to ensure that conflicts about or contact between fundamental beliefs and prejudices do not arise. The classroom does not, in other words, automatically function as a contact zone in the positive ways Pratt discovered in the Stanford course, where, she asserts: "Along with rage, incomprehension, and pain there were exhilarating moments of wonder and revelation, mutual understanding, and new wisdom—the joys of the contact zone" (39). As the conclusion of

Pratt's article makes clear, and the foregoing discussion of "Queers, Bums, and Magic" vividly illustrates, there is still a great deal of work to be done in constructing the "pedagogical arts of the contact zone." Thus, having acknowledged that, from this distance, we will never be able to resolve the question of whether or not "Queers, Bums, and Magic" is a factual or fictional account, I would like to turn now to my own efforts to create a place where more contact between the competing interpretive systems of the classroom and the worlds outside the classroom occurs and is made available for discussion.

There is a paradox, of course, in trying to establish a classroom that solicits "unsolicited oppositional discourse." There is also an attendant danger of a kind of "intellectual slumming," whereby investigating the disjunction between the ways of knowing fostered inside and outside the classroom might result in students deeming the former kind of knowledge "artificial" and the latter "authentic." Rather than perish in the abyss created by this killer dichotomy or put myself in the pedagogically questionable position of inviting my students to vent on the page so that we can discuss their feelings afterward, I have tried to develop a pedagogical practice that allows the classroom to function as a contact zone, where the central activity is investigating the range of literate practices available to those within asymmetrical power relationships. My primary concern as a composition instructor, in other words, is with the kinds of issues raised in Pratt's article and Lankford's student's essay insofar as they shape the ways of reading and writing that occur inside and outside the classroom. And, given the heightened racial tensions following the O. J. Simpson verdicts, the ongoing fear and ignorance about AIDS and the means of its transmission, the backlash against feminism, and a climate of diminished expectations and violence, it should come as no surprise that students bring to our classrooms the ill-formed, irrational, and even dangerous ideas fostered by the surrounding environment. The challenge, for teachers who are interested in teaching rather than indoctrinating their students, is to learn how to respond when such potentially threatening material makes its way into the classroom.

I would like to turn to one such instance, drawn from my own classroom, that emerged when my students set out to respond to Gloria Anzaldúa's "Entering the Serpent." Now, for many of the students in my class, the introduction of this text was itself perceived as a threatening act: in "Entering the Serpent," excerpted from Anzaldúa's *Borderlands/La Frontera,* Anzaldúa shifts back and forth between Anglo-American English, Castilian Spanish, Tex-Mex, Northern Mexican dialect, and Nahualt, writing in a mélange of languages to express the diversity of her heritage and her own unique position as lesbian, feminist, Chicana poet, and critic. While Anzaldúa's multilingual text places special—and many of the students argued, unfair—linguistic demands on its readers, it also makes relatively unique generic demands, moving between poetry and prose, personal narrative and revisionist history. Thus Anzaldúa occupies a range of positions, some of them contradictory, as she relates her efforts to reclaim the Aztec goddess Coatlicue, the "serpent goddess," split from the goddess Cihuacoatl by the "male dominated Azteca-Mexica culture" in order to drive "the powerful female deities underground" (26–27). After the Spanish Conquest, Cihuacoatl was further domesticated by the Christian Church and transformed by stages into the figure now known as the Virgin of Guadalupe. While Anzaldúa admires La Virgen de Guadalupe as "the symbol of ethnic identity and of the tolerance for ambiguity that Chicanos-*mexicanos,* people of mixed race, people who have Indian blood, people who cross cultures, by necessity possess" (29), she nevertheless insists on the importance of regaining access to Coatlicue, "the symbol of the dark sexual drive, the chthonic (underworld), the feminine, the serpentine movement of sexuality, of creativity, the basis of all energy and life" (33). Recovering this contact with the supernatural provides one with "*la facultad . . .* the capacity to see in surface phenomena the meaning of deeper realities, to see the deep structure below the surface" (36). Anzaldúa concludes this section by asserting that "[t]hose who are pounced on the most have [*la facultad*] the strongest—the females, the homosexuals of all races, the darkskinned, the outcast, the persecuted, the marginalized, the foreign" (36).

Here's how one of my students described his experience reading "Entering the Serpent":

> Even though I had barely read half of the first page, I was already disgusted. I found myself reading onward only to stop and ask "What is she trying to prove?" Scanning the words and skipping over the ones that were not english, I went from an egocentric personal story to a femo-nazi account of central american mythology that was occasionally interrupted by more poems. . . .
>
> From what I gather, she is trying to exorcise some personal demons. Her feelings of inadequacy and insecurity drove her to project her own problems not only onto the world, but into history and mythology. I'm surprised she didn't call history "herstory." It seems that she had no sense of self or worth. To overcome this, she fabricated a world, a past, and a scapegoat in her own image. Although her accusations do hold some truth, her incredible distortion of the world would lead me to believe that she has lost touch with reality and is obsessively driven by her social psychosis. She views herself as a gallant and brilliant member of a great culture that has been oppressed by the world. Her continuous references to females, sex, and the phallic symbols of snakes is most likely brought out by the lack of a man in her life. Rather than admit her faults, she cherishes them and calls them friends.

This was not an uncommon response to my assignment that began by asking the students to discuss the difficulties they encountered reading Anzaldúa's essay. This student, having made his way past the language barrier of the text, confronts the description of a world and a way of being in that world that he finds personally repugnant. Beginning with a variant of the Rush Limbaughism, "femo-nazi," the student then proceeds to document the many ways that "Entering the Serpent" offended him: it contains Anzaldúa's effort to "exorcise some personal demons"; it includes "her incredible distortion of the world"; the writer claims to be "a gallant and brilliant member of a great culture" of which the student is not a part. Given this reading, it is not too surprising that the student concludes that all the faults in the text are produced by "the lack of a man in [Anzaldúa's] life."

Taking offense with this response to Anzaldúa's essay strikes me as being exactly the wrong tactic here. It is of paramount importance, I believe, to begin where students are, rather than where one thinks they should or ought to be, and this student, by my reading, is trapped between the desire to produce a stereotypical critique of any feminist text ("I'm surprised she didn't call history 'herstory'") and the necessity of responding to this particular feminist text. He negotiates the tension between this desire and this necessity by producing a fairly detailed outline of Anzaldúa's essay and, simultaneously, mocking its argument ("Rather than admit her faults, she cherishes them and calls them friends."). However rudimentary or sophisticated one deems this kind of multivocalic writing to be, it is, as I have said, only a starting point for beginning more detailed work with Anzaldúa's text. For this reason, the assignment that elicited this response does not simply ask the students to revel in the difficulties they experienced reading Anzaldúa's essay; it also requests that they outline "a plan of action for addressing the difficulties [they] encountered." The goal, thus, is not to invite students simply to record their various levels of rage, incomprehension, and despair with an admittedly difficult text, but rather to have them reflect on how they might adjust their own ways of reading to meet the text halfway.

The results of having the students read their own readings and chart alternative ways of returning to the text can be startling indeed. Although this writer began by accusing Anzaldúa of being a "femo-nazi," he concluded by reflecting on what he had done with her text in the following way:

> If not for searching for her hidden motives and then using them to criticize/bash Anzaldúa and her story, I would not have been able to read the story in its entirety. Although my view is a bit harsh, it has been a way that allows me to counter Anzaldúa's extremities. In turn, I can now see her strategy of language and culture choice and placement to reveal the contact zone in her own life. All of my obstacles previously mentioned, (not liking the stories, poems, or their content) were overcome by "bashing" them. Unfortunately, doing that in addition to Anzaldúa's ridiculous disproportionism and over-intense, distorted beliefs created a mountain which was impossible for me to climb. This in effect made it impossible to have taken any part of her work seriously or to heart. I feel I need to set aside my personal values, outlook and social position in order to escape the bars of being offended and discouraged. Not only must I lessen my own barriers of understanding, but I must be able to comprehend and understand the argument of the other. It is these dif-

ferences between people and groups of people that lead to the
conflicts and struggles portrayed and created by this selection.

This strikes me as being an extraordinarily astute assessment of
the strengths and weaknesses of this writer's initial reading strategy: "bashing" Anzaldúa enabled a certain kind of work to be
accomplished (the reading was completed, the writing assignment
could be fulfilled), but it also prevented the writer from taking
"any part of her work seriously or to heart." Thus, by "bashing"
Anzaldúa, the student inadvertently ended up showing himself
that her description of her trying experiences within the straight
white world was, at least partly, accurate. The writer's proposed
solution to this problem—setting aside his "personal values, outlook and social position"—attests to the magnitude of the challenge Anzaldúa's position holds for him. Whether this proposed
solution proves, in practice, to be a workable plan can only be
known when the writer returns to Anzaldúa's essay to begin his
revision. What is important to notice here, however, is that the
writer's plan does make returning to her text an imaginable activity with an unforeseeable outcome. Given the way this student's
essay began, this is no small accomplishment.

Required self-reflexivity does not, of course, guarantee that
repugnant positions will be abandoned. At best, it ensures only
that the students' attention will be focused on the interconnec-
tions between the ways they read and the ways they write. This
can be a salutary experience, as in the previous example, where it
provided the student with an avenue for renegotiating a relationship with a difficult text and the wide range of concerns affiliated with that text, but it does not mean that this approach wields
sufficient power to transform the matrix of beliefs, values, and
prejudices that students (and teachers alike) bring to the classroom. This kind of wholesale transformation (or, to be more pre-
cise, the *appearance* of this kind of wholesale transformation) is
only possible in classrooms where the highly asymmetrical relations of power are fully reinstated and students are told either
implicitly or explicitly (as I was during a course in graduate
school), "No language that is racist, sexist, homophobic, or that
degrades the working class will be allowed in our discussions."

Reimagining the classroom as a contact zone is a potentially powerful pedagogical intervention only so long as it involves resisting the temptation either to silence or to celebrate the voices that seek to oppose, critique, and/or parody the work of constructing knowledge in the classroom. Scott Lankford achieved the kind of partial, imperfect, negotiated microvictory available to those who work in the contact zone when he found a way to respond to his student's essay that not only kept the student in his course, but eventually led to the student signing up to work with him in another course as well. By having my students interrogate literate practices inside and outside the classroom, by having them work with challenging essays that speak about issues of difference from a range of perspectives, and by having them pursue this work in the ways I have outlined here, I have been trying to create a course that allows the students to use their writing to investigate the cultural conflicts that serve to define and limit their lived experience.

In the uncharted realms of teaching and studying in the contact zone, the teacher's traditional claim to authority is thus constantly undermined and reconfigured, which, in turn, enables the real work of learning how to negotiate and to place oneself in dialogue with different ways of knowing to commence. This can be strangely disorienting work, requiring as it does the recognition that in many places what passes for reason is not something separate from rhetoric, but rather one of many rhetorical devices. This in turn quickly leads to the corollary concession that, in certain situations, reason exercises little or no persuasive force when vying against the combined powers of rage, fear, and prejudice, which together forge innumerable hateful ways of knowing the world that have their own internalized systems, self-sustaining logics, and justifications. For teachers who believe in education as a force for positive social change, the appropriate response to these new working conditions is not to exile students to the penitentiaries or the psychiatric wards for writing offensive, antisocial papers. Nor is it to give free rein to one's self-righteous indignation and call the resultant interchange a "political intervention." The most promising pedagogical response lies, rather, in closely attending to what our students say and write in an ongoing effort to learn how to read, understand, and respond to the strange, sometimes threatening, multivocal texts they produce while writing in the contact zone.

Works Cited

Anson, Chris, ed. *Writing and Response: Theory, Practice, and Research.* Urbana, IL: NCTE, 1989.

Anzaldúa, Gloria. "Entering into the Serpent." *Ways of Reading.* Ed. David Bartholomae and Anthony Petrosky. Boston: Bedford, 1993. 25–38.

Kennedy, X. J., and Dorothy M. Kennedy. *The Bedford Guide for College Writers.* Boston: Bedford, 1990. 41–42.

Lankford, Scott. "'Queers, Bums, and Magic': How Would You Grade a Gay-Bashing?" Myths of Correctness: Approaches to Grammar and Politics. Conference on College Composition and Communication. Cincinnati. 19 Mar. 1992.

Pratt, Mary Louise. "Arts of the Contact Zone." *Profession 91* (MLA 1991): 33–40.

White, Edward M. *Teaching and Assessing Writing.* San Francisco: Jossey-Bass, 1985.

CHAPTER FOURTEEN

Queer Pedagogy and Social Change: Teaching and Lesbian Identity in South Africa

ANN SMITH
University of the Witwatersrand, Johannesburg

[My] deepest impulse was the desire to make learning part of the process of social change itself.
RAYMOND WILLIAMS

In 1976 the Nationalist Party government overcame its Calvinistic dread of the evils of television viewing and permitted South Africans to watch, in the late afternoon and early evening, on one channel only, a few hours of strictly censored material on the small screen. Eight years later, on the first program ever to deal with what the producers agreed to call "gay rights"—*lesbian* still being *the* unspeakable word—I appeared on prime time in a few million homes arguing with a fundamentalist minister of religion and a patronizingly condescending medical doctor (both male) against the view that homosexuality was a sin and a disease (see Charlewood). I did not get to say much about rights—the emphasis was very much on how wrong it was. I was in no way prepared for this—expecting, in my naiveté, a rational discussion, a polite interchange of views. In my muddled and inelegant anticipation of Jeffrey Weeks's excellent discussion of how homophobic models of the etiology of homosexuality, especially around pathology, have become naturalized—whereby "you can be born with [it], seduced into [it] and catch [it] all at the same time" (qtd. in Sedgwick 146)—I came across, predictably enough, as angry and frustrated. I was described, equally predictably, in the print media as having been aggressive and strident. It was a disempowering event for me, but only years later was I able to articulate why. I was ostensibly given the space in which to present a case for the recognition of "gay rights" but was simultaneously denied that space. Although the show was conceptually antihomophobic, the dominant discourse ensured that it was anything but, and the results were predictably patriarchal, (hetero)sexist, and homophobic. Caught in the crossfire between the forces of "socially responsible television" and government censorship, I was a clay pigeon (mis)represented as a token spokesperson. Coming out to the nation in the repressive and often violent mid-1980s was difficult enough without the additional complication of having a persona imposed upon me; I recall vividly the terrible frustration of being forced to play out the stereotype of the aggressive man-hating lesbian-feminist and lacking the skills to resist it.

Subsequent appearances on television were much easier to handle, but as a lesbian activist and a founding member of the first national gay association in this country—The Gay Association of South Africa (GASA)—I inevitably became more and more aware of different manifestations of oppression in the public and private arenas. While the overwhelmingly racist agenda of the apartheid regime tended to make less visible to observers, both here and abroad, the extent of its homophobia and misogyny, lesbians and gay men in South Africa contended with the oppressive effects of this on a daily basis. I seized the opportunity to use this experience of lesbian activism openly and explicitly in my teaching when, as part of our engagement with the debate on the issues of the literary canon, the Department of English at the University of the Witwatersrand in 1995 increased the number and range of options available to students studying toward the English major. Among these was the first course in the history of the university curriculum to use the dreaded "L" word unequivocally: I offered a course titled The Lesbian in Literature as a semester-long open elective.

When I planned this course, I knew that I could incorporate my own experiences as a lesbian activist during those particularly vicious years of the apartheid era and at the same time position myself relative to the emerging "New" South Africa. This was a unique historical moment: the old homophobic laws were still in place but there was reason to hope that lesbian and gay rights would be protected under the new Constitution (as they now are). I knew that trying to ensure that the discursive space I created would be free from all personal uncertainties and political ambiguities was neither possible nor pedagogically desirable. For instance, I did not need to discount the part played by my own revulsion toward the authoritarianism evident in the insistence of my TV opponents that they, in their respective religious and secular heteronormative guardianship of the morality of the South African population, were indisputably right. Neither was it necessary for me to suppress the sense of failure that afflicted me then. I could use this, along with an account of the process of later empowerment, to illustrate the pragmatic importance of lived experience and the desirability of being able to locate the personal within specific historical and political contexts. I saw that what I could do was to foreground, within a cultural studies approach, the inevitability of ambiguities and conflicts of various sorts within a pedagogical context. If I planned to use what happened in the everyday world as a way into teaching a course on literature, linking experiences of ambiguity and conflict as related to lesbian identity, lived and fictional, why not extend this explicitly to transformative pedagogical practice? In (the "New") South Africa, the constituencies which now, quite rightly of course, "demand a say in how culture will be defined" are no longer part of a "relatively homogeneous class with a relatively common background," and these newly recognized constituencies now include blacks as well as lesbians and gay men among others. Here was an arena in which to dramatize, through a "less 'canonical' faculty [member] and student body . . . [and] a less canonical curriculum[,] . . . the fact that culture itself is a debate, not a monologue" (Graff 8).

This course was scheduled for the first semester of 1995 (which runs from mid-February until the end of May). During this time, the National Coalition for Gay and Lesbian Equality was heavily involved in lobbying support for the retention of the phrase "sexual orientation" in the Equality Clause of the new Constitution. Preparation for the course coincided with my helping with the organization of a campaign of letter and postcard writing to the Constitutional Assembly. The Equality Clause read: "No person shall be unfairly discriminated against on the grounds of race, gender, sex, ethnic or social origin, colour, sexual orientation, age, disability, religion, conscience, belief, culture, language, birth or marital status." But the Constitution was not due to be signed into law until May 1996. Feelings were running high in the country over this controversial inclusion: white church groups allied themselves in principle to the African Christian Democratic Party, and opposition to the inclusion was aggressive and vociferous, but so was support for it. There were radio and television talk shows, letters to the editor, press articles, public meetings and debates, and street parties. In contrast to my experience in that TV studio, where my voice had to be defensive and aggressive in order to be heard, gay voices were now being legitimated. We won, but I did not know that as I prepared this course.

My concerns about the course and the Equality Clause were similar in some ways: both were highly contentious, and the failure of either to get beyond the lobbying and planning stage would mean a setback. If the movement in favor of the Equality Clause did not prevail, it would be a great reversal for the lesbian and gay rights movement in South Africa; if the course did not run, it would be a blow, not only to me but to the lesbian and gay community within the university. The University of the Witwatersrand, an urban campus in Johannesburg, the largest city in South Africa, had long prided itself on working toward social change and fostering anti-establishment political practices during the years of apartheid. The successful implementation of The Lesbian in Literature course would demonstrate two things: the commitment of those who were directly involved in it as an academic course, and the commitment of the university itself to progressive, material change at the levels of teaching, learning, and curriculum. A great deal of publicity surrounded the inception of the course, and it became apparent to me that its success was important beyond the English department and that more than just academic change was at stake. Here was an opportunity for the university, long celebrated for its stand against racism, to indicate its opposition to forms of oppression which were becoming less "invisible" in the light of the emergent political change based on democratic accountability and the growing awareness that if one form of oppression is legitimated, all other forms are, by implication, made permissible. Through this course, the heady combination of the aims of political advocacy and transformative pedagogy could result in real social change, in however small a way.

Allied to the issue of social change was that of academic change: I had to remain aware of and combat the tendency in conservative academic circles to view lesbian and gay studies, along with women's studies, as suspect and unscholarly. As Tamsin Wilton, with wry humor, accurately observes: "Homophobia is the most respectable of prejudices, and it remains a majority viewpoint that a set of execrated, criminalised sexual practices is an inadequate foundation for an academic discipline" (11).

It seemed clear to me that in the context of what we were emerging from in South Africa, and the unfolding democratic process, a course in lesbian studies *must* concern itself with "the most respectable of prejudices." Far from being "an inadequate foundation for an academic discipline," it provided the perfect opportunity to begin to enact the proposition that educators can "transform how educational institutions, teachers and students define themselves as political subjects capable of exhibiting critical sensibilities, civic courage, and forms of solidarity rooted in a strong commitment to freedom and democracy" (Giroux 201).

In planning the course, I wanted to consider how I could put into practice a pedagogy in which the emphasis would not be on "the transmission of a particular skill, body of knowledge, or set of values" but would be " a cultural practice engaged in the production of knowledge, identities and desires" (Giroux 202). In addition, I needed to articulate some points in relation to the presentation of myself in this course that I thought needed careful consideration. It seemed to me that being unreservedly "out" as a lesbian and fairly well known locally as a lesbian activist might need to be negotiated in relation to the group as a whole. I know what being a lesbian is *for me,* but I do not have lived knowledge of what it means for any other woman. Although I had come out to the public on TV and in the press, I knew that coming out is never done once and for all: it has a constant performative component to it. I wondered what it would be like to stand in front of the class in those first few minutes, no longer "hovering at that threshold of indecision where the benefits of being out can be swiftly weighed against the liabilities" (Malinowitz xv). In the more typical university classroom, my primary role is that of educator, and I may only incidentally be seen as a lesbian activist. In this course, my role as activist would be foregrounded and inseparable from my role as teacher. For all of us as learners, this course would be unlike any other in which we had participated. In some teaching situations, pedagogical strategies developed earlier are often replicated: here I could not take any such repertoire for granted.

In addition to allowing fully for the multiplicity of positions held by the students according to race, ethnicity, social class, religion, age, and sexual identity, I knew I also would have to address the perception so common (perhaps inevitable?) among men who find themselves in seminar discussions on feminism and think that they are being targeted as the enemy, as representatives of patriarchy. I knew it would be a challenge to deal with the possible manifestation of patriarchal attitudes and beliefs some men (and some women) may bring to the course without seeming to attack the socialized individual transgressor and without seeming to hold all males responsible, given that being male in a course on lesbianism may in itself be a threatening scenario. The fact that male students choose such an option does not necessarily prepare them for the demands made by full participation in the course, or for the sociopolitical implications of their choice. The endorsement by women of various patriarchal beliefs and practices, particularly those women who are well served by them, would need to be handled just as carefully if I was to encourage students to see the course as interrogative of homophobia and sexism and not as antimale or antiheterosexual propaganda.

In the interests of parity with other courses being offered at that time, I assigned four primary texts. Since I wanted to offer the students a range of responses to lesbianism and to include different genres of text, I decided on two novels, a play, and a set of interrelated short stories. I chose texts which would be amenable to the investigation of how theoretical positions can be seen to be worked out in fictional practice. Instead of theoretical works on the etiology or the social and psychological construction of lesbianism, I wanted to use fictional texts in which these notions are textually represented and dramatized. Also, I hoped to show how representations of lesbian identity and experience have altered over the years in keeping with changing societal attitudes and norms. It was important, I felt, that the texts should not be drawn from the traditional canon of English literature, since, it seems to me, changes in societal attitude are reflected more readily and more accessibly in more contemporary, less canonized texts.

Radclyffe Hall's *The Well of Loneliness* (1928) offered a useful starting point given its status as a famous (infamous?) early novel of lesbian experience. Although its position within lesbian literary history is debatable, the controversy surrounding its publication ensured a mass audience for the work. In this novel, Hall situates herself squarely within the then current prevailing dominant discourse around lesbianism—that of the pathology of inversion, in place of the earlier model of criminality—so it seemed to me to be appropriate to use this novel to locate perceptions of homosexuality within the etiological model of homosexuality as disease. Although the historical trajectory was not the most important part of the course, I did want students to have some sense of it and of the importance of such contextualization.

The ways in which past suffering can be recognized and validated (as seen, for instance, in the South African Truth and Reconciliation Committee hearings) are of immediate concern in postapartheid South Africa, and many fear that subsequent enfranchisement may well result in institutionalized forgetting of the costs of the struggle that led to such enfranchisement within improved economic and political conditions. The opposing argument is based on the belief that only in forgetting the past and in forgiving the oppressors can new beginnings be made. For me, the institutionalized forgetting of past suffering is an appalling insult to those who have paid so dearly for this victory. Furthermore, such forgetting allows us to see the struggle as having been won, whereas remembering what it cost forces us into the realization that, in terms of reparation and redress, the struggle is only just beginning. Likewise, I think that the entrenchment of lesbian and gay rights in the new Constitution marks not only the end of one particular aspect of the struggle but also the beginning of another battle, in that legislation does not straightforwardly ensure a concomitant change in attitude and certainly not in practice, unless, of course, such practice is publicly observable. Lesbians and gay men in South Africa have been recategorized; we are citizens with equal rights and are no longer seen as deviant criminals, but this does not in itself recognize and validate the cost of past and present struggles against homophobia.

Through an investigation of Hall's use of what Raymond Williams calls "reverse discourse," in which the oppressed use the language of their oppressors to shape their identity, I wanted to foreground what Henry Giroux and Paulo Freire refer to as the ways in which institutionalized "forgetting" works to make it "more difficult for those who [are] victimized by such oppression to develop an ontological basis for challenging the ideological and political conditions that produced such suffering" (xi). In other words, I wanted to explore the debate around Hall's representation of lesbian subjectivity: did she do lesbian existence a disservice in her apparently unquestioning use of the very discourse of lesbianism as disease, as pathological inversion, or did she offer hope and comfort to lesbian readers in her location of her text within a discourse that was perhaps preferable to the earlier one based on lesbianism as criminally deviant? I wanted to direct discussion to the implications of Hall's use of the etiological model of disease as the basis for her plea for the acceptance of lesbianism in society—such women, for Hall, could not help being what they were, and they both needed and deserved to be pitied and tolerated—since it could be seen to have been based on the institutionalized forgetting of the suffering of lesbians under the earlier model of criminality in favor of a slightly more tolerant model of pathology. Hall's use of Stephen as a Christ-like martyr to the (seemingly lost) cause of lesbianism raises further questions about the validation of previous suffering. Through such an investigation, I hoped to encourage my students to discuss the significance of remembering and/or forgetting the forms of oppression they suffered under the old, as well as the new, government in order to further establish the connections between Hall's fictional world and the one in which my students and I live. Practical action directed at overcoming oppression must, I believe, include remembering and recounting the suffering so that the struggle for change in the classroom, as well as in the world outside of it, is "forged through human communities and forms of solidarity"(Giroux and Freire xi).

Lillian Hellman's play *The Children's Hour* (1934) was chosen as an illustration of the deep and troubling ambivalence felt toward female teachers who are suspected of having lesbian desires. I wanted to explore what is for me the central concern of this play: the power of popular prejudice, such as that which sees a necessary connection between lesbianism and the corruption of children, somewhat analogous to the popular belief that there is a direct relation between homosexuality in men and pedophilia. It was this belief which underlay many of the arguments submitted in favor of dropping what was then referred to as the "sexual orientation category" from the Equality Clause of the new Constitution. Letters appearing in the daily newspapers and other print media obsessively stressed the danger in which children would be placed if homosexual activity were to be decriminalized. Street protests around this issue saw fundamentalist group members carrying placards warning of the same danger, and radio talk shows gave a great deal of time to discussions of this point. Although most of the fear expressed had to do with homosexual male teachers molesting and raping boys, extrapolation to the corruption of children by lesbian teachers and caregivers was fairly frequent. This of course gave Hellman's play an immediate relevance to recent political attempts in South Africa to legislate against the enactment of similar homophobic prejudice and belief.

I planned to use this play, set as it is in a school, to provide the springboard for discussion of the significance of transformative pedagogy to social change, particularly in relation to the social construction of what counts as knowledge. I wanted to draw attention to the power of the dominant discourse—based in this case on what were seen as respectable heterosexist norms—to destroy the careers of two women and end the life of one of them because one woman desired another. I intended to introduce a collection of cuttings from recent newspapers and magazines, from South Africa and abroad, which dealt with the loss of jobs and lives of lesbians and gay men under similar circumstances of homophobic hatred, whether legislated or not.

The next text was Audre Lorde's *Zami: A New Spelling of My Name* (1982), which served the purpose of presenting a celebratory view of a woman's self-identification as lesbian and which could function to counter the model of medical pathology presented in Hall's work. Given Lorde's semiautobiographical investigation of the poststructuralist notion of identity as unfixed and amenable to personal choice, her representation of Zami as primarily a woman capable of great love who chooses a lesbian identity for herself only after exploring her heterosexual potential, would provide the opportunity for my students to consider the implications of lesbianism as an individual political choice. While for Hall lesbianism is both pathological and unavoidable, for Lorde it is a political position, and I hoped to use this huge difference to illustrate the shift in thinking about what constitutes lesbian subjectivity over the slightly more than fifty years that separate these novels.

Another reason behind this investigation of lesbianism as a subject position had to do with the then current discussion of the political and social significance of the global commodification of lesbianism that was becoming highly topical in South Africa because of the Equality Clause debate. I wanted my students to understand the political dangers of seeing the choice of a lesbian lifestyle as chic and fashionable, as well as the possible social advantages of such a standpoint. This, I thought, would relate well to the earlier consideration of the power that the institutionalized forgetting of past pain and suffering wields when a once forbidden aspect of identity becomes trendy.

Furthermore, Lorde's refusal to validate Western myths, such as the Sapphic tradition, as an explanation for black African and African American same-sex desire could serve to introduce alternative cultural perspectives on the historical and social construction of lesbianism—an important consideration given the cultural diversity of our students in South Africa and one that has particular relevance to nationalist propaganda, which sees homosexuality not as part of African culture but as a white colonial import.

I selected Gloria Naylor's *The Women of Brewster Place* (1980) because it investigates different kinds of relationships between women, ranging from an overtly lesbian relationship to the "female friendship and comradeship" which, for Adrienne Rich, is part of "a lesbian continuum" which locates the "erotic . . . as . . . unconfined to any single part of the body or solely to the body itself" (53), regardless of the sexuality of the women concerned. The well-known debate about Rich's controversial formulation centers on the notion that to universalize "lesbian existence as informing and structuring all interactions between women" is to deny the "minoritizing view that 'lesbian' refers to a specific, delineated population" which seeks its explicit definition in terms of genital sexuality (Jagose 11–12). The interesting ambivalence in this work regarding the only sexually defined lesbian couple in the stories could, I believed, be used as a springboard into further exploration of this debate. A text which raises questions about the implications of defining a couple as lesbian in specific terms appeared to me to have significant political ramifications, particularly in a country such as South Africa, which is obsessed with labels and taxonomies. This work could serve to show, as Eve Kosofsky Sedgwick puts it, "how preposterous is *anybody's* urbane pretense at having a clear, simple story to tell about the outlines and meanings of what and who is homosexual and heterosexual" (146). An exploration of the different ways in which Naylor has the two lesbians, Theresa and Lorraine, construct themselves in terms of their sexuality and the ways in which their neighbors construct them would, I thought, demonstrate just how preposterous this attempt to define what it means to be homosexual or heterosexual actually is.

As it turned out, many of my anxieties in planning the course were groundless: of the 139 students who had to choose from

ANN SMITH

five open electives, 33 opted for The Lesbian in Literature, making it by far the most popular course on offer. In 1996 and 1997, this enrollment pattern was repeated, and student response continues to be affirming, encouraging, and constructively critical. If student comment is any indication, the desire to effect social change through learning seems to have been realized, at least to some extent, as the later discussion of excerpts from student journals and other writings suggests.

Around that time, the Department of English was beginning an institutionalized reassessment of its pedagogical principles and practice as well as its curricular content. Consequently, for most students the experience of student-centered teaching and learning was new; the primary mode of teaching to which they had been exposed at school and at university was "transmission-style" teaching, in which the dominant discussion practices are nonegalitarian and often adversarial. This results in many students' perceived need for "coverage" of a given topic and a tendency to see the number of pages of notes taken down during a seminar as a measure of the worth of that particular class. I saw it as imperative that the course The Lesbian in Literature model in form its revolutionary content. I sought to integrate the personal as a vehicle for knowledge within an academic examination of the given texts. Although, of course, I promoted small-group work, informal class presentations, and other learner-centered activities, I needed to ensure that the seminars did not become an excuse for self-indulgent, emotive, anecdotal outpourings. Always aware of the charge of frivolousness leveled against noncanonical course content, and the inclination to deride democratic teaching practice and the use of the personal as pseudopsychotherapy, I tried to ensure academic rigor throughout the course. Class presentations, for example, had to be conceptually sound and located within a solid theoretical framework. I encouraged in class discussions the exploration of the connections between personal experience and socially entrenched norms and attitudes, and then went on to invite students to investigate the ways in which dominant discursive practices and power are related. The students were expected, in other words, to demonstrate an understanding of how various kinds of texts can be seen to play out, endorse, and/or interrogate, in different ways, their sociopolitical theoretical underpinnings.

Modes of assessment also needed to reflect the innovative nature of the course. Students accustomed only to formal expository essays were offered a range of possibilities for their course assignments. Precisely half the students chose to keep a journal over six weeks in which they responded to issues raised in class; offered personal reflections on the course; and commented on current TV shows and movies, media coverage of pertinent issues, cartoons, and bumper stickers, as well as other popular culture artifacts and phenomena, all in relation to the assigned texts. Others chose to write formal essays, while a few elected to offer presentations which included performative components.

While the course evaluation yielded some useful information, the student journals proved to be a more revealing indicator of the extent to which the course effected change in their thinking and practice. At the start of the semester, I indicated that I would be likely to make this course the subject of an essay dealing with its pedagogical practice in relation to lesbian and gay rights in South Africa, and I sounded them out about the possibility of using their writings about the class for data. Not only was agreement unanimous and readily granted, but the students also insisted that their own first names be used rather than having their comments attributed to "fictional" respondents. They wanted to make explicit their involvement in a course which had so much to do with historical change in the university and in the world outside. Not surprisingly, many of the students reflected on their own role as participants in a groundbreaking course. For Genevieve, in her experience the university pays lip service to traditions of liberalism, and this was the only course which "had changed [her] life in its raising of questions around race, sex and gender in its attempt to raise consciousness about those things we hide from ourselves in an effort to fit in." She makes explicit the connection between transformative pedagogy and social change. Ioanna and Ryan were both "thrilled to be making history" as participants in the course in its first year, and both spoke of change in their lives which would always be linked to this historical moment. Ryan sounded a warning note in his observation that some students chose this option because "along with nose-rings, dyed hair and 'docs,' this course has found its place with the 'trendy' students," but went on to say that he thought that those who had signed up for such "shallow reasons had learned more than they bargained for!" Here was evidence that this new course was being seen as part of an emergent and liberating new mood of political awareness in South Africa, and this is again apparent in Marlise's pride in doing "probably the only course in South Africa and possibly the whole of Africa which dealt with lesbian literature."

Many students elaborated on the value of integrating the personal with the political and showed an ability to theorize the personal. In her assessment of the course, Ingrid wrote: "There is a lot of stuff I have been quietly sweeping under the heterosexist carpet for a long time, and this course allowed me to start reclaiming some of the lost stuff." For Ashleigh, while the academic worth of the course lay in its "not entirely rejecting the established tradition but encouraging an approach whereby the dominant and the emergent are addressed as intricately connected," the personal value had to do with her experience of the course as dealing "with issues relevant to [her] own experience." She saw the selected texts in relation to the dominant discourses of their time as analogous to the conflict between the course itself and the traditional academic areas of literary investigation, and she expressed gratitude for "having been given the opportunity to study in such an encouraging and stimulating setting, one which has opened intellectual and personal space in which change can be effected."

Karen wrote about the value of being able to deal in seminars with emotional responses to a work of literature. Her mother felt that the course is the product of a member of the "gay minority that wants special rights," and a friend felt that if a course on homosexual literature is on offer, then a course on heterosexual literature should also be offered! Another friend is recorded as asking why "homosexual people always want to force themselves down other people's throats," and her father wanted to know if we are also going to offer a course "in the literature of left-handed people." Karen articulated a new awareness of how commonly held prejudices work to construct what is then held to be knowledge. Likewise, other students identified some of the ways in which even enrolling for a university course means having to deal with the pervasiveness of common prejudices and how it has helped them understand how marginalization operates. Lesley Anne said that attending this course has shown her that her "response to being marginalized, ignored and suppressed [as a student within a patriarchal university] should be defiance." I quote her final sentence: "When I informed a friend that I had opted to take a course in lesbian writing he responded by saying that maybe I would become lesbian. While I was quick to respond in the negative, I now wish I could have the conversation over, so that this time I could say that if it means embracing empowerment, strength and fortitude in [this] society then it certainly appears to be a reasonable option."

Parental attitudes play an even greater role in students' course choices than is customary when, as in South Africa, most young people are educated at their parents' expense. There is no free tertiary education in South Africa, and bursaries are scarce and difficult to obtain. Jennifer's father bought all the books she needed for her other courses, but he refused to purchase the texts for this option and she spoke of the extent to which being thus "marginalized for choosing this course has made [her] more aware of how oppression functions in the real world." Marlise's father was concerned though considerably less extreme; she says, "I suspect that my father had his reservations."

Societal and personal responses to homophobia found expression in many journal entries. Colin mentioned that "Fridays at Wits [University of the Witwatersrand] have taken on a new meaning," and he speaks of how liberating it has been to be able to speak so comfortably about the "forbidden subject of homosexuality." He also related stories of fellow student disgust and horror at his taking such a course but said he felt compelled to discuss the course as often as possible because of this antagonism. Significant change occurred in Anthony's thinking: he related how he was "signed up for the course in error by a friend" and how he "was too lazy to change course" and was determined to be a disruptive element, "a thorn in the side of the class." He acknowledged having been a "homophobe from hell" who after three weeks "began to look forward to the classes" as his "homophobic tapestry was slowing unweaving itself." He spoke of his homophobia being "subtly attacked by a lecturer who was having an amazing influence on [him]" and of "beginning to face his inner demons" by a teacher and fellow students who made him think about things long after the classes had ended. His journal ends thus: "Thank you Ms Smith, I owe you one."

One powerful example of how the academic can make room for and foster the personal lies in the fact that two students found the courage to come out in their journals: Thandiswe and Matthew spoke of how liberating it was to be free and to have a safe space in which to pursue the connection between the academic and the personal. Thandiswe used a commercially printed illustrated journal for her entries and signaled her coming out by crossing out the drawing of a heterosexual couple and pasting next to it a photograph of two women. Furthermore, this photograph was taken from the publication of a student group called Activate, which deliberately describes its agenda as "anti-homophobic" rather than "gay and lesbian" because it wishes to draw in as members all people opposed to homophobic beliefs and practices. Thandiswe used her academic investigation of the assigned texts of the course to help her deal with a personal confrontation with her father, whose attitude to lesbianism was that it was not only "un-African" but also "unnatural"—a widely held and culturally specific prejudice with which black lesbians and gay men in South Africa have constantly to contend. Her final entry told me that she had been a student at this university for four years and never had "a learning experience like this"; she told me too that "nothing [she] has learned has ever had any impact on [her] life apart from this course." Matthew thanked me for the "wonderful experience" and spoke of having been empowered "to grapple with concepts and apply them to the set texts and to [his] own life." He said that he "had thought it would be interesting to take such an 'unconventional' course so as to open [his] mind a little" but he concluded that "little did [he] know that it would have presented a whole new world to [him]."

In South Africa, as the TV program in 1984 made clear, a strongly Calvinist, deeply conservative Christian tradition underlay apartheid policies and the exercise of power based on them. Two very conservative, fundamentalist Christian women were brave enough to take this course, and they struggled hard with serious conflicts between their religious beliefs and practices and their academic commitments against the oppression of the Other. Both were hesitant at first to say anything they thought I might construe as homophobic and therefore hurtful to me personally, but they began to take great risks and emerged with a recognition of the ambiguities inevitably part of the attempt to reconcile their religious beliefs with their academic position. Debbie concluded thus: "I honestly feel that I've learned more about myself in this experience than in any other university assignment. I valued being challenged to think more deeply . . . and it saddens me that this is my last entry. This journal has become part of my life . . . thank you for your honesty and understanding." Bronya spoke of her longing to "have heterosexual children so as not to have to face the conflict with [her] religious beliefs." She was grateful to have learned to be unafraid of "expressing her conservative beliefs," which the journal writing allowed her to do in safety.

I needed to recognize that gratifying comments which complimented me as a teacher and paid tribute to the success of the course should be regarded warily, since even in the context of a democratically constituted classroom, power is not evenly distributed. This power dynamic is demonstrated by the fact that all assignments had to be graded according to externally determined departmental conventions and requirements. Nonetheless, not all students felt a need to be complimentary: some raised issues surrounding the pedagogical problems related to maintaining a free, open space for student interaction and participation while still exercising enough control to keep the classes academically rigorous—a balancing act which, as I have indicated, was an anxiety of my own from the start. Ingrid mentioned "the difficulty of reconciling the need for structure and intellectual rigor" in the course with what she described as my "friendliness, accessibility and generally relaxed and informal vibe." As she put it, "You maintained an open approach to things and pointed out ambiguities and problems rather than answers . . . and I just can't stand seeing people take advantage of the fact that you are not aloof and intimidating by not doing very much work. Know what I mean?" Clint made similar points in his observation that "in a course of this nature where the very binaries of constructed identity are challenged, any hegemonic teaching presence would negate the course at its most basic level, yet it was frustrating to find a few people slacking off because there was no penalty for doing so."

In addition to the student responses about the changes in their lives, I believe that the success of the course can be measured, at least in part, in the encouragement it has given to some of my departmental colleagues to offer their own courses in gay and lesbian studies. In 1997 four courses, all of which use in their titles some of those formerly unprintable, if speakable, words—*lesbian, homosexual,* and *queer*—were outlined in the publicly available University of the Witwatersrand Arts and Humanities Prospectus for 1998: on offer as open electives from two colleagues were The Homosexual Predicament and Lesbian Modernism, along with my The Lesbian in Literature, and, in addition to this, a new course from me entitled An(other) Reading: Queer Politics and Postmodernism (or, I Can See Queerly Now!). Of particular significance, though, is the way in which my new course marks a significant shift in departmental thinking: it takes the form of a series of lectures which are a component of the final year undergraduate core course and are therefore compulsory for all students. This demonstrates that gay and lesbian studies is becoming an integral part of our curriculum. As South Africa moves toward meaningfully implementing what has been hailed as the most progressive Constitution in the world, this course on The Lesbian in Literature will continue to provide a significant academic site from which the challenges of social change can be explored. I do believe that at least some of these students, with their awareness of the pervasiveness and ubiquitousness of politically and socially oppressive structures, will continue to work toward personal and social change long after they have left the university.

Works Cited

Charlewood, Carole. *Viewpoint.* SABC TV1. Gay and Lesbian Archives Collection. University of the Witwatersrand Libraries. 4 Sept.1984.

Giroux, Henry. "Resisting Difference: Cultural Studies and the Discourse of Critical Pedagogy." *Cultural Studies.* Ed. Lawrence Grossberg, Cary Nelson, and Paula Treichler. New York: Routledge, 1992. 199–212.

Giroux, Henry, and Paulo Friere. Series Introduction. *Critical Pedagogy and Cultural Power.* Ed. David W. Livingstone. South Hadley, MA: Bergin, 1987. xi–xvi.

Graff, Gerald. *Beyond the Culture Wars: How Teaching the Conflicts Can Revitalize American Education.* New York: Norton, 1992.

Grossberg, Lawrence, Cary Nelson, and Paula A. Treichler, eds. *Cultural Studies.* New York: Routledge, 1992.

Hall, Radclyffe. *The Well of Loneliness.* 1928. London: Falcon, 1949.

Hellman, Lillian. *The Children's Hour.* 1934. New York: Modern Library, 1942.

Jagose, Annemarie. *Lesbian Utopics.* New York: Routledge, 1994.

Lorde, Audre. *Zami: A New Spelling of My Name.* Freedom, CA: Crossing, 1982.

Malinowitz, Harriet. *Textual Orientations: Lesbian and Gay Students and the Making of Discourse Communities.* Portsmouth, NH: Heinemann, 1995.

Naylor, Gloria. *The Women of Brewster Place.* London: Hodder, 1982.

Rich, Adrienne. *Blood, Bread and Poetry: Selected Prose 1979–1985.* London: Virago, 1986.

Sedgwick, Eve Kosofsky. "Pedagogy in the Context of an Antihomophobic Project." *South Atlantic Quarterly* 89.1 (1990): 139–56.

Wilton, Tamsin. *Lesbian Studies: Setting an Agenda.* New York: Routledge, 1995.

CHAPTER FIFTEEN

The Straight Path to Postcolonial Salvation: Heterosexism and the Teaching of English in India Today

RUTH VANITA

University of Montana

Of all the schools of critical theory that have developed in academic studies in the West over the last few decades, postcolonial studies is the one that has been most eagerly embraced in the Indian academy and lesbian and gay studies the one most systematically avoided. This selection is not fortuitous. The proponents of postcolonial studies in India range from orthodox Marxists to right-wing nationalists, and what these apparent antagonists share is a stance of opposition to a monolith known as "the West," which, when deconstructed, turns out to be England in the role of a lesser Satan and the United States in the role of the archfiend himself! Given that postcolonial theory was imported from precisely this Western hell, the relationship with Satan becomes fraught, as relationships with Satan are wont to be. Scholars often seek to resolve this tension by wedding postcolonial studies to straight feminist theory and erasing any suggestion of lesbian and gay theory.

In India, the politics of canon formation—expressed in syllabi, choice of dissertation topics, works included in or excluded from bibliographies and hence bought or not bought for libraries—is based on a few unexamined assumptions derived from an undigested mix of feminism, deconstructionism, postcolonialism, and theories of popular culture. These assumptions include the following:

1. Any canonical text, especially if written by a white male, is bound to be patriarchal and conservative, and the less we read of such texts the better.

2. Anything written by an American (even a white woman and perhaps even an African American man) is written in a neo-imperialist context and hence is suspect. African American women writers are usually an exception.

3. Writing is determined by the writer's subject position; consequently, the writer's nationality is crucial. That the writer may happen to be explicitly critical of his or her country or government is irrelevant.

4. Nothing is adequately radical unless it is adequately postcolonial.

What are the consequences of these assumptions ? First, virtually all homoerotically charged writing in English literature that could provide lesbian and gay students with a sense of ancestry disappears. Critical work in lesbian and gay studies and queer theory is also almost entirely absent. In attempts to reframe English literature syllabi in India today, a case can be made for the inclusion of virtually any Indian or other postcolonial writer, a weaker case for a white female writer, but no case at all for a white male writer. Since same-sex desire is rarely ever mentioned in the Indian academy, its oppositional aspect is not acknowledged as a viable site of inquiry in literary studies. Thus a couple of years ago, in a debate around syllabus change for the B.A. Honours degree in English literature at a leading Indian university, *The Color Purple* was deemed unfit for undergraduate study because of its explicit descriptions of lesbian sex, and Emily Dickinson and Tennessee Williams were summarily dismissed because they were American.

Third, postcolonial and black writers are not considered sufficiently radical unless they assert their postcolonial or black identity. Assertion of a lesbian or gay identity by these writers is considered irrelevant. For example, one teacher of English at an Indian university who, in a dissertation on James Baldwin, had characterized Baldwin as a sell-out to white culture, had not even considered that Baldwin's foregrounding of homosexual themes might be potentially radical, and was surprised when I suggested this to him. The puritanical and hegemonic insistence on postcolonialism as the sole criterion of radicalism was demonstrated by one graduate student/teacher of English literature who remarked during an M.Phil. oral exam that the only English text he had ever read which was adequately radical and therefore satisfying to him was Ngugi's *Devil on the Cross,* because it was written by Ngugi in his own language and later translated into English and hence was, in his view, truly decolonized.

One time-tested strategy used to build a sense of identity and community by homosexually inclined people such as Wilde and Pater in Victorian England and lesbians and gays in the twentieth century has been the reclaiming of well-known historical figures.[1] This strategy is still very useful in societies where most homosexuals are invisible and silent. I have found that in the course of a debate, whether in the classroom or with family members, a gay reference to Plato, Shakespeare, Michelangelo, Virginia Woolf, or others incites much argument because most people are unwilling to denounce as unnatural or sick artists they consider "geniuses." In the Indian academy today, this strategy and the subsequent debates that surround it are undermined by an anticanonical approach that ignores artistic excellence, privileging instead texts that focus on victimization and resistance.

The Indian left, however, including dominant Indian feminism (when it says anything at all on the subject, which is rarely), tends to take, at best, the position that homosexuals are not and never have been persecuted in India, and that such persecution was imported from the West; at worst, it takes the position that homosexuality itself is a Western perversion imported through the capitalist free market.[2] The silence and invisibility of homosexuality, and the relentless glorification of heterosexuality, marriage, and childbearing, are neither acknowledged as problems nor characterized as oppressive. Instead, the focus of dominant Indian feminism is on the reform of marriage, the redressal of abuses within marriage, and the support of motherhood. The editor of India's leading feminist journal recently told me that since Indian homosexuals are not victimized, they have "no reason to make a fuss." Following this logic, since we are disqualified from victim status, we have nothing to resist and hence texts produced by us cannot be radical. At best, such texts are irrelevant; at worst, they are decadent and self-obsessed. It is no accident that in the last twenty years, not a single text by Oscar Wilde has figured in any undergraduate or graduate course in English at Delhi University.

In contrast to the situation in most western countries, the Indian academy is far behind the media in its ostrichlike approach to the subject of homosexuality. Gay people are highly visible in the urban India theater, the performing arts, and fashion and design.[3] The Indian mass media tend to take a generally sympathetic, even celebratory, view of those who dare to come out. The oppressive silence in the academy, however, ensures that in a huge university such as Delhi University, perhaps one or two faculty members are somewhat openly gay, while homosexuality is rarely, if ever, built into an academic discourse.

This silence has roots in the history of South Asian studies and has been reinforced by the heterosexist biases of postcolonial theory. There is a wealth of material relating to same-sex love in Indian languages, literatures, visual arts, and modern mass media. Without any extended history of overt persecution in precolonial India, same-sex love and romantic friendship have existed in various forms at different times and places on the subcontinent, tolerated if not always approved. Nineteenth-century British administrators and educationists imported their generally antisex and specifically homophobic attitudes into already heterosexist Indian society. The antisodomy law was put on the statute book in India in 1860 and remains in place today as Section 377 of the Indian Penal Code, even though homosexuality between consenting adults was decriminalized in England in 1967.

Indian nationalism inherited this new homophobia, which remains unexamined by postcolonial theorists. Even before the advent of postcolonial theory, South Asian scholarship, both in India and in the West, either ignored precolonial materials relating to same-sex desire or interpreted it as heterosexual. In the course of research for our recent collection of Indian writings on same-sex love, Saleem Kidwai and I have found that many such writings have been bowdlerized and even erased from the canon.[4] For instance, poems that openly describe sex between women are often missing in modern Indian editions of collected works of major medieval Urdu poets. In one case, the only edition that included these poems was published in Italy. The Indian historians who invented subaltern studies never considered that homosexuals might be a subaltern group. These attitudes have helped foster the popular belief in modern India that homosexuality is an aberration imported from Europe or West Asia and was non-existent in ancient India. The well-known tendency of postcolonial theorists in the Indian diaspora to ignore same-sex desire as a viable site of intellectual, literary, or cultural inquiry thus comfortably reinforced, rather than unsettled, the already well-established heterosexism of the Indian academy.

Of contemporary Indian writers in English, those who foreground and stress their "Indian-ness" are most often regarded as representative of postcolonial and/or popular culture. Given the political context I have outlined, any foregrounding of homosexuality runs the risk of being automatically disqualified as not indicative of "Indian-ness." This is compounded by the fact that most gay, lesbian, and bisexual Indian writers need to keep at least one foot in the West, and many of them emigrate, for the simple reason that they need an openly gay culture in order to live with some degree of freedom. Emigrant writers are viewed with suspicion in the Indian academy because they are considered to have sold out to the West; they are thought less pure than the supposedly truly nationalist writers who remain in India.[5] In this debate, the relation between nationalism and heterosexism remains untheorized. When academics and creative writers choose to return to India after an education abroad, this choice is often tied to the choice to marry and raise children. The simultaneity of the two choices is so heavily normalized that scholarship in postcolonial studies on/in India has not theorized them as related. An unacknowledged heterosexism does ensure, however, that the choice to return to India constitutes a powerful subtext in the constitution of these writers as more "authentically" Indian.

I will try to demonstrate the way this normalizing process works by looking at the recent fortunes of two Indian women writers—Shobha De and Suniti Namjoshi—both of whom have frequently represented lesbian subjects, but in contrasting ways. Shobha De, known as Shobha Kilachand before her marriage, was a writer of film gossip columns. She then took to writing novels, the titles of which adequately indicate their contents— *Socialite Evenings, Starry Nights,* and *Strange Obsession.* These novels deal with the sexual escapades of highly affluent people and present extended descriptions of their bodies, clothing, food and drink, and sexual activities. The novels are always sold and reviewed with photographs and accounts of the author packaged like one of her characters—a beautiful and fashionable member of the jet set, accompanied by inevitable references to her pride in being a wife and the mother of six children. This mix is crucial. Everything about the text and the author is highly Westernized except—and it is a crucial exception—the impeccable focus on marriage and prolific childbearing, which is constituted as a stamp of Indian-ness. All of this is not surprising. What is surprising is that novels by Shobha De have been included in courses on popular culture at the University of London and in the English department at Bombay University. At a recent seminar on Jane Austen, a Delhi University English Honours undergraduate student, well trained in postcolonial discourse, asked me why students have to study Austen and Dickens rather than something more relevant. When I asked what she would like to study instead, she named Shobha De and Khushwant Singh (De's admirer and collaborator on a book on Indian sexuality; read: heterosexuality).

What about De's postcolonial texts is "more relevant"? One important feature is their overt heterosexism. Lesbian episodes occur quite frequently in her novels, as do stereotyped lesbian characters, frequently portrayed negatively. Her most extended portrayal of a lesbian occurs in her novel *Strange Obsession,* where the title refers to a lesbian passion. In my reading of the novel, I focus on its use of animal imagery. There are powerful traditions in Indian literatures of using animals as sites for ungendering and for the development of alternative emotional engagements and eroticisms. There are also traditions in English literature of animals as stand-ins for the homosexual beloved and for the hunted, persecuted, but innocent woman or homosexual. In the work of contemporary Indian writers such as Suniti Namjoshi and Vikram Seth, these traditions encounter and enrich one another, and I will examine examples of this in Namjoshi's work later. Shobha De's writing, on the other hand, uses animal imagery in a completely stereotyped and homophobic way, characterizing homosexuality as bestial. In the context of her flaunting of Indian-ness, it is worth pointing out that Indian philosophical traditions do not generally take such a view of animals. In Hindu tradition, there is no essential difference between human and nonhuman beings since the soul can inhabit human and nonhuman bodies in different births. Animals in Hindu texts, both written and oral, participate as agents in the action, speak rationally as a matter of course (rather than by miracle), and are often cherished allies and friends of humans as well as models for humans to imitate.

Shobha De's heroine Amrita (the name means "heavenly nectar") is introduced as "the most beautiful woman in the world" (2). The excitement in India following the winning of the Miss World and Miss Universe titles by two Indian women in 1994 suggests the sort of nationalism De is appealing to here. Amrita is "no more than an average student" but makes up for this by her "magnificently structured body, with its long toast-brown legs, narrow waist, and breasts that stood out—proud, high and firm" (2). In Chapter 2, Amrita encounters the lesbian Meenakshi, "buying a pack of imported cigarettes" (5). The action is significant—on Amrita's first date with her future husband Rakesh, he will forbid her to smoke, telling her that smoking is a "foul habit" (143). Meenakshi's nickname, by which she is known throughout the novel, is "Minx." Minx has short hair, always dresses in black, almost always wears men's clothes, and operates in the Bombay underworld as the only woman amongst men. She uses all the weapons of the mafia, from blackmail, to acid throwing, to staged street accidents and shoot-outs. Amrita sees Minx as "ugly," with a "flaky, mottled skin that gave her a reptilian appearance" (30). She woos Amrita aggressively, loading her with expensive gifts and warding off all rivals with violence. Amrita responds by telling her repeatedly that she is "abnormal," "weird," and "sick" (22, 42).

Amrita's perception is soon reinforced for the reader by Minx's penchant for shedding the blood of animals. She slaughters a piglet in Amrita's sink, leaves a dead calf's heart in her fridge, and sacrifices a goat to the goddess after Amrita first sleeps with her. Explicit descriptions of sex between the two women all represent Minx in the active role and Amrita passively moaning with the pleasure of multiple orgasms. Apart from making love to Amrita, Minx is shown masturbating, but there is no indication that Amrita makes love to Minx until, very near the end of the novel when the affair is over and Amrita is married to a man, Minx tells Amrita after abducting her: "Use your fingers . . . like you used them on me" (199). Minx throws acid on one of Amrita's professional rivals and also mutilates this female fashion model by knifing her in the vagina. She forces Amrita into a wedding ceremony with her and undergoes surgery to reduce the size of her own breasts.

Pursued, threatened, and fascinated by Minx, Amrita succumbs, and they live together for six months. During this period, Minx continues to pamper Amrita and shower her with expensive gifts but keeps close watch over her and goes into jealous rages if Amrita so much as looks at a man. In debates over the validity of their relationship, Minx argues persuasively that her love is genuine and not abnormal. Amrita persists in calling theirs "an unnatural relationship" (204) that is "kinky," "crazy," "wrong," and the product of Minx's "lunacy" (109–110). Amrita's homophobic views are bolstered and Minx's arguments undercut by the novel's representation of Minx as indeed a raving lunatic who reacts to Amrita's having coffee with a man by tying Amrita down and singeing her pubic hair with a lighted cigarette and, later, after Amrita's marriage, abducting her husband and nearly killing him as well as Amrita and herself.

Homophobic prejudices expressed by heterosexual characters are heavily reinforced by the action. Amrita's friend Partha, presented as an intellectual and the editor of a newsmagazine, sums up the debate in his contemptuous comment: "I get it— she's one of those. I won't call her a lesbo. The correct term these days for them is, I believe, people who practise alternative sexuality" (113). The reason for this contempt becomes evident in

Amrita's ultimate challenge, delivered when Minx desperately offers to undergo a sex change operation. In a variant of Angela Crossby's question "Could you marry me, Stephen?," Amrita demands: "Will you be able to fill my womb with a child? Answer me" (110). When Amrita finally deserts Minx for an arranged marriage with Rakesh, a New York–based industrialist who is Indian enough to touch his mother-in-law's feet and to seek his parents' blessings before finalizing the match, he proves his credentials by filling her womb. The last pages of the novel tell us: "Her enormous belly had begun to get in the way already. And it wasn't even five months yet. Twins? Everybody seemed to think so" (207).

But the birth of more Amritas and Rakeshes is not enough. The death of the lesbian is also necessary. So, after Minx has attempted suicide, kidnapped Rakesh, tortured him and Amrita, and tried to burn them and herself to death, she is taken into custody by her father. Early in the novel, Minx had won Amrita's sympathy by telling her that she had been beaten and raped by her father when she was a child and subsequently rejected by her mother. This is the only passage in the novel in which Minx is sympathetically represented; we are told that "she was less wary and almost feminine at that moment" (46). This is the only extenuating circumstance offered throughout the novel for Minx's behavior. And right at the end, it is withdrawn. Amrita meets Minx's father, who is horrified when told about Minx's accusation. It turns out that Minx had inherited her madness from her mother, who was in a mental institution. "God almighty knows the truth. The psychiatrist who treated her mother knows it too" (203), he tells Amrita, who apologizes. Two years later, the pregnant Amrita reads Minx's obituary in a newspaper and the novel ends: "She felt herself shiver involuntarily. Amrita was free at last" (208). The moral of the story: the good Indian woman can only be freed into normative heterosexuality when the bestial lesbian dies.

Minx's animality is an important theme in the novel. Apart from her name, her black cat, and her killing of animals, she is also referred to as a loathsome animal. Amrita sees her as a reptile; Rakesh says "we'll pick her up like a stray rat and chuck her into the dustbin" (157); and when she kidnaps Rakesh, the local rustics remark that human beings don't hurt each other in this rural area but "who can say anything about wild animals?" (179). When they find a pool of Rakesh's blood, it is clear who the wild animal is. A strong link is thus established between homosexuality and animality. Amrita's first lover, who turns out to be bisexual, is named "Rover" and sleeps with her in the presence of his dog. In contrast to Rover's unimaginative lovemaking, Rakesh is described as doing to Amrita everything Minx did but in "a new" way "she'd never experienced before" (160). In addition, on his honeymoon Rakesh develops the trait, unique to him in the novel, of referring to men whom he dislikes as "eunuchs" and "buggers" (176–77).

Women's organizations in India frequently protest what they see as obscene, pornographic, or degrading representations of women in books, film, television, and popular culture, including a World Beauty Pageant held in Bangalore in 1996. Feminist organizations, however, have not protested De's viciously homophobic text. On the contrary, De is increasingly acquiring intellectual respectability, nationally and internationally, as an icon of so-called popular culture. On the other hand, Suniti Namjoshi, who is an ideal candidate for syllabus inclusion as a postcolonial feminist writer, working creatively as she does with several traditions and genres such as fables, utopian fantasies, and poetry, is virtually ignored in the Indian academy. Her positive foregrounding of lesbian themes seems to me the only possible reason for this. Namjoshi lives with and often writes in collaboration with Gillian Hanscombe. Indian editions of her books rarely carry her picture and merely state cryptically that "she lives and writes in Devon."

One of the secrets of De's success is that she says nothing at all unexpected. She reheats and serves up the lukewarm leftovers from agony aunt columns, fashion spreads, and magazine stories. Suniti Namjoshi also rewrites the old, but in such a way as to make more explosive its already explosive potential. One set of images her work frequently engages with is that of beasts. In her fable "A Moral Tale," she deconstructs the narrative of the monstrous beast in love with beauty and shows how the ancient idea of metamorphosis may contain both tragedy and utopia. The tale begins: "The Beast wasn't a nobleman. The Beast was a woman. That's why its love for Beauty was so monstrous" (*Femi-*

nist Fables 23). Rejected by her female beloved and ridiculed by society, the Beast finds refuge in books and realizes: "I know what's wrong: I am not human. The only story that fits me at all is the one about the Beast. But the Beast doesn't change from a Beast to a human because of its love. It's just the reverse. And the Beast isn't fierce. It's extremely gentle. It loves Beauty, but it lives alone and dies alone" (23).

In Namjoshi's fable "A Quiet Life," the unnamed female protagonist is described as not exceptional in any way and as having "kept her sufferings largely to herself, the nature of her pain not being admissible" (*Feminist Fables* 51). When asked what she wants, she replies, "I don't want to be a woman." She is then asked, "Do you want to be a man?" and replies "No." Finally, she says, "I want to hide, to live in the bushes, be a rabbit or a squirrel or a mythical animal . . . when there's nobody about, be what I am; and when people are present, disguise myself." "As what?" "As a fake woman." (51). The text here engages with that aspect of imagination, individual and collective, which resists compulsory heterosexuality. The mixture of fascination, fear, amusement, awe, and ludic attraction with which *hijra*, or eunuch communities, are viewed in India indicates the tensions at work. More than one older Indian woman friend has told me, half playfully, half seriously, "I'm a *hijra*," which reminds me of Virginia Woolf's statement that she was neither a man nor a woman. Indian lesbian friends have expressed to me feelings similar to my own, to the effect that they do not think of themselves as women or as men. As an experiment, I have asked many nonfeminist Indian women friends of differing class, age, and sexuality whether they would like to be reborn as men or as women, and have almost invariably received the answer, "Not as a woman." Some have said they would like to be birds.

In Namjoshi's work, animal tropes suggest crossings of the boundaries of race, gender, culture, nationality, and sexuality. Her beasts, with their capacity to transform themselves and to live at ease in more than one skin, are less containable than human beings already positioned in categories of nationality and gender. The beasts often reveal the surprising commonalties of apparently distinct traditions and mythologies. Thus the donkey in both Western and Eastern folk traditions has a reputation for stupidity. But in the Biblical tradition (which can be considered both Middle Eastern and European), it is meek and humble, and it is also the only beast that speaks to give its master good advice. Blue is a heavenly color in both European and Indian iconography—it is the color of the Virgin's mantle and also of Sri Krishna's complexion. Namjoshi's wise, unheroically heroic, and self-parodic blue donkey appropriates and plays with these, among other, traditions.

Even more interesting are her cows. Used in the West to put down women ("stupid cow"), Hindus ("cow worshippers"), and India generally ("cows wandering on the streets"), and used in India to express horror against non-Hindus (beef eaters), the cow is a symbol of many kinds of prejudice. Namjoshi's cow Bhadravati, in *The Conversations of Cow,* recalls the mythological cornucopian cow Kamadhenu, fulfiller of all wishes. In Hindu tradition, *Kama* is one of the four aims of life and the third stage in the achievement of self-realization or liberation. *Kama* means "wish" and *dhenu* means "cow"; another meaning of *kama* is "work" and yet another meaning is "eroticism" or "sex," as in *Kamasutra.* Bhadravati is therefore quite appropriately a lesbian who has the disconcerting ability to turn herself into anything— a white man, an Indian woman, and, in a comic transformation of Indian omnivorous scavenger cows, a devourer of the universe. This last incarnation is somewhat alarming to the narrator, Suniti, since Bhadravati naturally objects to beef eating and reflects in an ecologically sound manner that a change in the diet of cows would "change the world balance" (22). Scavenger cows on streets in India today travel in all-female groups, accompanied by calves, and are often to be seen licking, caressing, and playing with each other at traffic intersections and other convenient spots. Bulls, on the other hand, roam alone. So Namjoshi's community of separatist lesbian cows has a material base in urban India as well as in Western feminism!

Namjoshi's latest work, *Saint Suniti and the Dragon,* attempts to confront the frightening dragon within the self, that which is hated as ugly and reptilian. Her earlier attempts to demystify the Other, in poems such as "Among Tigers," dwell on keeping an uneasy distance from the "massive jaws" of that "lordly race" (*The Blue Donkey Fables* 70). In another early poem titled "If somehow I might . . . ," she wishes she had the "vision" that would enable her to see "some strutting and well-nourished male" as merely a "beautiful animal" and treat this as "occasion to feel blessed and bless" (56). In *Saint Suniti and the Dragon*, the narrator encounters the monstrous oppressor's humanity, even as expressed in his greed and violence, and is forced to recognize in herself elements that mirror both him and his equally monstrous female parent. In the last section "On the Extinction of Dragons," Suniti and the dragon are both bleeding to death. The dragon writes a beautiful elegy for her, and the text closes with the dragon's unanswered question: "But wouldn't the extinction of dragons be very sad?" (*Feminist Fables* 183).

Namjoshi arguably makes far more creative use than does De of Indian literary conventions, as of Western literary conventions, not only in her use of beast tropes but also in her narrative strategies and allusions. De's narrative predictably follows the conventions of the realistic English novel. It would seem that the inclusion of De in a course at Bombay University is based on a postcolonialism that in practice gets reduced to nationalism, which in turn is heavily invested in heterosexism.

If the beast metaphor indicates the potential of lesbian and gay texts to cross boundaries of gender, nationality, and culture, the metaphor of aggressive male sport indicates the dominant direction of postcolonial theory in India today. In his concluding remarks in a recent collection of essays on postcolonialism, Harish Trivedi proposes a strategy of "combative engagement" by Indian critics with postcolonial theory that originates in Euramerica. The metaphor he uses to advocate this strategy is that of boxing: "this would mean neither a craven throwing-in of the towel by us, nor a knock-out victory over the rival which is in any case too wishful to come true, but rather, after many rounds of short-armed jabs and much close body punching while locked together in a clinch which may look like an embrace but is still combat, a decision finally on points" (245). One unintended irony here is that boxing is an extremely bloody and masculinist sport which originated in imperialist Rome and was revived in imperialist England in the eighteenth century. Its rules were codified by the Marquis of Queensberry, notorious for his persecution of his son's lover, Oscar Wilde. To suggest this sport as a metaphoric model for Indian postcolonial theorists is to unwittingly evoke the heterosexist homosociality of both the sport and the theory: "a clinch which may look like an embrace but is still combat."

The metaphor is an apt one for the hidden agenda of postcolonial theory in the Indian academy today. Postcolonial theory functions to legitimize the praxis of nationalism, which in modern India is heavily masculinist and heterosexist. This legitimation occurs in such enterprises as syllabi formation, wherein writers ostensibly chosen for their Indian-ness are generally those whose writings foreground normative heterosexuality. Indian postcolonial theorists' ignoring of queer studies ensures that the equation of Indian-ness with heterosexuality has become so normalized that it remains almost completely unexamined.

Recently, however, a number of scholars outside the ambit of postcolonial theory and outside the Indian academy have begun to research same-sex desire in India. Amongst the works reflecting this interest are Jeffrey Kripal's biography of Sri Ramakrishna; Giti Thadani's short book on lesbianism, *Sakhiyani,* which is flawed by an unaccountable erasure of medieval, especially Muslim materials; and Serena Nanda's study of *hijras*. In addition, there are a few essays by scholars such as Michael Sweet and Leonard Zwilling on some ancient texts.

Much more important than importing queer theory into India, however, is the need to develop theories that arise out of research on South Asian texts on same-sex attachment. Kidwai and I hope that our anthology will provide materials for a new generation of scholars in India to conduct extended research into different Indian languages and literatures, including Indian writings in English (see Vanita and Kidwai). Some patterns we discovered that are significantly different from patterns of representation in Western texts relate to indigenous literary traditions and belief systems; for example, the belief in rebirth often works in texts, as in life, to legitimize same-sex attachment by making gender appear fluid and changeable from one birth to another. We also found several instances, in both medieval and ancient Indian texts, of linguistic terms being used to categorize persons by sexual preference. This suggests that Foucault's thesis regarding the invention of homosexual identity in the nineteenth century, which has been challenged even in the West, is certainly not true for the entire world. Taking into account South Asian perspectives will enrich lesbian and gay studies in the West, which has hitherto almost altogether ignored them. Research by young Indian scholars, some of whom will go on to become teachers of English at Indian universities, will hopefully make it increasingly difficult for the Indian academy and its postcolonial theorists to perpetuate the normalization and normativization of heterosexuality.

Notes

1. Walter Pater, in his collection of essays titled *The Renaissance* (1873), used this strategy to homoeroticize famous figures, such as Michelangelo and Leonardo da Vinci, as did Oscar Wilde in his essay on Shakespeare's sonnets, "The Portrait of Mr. W. H." and Edward Carpenter in his *Iolaus: An Anthology of Friendship*. For detailed analyses of these texts and of the tradition of constructing a homosexual literary ancestry, see my *Sappho and the Virgin Mary: Same-Sex Love and the English Literary Imagination,* especially Chapters 3, 4, and 7.

2. The Communist Party of India's women's front, The National Federation of Indian Women, issued through its spokeswoman, Vimla Farooqui, newspaper statements making this claim, recently asking the government to ban a gay conference in Bombay.

3. Many plays focusing on lesbian and gay issues have been staged in the urban centers of India over the last two decades. *The Importance of Being Earnest* remains a perennial favorite with theater groups, including dramatic societies at colleges.

4. An anthology of such materials from the earliest times to the present, translated from Indian languages and edited by Ruth Vanita and Saleem Kidwai, was recently published by St. Martin's Press.

5. For further elaboration of this argument, see Makarand Paranjape's "Coping with Post-Colonialism," in Trivedi and Mukherjee.

Works Cited

Carpenter, Edward. *Iolaus: An Anthology of Friendship*. London: Allen, 1902.

De, Shobha. *Strange Obsession*. New Delhi: Penguin, 1992.

Kripal, Jeffrey. *Kali's Child: The Mystical and the Erotic in the Life and Teachings of Ramakrishna*. Chicago: U of Chicago P, 1995.

Nanda, Serena. *Neither Man nor Woman: The Hijras of India*. Belmont, CA: Wadsworth, 1990.

Namjoshi, Suniti. *The Blue Donkey Fables*. New Delhi: Penguin, 1991.

———. *The Conversations of Cow*. London: Women's, 1985.

———. *Feminist Fables; Saint Suniti and The Dragon*. New Delhi: Penguin, 1995.

Paranjape, Makarand. "Coping with Post-Colonialism." Trivedi and Mukherjee 37–48.

Pater, Walter. *The Renaissance: Studies in Art and Poetry*. Ed. Adam Phillips. Oxford: Oxford UP, 1985.

Sweet, Michael, and Leonard Zwilling. "The First Medicalization: The Taxonomy and Etiology of Queerness in Classical Indian Medicine." *Journal of the History of Sexuality* 4 (1993): 590–607.

Thadani, Giti. *Sakhiyani: Lesbian Desire in Ancient and Modern India*. New York: Cassell, 1996.

Trivedi, Harish, and Meenakshi Mukherjee, eds. *Interrogating Post-Colonialism: Theory, Text, and Context*. Simla: Indian Inst. of Advanced Studies, 1996.

Vanita, Ruth. *Sappho and the Virgin Mary: Same-Sex Love and the English Literary Imagination*. New York: Columbia UP, 1996.

Vanita, Ruth, and Saleem Kidwai, eds. *Same-Sex Love in India: Readings from Literature and History*. New York: St. Martin's, 2000.

Wilde, Oscar. "The Portrait of Mr. W. H." *Complete Works of Oscar Wilde*. 1966. Ed. Vyvyan Holland. London: Collins, 1983.

CHAPTER SIXTEEN

Rememorating: Quilt Readings

MARCIA BLUMBERG

The Open University, Milton Keynes, England

[W]e have no alternative but to involve ourselves and mire ourselves in what we are calling the textuality of the socius. The real task here is to displace and undo that killing opposition between text narrowly conceived as the verbal text and activism narrowly conceived as some sort of mindless engagement.

GAYATRI CHAKRAVORTY SPIVAK, "The *Intervention* Interview"

AIDS activists know that silence equals death, but we also know that this cannot be said, it must be performed.

CINDY PATTON, *Inventing AIDS*

The quilt works as a symbol, but it also works as rhetoric. . . .[It] quite literally invites a reading—the panels are the leaves of an enormous textile text. Speaking its complex visual, verbal, and nonverbal language, the Names Project quilt sets about claiming power for people with AIDS by creating a story of their own making.

JUDY ELSLEY, "The Rhetoric of the NAMES Project AIDS Quilt: Reading the Text(ile)"

It is essential to put a human face on this epidemic. . . . We can talk about statistics or money, but this quilt is about people, person by person, panel by panel.

ANTHONY TURNEY, "The Power of a Single Pebble"

My epigraphs address the fluid yet vital relations between art and lived experience, between text and context, between pedagogical theory and praxis, between the performativity of activism and the activism of performance. What informs the dynamic when these linkages are situated within a time-space of AIDS? Reading the densely woven text of the AIDS Memorial Quilt, I examine different approaches, agendas, positionings, and responses to the Quilt display that was last performed in its entirety from October 11 to 13, 1996, in Washington, D.C. These readings investigate the conditions of representation, the sites of struggle, and the imperatives for readers/spectators to engage with the complexities at the nexus of AIDS: the arts, class, race, gender, and sexual identity, as well as other issues.

The AIDS Memorial Quilt came into being in the United States out of a sense of desperation at the growing numbers of deaths from AIDS-related causes, and anger at the disease of prejudice and the resulting marginalization that rendered these deaths invisible. Cindy Ruskin asserts: "As a nation, we have struggled not only against a disease, but also against the equally destructive enemies of ignorance, hysteria, and bigotry" (157). The originator of the Quilt, Cleve Jones, a gay rights activist from San Francisco, was planning a candlelight memorial march in 1985 for San Francisco officials Harvey Milk, the gay city supervisor, and mayor George Moscone, both of whom had been murdered seven years earlier. Noticing a headline in the *San Francisco Examiner,* "1,000 AIDS Deaths in S.F.," Jones was disturbed to re-

I would like to honor the memory of South African activist Simon Nkoli, who died of AIDS-related causes on November 30, 1998. His warmth, vitality, gentleness, and resolute commitment touched me, as did his life and legacy of activism, which will continue to make a difference in international venues and throughout South Africa, particularly in Johannesburg and Soweto, where he founded GLOW (Gay and Lesbian Organization of the Witwatersrand), TAP (Township AIDS Project), and PAMP (Postive African Men Project).

My thanks to Ed Nyman for reading an earlier version of this essay. I owe a special debt of gratitude to Stephen Barber for his inspiration and an ongoing engagement with my work. My sincere appreciation to William Spurlin for his detailed and constructive editing of this essay and to the Social Sciences and Humanities Council of Canada for a postdoctoral fellowship supporting my work.

alize that many of these people were acquaintances or friends who lived nearby; yet, as he expresses it: "There was no evidence we were standing at Ground Zero. . . . If this were just a field with a thousand corpses lying in the sunlight . . . then people would see it and understand and be compelled to respond" ("Blanket Judgment" 32). Jones raises an important concern regarding activist and pedagogical methodologies: How can statistics, especially numbers of deaths, be rendered metaphorically concrete and potentially imaginable yet still be finally inexplicable? Can art ever adequately realize both the immensity of loss in general and the value of each specific individual who constitutes one unit of the mass? These and many other questions raised throughout this essay should be asked when teaching the Quilt in literature, cultural studies, language arts, or other arenas. The planning and actualization of the Quilt attempts to address these issues, nowhere more effectively than when displayed and performed in its entirety.

How do we conceptualize the art of quilting? According to the *Oxford English Dictionary*, the word is both "the action of padding, sewing together" and the "material for making a quilt." We often read quilting as a performative process and a product that are gendered female and signify a pleasurable collaboration. Writing on American quilts, Patsy Orlofsky and Myron Orlofsky accord the activity a significance when viewed as part of a gender-stereotyped process anticipating future events: "When a girl gained proficiency, she would embark on a series of quilts for her own hope chest, to be completed by the time she was engaged" (27). Other quilts signified death: the Mourning Quilts, black and white or grey with a black border, were used during a bereavement; Memory Quilts were "made of pieces of material taken from the clothing of a deceased member of a family or friend. . . . The center of the block . . . [was] embroidered with the name of the deceased, the date of death and sometimes a sorrowful verse" (226). At the close of the twentieth century, quilting retains its traditional connotations; yet in the AIDS Memorial Quilt, quilt-ing simultaneously employs and displaces the conventional art form in a postmodern performance of mourning that celebrates lives, creates healing narratives, challenges and refuses elitism, values creativity, raises awareness, and inspires action. Pedagogi-cal methodologies can emphasize these aspects by reading *with* the Quilt as text; at the same time, reading *against* the text(s) problematizes the universalizing impetus behind the Quilt and its panels, the apparent heterogeneity of individuals memorial-ized in panels, and the economic and political questions raised or elided in this powerful interventionary vehicle.

The first display of the AIDS Memorial Quilt, organized by the NAMES Project in 1987, comprised under two thousand panels and formed one of the events of the March on Washing-ton for gay and lesbian rights. Displays thereafter focused on the Quilt, which comprised an ever-increasing number of panels: approximately eight thousand in 1988, ten thousand in 1989, twenty thousand in 1992, and a staggering forty thousand pan-els containing seventy thousand names in 1996. Over the years, these changing figures affected the mode of the Quilt's reception, which is also intricately related to medical knowledge about the pandemic and the particular positioning of the spectator within the time-space of AIDS. For Jones the fulfillment of his dream bears testimony to the cooperation of thousands of diverse people, whose shared devastating grief and healing are performed and realized in the Quilt in a personal and concomitantly highly po-litical public celebration of mourning. This project emphasizes individual and collective loss while insisting on the ceremonial manifestation of valuing and remembering people's lives rather than their data. The making of the three-by-six-foot quilt panels, evocative of graves, usually involves collaboration by lovers, friends, co-workers, and sometimes family in private venues, but groups of strangers often pool resources in specially organized public "Quilt shops." Participants share mourning, solace, and even joy as they realize the special attributes of those remem-bered in ways that range from simple panels featuring just a name, or name and dates, to the most elaborate and artistic panels that also incorporate, in an often vibrant splash of colors, sequins, buttons, lace, fur, leather, red ribbons, jewelry, photographs, newspaper reports, documents, passports, credit cards, items of clothing, masks, silk flowers, teddy bears, toys, poems, badges, pennants, flags, letters, maps, shoes, hats, and even pouches with ashes. Presentation of the individual panel to the project forms another difficult stage of separation; thereafter, the stitching of eight panels into a quilt twelve feet by twelve feet, which is then placed on public view, rehearses the memorial performance.

The massive spectacle, performed at different locales and occasions using thousands of panels separated by "walkways," constitutes a portable cemetery, a Foucauldian heterotopia (Foucault 22). This temporary site of mourning is a "real unreal place" and performs another version of the concept of cemetery, which Foucault argues changes location from the city center site, with its accent on resurrection and immortality, to the outskirts of the city in the nineteenth century, when corrosion of faith emphasized body rather than soul and recoded the cemetery as a place of death from illness. The Quilt as portable cemetery deemphasizes religion and refuses to be limited to the spectre of illness and decay so often portrayed in death from AIDS; instead, it performs a postmodern ritual of memorial to celebrate life in a shared community festival that, like a theatrical performance, is set up, packed away, and remounted in these periodic large displays, while twelve-by-twelve blocks of eight stitched panels travel to different continents in varying formats for disparate audiences—hospitals, theaters, and schools—to accompany a vibrant education program.

The National High School Quilt Program founded in 1995 provides on request to high schools up to four of these twelve-by-twelves specially chosen for their relevance to teenagers. Jerry Roberts argues that "displaying panels of the quilt, particularly those made for young adults who died of AIDS, increases awareness of the causes of the epidemic among teenagers in a way that no lecture—whether about abstinence or how to put on a condom—could ever do" (E8). The panels are accompanied by lesson plans, student guides, posters, books, and videos. Further sessions conducted by teachers may include discussions with invited doctors, social workers, community activists, and people living with HIV/AIDS, as well as visits to relevant plays, movies, or art installations. The Quilt in and of itself is a rich pedagogical vehicle providing critical links to social issues. Anthony Turney, the executive director of the Quilt Foundation, foregrounds the significance of this school project: "There's a role for this Quilt at a time when it seems that AIDS is slipping off the radar screen, that its place in the national consciousness is slipping. It is becoming ordinary, it is becoming a fact of life . . . like cancer. We believe that *that* is something the Quilt can help to turn around, by its very presence (qtd. in Enoicaras 19).

Open discussions on various aspects of AIDS and HIV transmission form the basis for attaining knowledge about prevention, since teenagers and young adults compose approximately 25 percent of the new cases of HIV infections recorded in the United States. While prevention of HIV transmission is the primary aim of this program, ethical pedagogical strategies will call attention to the scope and complexity of HIV/AIDS issues and should include not only a discussion of sexual practices and various options for safer sex, but also call attention to the detrimental effects of media misinformation and cultural myths that perpetuate stereotyping and homophobia. If health promotion is a primary aim of the program, then prevention of disease should operate within the parameters of bodies, as well as practices and attitudes. Pedagogical sessions should always acknowledge and be sensitive to the diversity of participants' subject positions and cultural baggage; the latter, Susan Bennett remarks in another context, is "not an optional extra; it must be carried everywhere" (108). Important too is the humanization and deconstruction of statistics. Michael Shower's speech read on the first World AIDS Day, December 1, 1988, is instructive when considering the significance of the school Quilt program and the value of the Quilt itself: "Numbers are numbing. They tell us of the masses but they do not tell us of people. They allow us to avoid the reality with which people throughout the world are confronted: people do not die as masses; they die one by one" (qtd. in Williams 5). Most important, when viewing the Quilt it is necessary to call attention to the many thousands of people, especially those in the developing countries, whose names and lives are not remembered in quilt panels.

Although only the twelve-by-twelves in the quilt are permanently joined panels, there is no guarantee of an eternal memorial of quilts even though restorative needlework lovingly keeps memories alive. An important new initiative addresses the necessary impermanence of cloth panels and is also an invaluable educational resource: The AIDS Memorial Quilt Archive Project has undertaken the mammoth task of photographing and documenting every panel of the world's largest funerary art installation so that a full record of electronic images of the Quilt is available on the World Wide Web. At present some panels are displayed according to categories. Each name page displays the individual panel and its location within the twelve-by-twelve. Some pages also include quotations from letters that accompanied the panel. For example, the category "Gay and Lesbian" shows a range of panels and people. Marvin Feldman's panel is accompanied by a comment: "Marvin wouldn't approve; he would have wanted something to be displayed at the Museum of Modern Art, or in Bloomingdales windows." Panels are included for well-known personalities such as filmmaker Marlon Riggs, whose 1989 movie *Tongues Untied* offered for the first time the voices of black men through a collage of music, dance, poetry, and the spoken word. The panel for pop artist Keith Haring, who melded icons and activism, cartoons and chalk drawings in venues as disparate as the New York subway, streets, and art galleries, is accompanied by a letter that asks the viewer to respond: "Don't just watch. Do Something!" In a different vein, the panel for Sergeant Matlovich, a hero of the Vietnam War, is informative and politically powerful since he was discharged on the grounds of his sexual orientation and won his court case against the U.S. military. Group panels feature twelve-by-twelves devoted, for example, to the Sisters of Perpetual Indulgence, a group of drag activist nuns with fellow sisters in Australia, Britain, and the United States, who promulgate universal joy and expiate stigmatic guilt. Members of the order work to raise funds, provide HIV/AIDS education, and services. Here multiple names speak of the loss of groups within the "community." This small sampling of panels, in its diversity and valuing of lives, refuses stereotypical homophobic representations of gay men and serves as another means of resisting bigotry.

Large performances of the Quilt are constructed according to specific methods of folding/unfolding. The lotus fold, used for the opening ritual, transforms the usually flat object into the shape of a lotus, a plant well known in Greek mythology for its fruit which, when eaten, produced states of forgetfulness, contentment, and pleasure. For me, however, these evocative images were instantly replaced by the harsh reality of the scene I witnessed when I arrived at the Washington Mall long before the arrival of the crowds for the three-day display in 1996—huge areas of grass were dotted with what from afar appeared to be crumpled bodies. The resulting overwhelming sense of devastation and loss was the most difficult moment of the entire event and in retrospect has rendered concrete for me Cleve Jones' wished-for image: I saw what appeared to be many "thousand[s] of corpses lying in the sunlight . . . and [felt] compelled to respond" ("Blanket Judgment" 32). In the opening ritual, the lotus fold engenders a slow and deliberate ceremonial performance that anticipates the disclosure of the individual quilt panel and its reconnection with mourners and other spectators, while the simpler closing fold more quickly enacts each quilt panel's farewell. In contrast, the emergency-rain-fold procedure, if properly executed, enables the entire massive Quilt to be closed in forty-five seconds and then wrapped in plastic.

Although the panels are treated with reverence, one organizer's instructions to volunteers demonstrate the complex physical and emotional involvement in the process: "You're laying people's possessions—parts of people—on the ground . . . but you can't be afraid of the Quilt. In order to fold it up you have to walk on it" (Ruskin 112). Taking physical care of the panels and showing concern for the emotional healing process experienced by the makers and other spectators are vital aspects of the performance. Special volunteers known as Hand Maidens of the Quilt tend the twelve-by-twelves; they move around the entire display making repairs or refastening individual quilts so that the panel remains as originally submitted in order to achieve a stability and a degree of permanence ultimately dictated by the materials of construction. The very organization of the performance reflects concern about the healing quality of the Quilt. Boxes of tissues placed around the perimeter of each twelve-by-twelve are practical markers that demonstrate that the organizers recognize the value of expressions of sorrow. Most important, Emotional Support volunteers, a designated category of people professionally trained in grief counseling who also have particular experience with AIDS, provide comfort for quilt makers, mourners, spectators, and other volunteers alike. A culture of caring operates within the NAMES Project that attempts to transform an artwork into a powerful force for emotional well-being at the same time that it demonstrates, on an immense scale, the enormity of the problem and the necessity to be informed and engaged. Volunteers, while instructed never to be intrusive, are available to hear expressions of emotion, answer questions, or just provide a hug. This caring component is only one aspect of the multivalent performance of the Quilt.

The ritualized reading of a litany of names initiates the opening ceremony and continues until the final moments of the closing ceremony. Huge amplifiers placed strategically at many locations within the immense expanse of the display relay the names as an integral part of the experience of the Quilt wherever one is positioned. This performance of reading foregrounds the significance of the public recitation of names of those who have died as one of many possible readings of the Quilt, both in its component panels and as a whole. Tellingly, Cleve Jones begins and ends with the name of Marvin Feldman, the friend memorialized in the first quilt panel. In so doing, Jones frames and encapsulates the very history of the Quilt and the determination never to forget those who died from AIDS in years past and in recent times. Readers include prominent political figures, artists, and personalities from popular culture as well as service providers, care providers, activists, and those infected and affected by HIV/AIDS. The continuous reading of names—in 1996 seventy thousand over three days—corroborates Peter Hawkins's view that "the Quilt in any of its forms is most profoundly about the naming of names. . . . As with the Vietnam Veterans Memorial, the names themselves are the memorial" (760). Mourners, makers of the Quilt, volunteers, and visitors celebrate the dynamism of the lives behind the names that are realized in a range of materials and modes, from solemn panels to those with riotous colors and an infinite variety of decorations and memorabilia. Elinor Fuchs argues that the Quilt is "cemetery as All Fool's Day, a carnival of the sacred, the homely, the joyous and the downright tacky, resisting even *in extremis,* the solemnity of mourning" (17).

In a challenge to the stigma and disinformation constructed through the complex discourse of AIDS, the Quilt celebrates mourning and actively politicizes and renders problematic the AIDS epidemic "with its genuine potential for global devastation—[which] is simultaneously an epidemic of a transmissible lethal disease and an epidemic of meanings or signification" (Treichler 32). The public celebration of mourning performed in the display of the massive Quilt thus comprises both ritual and consciousness-raising to enact the AIDS slogan, Silence = Death. White lettering on a black background, accompanied only by an upturned pink triangle, situates early activism within the gay community and represents gay pride and a challenge to the silence and oppression of the down-turned pink triangle of the Nazi regime. The Quilt can, therefore, also form a healing narrative when its mammoth presence and ramifications represent a catalyst to lessen the impact of the disease of prejudice. Another strategy employed in the display is the use of blank twelve-by-twelves, known as signature squares. Here spectators remove their shoes to reach a central place on the blank square and record in colored markers their message of hope or pain. This spontaneous act of expression is inclusive and at the same time comforting and upsetting; furthermore, it makes the writer a small part of what the organizers term "the Quilt family." This nomenclature gives a homely feeling to bolster what Hawkins argues is "the primary strategy . . . to create a consensus, a myth of inclusion" (777).

Yet, further analysis offers a much needed opportunity to problematize the notion of family, assumed in heteronormative structures to be the traditional nuclear family; since the beginning of the AIDS pandemic, this family has often distanced itself from or abandoned a relative living with AIDS. The dynamic of denial is evident in veiled or deliberately misleading obituaries and in the panels in which names have been deleted out of shame. These families have not only robbed the individual of what was central to his or her life but have also attempted an erasure in death. All too often, when birth families have totally rejected a person living with HIV/AIDS, this relative has chosen a new family of lovers and friends who, at the appropriate time, together with support workers become caregivers. In the case of gay men, this revisioning of "family" has often occurred if their coming out was greeted with disapproval or ostracism. The reading of the Quilt performance, therefore, demands an awareness of presence, absence, voicing, silence, and the nuances of the in-between, all of which constitute material for interrogation when speaking about or teaching the Quilt.

For Cindy Patton, "the narrative of AIDS overdetermines the virus, HIV" (*Inventing AIDS* 128), yet she cautions against what she categorizes as silence: "the unspeakable, the perceived but best not said, the ignored, the safely tucked away, the camouflaged" (129). The Quilt as memorial speaks eloquently of loss, love, and healing in its individual panels and enormous scope. Despite Reverend Fred Phelps's egregious, homophobic designation of the Quilt as "that filthy fag blanket" (qtd. in Jones, "Blanket Judgment" 32), it resists the simplistic equation of AIDS with gay men since the multiplicity of panels of men, women, and children emphasizes the nexus of gender, race, class, religion, sexual identity, and ethnicity. Yet, particularly in the context of the apparently heterogeneous community evidenced by the Quilt, further mention should be made of the many gay men who have suffered loss in this pandemic on an unprecedented scale; this "community," however problematic a term in its reductiveness and apparent homogeneity, has, despite ongoing stigmatization, resisted apathy, insisted on improved research and facilities, challenged heterosexist norms, imbued the term "activism" with new vitality, and demanded that attention be paid. Douglas Crimp acknowledged the situation of his constituency in 1989:

> Seldom has a society so savaged people during their hour of loss. . . . The violence we encounter is relentless, the violence of silence and omission almost as impossible to endure as the violence of unleashed hatred and outright murder. Because this violence also desecrates the memories of our dead, we rise in anger to vindicate them. For many of us, mourning *becomes* militancy. ("Mourning" 8–9)

The added ramification of an inherently militant performance of mourning intricately and urgently combines the threads of memorial, celebration, activism, and healing. Refusing, both physically and semiotically, to be "safely tucked away," the Quilt demands explicitness, education, research, and reevaluated hegemonic power and priorities.

People with AIDS who care less about the beneficial aspects for quilt makers of making the Quilt and concentrate on the person behind the name may regard the Quilt as a sentimentalizing of an individual's struggle with AIDS. Derek Jarman, the British artist and filmmaker, reacted vehemently when he saw a display of panels:

> When the AIDS quilt came to Edinburgh during the film festival, I attended just out of duty. I could see it was an emotional work, it got the heartstrings. But when the panels were unveiled a truly awful ceremony took place, in which a group of what looked like refrigerated karate experts, all dressed in white, turned and chanted some mumbo jumbo—horrible, quasi religious, false. I shall haunt anyone who ever makes a panel for me. (91)

This discomfort at the performance of the ritual provides one objection. Some activists also rail against the Quilt as a distraction from the weightier issues of accessibility to medication, better care and services for people with HIV/AIDS, and an intensification of various avenues of research. Not only do they feel that attention is deflected from these matters, but they also consider the sponsorships and fund-raising efforts for the Quilt a financial drain and a diversion from needs which they deem more valuable for the use of these funds. Other criticisms point to the paucity of panels memorializing black people with AIDS and an absence of panels for IV drug users who have died from AIDS-related causes. This observation foregrounds the element of luxury associated with the time and energy to devote to quilt making, let alone having the money for materials. Here the differentials of marginality play a part in the Quilt, as they do in life, and emphasize how much more needs to be accomplished. Another imperative in reading or teaching the Quilt as text is the acknowledgment of these apparently silent subtexts. The nexus of working-class pressures, poverty, and racial marginalization constitutes a trajectory of exclusion from these activities when mere survival heads the agenda.

Hal Rubenstein's decision not to see the Quilt again stems from the emotional lacuna that develops when someone deeply affected within the pandemic has experienced multiple loss on a scale usually experienced only in times of war. Except, here the dead are *all* loved ones, close friends, and acquaintances; in short, they represent his entire world:

> I've had enough of feeling devastated by its acreage. . . . I'm tired of being almost too exhausted to remain still by the time I find the crafted tombstones of my friends and lovers. I don't want to be surprised anymore by the sudden appearance of a patch of fabric embroidered with a name of someone I hadn't known had passed away. I don't want to be beat up anymore. Been there. Done that. . . . Flippant? No. How can you be if you've been there from the beginning and are still standing? It's just that now there's hope. And I want to believe it. I don't want things to remind me that besides the glass's being half full or half empty, it can also shatter. . . . I want to remember. I have to. I've no choice. But I don't want to be overwhelmed anymore. . . . When the heart wants to be touched, it goes down the list of those who aren't here, one by one. (57)

This eloquent personal statement signifies a limit situation wherein the sheer extent of numbers, the degree of one individual's loss, precludes a healing narrative; here, onlookers as well as the so-called "community" of mourners only foreground the distance between their experience and the trauma of Rubenstein's "community" scattered amongst the seventy thousand names in various locales within the huge expanse of panels covering the Mall in Washington. For Rubenstein the haphazardly separated panels of friends intensify the disjunctions and emotional dislocations that spell one actuality in his volatile existence—the certainty of loss. The difference in positionality and perspective between the infected, the affected on an individual scale, and those affected by immense and seemingly unstoppable loss translates into very different experiences of the world in this time of AIDS. It is instructive to recall Douglas Crimp's 1991 explication of "the incommensurability of experience. . . . [C]ertain people are experiencing the AIDS crisis while the society as a whole doesn't appear to be experiencing it at all" (Caruth and Keenan 539). This excruciating disjunction between the suffering of people experiencing the AIDS crisis (both those infected and affected) and a general societal inaction is compounded and rendered more urgent by a situation described by Cindy Patton at the Acting on AIDS Conference in London in March 1996 as an "epidemic of discrimination." Even for those who may disagree with Jarman or be positioned differently from Rubenstein and praise the Quilt, Michael Musto's caveat that "the Quilt should always come with a warning sticker that reads, 'Don't feel that by crying over this, you've really done something for AIDS'" (46), raises valid problems of catharsis and passivity and deserves ongoing discussion. In ancient Greece, the ritual performances of tragedy achieved, according to Aristotle, the purgation of fear and sorrow. This very criterion has been read by feminist dramatists and others as a problematic position. After all, when emotions have been heightened and then released, there seems to be a closure and thus little incentive to continue an engagement with the problem. Critics of the Quilt consider that the emotional release expended during the performance of the Quilt engenders passivity and a missed opportunity to continue active engagement not only with the Quilt but, most important, with the issues it raises. Certainly the problems of catharsis and ensuing passivity generate implications applicable to the teaching of the Quilt or literature on AIDS, both of which can be moving, sad, or even tragic. Since passive responses bring no social transformation, it is imperative that pedagogical approaches to the Quilt and/or literature on AIDS be ethically responsible and foreground the necessity for ongoing engagement in the classroom and in society at large.

Various related events occurred during the three-day display in Washington, D.C. that attempted to mitigate against catharsis and passivity. The 1996 gathering heralded a series of performances, from dance and choral benefit evenings, to an interfaith religious service, to a cycle race for AIDS. "The Rage against the Dying of the Light," the candlelight vigil supported by Elizabeth Taylor, attracted thousands of marchers. In a series of short presentations, they emphasized the diversity of people infected with or affected by HIV/AIDS, providing glimpses of the lives of people who defy that hated term "AIDS victim"; each speaker ended with the phrase, "I am the face of AIDS." While these projects raised money and awareness of HIV/AIDS, another event positioned volunteers around the perimeter of the Quilt to hand out buttons exhorting wearers to "Remember Them with Your Vote";

the proximity of the quilt panels, juxtaposed with the direct linkage of an individual's responsibility to choose political candidates based on their platform and record, provided a reading of the Quilt that spoke clearly of cause and effect in the 1996 U.S. elections, as well as of the former lack of political will and the inactivity to the point of negligence, so clearly visible in the thousands of panels. Cleve Jones articulates this massive governmental neglect:

> The Quilt . . . is terrible evidence of the consequences of our government's failure. For fifteen years the struggle against AIDS has been sabotaged by outright bigotry, political cowardice and mind-numbing stupidity from Congress and the White House. The cost of this failure is incalculable, although now measured in thousands of American lives. ("Blanket Judgment" 33)

At other times, demonstrations by ACT UP, the AIDS Coalition to Unleash Power, attended by members from different parts of the United States, used the occasion of the Quilt display to target the pharmaceutical companies and the American president. In the first demonstration, protesters staged a die-in outside the sumptuous offices of one pharmaceutical company and named other companies, indicting them for causing unnecessary death through the relentless pursuit of profits. Two issues were and still are pertinent: first, extended periods of drug testing exclude people who are terminally ill and who cling to any opportunity to participate in trials; second, another exclusionary practice concerns the exorbitant prices charged for many commonly used drugs as well as for the new antiviral cocktails that are making a startling difference to some people living with AIDS and who, thanks to these cocktails, are now experiencing what is called "The Lazarus Syndrome"—a seemingly miraculous improvement in health and T-cell levels—and the apparent "disappearance" of the virus. Since the 1996 Quilt display, as ever more effective drug cocktails are developed, new aspects cause ongoing concern, such as the development of immunity to the new cocktails by some people living with AIDS, and viral latency (the probability that the seemingly eliminated virus lurks in certain organs). The Quilt reminds all spectators/readers not to succumb to complacency. The second ACT UP demonstration involved a march to the White House to scatter "cremains" on the lawn of the presidential home; those who had left explicit instructions for the disposal of their ashes regarded this action as a way of drawing attention to the urgency of certain issues, such as universal health care.

Since the 1987 showing of the Quilt, which was expressly initiated to draw attention to the existence of the AIDS pandemic, subsequent displays maintain this consciousness-raising component as well as generate healing narratives. The context, however, is vital: as the number of panels and deaths increased and the hoped-for cure never materialized, the Quilt display—especially that of 1992—emphasized that the performance of mourning and private healing often gives way to a sense of hopelessness. The 1996 Quilt realized a markedly different performance. The healing of personal grief and the confrontation of the enormity of loss continues, but now the normalization of AIDS places the issues within a panoply of social problems and thereby denies its urgency. Another vital aspect of the 1996 Quilt display follows from the newly discovered antiviral cocktails just mentioned, which have initiated dramatic health reversals and concomitantly engendered enormous anger because of subject exclusion, usually on financial grounds. Cleve Jones articulated that "the challenge of displaying the Quilt [in 1996] . . . is to attempt to transform what has been a symbol of grief and loss into a symbol of hope and determination" (qtd. in Raine C8). Anthony Turney further extrapolated this notion: "Our mission . . . is to put ourselves out of business" (qtd. in Roberts E8). At this time, however, while the pandemic still rages, the healing narratives of the Quilt *do* provide something tangible. Robert Rankin articulates what he considers the "miracle of the Quilt": "[I]t allows us to come to terms with our grief, and at the same time inspires us to greater compassion, commitment, and strength for those who need us" (17). The penultimate words about this Quilt performance belong to two men deeply committed to the project. Cleve Jones, the Quilt's founder, makes a plea:

> Those of us battling AIDS did not watch in silence as the quilt grew. Through education and activism, we fought against ignorance and prejudice. . . .We have cared for the sick, com-

forted the dying, built hospices, joined speakers' bureaus, written checks, signed petitions, demonstrated, testified, been ar-
rested, worn red ribbons, sewn quilts for our dead and raised
our candles against an ever-darkening sky. And yet, none of
these actions will save my life or the life of any other person
already infected with HIV. The plain truth is only one thing
can: Research—and more of it. ("AIDS Quilt" E8)

Anthony Turney addresses the immensity of the task by quoting
a Zen proverb: "When you pick up a pebble on the beach, you
disturb the ocean. . . . We must use every means and every opportunity to keep disturbing that ocean regardless of its size, because every pebble has the potential to be the one that makes *the*
difference" (5). These impassioned statements influence our readings of the Quilt and make it imperative to ask: "How many
pebbles will *we* pick up, what will *we* disturb?"

In choosing to teach the Quilt as a text in a gay and lesbian
studies/English studies environment, my question raises two imperatives: that we pick up pebbles, thus becoming more actively
involved in the time-space of HIV/AIDS, and that we seize any
opportunity to disturb the heteronormative status quo. In a classroom space explicitly made safe by openness and respect for difference, the Quilt functions as a vehicle for examining the specifics
of the Quilt's materiality and the multiplicity of issues relevant to
society at large that intersect with questions arising from its performance as an event. In asking if there is a queer pedagogy,
Deborah Britzman issues a caveat—"Stop reading straight"—
and questions whether the "educational apparatus and its
pedagogies [can] exceed their own readings" (164). By asking
new questions, conventional binaries can be rethought. In identifying the attributes of a queer pedagogy, Britzman foregrounds
its "refusal of normalcy" and calls for an "ethical concern with
one's *own* reading practices" (165). The teaching of the Quilt,
especially in the context of English studies and language arts,
demands an emphasis on political connections of the performance
of art—the inextricability of politics in language, iconography,
and culture. The structure of these elements is never immutable
but rather is contingent upon the spatio-temporal context, the
perspective and positioning of the reader/spectator, and the differing sites of struggle. Henry Giroux identifies the main chal-

lenge for educators as redefining "the central relationship between culture and politics in order to deepen and extend the basis for transformative and emancipatory practice. . . . [T]he political side of culture must be given primacy as an act of resistance and transformation by addressing issues of difference, identity, and textuality within rather than outside of the problematics of power, agency, and history" (30). This essay offers readings of the Quilt from perspectives that are inextricably related to the politics of culture; however, the context of gay and lesbian studies offers a specific focus which addresses queer issues as an ethical obligation. Although I have already addressed some of these within other readings of the Quilt, more specific attention should be paid to a range of questions.

At the outset, no assumptions should be made regarding the sexual identity of students participating in English studies or, more important, in a gay and lesbian studies course within that program, or about their levels of knowledge and experience with HIV/AIDS. Peter Bowen offers his perspective on teaching AIDS: "[It] becomes a practice of unlearning, of untangling the complicated ideological weaving of cultural misconceptions, media misrepresentation, and medical misinformation so that students can begin to recognize their relation to AIDS as both frighteningly real *and* discursively constructed" (141). Particular sensitivity should be exercised in accordance with an awareness of different subject positions, not only those of the infected and the affected, but those spectators/readers/students with an HIV-negative sero status as well. Walt Odets has documented survivor guilt, overprotectiveness, fear of sero conversion, and multiple loss: "The AIDS epidemic has spawned an epidemic of denial" (220). The Quilt panels are understandably silent about the trauma experienced by these gay men even while they offer powerful representations of those who have died. The Quilt replicates the greater prominence accorded to gay issues through the larger number of panels for gay men—which is in line with the death statistics; women appear on fewer panels, and little attention has been paid to lesbians in particular and women in general who are living with AIDS. Cindy Patton problematizes the categorization of women in the pandemic: "Women's position in the epidemic is understood radically differently depending on whether women's concerns are posed by governments of developed or developing countries, by gay groups, by women influenced by the women's health movement or by women influenced principally by AIDS activism" (*Last Served* 2). Moreover, the different positions and agendas of gay men and lesbians need to be deconstructed in relation to the Quilt and societal structures. HIV/AIDS issues do not impinge in the same way on everyone, and classroom practices require sensitive analyses that acknowledge the complexity of a range of subject positions and the differentials of marginality, which may shift according to the specifics of a situation. For example, while gays and lesbians are often marginalized in juridical terms and repeatedly face discriminatory practices in institutional life, they have mobilized as a political force and voice for HIV/AIDS issues and achieved many goals. Most important, this emphasizes the empowerment of an activist stance and the refusal in many instances by people living with HIV/AIDS to entertain the notion of victimhood.

Another phenomenon evident in a close reading of the Quilt distinguishes between "innocent" and supposedly "guilty" scenarios surrounding death. According to what he terms "cemeterial apartheid," Timothy Murphy notes that certain panels state the "route of infection" (317), such as blood transfusions, artificial insemination, or mother to baby transmission, to dissociate the deceased from any connection to the gay community. This practice calls for a reiteration of the fact that guilt has no place in the transmission of a virus; yet Douglas Crimp reminds us that Kimberly Bergalis "spoke not as a person with AIDS . . . but as the 'victim' of people with AIDS" ("Right On" 303). Furthermore, contrary to homophobic pronouncements that equate AIDS with the "curse" of being gay, there are no risk groups, only risky practices. Cindy Patton argues that this "blaming ethos was reorientated by promoting safe sex not only as an individual risk reduction, but as a practice of community-building through resistance" ("Visualizing" 381). Further questions can be raised about the complexity of safe-sex practices and the necessity of carefully choosing a target audience for efficacious advertising.

In seeking greater awareness of the problematics of AIDS, British gay activist Simon Watney cautions against the implications of generally accepted practices such as "AIDS awareness" and points toward different agendas:

> Vast bonfires of money have been squandered in the name of "AIDS awareness" in [Britain]. . . . [E]ducation campaigns have been targeted at those at least risk of contracting HIV, as if the priority of preventing an epidemic amongst heterosexuals had been established at the expense of halting the epidemics that are actually raging throughout the developed world. (*Practices* 263)

His objections are spelled out in an article in which he argues against the "generalist outlook," which equates the possible risk of infection for anyone with a supposedly equal risk to everyone; "the globalisation of AIDS," which elides the specificities of local issues; and "the de-gaying of AIDS," which regards the syndrome from the perspective of the heterosexual population and relegates to the margins the needs of the gay community, which, in terms of pro rata percentage, represents the highest statistic of people infected with HIV in North America and Europe. Watney also protests "highly individualistic" approaches to AIDS, which range from its designation as a "tragedy"—with the subtextual implication that it was predestined—to "glibly optimistic" approaches that dismiss the enormity of medical and other problems, and the "normalizing" of AIDS in the calls for tolerance that do not examine how prejudice is meted out ("AIDS Awareness" 8–9). In all of these arenas, Watney requires of us a more careful analysis of interest groups and perspectives. His conviction that "HIV is not an 'Equal Opportunities' virus[; i]t does *not* affect everybody equally, and least of all does it do so at the global level" ("Signifying" 202), is a reminder that positionings within race, class, gender, and sexual identity formulations variously intersect with homophobia, racism, and poverty.

By reading the AIDS Memorial Quilt as a process of rememoration, we bring the past into the present and foreground the history of gay and lesbian communities since the 1980s, a period inextricably and complexly linked to the trajectory of HIV/AIDS; remembering individual and community losses and lives is part of the performative structure of the Quilt, as is the governmental neglect and violence. At a time when some term this a "post-AIDS" era, the Web site of the NAMES Project Foundation offers a mid-1997 article titled "AIDS Is Not Over," which combines cautious optimism about some responses to new drugs with cautionary tales about the increasing global pandemic, decreasing funds, and the effects of complacency. In response, through our readings of the Quilt inside and outside of the classroom, we should also continue to ask an old question: "How many pebbles will *we* pick up, what will *we* disturb?"

Works Cited

Bennett, Susan. "Mother Tongue: Colonized Bodies and Performing Cultures." *Contemporary Theatre Review* 2.3 (1995): 101–09.

Bowen, Peter M. "AIDS 101." *Writing AIDS: Gay Literature, Language, and Analysis.* Ed. Timothy Murphy and Susanne Poirier. New York: Columbia UP, 1993: 140–60.

Britzman, Deborah. "Is There a Queer Pedagogy? or, Stop Reading Straight." *Educational Theory* 45.2 (1995): 151–65.

Caruth, Cathy, and Thomas Keenan. "'The AIDS Crisis Is Not Over': A Conversation with Gregg Bordowitz, Douglas Crimp and Laura Pinsky." *American Imago* 48.4 (1991): 539–56.

Crimp, Douglas. "Mourning and Militancy." *October* 51 (1989): 3–18.

———. "Right On, Girlfriend." *Fear of a Queer Planet: Queer Politics and Social Theory.* Ed. Michael Warner. Minneapolis: U of Minnesota P, 1993. 300–19.

Elsley, Judy. "The Rhetoric of the NAMES Project AIDS Quilt: Reading the Text(ile)." *AIDS: The Literary Response.* Ed. Emmanuel S. Nelson. New York: Twayne, 1992. 187–96.

Enoicaras, T. X. "The AIDS Memorial Quilt Travels to D.C." *San Francisco Frontiers* 15.7 (1 Aug. 1996): 18–22.

Foucault, Michel. "Of Other Spaces." *Diacritics* 16 (Spring 1986): 22–27.

Fuchs, Elinor. "The Performance of Mourning." *American Theatre* 9.9 (Jan. 1993). 14–17.

Giroux, Henry A. "Living Dangerously: Identity Politics and the New Cultural Racism." *Between Borders: Pedagogy and the Politics of Cultural Studies*. Ed. Henry A. Giroux and Peter McLaren. London: Routledge, 1994. 29–55.

Hawkins, Peter S. "Naming Names: The Art of Memory and the NAMES Project AIDS Quilt." *Critical Inquiry* 19.4 (1993): 752–79.

Jarman, Derek. *Derek Jarman's Garden*. London: Thames, 1995.

Jones, Cleve. "AIDS Quilt: A Call for Research." *San Francisco Examiner* 30 Nov. 1995: E8.

———. "Blanket Judgment." *POZ* (Oct. 1996): 32–33.

Murphy, Timothy. "Testimony." *Writing AIDS: Gay Literature, Language, and Analysis*. Ed. Timothy Murphy and Suzanne Poirier. New York: Columbia UP, 1993. 306–20.

Musto, Michael. "La Dolce Musto." *Village Voice* 25 Oct. 1988: 46.

Odets, Walt. *In the Shadow of the Epidemic: Being HIV-Negative in the Age of AIDS*. Durham: Duke UP, 1995.

Orlofsky, Patsy, and Myron Orlofsky. *Quilts in America*. New York: McGraw-Hill, 1974.

Patton, Cindy. *Inventing AIDS*. New York: Routledge, 1990.

———. *Last Served: Gendering the HIV Pandemic*. London: Taylor, 1994.

———. "Visualizing Safe Sex: When Pedagogy and Pornography Collide." *Inside/out: Lesbian Theories, Gay Theories*. Ed. Diana Fuss. London: Routledge, 1991. 373–86.

Raine, George. "Man behind Quilt Winning Own AIDS Battle." *San Francisco Examiner* 15 Sept. 1996: C8.

Rankin, Robert. "The Quilt Remembrance." *Reform Judaism* 17.4 (1989): 16–17.

Roberts, Jerry. "The AIDS Quilt Comes of Age." *San Francisco Examiner-Chronicle*. 3 Dec. 1995: E8.

Rubenstein, Hal. "Quilt Guilt." *The Advocate* 3 Sept. 1996: 57–58.

Ruskin, Cindy. *The Quilt—Stories from the NAMES Project*. New York: Pocket, 1988.

Spivak, Gayatri Chakravorty. "The *Intervention* Interview." *The Post-Colonial Critic: Interviews, Strategies, Dialogues*. Ed. Sarah Harasym. New York: Routledge, 1990. 113–32.

Struck, Doug. "Visitors Marvel, Grieve over a Living Monument to the Tragedy of AIDS." *Washington Post* 13 Oct. 1996: A33.

Treichler, Paula A. "AIDS, Homophobia and Biomedical Discourse: An Epidemic of Signification." *AIDS; Cultural Analysis, Cultural Activism*. Ed. Douglas Crimp. Cambridge: MIT P, 1988.

Turney, Anthony. "The Power of a Single Pebble." *Namesletter* 8.3 (1995): 2+.

Watney, Simon. "AIDS Awareness?—Some Reflections on the Debates about AIDS and Representation." *Oxford* 1 (1995): 6–9.

———. *Practices of Freedom: Selected Writings on HIV and AIDS*. Durham: Duke UP, 1994.

———. "Signifying AIDS: 'Global AIDS,' Red Ribbons and Other Controversies." *Random Access: On Crisis and Its Metaphors*. Ed. P. Buchler and N. Papastergiadis. London: Rivers Oram, 1995: 193–211.

Williams, Scott. "Pennies from Heaven." *Namesletter* 8.3 (1995): 5.

Index

Freire, Paulo, xv, 171, 193, 260–61
Fuchs, Elinor, 296
Fuoss, Kirk, 122
Fuss, Diana, xix, 194

Gallop, Jane, 66, 83
Garber, Marjorie, 160
Garden, Nancy, *Annie on My Mind*, 127
Gay and lesbian studies. *See* Lesbian and gay studies
Gender
binary model of, 85–88
connotations of, 79–80
as creative play, 86–87
dynamics of, 218–19
in popular discourse, 86
in primary school children, 213–32
Gender performance, and sexual orientation, 37
Gender play, 219
Gilbert, Sandra, 82
Girls in Three-B, The (Taylor), 8
Giroux, Henry, 39, 172, 193, 257, 260–61, 304–5
Gloria Goes to Gay Pride (Newman), 116–17
Goldberg, Jonathan, 151, 153, 158, 162
González, Deena J., 177
Gould, Janice, 201
Graff, Gerald, 150, 255
Grahn, Judy, *Another Mother Tongue*, 12
Greene, Bette, *The Drowning of Stephan Jones*, 123, 124
Greene, Thomas C., 148
Grosz, Elizabeth, 73
Gubar, Susan, 82

Haggerty, George, 48, 55, 148
Hairston, Maxine, 170–71, 174
Hall, Radclyffe, 4, 7, 12

The Well of Loneliness, 4, 5, 7, 259–61
Halperin, David, 45
Halpin, Tony, 213
Harbeck, Karen, 15, 132
Hardiman, Rita, 115
Harper, Phillip Brian, xix
Harris, Christie, 203
Hate crimes, 172
Hausman, Gerald, 203
Hawkins, Peter, 296, 297
Heart Is a Lonely Hunter, The (McCullers), 4
Hellman, Lillian, *The Children's Hour*, 261–62
Herford, C. H., 155, 156
"Her Name Is Helen" (Brant), 203
Heterosexism, in India, 272–86
Heterosexuality, normalization of, 219–22
Hirsch, Marianne, 83
Hitchcock, Alfred, *Rope*, 45–46
"Holding" (Lowry), 121
Holford, Vanessa, 195
Homophobia, xvii–xviii
AIDS and, 293
in cold war era, 49, 149
as hate speech, 241
hidden curriculum of, 39
and homosexuality of canonical authors, xviii
in India, 275–76
institutionalization of, xviii, 132
in "Queers, Bums, and Magic," 236–46
responding to, 237–43, 248–51
in secondary schools, 132–33
in South Africa, 253–70
in student writing, 234–52
in *The Catcher in the Rye*, 143
Homosexuality
awareness of, 133, 168–89
Catholic Church's view on, 16
as deviancy, 17–18
discourse community examining, 112–13

EDITOR

William J. Spurlin has co-edited *The New Criticism and Contemporary Literary Theory: Connections and Continuities* (1995) and *Reclaiming the Heartland: Lesbian and Gay Voices from the Midwest* (1996). His essays on queer studies, American literature and culture, and critical theory have appeared in numerous journals and anthologies, most recently in *De-Centring Sexualities* (2000); *Mourning Diana: Nation, Culture and the Performance of Grief* (1999); *James Baldwin Now* (1999); *Coming Out of Feminism?* (1998); and *Reconceptualizing American Literary/Cultural Studies: Rhetoric, History, and Politics in the Humanities* (1996). He has lectured on queer studies at academic conferences and symposia, and as an invited speaker, in Europe, Africa, Asia, and across North America. Spurlin is presently working on his book "Imperialism within the Margins: The Cultural Politics of Queer Identity in Postcolonial Contexts," and he teaches twentieth-century literature, critical and cultural theory, and queer studies at Cardiff University.

CONTRIBUTORS

Marcia Blumberg is visiting research fellow at the Open University, Milton Keynes, England. She has taught drama courses at York University, Toronto, and theater courses at the festival for Edinburgh University. She has co-edited *South African Theatre as/and Intervention* with Dennis Walder (1999) and she is completing her book *Engendering Intervention in South African Theatre*. Her articles on contemporary theater appear in *Staging Resistance, Hollywood on Stage, New Theatre Quarterly, Performance Research, Theatre Research in Canada, South African Theatre Journal*, and in other anthologies and journals. The essay in this volume forms part of a larger project tentatively titled "Making AIDS Visible: Theatre as/and Activism."

tatiana de la tierra is a bilingual, bicultural writer and *activista*. She has taught English composition at the University of Texas at El Paso, where she obtained her M.F.A. in creative writing in 1999. She is former editor of the Latina lesbian publications *esto no tiene nombre, conmoción*, and *el telarañazo*. Her fiction, poetry, and creative nonfiction have appeared in journals and anthologies such as *Cimarron Review, Chasing the American Dykedream, Hot & Bothered, Journal of Internal Medicine, Mid-American Review, Tropic Magazine, Queer View Mirror, Perral, Compañeras*, and *Gay and Lesbian Poetry in Our Time*. She is currently in residence as a reference librarian at the State University of New York, Buffalo, where she obtained an M.L.S. degree in 2000.

Mario DiGangi is assistant professor of English at Lehman College, City University of New York, where he teaches courses in Shakespeare and Renaissance culture. He is the author of *The Homoerotics of Early Modern Drama* (1997) and of articles in *Shakespeare Quarterly, ELH, English Literary Renaissance, Textual Practice*, and *GLQ*. His work also appears in the anthologies *MLA Approaches to Teaching: Shorter Elizabethan Poetry; Marlowe, History, and Sexuality;* and *Essays to Celebrate Richard Barnfield: Four Hundred Years of* The Affectionate Shepheard. He is currently working on a study of sexuality, gender, and work in early modern England.

Debbie Epstein is reader in education at the University of London's Institute of Education, where she teaches women's studies, cultural studies, and research methodologies. Her scholarship addresses the shaping of inequalities, particularly in relation to gender, race, and sexuality, in schooling and in popular culture. Recent books include *Schooling Sexualities,* co-authored with Richard Johnson (1998), and a number of co-edited volumes, including *Failing Boys? Issues in Gender and Education* (1998), *Border Patrols: Policing the Boundaries of Heterosexuality* (1997), and *A Dangerous Knowing: Sexuality, Pedagogy, and Popular Culture* (1999).

Lillian Faderman is the author of several books of lesbian history, including *Surpassing the Love of Men: Romantic Friendship and Love between Women from the Renaissance to the Present* (1981; reissued with a new introduction, 1998), *Odd Girls and Twilight Lovers: A History of Lesbian Life in Twentieth-Century America* (1991), and *To Believe in Women: What Lesbians Have Done for America— A History* (1999). She is professor of English at California State University, Fresno. For her outstanding contributions to gay and lesbian studies, she was the 1998 recipient of the Monette/Horowitz Award.

Edward J. Ingebretsen is associate professor of English at Georgetown University. He is the author of *Robert Frost: A Star in a Stone-Boat* (1995) and *Maps of Heaven, Maps of Hell: Religious Terror as Memory from the Puritans to Stephen King* (1996). His essays have appeared in *The Journal of Gay, Lesbian and Bisexual Identity; Journal of American Culture; Religion and American Culture; Thought;* and *The International Journal of Sexuality.* He is currently finishing a study of American political gothic titled *Making Monsters: Politics and Persuasion* (forthcoming 2001).

Jay Kent Lorenz is a doctoral candidate in visual culture at the University of California, Irvine. He holds an M.A. from Georgetown University in English, where he also taught cultural studies. His writing on cinema has appeared in *Film Quarterly, Film and History, Psychotronic,* and the *Miami Herald;* he has been a commentator on film for Britain's Channel Four and is co-editing an anthology on global sex.

Lee Lynch has written eleven books, among them *Cactus Love* (1994) and *The Swashbuckler* (1985). Her column "The Amazon Trail" appears in over a dozen newspapers in the United States. She lives with Akia Woods on the Oregon coast, where she earns her living in social service work. Akia and Lee co-edited *Off the Rag: Lesbians Writing on Menopause* (1996), and Lynch's most recent book is the novel *Rafferty Street* (1998), the third volume in the Morton River Valley trilogy.

Richard E. Miller is associate professor of English and associate director of the Writing Program at Rutgers University. He is the author of *As If Learning Mattered: Reforming Higher Education* (1998). His essays have appeared in *College English, CCC, JAC,* and *Cultural Studies.*

Claudia Mitchell is associate professor of education at McGill University, Montreal, where she teaches and conducts research in the areas of childhood as a cultural space, literacy, gender, popular culture, teacher education, and gay and lesbian literature for children and young adults. She has co-authored with Sandra Weber *That's Funny, You Don't Look Like a Teacher: Interrogating Images of Identity in Popular Culture* (1995) and *Reinventing Ourselves as Teachers: Beyond Nostalgia* (1999).

Jody Norton is a lecturer in English language and literature and in women's studies at Eastern Michigan University. S/he is the author of *Narcissus* Sous Rature: *Male Subjectivity in Contemporary American Poetry* (2000) and is currently writing a book on the cultural origins of transphobia. S/he has published in *Centennial Review; Women and Language; College Literature; Contemporary Literature; The Journal of Gay, Lesbian, and Bisexual Identity; Journal of Medical Humanities; Sulfur; The American Poetry Review; The Journal of the Midwest Modern Language Association; Sexuality and Culture; Twentieth Century Literature,* and other journals and collections.

Karen Lee Osborne is the author of the novels *Carlyle Simpson* (1986) and *Hawkwings* (1991), the editor of *The Country of Herself: Short Fiction by Chicago Women* (1993), and co-editor, with William J. Spurlin, of *Reclaiming the Heartland: Lesbian and Gay Voices from the Midwest* (1996). Her essays have appeared in *American Book Review, The Denver Quarterly,* and *The Literary Review.* She teaches at Columbia College of Chicago, where she was named 1996 Teacher of the Year, and where she developed and teaches the courses Introduction to Native American Literature and The Contemporary Native American Novel.

Jim Reese is head of high school English at the International School of Brussels, Belgium; he has also taught at the British School of Brussels and at Oakton High School in Virginia. He currently serves as coordinator of Project Safe Place, a teacher-led effort to educate his school community on issues affecting lesbian and gay youth and adults. He published articles in *English Journal* and the *International Schools Journal* in 1995 and 1998, respectively.

Ann Smith teaches literature at the University of the Witwatersrand, Johannesburg, South Africa. Her research is in the areas of queer studies, gender studies, and young adult literature; her essay "Teaching as a Feminist in South Africa: Some Aspects of the Politics of Gender, Race and Education" appeared in *Textual Studies in Canada: Canada's Journal of Cultural Literacy* (1996).

Susan Talburt is assistant professor of educational policy studies at Georgia State University, where she teaches courses in anthropology of education, curriculum and higher education, poststructuralist and feminist theory, and women's studies. She has published essays on queer theory and ethnographic research, identity politics in higher education, and curriculum and pedagogy in the *Journal of Curriculum Theorizing*, the *International Journal of Qualitative Studies in Education*, and *Review of Education/Pedagogy/Cultural Studies*, as well as a book, *Subject to Identity: Knowledge, Sexuality, and Academic Practices in Higher Education* (2000).

Ruth Vanita, formerly reader in English at Delhi University, is now associate professor of liberal studies at the University of Montana. She is author of *Sappho and the Virgin Mary: Same-Sex Love and the English Literary Imagination* (1996) and *A Play of Light: Selected Poems* (1994). She was a founder and co-editor of *Manushi*, India's first feminist journal, from 1979 to 1990, and she recently co-edited an anthology, *Same-Sex Love in India: Readings from Literature and History* (2000), with Saleem Kidwai.

This book was typeset in Adobe Sabon by Electronic Imaging.
Typefaces used on the cover include variations of Esprit.
The book was printed on 50-lb. Husky Offset
by IPC Communication Services.